Taking Stock of Delinquency

LONGITUDINAL RESEARCH IN THE SOCIAL AND BEHAVIORAL SCIENCES

An Interdisciplinary Series

Series Editors:

Howard B. Kaplan, *Texas A&M University, College Station, Texas*
Adele Eskeles Gottfried, *California State University, Northridge, California*
Allen W. Gottfried, *California State University, Fullerton, California*

A Continuation Order Plan is available for this series. A continuation order will bring delivery of each new volume immediately upon publication. Volumes are billed only upon actual shipment. For further information please contact the publisher.

Taking Stock of Delinquency

An Overview of Findings from Contemporary Longitudinal Studies

Terence P. Thornberry
University at Albany, Albany, New York

and

Marvin D. Krohn
University at Albany, Albany, New York

Kluwer Academic/Plenum Publishers
New York, Boston, Dordrecht, London, Moscow

ISBN 0-306-47364-X

©2003 Kluwer Academic / Plenum Publishers, New York
233 Spring Street, New York, New York 10013

http://www.wkap.nl/

10 9 8 7 6 5 4 3 2 1

A C.I.P. record for this book is available from the Library of Congress

Printed in the United States of America

Contributors

Robert D. Abbott is Chair and Professor of Educational Psychology in the University of Washington College of Education. He and colleagues are engaged in a research project that focuses on learning disabilities in children and ways in which teachers can help them learn more effectively. Dr. Abbott is a Fellow of the American Psychological Association.

Jennifer M. Beyers is a Research Analyst at the Social Development Research Group, School of Social Work, University of Washington, Seattle, WA.

Avshalom Caspi is Professor of Psychology at the University of Wisconsin—Madison, and Professor of Personality and Social Psychology at the Institute of Psychiatry, King's College, London. He has a long-standing interest in life-course models of antisocial behavior.

Richard F. Catalano is Professor and the Associate Director of the Social Development Research Group, School of Social Work, University of Washington. He is the Principal Investigator on a number of federal grants, which include family, school, and community-based prevention approaches to reduce risk while enhancing the protective factors of bonding and promotion of healthy beliefs and clear standards.

Finn-Aage Esbensen is the E. Desmond Lee Professor of Youth Crime and Violence in the Department of Criminology and Criminal Justice at the University of Missouri – St. Louis. He served as a Research Associate on the Denver Youth Survey (1987–1992) and Principal Investigator of the NIJ funded National Evaluation of the Gang Resistance Education and Training (G.R.E.A.T.) Program (1994–2001).

Rachele C. Espiritu is a Senior Research Associate at EMT Associates, Inc. in Sacramento, California. She is the Principal Investigator of a national cross-site evaluation examining the effectiveness of a mentoring program in preventing alcohol and drug use among high-risk youths. Her research interests include developmental gender differences in the causes of delinquency and drug use, child and adolescent mental health issues, and program evaluation of prevention programs for high-risk youths.

David P. Farrington is Professor of Psychological Criminology at Cambridge University and Director of the Cambridge Study in Delinquent Development. He has been president of the American Society of Criminology, the British Society of Criminology, and the European Association of Psychology and Law. His main research interest is in the development of offending and antisocial behavior from childhood to adulthood.

J. David Hawkins is Kozmetsky Professor of Prevention, School of Social Work, and Director of the Social Development Research Group, University of Washington. Dr. Hawkins is co-author of Preparing for the Drug-Free Years and Parents Who Care, prevention programs that empower parents to strengthen family bonding and reduce the risks for health and behavior problems in their families.

Karl G. Hill is with the Social Development Research Group, School of Social Work, University of Washington. He is the Project Director of the Seattle Social Development Project, and Principal Investigator on the NIDA-funded study Intergenerational Influences of Substance Use on Children. In addition, he directs activities on the study of Early Adulthood Consequences of Adolescent Substance Use.

David Huizinga is a Senior Research Associate at the Institute of Behavioral Science at the University of Colorado. He is the Principal Investigator of the Denver Youth Survey (1986–2003), Co-Principal Investigator of the National Youth Survey (1976–2004), and the Principal Investigator of two cross-national longitudinal projects on delinquency. For over two decades he has conducted basic and evaluation research on developmental lifespan issues.

Howard B. Kaplan is Distinguished Professor of Sociology and Mary Thomas Marshall Professor of Liberal Arts at Texas A & M University. He directs a multi-generational longitudinal study of drug abuse and other deviant adaptations to stress. Among his works are *Patterns of Juvenile Delinquency; Social Psychology of Self-Referent Behavior; Deviant Behavior in Defense of Self; Drugs, Crime, and Other Deviant Adaptations;* and *Social Deviance: Testing a General Theory* (with Robert J. Johnson).

Rick Kosterman is Project Director and Research Scientist at the Social Development Research Group, School of Social Work, University of Washington.

His current research interests include developmental risks for mental health problems and violence, rural family and community prevention, and early adult consequences of childhood and adolescent problem behaviors. Implications for prevention are an ongoing focus.

Marvin D. Krohn is Professor of Sociology at the University at Albany with a joint appointment in the School of Criminal Justice. In addition, he is a Co-Principal Investigator of the Rochester Youth Development Study. His research focuses on theoretical explanations of juvenile delinquency and adolescent drug use with special attention to social network and interactional theories.

Alan J. Lizotte is Professor of Criminal Justice at the University at Albany and a Co-Principal Investigator of the Rochester Youth Development Study. Among other things, his research interests include all aspects of firearms policy, owner-ship, and use, as well as using quantitative research methods to study the causes and consequences of various forms of antisocial behavior.

Rolf Loeber is Professor of Psychiatry, Psychology, and Epidemiology at the University of Pittsburgh, Pittsburgh, PA, and Professor of Developmental Psychopathology at the Free University, Amsterdam, Netherlands. He is the Principal Investigator of the Pittsburgh Youth Study. His research interests focus on developmental criminology and on understanding developmental pathways to offending.

Terrie E. Moffitt is Professor of Social Behaviour and Development at the Institute of Psychiatry, King's College London, and Professor of Clinical Psychology at the University of Wisconsin – Madison. Her research has focused on the neuropsychological bases of antisocial behavior and in the development of typological theories of delinquency.

Daniel S. Nagin is Teresa and H. John III Heinz Professor of Public Policy at the Heinz School of Public Policy and Management, Carnegie Mellon University. His research focuses on the evolution of criminal and antisocial behaviors over the life course, the deterrent effect of criminal and non-criminal penalties on illegal behaviors, and the development of statistical methods for analyzing longitudinal data.

Linda Pagani is Associate Professor (School of Psycho-Education) and Researcher (Research Unit on Children's Psycho-Social Maladjustment and Ste-Justine's Hospital FRSQ Research Centre) at the University of Montreal. Her research focuses on understanding the impact of poverty and family processes on children's adjustment. In 1997, she launched a major longitudinal-experimental study to evaluate the long-term effects of the Montreal Head Start Program for children from impoverished areas of the city.

Pamela K. Porter is the Research Coordinator for the Rochester Youth Development Study at the Hindelang Criminal Justice Research Center, University at Albany. In addition to her coordinating role, she is interested in the construction and evaluation of developmentally specific measures of antisocial behavior and its predictors.

Jean Séguin is a Research Scientist at the University of Montreal. His research focuses on the neuropsychology of physical aggression, hyperactivity, and other forms of externalizing behavior problems. In the past five years, he has undertaken a longitudinal study to examine the development of externalizing disorders in pre-schoolers from an executive function perspective.

Brian H. Smith is a Ph.D. student in the School of Social Work and a Research Assistant for the Social Development Research Group at the University of Washington. He has a background in social work and counseling in schools. His current research interests are in the dissemination of effective prevention interventions for children and youth.

Carolyn A. Smith is Associate Professor of Social Welfare at the University at Albany and a Co-Principal Investigator of the Rochester Youth Development Study. She has international social work practice experience in child and family mental health, and in delinquency intervention. Her primary research interest is in the family etiology of delinquency and other problem behaviors, as well as the impact of child maltreatment on the life course.

Magda Stouthamer-Loeber is Associate Professor of Psychiatry and Psychology at the University of Pittsburgh, Pittsburgh, PA. She is the Co-Principal Investigator of the ongoing Pittsburgh Youth Study. She has particular interest in the study of family factors as both risk and protective factors for delinquency.

Terence P. Thornberry is Distinguished Professor at the School of Criminal Justice, the University at Albany, and Director of the Hindelang Criminal Justice Research Center. Since 1986 he has been the Director of the Rochester Youth Development Study. His research interests focus on understanding the development of delinquency and crime over the life course and in examining intergenerational continuity in antisocial behavior.

Richard E. Tremblay is Canada Research Chair in Child Development, Director of the Centre of Excellence for Early Childhood Development, and Director of the Research Unit on Children's Psychosocial Maladjustment. He is a professor of pediatrics, psychiatry, and psychology at the University of Montreal. Since 1982 he has been conducting a series of longitudinal and experimental studies on the development of behavior problems from fetal life to adulthood.

Frank Vitaro is a Professor at the School of Psycho-Education of the University of Montreal and a Researcher at the Research Unit on Children's Psychosocial Maladjustment. His work focuses on the role of peers in the development of deviant behaviors, the comorbidity of adjustment problems, and the prevention of these problems.

Evelyn H. Wei is a Senior Research Principal at Western Psychiatric Institute and Clinic, University of Pittsburgh Medical Center, Pittsburgh, PA.

Anne Wylie Weiher is a Research Associate at the Institute of Behavioral Science at the University of Colorado. Her research interests include developmental psychology, prosocial and antisocial behavior during the teen years, and domestic violence. She also serves as an adjunct professor in the Department of Psychology, Metropolitan State College, Denver, Colorado.

Helene Raskin White is a Professor of Sociology in the Center of Alcohol Studies and the Sociology Department at Rutgers University, Piscataway, NJ. Her major research interests focus on describing patterns of, and in identifying risk factors for, substance use.

Preface

The latter part of the 20th century saw a tremendous burgeoning of information about the causes, course, and consequences of delinquent careers. During this period, our knowledge about the epidemiology of delinquency and crime, risk and protective factors for this type of behavior, etiological theories, and life-course consequences of adolescent deviance expanded exponentially. All of these topics were examined from multidisciplinary perspectives and the rate at which our knowledge base expanded was revolutionary.

Although many research approaches contributed to this increased understanding of delinquency, no approach was more central than the one based on longitudinal research designs. Longitudinal studies vary considerably in size and orientation, but they all trace the development of delinquent and criminal careers over time. Doing so allowed them to address a host of new issues and to reexamine a host of old ones with new rigor and precision. Their empirical findings have led to new theoretical perspectives and to new policies for prevention and treatment.

In this volume, the principal scientists from seven contemporary longitudinal studies of delinquency pause for a moment to reflect upon and to take stock of their empirical results. Our basic objective is to summarize major findings, both within each of these longitudinal studies and across them, so that common themes can be identified.

The seven studies include the three projects of the Office of Juvenile Justice and Delinquency Prevention's Program of Research on the Causes and Correlates of Delinquency. These studies are the Denver Youth Survey, the Pittsburgh Youth Study, and the Rochester Youth Development Study. The Cambridge Study in Delinquent Development, the Houston Longitudinal Study, the Montreal Longitudinal and Experimental Study, and the Seattle Social Development Project are also represented. There are, obviously, many other excellent longitudinal studies that are not represented in this volume, but the ones that are included are among the better known and represent a substantial portion of the theoretical, temporal, and geographical diversity of the full set of longitudinal studies. We hope that a volume summarizing the major results of these seven studies will yield a starting point for the even more general enterprise of synthesizing and reconciling the empirical results from the full range of contemporary longitudinal studies of delinquency.

Longitudinal panel studies by design are major undertakings typically involving the efforts of a number of scholars and support staff and requiring substantial financial backing. Being responsible for such an enterprise along with the production of the quality and quantity of information represented in this volume is a most labor-intensive task. So we are especially grateful to the contributing authors for taking the time to write such thoughtful summaries of the products of their labors.

The research reviewed here could not have been conducted if the various funding agencies had not had the foresight to provide support for these projects and to continue to provide money for data collection and analyses over the many years that the studies have been ongoing. The initial funding for the three projects that served to stimulate interest in producing this compendium was provided by the Office of Juvenile Justice and Delinquency Prevention. However, the seven projects included in this volume have been sponsored by a multitude of agencies and foundations. We are sure that all of the contributing authors would join us in thanking these agencies and the people who work in them for the confidence they have displayed in us.

Projects of this size and complexity require the efforts of more than just the principal and co-principal investigators. The research reviewed in these chapters is a result of the work of many collaborators, support staff, field workers, and research assistants whose names may not appear on the byline of these chapters. In many ways though, this compendium is a tribute to their efforts.

The editors of this volume would like to especially thank our co-workers on the Rochester Youth Development Study who have contributed to its production. Alan Lizotte, Carolyn Smith, and Pam Porter have been involved in all phases of the Rochester Study and their contributions to this volume exceed their work on our chapter. We would especially like to thank Patricia Lambrecht for her editorial assistance in making seven somewhat different chapters appear as a coherent whole.

Terence P. Thornberry
Marvin D. Krohn

Contents

David Huizinga, Anne Wylie Weiher, Rachele Espiritu et al.

Rolf Loeber, David P. Farrington, Magda Stouthamer-Loeber et al.

6. Testing an Integrative Theory of Deviant Behavior: Theory-Syntonic Findings from a Long-Term Multi-Generation Study

Howard B. Kaplan

1

The Development of Panel Studies of Delinquency

Terence P. Thornberry and Marvin D. Krohn

Introduction

Etiological studies of delinquency and crime have come to rely almost exclusively on longitudinal panel designs to investigate the social and psychological forces associated with antisocial careers. While there can be considerable variation in the design of this type of study, all panel studies share a set of core features. They typically are based on a representative sample of individual subjects selected at some point in their life course and then followed across time with repeated measures being taken. Doing so allows for a description of the onset and course of antisocial careers and, if the individuals are followed long enough, the termination of these careers. Panel designs also allow investigators to identify antecedent risk factors and causal processes that lead to antisocial behavior as well as the developmental consequences of such behavior.

Contemporary panel studies emerged from two long-established research traditions in criminology. The first were cross-sectional tests of various theories of delinquency and crime. The second were longitudinal studies describing delinquent or criminal careers.

For the better part of the 20th century, research to test the validity of theoretical models was, by and large, limited to cross-sectional surveys in which individuals were assessed at a single point in time and attempts were made to draw causal inferences from the data collected. There are numerous examples of this

Taking Stock of Delinquency: An Overview of Findings from Contemporary Longitudinal Studies, edited by Thornberry and Krohn. Kluwer Academic/Plenum Publishers, New York, 2003.

type of study. Good illustrations can be found in the works by Akers, Krohn, Lanza-Kaduce, and Radosevich (1979), Hirschi (1969), Hindelang (1973), Johnson (1979), and Short (1957). Although these and related studies have greatly informed our understanding of the correlates of delinquency, they are severely limited in their ability to test the causal processes implied by the various theories. The fundamental stumbling block, of course, is the establishment of temporal order and, therefore, of causal order among the concepts. Because data on the explanatory variable and the outcome variable are collected simultaneously, only a single association or correlation is generated by the data. As a result, it is logically impossible to determine whether the purported cause leads to delinquency. Several other possible relationships, including delinquency leading to the purported cause, reciprocal causality, and a spurious relationship between the concepts, could also generate the observed correlation. Thus, the rich tradition of cross-sectional studies, while informing our understanding of the correlates of delinquency, foundered in its efforts to uncover its causes.

The second important origin of contemporary panel studies is in cohort studies of delinquent and criminal careers. Perhaps the most important are the Philadelphia birth cohort studies conducted by Wolfgang and his colleagues (Tracy, Wolfgang, & Figlio, 1990; Wolfgang, Figlio, & Sellin, 1972; Wolfgang, Thornberry, & Figlio, 1987). Cohort studies were conducted in several other American settings, for example, Racine, Wisconsin (Shannon, 1988), and Columbus, Ohio (Hamparian, Shuster, Dinitz, & Conrad, 1978), and many settings abroad (see, for example, Janson, 2000; Magnusson, Bergman, Rudinger, & Törestad, 1991).

Unlike cross-sectional studies, the hallmark of these cohort studies is the following of a sample of individuals over time. The first Philadelphia birth cohort study, for example, sampled 9,945 males born in 1945 who grew up in Philadelphia. Information on their delinquent and criminal careers, out to age 30, was gathered from their official arrest histories. These studies provided rich, detailed information on numerous issues such as the prevalence and frequency of delinquency, patterns of onset, the length, duration, and severity of criminal careers, and patterns of termination.

Although they took time into account, these longitudinal studies were also very limited in their ability to inform our understanding of the causes of delinquency and crime. Here the problem was not with temporal order, but with the absence of detailed measures of explanatory variables. Typically, these cohort studies had large samples and measures were drawn almost exclusively from official documents such as school and police records. As a result, there were few, if any, good indicators of important causal processes such as family relationships, commitment to school, peer associations, and so forth.

In the end, therefore, the research tradition in criminology that existed for the better part of the 20th century failed to investigate satisfactorily the causal processes associated with criminal careers. Most empirical tests of theory relied on cross-sectional designs that could not disentangle temporal order; cohort studies could, but by design they were primarily descriptive and had little data on explanatory variables.

To address these limitations, the style of both criminological theory and empirical study has changed to take time more explicitly into account. The intriguing empirical descriptions of delinquent and criminal careers generated by cohort studies led to developmental theories of delinquency. For example, the theories offered by Hawkins and Weis (1985), Thornberry (1987), and Loeber and LeBlanc (1990) were early efforts to move beyond static models and to present theoretical explanations informed by longitudinal data. In turn, individual-based panel studies emerged as the primary way of testing the dynamic hypotheses that are at the core of developmental models.

Panel Studies of Crime and Delinquency

Panel studies of crime and delinquency share a core set of design features, while at the same time exhibiting substantial variation in approach. We will begin our discussion by describing the common elements of these studies, at least of the type of panel study included in this book. In many ways, we describe an ideal type of panel study and actual studies conform to them in varying degrees.

Common Elements

The core unit of analysis is the individual, typically selected in childhood or early adolescence. While data on other units—for example, family, peer group, and neighborhood—may be collected and analyzed, the study ultimately emanates from, and revolves around, a focal subject. That subject is typically selected before or at the normal age of onset of delinquent careers to allow for an examination of the precursors of antisocial behavior and to better estimate temporal order among the constructs.

Panel studies are usually based on probability samples selected from a representative, community population. By definition, nondelinquents and delinquents are included, and, among the latter, a full range of offending patterns in terms of frequency, severity, and types of careers should be represented. Using community samples allows for inferences to the general population and avoids the biases produced by selected samples such as clinical samples, incarcerated populations, known gang members, and the like. The samples used in these panel studies also tend to be relatively large to allow for precise estimation of complex statistical models.

All panel studies involve following subjects over time with repeated measures. Preferably, the follow-up period will extend across long portions of the life course, beginning prior to the onset of offending, moving through the peak offending periods of adolescence and early adulthood, and including the adult years when most antisocial careers wind down. The follow-up period should also extend across major developmental stages—childhood, adolescence, emerging adulthood, and adulthood—to maximize our ability to use developmental change to help understand the onset, course, and termination of delinquent careers.

Measures are gathered at regular intervals throughout this period and, within reason, more measurement points are better than fewer. Practical concerns of budget, respondent fatigue, and attrition usually place a natural break on the number of assessments conducted.

At a minimum, measures need to provide an assessment of involvement in the full range of antisocial behaviors and the major risk factors and presumed causes of delinquency and crime. The latter, of course, are heavily theory-dependent and the underlying theory guiding the study should be presented as explicitly as possible. Core measures are typically repeated to gauge stability and change in these constructs, but some measures need to be deleted or modified and new measures need to be added to reflect the developmental changes experienced by the focal subjects.

There are several basic purposes of individual panel studies of this sort. Among them is the description of delinquent and criminal careers, for example, estimating the prevalence and frequency of offending, age of onset patterns, trajectories of offending, and termination. The primary purpose is explanatory or etiological, however. These studies are designed to investigate the antecedent risk factors and causal processes that lead to delinquent careers and to different types of delinquent careers. While survey designs can never examine causal processes as definitively as experimental designs, the long-term, repeated measurement approach of individual panel studies comes closest to doing so, especially if the study extends across major developmental periods and begins prior to the age of onset. A third basic purpose of these studies is to examine the consequences of antisocial behavior, both in terms of disruption to normal life-course development and in terms of the perpetuation of delinquent careers themselves.

Diversity of Panel Studies

While individual panel studies share a common approach to research, these core design features are, in many ways, a platform from which a host of specific projects can be launched. And, indeed, actual panel studies vary considerably in how they examine delinquent and criminal careers.

There are many different conceptual orientations represented in panel studies of crime and delinquency. Some are more biological or psychological in orientation, others more sociological and structural. Some are more theory-driven, guided by a specific theoretical model; others are more eclectic, studying a broad array of risk factors and antecedents. Some studies are more interdisciplinary; others are more monothematic in approach.

Panel studies also differ in their specific research designs. They start at different ages and have varying numbers of assessments. In some studies, assessments are conducted at regularly spaced intervals, while in others, they are done at varyingly spaced intervals. Some studies select and focus on a single or tightly bunched age cohort, while others use an accelerated longitudinal design in which multiple, overlapping age cohorts are selected and followed.

Individual panel studies also vary considerably in their approach to measurement. All of these studies conduct interviews with the focal subject, but around that core there is substantial variation in the inclusion of other respondents and in the use of other methods. Among the many choices are interviews with parents, peers, and partners; the collection of archival data from school, juvenile and criminal justice agencies, and social service agencies; teacher reports; and observing the focal subjects interacting with others.

Panel studies also vary in the inclusion of other programmatic elements. Some embed substudies in the core study to examine specific issues, often using a subsample of the total panel. Some offer prevention or treatment programs to a subsample and use the remainder as the control group.

These are just a few of the conceptual, design, and programmatic dimensions along which individual panel studies of antisocial behavior actually vary. When the possible combinations of all these dimensions are taken into account, it is quite literally true that every panel study of delinquency and crime is unique. By sharing a common approach to the scientific investigation of delinquency and crime, these studies allow for replication and the accumulation of knowledge. At the same time though, the specific design decisions that are made yield a rich diversity of approach that allows for the investigation of unique issues and for testing the robustness and generalizability of core relationships with somewhat different methods. These twin features—common core design elements and diversity of approach—are perhaps the greatest strengths of individual panel studies of delinquency and crime.

Limitations of Panel Studies

Although panel studies have many strengths, they are certainly not without their limitations. There are a number of important theoretical questions that are hard to examine within the basic design features described above. For example, examining the impact of situational dynamics and group processes on antisocial behavior is hampered by the individual-level unit of analysis and focus of these studies. Although not impossible to investigate within the confines of panel studies, the individual-level focus of these studies hampers our ability to examine them fully.

Individual panel studies also lack the rigor of true experimental designs for testing causal propositions. Although clearly superior to cross-sectional designs, they still fail to rule out as many threats to internal validity as experiments do.

Also, panel studies are admittedly expensive and time-consuming. Maintaining a sample across time to reinterview at regular intervals is expensive and the analyses and results can only unfold as quickly (or as slowly) as the data are collected. Results are often not produced as rapidly as policy makers, funding agencies, and colleagues would like.

A final limitation we wish to raise, and one which in many ways gives rise to this volume, concerns the dissemination of results. One strength of panel studies is the sheer range of substantive issues they can address, especially as the subjects age and enter new developmental stages. What begins as a study of adolescent delinquency can eventually lead to an examination of marital formation, parenthood, employment careers, and many other issues. But, this diversity also leads to a certain fragmentation. Empirical findings tend to be published in a number of different journals in different disciplines. It is often hard for the field, and to some extent for the investigators, to obtain an overall picture of the pattern of results and of their interrelationships. Relationships that appear idiosyncratic at first glance, say with respect to risk factors for different outcomes, may conform to a very clear pattern when placed in juxtaposition. Because of this, we thought it wise to step back and "take stock" of the results that have already been presented by some, but certainly not all, of the leading contemporary panel studies of antisocial behavior. Our aim was, first, to summarize the findings within each of the studies and, second, by compiling them into one volume to create a database, if you will, to help identify commonalities and differences across the projects. We hope that doing so will identify common themes and begin to pave over the fragmentation that sometimes occurs in these long-term investigations of human development, and in the role of antisocial behavior in that development.

Taking Stock

The present volume initially began with the three projects of the Program of Research on the Causes and Correlates of Delinquency. These projects—the Denver Youth Survey, the Pittsburgh Youth Study, and the Rochester Youth Development Study—began in 1986 with support from the Office of Juvenile Justice and Delinquency Prevention (OJJDP). The projects have been ongoing since then with continuing support from OJJDP and with support from a variety of other funding agencies (see Chapters 2–4). Initially, all three projects were designed to investigate the causes, correlates, and consequences of delinquent behavior, especially serious and chronic delinquency. In the ensuing years, however, the projects have branched out to investigate many additional issues as well, for example, developmental psychopathology, teenage parenthood, transitions to adulthood, patterns of work, and cross-national comparisons. Many of these topics emerged as the subjects aged and entered different developmental stages and an examination of these issues became necessary both to understand better the origins of delinquency as well as to understand its consequences.

By the late 1990s, the results of the projects of the Program of Research on the Causes and Correlates of Delinquency had been reported in well over 100 articles, chapters, books, and reports. For the 1998 meeting of the American Society of Criminology, we paused to examine the findings up to that point and presented those papers in a session entitled "Taking Stock: Ten Years of Findings From the Program of Research on the Causes and Correlates of Delinquency." The three papers were well-received and the investigators decided to formalize them in the chapters that begin this book.

We also realized that there are many other panel studies of delinquency and crime and that this volume would benefit immensely if it were expanded to include some of them. In inviting other projects to join the effort, we tried to include as many contemporary panel studies of antisocial behavior as possible that are ongoing and that have collected data regularly over at least a ten-year period. There are other studies that could have been included; indeed, the directors of several other projects were invited to contribute to this volume, but because of other personal and professional obligations, they could not. Nevertheless, the longitudinal studies that are represented here conform rather nicely to the twin themes of common design elements and diversity of approach discussed earlier.

All seven projects are based on rather large community samples selected either in childhood or adolescence. The subjects have been followed over many years, typically well into their twenties. There have been multiple measurement points with core measures repeated over time to assess stability and change in development. All projects have excelled at subject retention and all have contributed substantially to our growing understanding of the origins of antisocial behavior.

At the same time, the seven studies included in this volume represent much of the diversity found in individual-based panel studies of antisocial behavior. In addition to the three projects of the Program of Research on the Causes and Correlates of Delinquency, the Seattle Social Development Project and the Houston Longitudinal Study are based on American samples, while the Cambridge Study in Delinquent Development is based on a British sample, and the Montreal Longitudinal Study is based on a Francophone Canadian sample. Although all seven studies have urban samples, the study sites vary considerably in the size of the metropolitan area—from London, England, one of the world's great cities, to Rochester, NY, the smallest of the cities represented here.

The studies also vary on more substantive theoretical and methodological grounds. Some are more explicitly focused on testing a specific theoretical model, while others are more guided by a risk factor approach designed to identify major antecedents of delinquency. Some are more psychological in orientation, while others are more sociological. But, all share an interest in and respect for interdisciplinary approaches to explaining delinquent and criminal behavior.

These studies began when the subjects were different ages, ranging from childhood to early adolescence, and they have followed them to varying points of adulthood. Some studies have chosen to focus on a single cohort, for example, the Houston study selected seventh graders; other studies sampled multiple age groups, for example, the Denver study initially sampled 7, 9, 11, 13, and 15-year-olds. Some studies included males and females, while others included only males. There is also substantial racial and ethnic diversity; some studies include only White subjects, while other samples are predominantly African American and Latino.

The seven projects also differ in their approach to measurement. They used different data collection techniques, such as interviews, questionnaires, and observations. They included different informants, for example, parents, peers, and teachers. Some rely more on official measures of delinquency and crime, while others rely almost exclusively on self-reported measures. Some measures are common across all the projects—especially across the three projects of the Program of Research on the Causes and Correlates of Delinquency—while others are unique to a single project.

But, despite these and other differences, all of these projects have two overriding common features. First, they are all individual-based panel studies that have followed a focal subject over time with repeated measures. Second, they are all focused on the same basic question: What are the origins and consequences of delinquent and criminal careers? For example, all are interested in examining the role of family, school, and peer effects in causing delinquency and all are interested in what delinquency does to the individual and his or her course of development. One of the fundamental purposes of this book, therefore, is to examine the extent to which the answers to these basic questions are similar across these studies with their somewhat different guiding theories, methods, and settings. For if they are, it would suggest that these results are robust and indicate something fundamental about the origins and consequences of antisocial behavior that go beyond the idiosyncrasies of any one study. We return to this issue in the concluding chapter.

Reflecting the origins of this volume, we begin with summaries from each of the projects of the Program of Research on the Causes and Correlates of Delinquency. We then present the other studies in chronological order, beginning with the oldest study represented here, the Cambridge Study in Delinquent Development. In the ensuing chapters, the investigators of these studies briefly describe the studies and their basic designs, and then summarize some of the core findings that have emerged from these individual-based panel studies of delinquent and criminal careers.

References

Akers, R. L., Krohn, M. D., Lanza-Kaduce, L., & Radosevich, M. (1979). Social learning and deviant behavior: A specific test of a general theory. *American Sociological Review, 4*, 635–655.

Hamparian, D. M., Shuster, R. S., Dinitz, S., & Conrad, J. P. (1978). *The violent few: A study of dangerous juvenile offenders.* Lexington, MA: D. C. Heath.

Hawkins, J. D., & Weis, J. G. (1985). The social development model: An integrated approach to delinquency prevention. *Journal of Primary Prevention, 6*, 73–97.

Hindelang, M. J. (1973). Causes of delinquency: A partial replication and extension. *Social Problems, 20*, 471–487.

Hirschi, T. (1969). *Causes of delinquency.* Berkeley, CA: University of California Press.

Janson, C.-G. (Ed.). (2000). *Seven Swedish longitudinal studies in the behavioral sciences.* Stockholm, Sweden: Swedish Council for Planning and Coordination of Research.

Johnson, R. E. (1979). *Juvenile delinquency and its origins.* New York: Cambridge University Press.

Loeber, R., & LeBlanc, M. (1990). Toward a developmental criminology. In M. Tonry & N. Morris (Eds.), *Crime and justice: An annual review of research* (Vol. 12, pp. 375–473). Chicago: University of Chicago Press.

Magnusson, D., Bergman, L. R., Rudinger, G., & Törestad, B. (1991). (Eds.), *Problems and methods in longitudinal research: Stability and change.* New York: Cambridge University Press.

Shannon, L. W. (1988). *Criminal career continuity: Its social context.* New York: Human Sciences Press.

Short, J. F. (1957). Differential association and delinquency. *Social Problems, 4*, 233–239.

Thornberry, T. P. (1987). Toward an interactional theory of delinquency. *Criminology, 25*, 863–891.

Tracy, P. E., Wolfgang, M. E., & Figlio, R. (1990). *Delinquency careers in two birth cohorts.* New York: Plenum.

Wolfgang, M. E., Figlio, R. M., & Sellin, T. (1972). *Delinquency in a birth cohort.* Chicago: University of Chicago Press.

Wolfgang, M. E., Thornberry, T. P., & Figlio, R. M. (1987). *From boy to man, from delinquency to crime.* Chicago: University of Chicago Press.

2

Causes and Consequences of Delinquency

Findings from the Rochester Youth Development Study

Terence P. Thornberry, Alan J. Lizotte, Marvin D. Krohn, Carolyn A. Smith, and Pamela K. Porter

Introduction

The Rochester Youth Development Study began in 1986 as one of three projects in the Office of Juvenile Justice and Delinquency Prevention's Program of Research on the Causes and Correlates of Delinquency. The purpose of the Rochester study is to investigate the causes and consequences of adolescent delinquency, with a particular focus on serious, chronic offenders.

While the initial aim was to study adolescent delinquency and drug use, over the years the project has expanded into a broader investigation of both prosocial and antisocial development across the life course. We have reported our findings in scores of publications, reports, dissertations, and presentations. We have investigated a number of interrelated analytic topics, and in this paper we try to "take stock" of at least some of what we have learned. We first summarize the theoretical and methodological approaches of the Rochester Youth Development Study and then discuss some of our key empirical findings.

Taking Stock of Delinquency: An Overview of Findings from Contemporary Longitudinal Studies, edited by Thornberry and Krohn. Kluwer Academic/Plenum Publishers, New York, 2003.

Theoretical Framework

The overall design of the Rochester study is guided by two theoretical models—interactional theory and social network theory. Interactional theory, first presented by Thornberry in 1987 and extended by Thornberry and Krohn in 2001, provides the core conceptual framework for hypotheses concerning the causes and consequences of delinquency. Social network theory was developed by Krohn in 1986 and its complementary perspective has been used to expand the theoretical purview of interactional theory. While these conceptual models help to guide the research design and measurement space of the Rochester project, the results of the study also help us to revise, expand, and better integrate our conceptual models of delinquency (see especially, Thornberry & Krohn, 2001). In this section we provide brief overviews of these theoretical models.

Interactional Theory

There are three fundamental premises to an interactional theory of delinquency. First, the theory adopts a developmental or life-course perspective; second, it emphasizes bidirectional causality; and third, it incorporates social structural influences into the explanation of individual delinquent careers.

Based on this framework, interactional theory posits that the basic cause of delinquency is a weakening of social controls caused by an attenuation of the person's bond to conventional society. For adolescents in particular, the bond is formed by strong relationships to parents and family, by commitment to and success in school, and by aspirations for and belief in conventional success goals. Adolescents who are strongly attached to, monitored by, and involved with their families are unlikely candidates for prolonged involvement in delinquency. The affective and control elements of these family processes should place bounds on the behavioral freedom of the adolescent. Similar arguments can be made with regard to both school and belief variables (see Thornberry, 1987).

In contrast, adolescents who have brittle relationships with their parents, who are alienated from school, and who lack conventional success goals have fewer social constraints to channel their behavior toward prosocial arenas. They have greater behavioral freedom and are more likely to become involved in delinquency.

For these youth to become seriously and persistently involved in delinquency, however, they need a social environment in which their new-found freedom is channeled in that particular direction. That environment is epitomized by the delinquent peer group which provides delinquent models and reinforcements for both delinquent behavior and delinquent beliefs. As youth freed from the constraints of the conventional world gravitate together, they find a social environment that supports and encourages prolonged involvement in delinquency.

At a very general level, therefore, interactional theory offers a two-stage explanation of delinquency. The causally prior stage is a weakening of social bonds which then leads to involvement in delinquent networks.

While the theoretical model begins here, it is more complex than this, as suggested by the earlier discussion of interactional theory's basic premises. First, interactional theory does not view these causal influences as static or unidirectional. Indeed, a core argument is that delinquent behavior feeds back upon and produces changes in both bonding and associations. The more the individual engages in delinquency, the more that involvement is likely to increase alienation from parents, reduce commitment to school, and render conventional success goals moot. To illustrate, interactional theory does not assume, as many static theoretical models do, that extensive drug use has no causal impact on school performance. Quite the contrary, interactional theory explicitly argues that prolonged drug use has profound effects on school performance and other sources of social control. Interactional theory also says that involvement in deviance will increase both associations with deviant peers and the formation of deviant belief systems.

Second, interactional theory argues that these causal influences vary developmentally. For example, during childhood, family influences are predicted to be more powerful than school or peer influences in shaping behavior. As the individual moves through adolescence, the burgeoning search for and attainment of autonomy increases the impact of school and peer influences, while the impact of the family fades.

These developmental stages are not discrete realms but are themselves causally interrelated. The more successful the individual is in meeting the developmental challenges of earlier stages, the more likely they are to succeed as they reach later stages. For example, children who form strong family attachments during childhood are better positioned to successfully negotiate autonomy during adolescence without resorting to extensive involvement in delinquency. Similarly, the more successful the person is at forming prosocial competencies and avoiding strong antisocial influences during adolescence, the easier the transition to adulthood should be and the easier it should be for the person to escape any involvement in delinquency.

Finally, interactional theory posits that all of these processes vary by structural position. Youth growing up in socially disadvantaged families and neighborhoods, especially if they are people of color, are apt to have more difficult life-course trajectories in which the previous processes leading to delinquent careers are exacerbated. Their environment diminishes the chances that strong prosocial bonds and opportunities will be available and heightens the chances that deviant opportunities—such as delinquent peers, street gangs, and drug markets—will be available as they reach adolescence. Given that, the bidirectional causal effects and their developmental consequences described earlier have fertile ground in which to unfold, and these youngsters are more likely to have serious and persistent delinquent careers.

Recently, Thornberry and Krohn (2001) presented a life-course extension of interactional theory stemming from the work of Glen Elder (1985, 1997). One of the great challenges to criminological theory is to account for both the continuity and change that is observed in criminal careers. While some offenders begin early and persist in offending over long portions of the life course, other careers are marked by change, either from offending to desistance or from prosocial behavior patterns to an onset of antisocial behavior patterns at a later age.

Unlike early starter/late starter typological models of delinquency (e.g., Moffitt, 1993, 1997; Patterson, Capaldi, & Bank, 1991), interactional theory starts from the assumption that the onset of delinquent careers is *continuously* distributed and that the correlation between onset and the duration of careers is moderate (see Krohn, Thornberry, Rivera, & LeBlanc, 2001). The model attempts to account for both of these observations rather than assuming that there are different etiological theories for two different types of offenders.

At one extreme are offenders who have an onset of aggressive, antisocial behavior sometime during early childhood *and* who persist in offending over long portions of the life course. This precocious and persistent offending is caused by the confluence of severe structural disadvantage, ineffective parenting, and individual deficits. These children have multiple risk factors to generate, and very few protective factors to ward off, an early onset of antisocial behavior. They also have few resources to ward off the reciprocal consequences of their early antisocial behavior, e.g., school failure, peer rejection, and embeddedness in deviant social networks. As a result, they are more likely to become entrapped in delinquent careers, in part because of continuity in the underlying causes and in part because of the adverse consequences of their own behavior. Escape becomes increasingly difficult as more and more avenues to prosocial careers become closed and long-term careers in criminal behavior become more likely.

Relatively few children are exposed to the potent mix of extreme structural disadvantage, ineffective parenting, and individual deficits, however. As these causal influences weaken in strength and as they become uncoupled, the impetus for a very early onset of delinquency diminishes and the onset of offending starts later and later. The severity of offending also diminishes as the potency of the causal factors diminishes. Given the uncoupling of these causal factors, these youth are also more likely to have protective factors to buffer them from whatever adverse consequences their antisocial behavior generates. As a result, escape from or desistance from their antisocial careers becomes more likely in light of the greater human and social capital available to these youth, as compared to the truly early onset offenders.

Thornberry and Krohn (2001) also discuss youth who begin offending even later, during adolescence. Their relatively mild and short-lived involvement in delinquency is in large part generated by the search for autonomy that typifies adolescence. Their movement away from parental control and their engrossment in adolescent social networks is a fertile field for minor forms of deviance—drinking, precocious sexual behavior, disorderly conduct, and the like. Unlike serious aggressive and covert forms of antisocial behavior, however, these manifestations are relatively nonconsequential in terms of formal reactions (e.g., labeling) or informal reactions (e.g., peer rejection). For these reasons, as well as the abundant human and social capital that delayed their onset of delinquency in the first place, they are unlikely to persist in their delinquent involvement.

Social Network Theory

To complement interactional theory's focus on the importance of the relationships between adolescents and both their peers and parents, the Rochester Youth Development Study has employed social network theory (Krohn, 1986) to better understand the structure and dynamics of those relationships. A social network is defined as a "specified set of links among social actors" (Fischer et al., 1977, p. 33). Thus, the focus of network analysis is on the structure and content of those links, rather than on the individual characteristics of the actors. How a network is structured and where a particular individual lies within that set of relationships are considered important in determining the behaviors of the individual actors involved in the network.

The social network perspective assumes that all social networks constrain the behavior of their participants to some extent. However, the degree of constraint depends on the structure of the social network. The type of behavior in which network members participate affects the type of behavior to which any member is constrained.

The structural characteristics of the social networks include homophily, density, intimacy, multiplexity, and stability. Homophily refers to the similarity of friends in terms of a number of attributes, including both personal characteristics, such as race, and attitudes and behaviors, such as drug use. Density is the degree to which each member of a social network knows or likes all other members of the network. Social networks can also be characterized by how intimate or supportive the relationships are among members. Multiplexity refers to the number of different role relations any two people have with one another or the number of contexts in a relationship. Stability of friendship networks is the degree to which individuals report having the same friends over time. All of these structural characteristics can be used to describe peer social networks while only homophily, intimacy, and multiplexity can be used to describe the family network.

Delinquent behavior is expected when the individual is enmeshed in some, and especially many, networks that allow or encourage such behavior. This is particularly the case if the networks are interlocking (multiplex), dense, intimate, stable, and have members who exhibit similar behaviors and attitudes.

Design of the Rochester Youth Development Study

The Rochester Youth Development Study (RYDS) utilizes a longitudinal research design to follow a panel of juveniles from their early teenage years through their early adult years. To date, we have collected 12 waves of data spanning the ages of 13 through 22.

Each subject and a primary caretaker (the biological mother in 85% of the cases) were interviewed at six-month intervals from the spring of 1988 until the spring of 1992. After a $2\frac{1}{2}$-year gap in data collection, annual interviews began in 1994. At the end of Wave 12, in the spring of 1997, we reinterviewed 846 of the initial 1,000 subjects in the study, a retention rate of 85%.

The interviews covered a wide range of topics, including family, school, social class, peers, neighborhood, delinquency and drug use, psychological functioning, and social support. We also collected data from official agencies, including the schools, police department, probation department, family court, and social services.

Sample

Because we know that the base rates for serious delinquency and drug use are relatively low, youth at high risk for these behaviors were oversampled. This was accomplished by (1) limiting the target population to 7th- and 8th-grade students in the public schools of Rochester, New York—a city with a diverse population and a relatively high crime rate—and (2) selecting a stratified sample so that high-risk youth are overrepresented.

To oversample high-risk youth, the sample was stratified on two dimensions. First, males were oversampled (75% versus 25%) because they are more likely than females to be chronic offenders and to engage in serious delinquency. Second, students from high arrest rate areas of the city were oversampled based on the assumption that adolescents who live in high arrest rate areas are at greater risk for offending. Since the probability of selection into the study is known for all the students, we can weight the data to represent the target population—the total cohort of 7th and 8th graders in the public schools of Rochester in 1988.

A final panel of 1,000 students and their primary caretakers was selected for study. The sample is 68% African American, 17% Hispanic, and 15% White. Virtually all of the Hispanic respondents in the sample are of Puerto Rican descent. Males represent 72.9% of the sample and females 27.1%. More detailed discussions of the sampling plan for the Rochester project can be found in a number of project publications, including Thornberry, Bjerregaard, and Miles (1993a), Krohn and Thornberry (1999), and Thornberry, Krohn, Lizotte, Smith, and Tobin (in press).

Subject Retention

Subject attrition is a potentially serious threat to the validity of inferences drawn from panel studies of delinquency and drug use. The importance of maintaining high levels of retention is underscored in an examination of the consequences of attrition (Thornberry et al., 1993a). Higher levels of attrition than those actually found in the Rochester sample were simulated and two sets of results were compared: those obtained when the more elusive subjects (those who were more mobile) and the less cooperative subjects (those who required more contacts) were included and those obtained when these hard-to-interview respondents were excluded. This simulation demonstrated that concerns about subject attrition were warranted. When the more elusive respondents were excluded from analyses, estimates of the prevalence and frequency of delinquency, as well as results from basic regression analyses, were biased. Similar results were obtained for the less cooperative respondents, although the differences were smaller.

Because of these implications for validity, considerable effort has been devoted to maximizing subject retention over the course of the Rochester study, particularly given the low income, highly mobile nature of many of our subjects, and the expectation that delinquent youth would be more difficult to contact and track. First, there was no a priori limit to the number of attempted contacts that were made at each wave of data collection. Second, all subjects who moved from Rochester were followed and interviewed whenever possible. Third, even though we conducted most of the adolescent interviews in the Rochester schools, adolescents who left the Rochester schools remained in the panel. Finally, we attempted to maintain cooperation by incentive payments, newsletters, and routine reminders to the subjects of the importance of the study and of their participation in it.

As a result of these procedures, the Rochester study has an excellent record of retaining these predominantly high-risk youth over a nine-year period involving 12 waves of data collection. In an initial analysis of potential attrition bias, Thornberry et al. (1993a) examined the level of attrition over the first six waves of the study and compared those who remained with those who left the panel. The retention rate at Wave 6 was 90%. Comparisons by race/ethnicity, gender, census tract of residence, and Wave 1 measures of delinquency and drug use showed that the subjects who remained in the study at Wave 6 were still representative of the overall panel. In other words, there was no evidence of differential attrition.

Krohn and Thornberry (1999) extended the investigation of subject retention through Wave 10. Over the course of the study, about 1% of the focal subjects were lost per year. Even with the $2\frac{1}{2}$-year gap in data collection between Waves 9 and 10 when the subjects moved from being high school students to the much more mobile and diverse stage of young adulthood, retention only dropped from 88% to 86%.

Parent attrition was slightly higher and more uneven across the waves. There was a larger drop in parent retention from Wave 5 to Wave 6 than there had previously been (from 86% to 81%). This was primarily due to an increasing number of adolescents who no longer lived with their parents at those ages. Since the vast majority of adolescent respondents continued to live with their parents, however, the interview schedule reflected this reality and was somewhat inappropriate for the parents who had little or no contact with the subject. Starting in Wave 10, when many subjects no longer lived with their parents, the interview schedule was revised to reflect this, and retention increased from 79% at Wave 8 to 83% at Wave 10.[1]

Krohn and Thornberry (1999) also examined whether there was selection bias due to attrition by comparing the respondents who were retained in the study with those who were not retained. These groups were compared on gender, social class, and family structure within racial/ethnic categories. Only small differences were evident and *none* of these differences were statistically significant, indicating that the loss of respondents over 10 waves of data collection did not affect the demographic portrait of our respondents.

When Wave 1 delinquency and drug use of the respondents who were retained in the study at Wave 10 were compared to the Wave 1 values for those who were not retained, differences were small and not statistically significant. This finding also holds for different racial/ethnic groups. Overall, evidence points to low levels of attrition and small differences in attrition across various subgroups in the sample.[2]

Measurement

The Rochester project contains a wealth of measures on youth behaviors, as well as measures on a wide range of environmental, social, and psychological forces that contribute to these behaviors. Because of the longitudinal nature of the project, we have multiple measures of the same variable over time, enabling us to track developmental progressions and changes in behaviors. To allow for replication of analyses across the three projects of the Program of Research on the Causes and Correlates of Delinquency, over half of the measures are drawn from a set of common measures developed at the beginning of the study.

Delinquency

At each wave, respondents were asked if they committed each of 36 delinquent acts and, if so, how often they had done so. All responses were screened to

---

[1] There were no parent interviews at Wave 9.

[2] Although not published, these comparisons have been extended to Wave 12 with the same results. There is no evidence of differential subject loss.

make sure they were categorized appropriately and then grouped into meaningful indices. For example, the general offending index includes 32 items covering a range of delinquent behaviors from status offenses, vandalism, and minor property crimes to serious violent and property crimes. Violent offending is comprised of six items, including attacking someone with a weapon and throwing objects such as rocks or bottles at people. Similar indices are constructed for a variety of other categories, including both severity and type of offending, as well as for drug use and drug sales. In addition to self-reported data on offending, other related behaviors, including self-reported gang membership and illegal gun carrying, were measured.

Official data on involvement with the police were obtained from the records of the Rochester Police Department and the New York State Division of Criminal Justice Services (DCJS). For the juvenile years, our data include official police contacts and arrests that were eventually sealed by the Juvenile Court because we searched the police files on an ongoing basis. Also, because the Rochester Police Department is a central repository for arrest records from other law enforcement agencies in Monroe County, arrests from surrounding communities are included. For the adult years, the Rochester data include all arrests in Rochester and the surrounding communities. In 1998, we searched the statewide files of DCJS to identify arrests that occurred outside of the Rochester area. Only unsealed records were available in the DCJS files. Probation and family court data were also collected.

Other Variables

We have measured a wide range of other variables that can be categorized into seven domains: parent-child relations, school factors, peer relationships, family sociodemographic characteristics, parental stressors, area characteristics, and individual characteristics. Most of these variables come from parent and youth interviews, but some were drawn from school records, social services records, and census data.

Analytic Themes

The Rochester study is a wide-ranging investigation of the development of delinquent behavior, following a high-risk sample from early adolescence through early adulthood and assessing multiple domains of the subjects' lives. Our analytic approach is also wide-ranging. Given the breadth of our measures, we have been able to investigate a variety of substantive topics related to the causes and consequences of delinquency and drug use. In this paper, we group these individual investigations into broader themes to summarize our empirical findings.

Some of these themes test hypotheses that flow directly from the conceptual models that guide the study. For example, both interactional theory and social network theory emphasize the importance of family and peers in the explanation of adolescent delinquency, and several publications have focused on these issues. In them, we have tried to examine the various conceptual premises that underlie interactional and network theories. For example, we have examined bidirectional causal influences, developmental changes in causal effects, and how family and peer networks coincide to produce delinquency and drug use.

While many of our investigations stem from the conceptual models that guide this project, others have been responsive to the environmental and life-course changes that have occurred during the course of the study. For example, during the late 1980s and early 1990s two secular changes occurred that could not have been anticipated at the outset of this longitudinal study. One was the sharp and rapid increase in youth violence, both nationally and in Rochester. The other was the tremendous spread of adolescent street gangs to more and more American cities, including Rochester. One of the great advantages of longitudinal studies is their ability to investigate new issues such as these as they unfold during the course of the study. Because of that, we added measures of both gang membership and gun ownership and use, the latter benefiting greatly from Lizotte's earlier work in this area (Lizotte & Bordua, 1980).

Other themes emerged as a result of our ability to continue following these subjects past their adolescent years. Early in the study, for example, we noted a high rate of teen pregnancy and parenthood among the sample members which led to an interest in assessing this behavioral area and, ultimately, to a study of intergenerational continuity and discontinuity in antisocial behavior.

In the following pages, we identify these themes and summarize the empirical findings to date for each. We begin with themes testing our theoretical models and then move to the themes that emerged as the study unfolded.

Family and Delinquency

The effectiveness and quality of parenting and the warmth of relationships among family members play important roles in interactional theory. What occurs in the home, particularly in the early adolescent years, is hypothesized to influence adolescents' attitudes to and performance in school, adherence to prosocial and deviant beliefs, their choice of friends, and their participation in delinquent behavior. Interactional theory also recognizes that participation in delinquent behavior and association with delinquent peers will have feedback effects on the quality of child-parent interactions, causing strain in those relationships. As adolescents mature, other social influences become more salient in their lives and the influence of the family begins to fade. Because of the important role that the family is hypothesized to play during the early adolescent years, we have explored its influence in some depth.

Measurement Issues

Our first step was to investigate alternative ways to measure family processes (Krohn, Stern, Thornberry, & Jang, 1992). Prior research had identified three general clusters of family processes: (1) the provision of control, (2) the provision of guidance, and (3) affective attachment. Much of the research on these clusters of variables had been limited to measuring the children's perception of what parents did and how youth felt about their parents. Recognizing that family processes involve the interaction of children and their parents, we examined the extent to which the perceptions of parents could shed additional light on the relationship between delinquency and family processes.

Krohn et al. (1992) measured nine different family processes with parallel measures asked of both children and their parents. Not surprisingly, adolescent and parent perceptions were not very highly correlated. (Pearson correlation coefficients ranged from .05 to .31.) Parent and child perceptions of control mechanisms such as supervision and discipline were particularly discordant. When family processes were correlated to both official and self-reported measures of delinquency, differences in the performance of child and parent measures were observed. Both child and parent measures of family processes contributed independently to the explanation of delinquency. However, child measures of family processes were more strongly related to self-reported delinquency, whereas parent measures were more strongly related to official delinquency. Of the nine different measures of family process, attachment and involvement were the most highly correlated, whether measured with child or parent data, for both self-reported and official delinquency. This study highlights the importance of acquiring information on parent–child relationships from sources other than the child.

The Impact of Structure

Having found that family process variables are related to delinquency, we examined whether the effect of family variables might be different for children from different racial or ethnic backgrounds. Smith and Krohn (1995) posited a causal model that included measures of economic hardship and single-parent families as exogenous variables to the family process variables of attachment (parent perception), involvement (adolescent perception), and control (adolescent perception). All five variables were predicted to have direct effects on self-reported delinquency. Path coefficients were computed separately for African American, Hispanic, and White males.

Although the results indicate that family processes play a role for all families in the determination of who will be law abiding, the impact of family life on adolescents does not appear to be uniform across different racial and ethnic contexts. Family socialization has a relatively weak impact on delinquency in African American and White families but has a stronger impact on Hispanic families. Hispanic males appear to be more adversely affected (in terms of delinquent outcomes) by not having a father present in the home than are either Whites or African Americans. In addition, parental involvement in the lives of children is directly related to delinquency for Hispanic males but is not directly related for White or African American males. In contrast, parental attachment and control are directly related to delinquency for Whites and African Americans, but not for Hispanics.

These findings suggest that there may be interactions between the family process variables and the racial or ethnic background of the family. We need to place these findings in the context of what is known about the differences among the different racial and ethnic groups in order to better understand how the family influences an adolescent's involvement in delinquent or prosocial behavior.

Although not a central focus of this research, Smith and Krohn did find some support for interactional theory's hypothesis that social structural variables like economic hardship and family structure were related to family process variables. Stern and Smith (1995) extended this analysis by incorporating several dimensions of what we refer to as family context measures: economic hardship, disadvantaged neighborhood, life distress, social isolation, and lack of partner support. Using the entire RYDS sample, we found that the family's disadvantaged neighborhood, life distress, social isolation, and lack of partner support were associated with dysfunctional parenting. Surprisingly, economic hardship per se was not associated with dysfunctional parenting. Life distress, a dimension that included recent life events, parental depression, and perceived inability to cope with stress, was particularly influential in adversely affecting the quality of the relationship between parents and their children.

In a continuation of this line of research, Stern, Smith, and Jang (1999) looked at the impact of social and economic disadvantage on parent distress, family processes, and adolescent mental health. The outcomes of interest in this paper included symptoms of adolescent depression and low self-esteem, as well as externalizing problems such as aggression and noncompliance. We found that poverty, life stressors, and isolation negatively affect parental mood, and this disrupts family processes (e.g., support and discipline). Disrupted family processes are, in turn, linked to adolescent internalizing and externalizing problems. Parental distress mediates the relationship between family adversity and disrupted family processes. It appears that parental discipline has more influence on externalizing problems, whereas adolescent perceptions of unsupportive parenting mediate the effects of distress and disrupted discipline on internalizing problems. Overall, it is important to note that the social and family context plays a key role in producing delinquent and disrupted behavior through its effect on parenting.

Family composition is another aspect of family life that is associated with delinquency. Thornberry, Smith, Rivera, Huizinga, and Stouthamer-Loeber (1999) examined the effect that the number of changes in family structure has on adolescent delinquency and drug use. Family transitions were counted by comparing family structure at six-month interview intervals over four years for a maximum of eight possible transitions. Family transitions are significantly related to subsequent increases in both delinquency and drug use.

Reciprocal Effects

Much of the research on family and delinquency, including the RYDS studies reviewed in this section, limits the analysis to the unidirectional effect of family variables on delinquent behavior. Interactional theory emphasizes the role that delinquent behavior can play in leading to disruption in the relationship between parent and child and to the further deterioration of this relationship. Several studies have examined the reciprocal nature of the relationship between family process variables and delinquency.

Thornberry, Lizotte, Krohn, Farnworth, and Jang (1991) investigated the hypothesized interrelationships between attachment to parents, commitment to school, and delinquent behavior using the first three waves of adolescent interviews. We found a complex pattern of relationships between attachment to parents and delinquency. From Wave 1 to Wave 2, these variables are reciprocally related. However, from Wave 2 to Wave 3, the relationship is unidirectional; delinquent behavior has a negative impact on attachment, but attachment does not have a significant effect on delinquency. This latter finding is consistent with interactional theory's hypothesis that family influences on delinquency begin to fade as the youth moves into middle adolescence.

Jang and Smith (1997) included both attachment to parents and parental supervision in a three-wave panel model and found that parental supervision is involved in a reciprocal relationship with delinquent behavior. Low parental supervision increases the likelihood of delinquent behavior, and delinquent behavior, in turn, attenuates subsequent parental supervision. However, the findings regarding attachment to parents do not support the bidirectional hypothesis. Consistent with Thornberry et al. (1991), the relationship between delinquency and attachment to parents is unidirectional; delinquent behavior decreases attachment to parents, but attachment to parents has no significant effect on delinquent behavior. This is not a surprising finding since Jang and Smith used data from Waves 2 through 4, when respondents were moving into middle adolescence.

The failure to find an effect of attachment on delinquent behavior may further support interactional theory's hypothesis concerning the fading effect of family influences, especially attachment, on delinquency during middle adolescence. Stern et al. (1999) and Smith and Stern (1997) discuss the implications of findings on reciprocal relationships, and particularly of the impact of delinquency on family processes for interventions with antisocial and delinquent youth.

The decreasing effect of family processes on delinquent behavior as youth traverse their teenage years is also illustrated in a study by Jang and Krohn (1995). The focus of this study was on whether differences in the rates of delinquency between males and females are invariant over the developmental stages of adolescence. As part of the analysis, Jang and Krohn examined whether parental supervision could account for the differences in the rates of delinquency between males and females. Parental supervision was chosen because it has been suggested that one of the differences in how females are raised as compared to males is that parents are much more concerned about monitoring their daughters' whereabouts and behavior than they are their sons'.

Jang and Krohn found that, for the first five waves of data, parental supervision could, indeed, account for the sex differences in delinquency. However, for Waves 6 through 9, supervision does not explain the sex differences in delinquency. Further analysis revealed that this is due to the declining effect of parental supervision on delinquency rather than any systematic changes in sex differences in the level of parental supervision. Again, these results lend credence to interactional theory's hypothesis concerning the fading effect of family process variables on delinquency as adolescents age.

Summary

Overall, our research on the effect of dimensions of family life on delinquent behavior has supported the major hypotheses from interactional theory. First, several family process variables were found to be related to delinquent behavior, including both parent and child measures. Second, social and family structural variables were found to be indirectly related to delinquent behavior through their effect on these family process variables. Third, the relationship between family process variables and delinquency is a reciprocal one: poor parenting increases the probability of delinquent behavior, and delinquent behavior further attenuates the relationship between parent and child. Finally, we found that the impact of family variables does appear to fade as adolescents age and become more independent from their parents, but that the pattern of these developmental changes is more complex than originally thought. At the earlier waves, delinquency and family process variables are reciprocally related. Over time, the impact of family process variables on delinquency fades, but the impact of delinquency on family processes appears to remain.

Maltreatment and Delinquency

The studies reviewed up to this point focus on the varying impact that parent-child relationships and normal parenting behaviors have on adolescent development, especially delinquency. In a series of papers, we have also examined the consequences of more extreme or aberrant forms of parenting, that is, child abuse and maltreatment. In the first paper, Smith and Thornberry (1995) found that 13.6% of the RYDS sample had substantiated abuse or maltreatment cases prior to the age of 12. As hypothesized, respondents who had been the victims of childhood maltreatment were more likely to have both self-reported and official delinquency during the teenage years, even when a number of control variables, including social class, were included in the analysis. The relationship was particularly strong and robust for the more serious forms of delinquent behavior. Smith and Thornberry also examined the effect of more serious and extensive child maltreatment and found that more extensive maltreatment predicts higher rates of delinquency.

Smith (1996) also linked childhood maltreatment to teen pregnancy, again when controlling for social structural variables such as social class and single-parent status. Kelley, Thornberry, and Smith (1997) extended this research by looking at a range of problematic outcomes that develop in the wake of childhood maltreatment. Although social class and family structure were not controlled in this analysis, there were indications of links between maltreatment and substance use, mental health problems, and academic achievement problems. Maltreatment appears to be an important aspect of family life that must be taken into account when assessing the family's impact on delinquent and high-risk behaviors.

In more recent work, we capitalized on the longitudinal design of the Rochester project to examine the relationship between maltreatment and adolescent outcomes with greater precision. In particular, we took the developmental stage during which the maltreatment occurred into account.

Ireland, Smith, and Thornberry (2002) evaluated the extent to which the timing of maltreatment affects the strength of its impact on delinquency and drug use. Focusing on maltreatment in the context of three developmental periods—childhood-only maltreatment (birth to age 11), adolescence-only maltreatment (12 to 17), and persistent maltreatment that occurs in both developmental periods—we looked at whether the developmental stage in which maltreatment occurs affects its impact on official delinquency, self-reported delinquency, and drug use. Ireland et al. controlled for several variables potentially linked with maltreatment and delinquency, including economic disadvantage, single-parent families, community poverty, lack of parent education, and race/ethnicity. Findings consistently indicate that maltreatment during adolescence and maltreatment that persists from childhood into adolescence are significantly related to official and self-reported delinquency and to self-reported drug use. However, and in contrast to what earlier studies have indicated, maltreatment that occurs only in childhood does not place adolescents at risk for these outcomes. The effect of maltreatment appears to be more short-term than long-term in its consequences.

Thornberry, Ireland, and Smith (2001) extended the examination of developmental stages by studying multiple adolescent outcomes, including delinquency, drug use, problem alcohol use, depressive symptoms, externalizing and internalizing behaviors, teen pregnancy, and dropping out of school, as well as the total number of these outcomes experienced by an individual. Outcomes were measured during both early and late adolescence. Thornberry et al. also examined the impact that different types of maltreatment—physical abuse, sexual abuse (during adolescence only), and neglect—had on these outcomes.

Consistent with the findings of Ireland et al. (2002), Thornberry et al. concluded that "Substantiated maltreatment that begins and ends in childhood ... is, by and large, not significantly related to the range of adolescent outcomes measured in the RYDS study" (2001, p. 975). In contrast, maltreatment that occurs in adolescence or that begins in childhood and persists into adolescence is significantly related to these outcomes. These findings suggest that the impact of risk factors such as maltreatment on delinquency and other adverse outcomes may be more developmentally nuanced than originally thought. The theoretical and policy implications of these findings, especially the need for greater attention to adolescent maltreatment, are discussed in Ireland et al. and Thornberry et al.

School and Delinquency

Another core prediction of interactional theory is that commitment to and success in school will reduce the likelihood that adolescents will engage in delinquent behavior. If they do become enmeshed in delinquency, however, interactional theory predicts that their involvement will have feedback effects that reduce school performance. The interplay between educational factors and delinquency has been examined in four publications.

The most explicit examination of the hypothesized reciprocal relationships was conducted by Thornberry et al. (1991) in which we analyzed a panel model covering the first three waves of the study. We found significant lagged effects from commitment to school to delinquency, as well as significant contemporaneous effects from delinquency to commitment to school. All effects are negative, as predicted. Thus, higher commitment to school reduces delinquent behavior and delinquent behavior also reduces commitment to school, at least during the early adolescent years.

An alternate way of examining the impact of schooling factors on delinquency is to see if educational success provides resilience or protection for youth at high risk for delinquency. This was the approach adopted by Smith, Lizotte, Thornberry, and Krohn (1995) who identified sample members at high risk for delinquency and drug use in terms of nine family-based measures, including low parental education and social class, high residential mobility, and childhood maltreatment. To be considered high risk, the youth had to experience five or more of the nine risk factors. Approximately one-fifth of the sample is considered at risk by this criterion. Over 60% of adolescents identified as high risk are resilient to negative outcomes such as delinquency and drug use in early adolescence

(Waves 2 and 3). Resilience is attributed to the protective factors that distinguish between high-risk youth who do have negative outcomes and those who do not.

The most salient factors for resilience to both delinquency and drug use are school factors. Those who avoided delinquency have higher standardized reading and math scores, are more committed to school and attached to teachers, have higher aspirations and expectations about attending college, and have parents who have higher expectations about their college attendance. With the exception of the adolescent's aspirations for attending college, all of these variables also discriminate between drug users and nonusers.

Overall, therefore, Smith et al. (1995) found that educational commitment and performance reduce the level of both delinquency and drug use, even for high-risk youth. This protective effect appears to fade over time for delinquency, but those with many protective factors are still resilient to drug use three years later.

While school performance unfolds over the adolescent years, in many ways it culminates in either graduating from or dropping out of school. Graduation is a significant marker for the transition to adult status, and failure to graduate may confirm and reinforce a problematic behavioral trajectory. Krohn, Thornberry, Collins-Hall, and Lizotte (1995) examined the interplay between dropping out of high school and involvement in drug use and delinquency. Prior drug use is significantly related to dropping out of school, even after demographic, family, and school performance measures are held constant. Prior involvement in serious delinquency is not related to dropout status, however.

Examining the impact of dropout status on later deviance, Krohn et al. (1995) found that dropout status is not related to later involvement in either drug use or serious delinquency once school commitment and performance variables are held constant. Several of the school variables themselves are related to later delinquency and drug use, however.

The relationship between drug use and and dropping out of school was further explored in a paper by McCluskey, Krohn, Lizotte, and Rodriguez (in press) where we examined whether the relationship between early drug use and failing to graduate from high school was due to the effect of early drug use on family relationships, school variables, or other precocious transitions such as pregnancy, parenthood, or living independently from the family of origin. We were particularly interested in whether the process by which early drug use led to failure to graduate from high school varied by ethnicity or race.

For African American and Hispanic males the effect of early drug use on failure to complete high school is mediated by impregnation. Early drug use significantly increases the likelihood that a minority boy will impregnate a girl. Impregnating a girl increases the probability that minority boys will not graduate from school. This indirect effect is not apparent for white boys. Rather, for whites, early drug use has a direct effect on school dropout regardless of whether these boys impregnated anyone.

Overall, the results of the Rochester Youth Development Study indicate that school is an important domain for understanding adolescent behavior. Weak school commitment and performance are related to involvement in delinquency and drug use (Krohn et al., 1995; Smith et al., 1995; Thornberry et al., 1991), and school success is associated with resilience (Smith et al., 1995). In turn, involvement in delinquency reduces commitment to school (Thornberry et al., 1991), and involvement in drug use (but not delinquency) increases the chances of dropping out of high school (Krohn et al., 1995; McCluskey et al., in press).

Peers, Beliefs, and Delinquency

The role that friends play in generating delinquent behavior has been the focus of much prior research (Thornberry & Krohn, 1997): having friends who participate in delinquent behavior is one of the most consistent and robust correlates of delinquent behavior. Delinquent belief systems are also a robust correlate of involvement in delinquency. Research using the RYDS data finds strong relationships among these variables (Krohn & Thornberry, 1993; Krohn, Lizotte, Thornberry, Smith, & McDowall, 1996; Thornberry, Krohn, Lizotte, & Chard-Wierschem, 1993b; Thornberry, Lizotte, Krohn, Farnworth, & Jang, 1994). Following one of the major premises of interactional theory, our research has focused on the reciprocal relationships among associating with delinquent peers, holding delinquent beliefs, and delinquency.

Using three waves of the RYDS data, Thornberry et al. (1994) examined the hypothesized relationships between associating with delinquent peers and delinquency. The theoretical model specifies that delinquent peers provide a social environment in which delinquency is reinforced and, because of that reinforcement, members of the network are likely to engage in delinquent behavior. In turn, adolescents who engage in delinquency are likely to seek out or be forced into associational patterns with others who engage in delinquency. Delinquent beliefs are also hypothesized to be involved in a reciprocal relationship with both delinquent peers and delinquent behavior.

The results from the analysis largely support the tenets of interactional theory. Association with delinquent peers has an indirect effect on delinquency, operating through the reinforcing environment of the peer network. In turn, engaging in delinquent behavior leads to increases in associations with delinquent peers. The predicted reciprocal effect between beliefs and delinquency was also supported as delinquent beliefs exert lagged effects on peers and behavior, which, in turn, tend to harden the formation of delinquent beliefs.

Krohn et al. (1996) extended this analysis by using five waves of data and focusing on drug use rather than delinquency. We estimated a model including a contemporaneous loop between drug use, drug using peers, and peer reactions to drug use, as well as a cross-lagged model. Results from estimating the first model indicate that there are contemporaneous causal loops from drug use to peer drug use, and then from peer drug use to peer reactions, and back to drug use. It is evident that a spiraling process is taking place in which those who use drugs associate with others who use. In turn, the peer network serves to reinforce drug use and thereby increases the likelihood of continued drug use.

In the second model, the contemporaneous loop among these three variables was replaced by a direct, cross-lagged effect of peer drug use at each time on drug use at the next time, and an indirect lagged effect via peer reactions. Drug use is also expected to have a direct effect on peer drug use across time. With the exception of the indirect effect of peer drug use on drug use through peer reactions, the results support the hypothesized effects.

The analysis by Krohn et al. (1996) also examined the interplay between beliefs about drug use and drug use, as well as between peers and beliefs. Bidirectional effects were consistently observed. In general, the effects from peers and from drug use to beliefs were somewhat larger than the effects from beliefs to either peers or to drug use. This is consistent with interactional theory's developmental predictions about the formation of deviant belief systems during early to mid-adolescence.

The results from these two studies suggest that simple models including only unidirectional relationships among peer associations, beliefs, and behavior are not adequate to capture the social dynamics that produce deviant careers. The reciprocal effects among peer-related variables specified by interactional theory apply equally well to the explanations of drug use and delinquent behavior.

In addition to focusing on the reciprocal relationship between peers and delinquency, Jang and Thornberry (1998) examined the role that delinquent peers play in the relationship between self-esteem and delinquency. There is no significant impact of self-esteem on delinquency, nor of delinquency on self-esteem. There is, however, a significant self-enhancing effect of delinquent peers; that is, associating with delinquent peers leads to an increase in later self-esteem. Moreover, delinquent peers tend to mediate the impact of delinquency on self-esteem. Earlier delinquency increases associations with delinquent peers and, as just noted, that leads to enhanced self-esteem.

Social Networks and Delinquent Behavior

An impressive amount of research, including our own, has established that youth are likely to behave in a manner consistent with the behavior of their friends. However, there have been fewer investigations into why this relationship exists. The Rochester project addresses this question from a social network perspective (Krohn, 1986), which assumes that all social networks constrain the behavior of their participants to some extent. The degree of constraint depends on the structure of the social network, how tightly the person is integrated into it, how central it is in the person's life, how it links to the person's other networks, and how stable the network is over time.

Krohn and Thornberry (1993) examined the impact of the network characteristics of homophily, density, intimacy, multiplexity, and stability on alcohol and marijuana use. We did not find significant differences between drug users and nonusers in terms of density or multiplexity, but found interesting differences in regard to homophily, intimacy, and stability. Homophily refers to the similarity in the background and attitudes of friends. Users are more likely to have friends who are of a different sex, attend a different school, and are in a different grade than are nonusers. However, users' friends are more likely to be from the same neighborhood, lending support to the notion that we need to understand the dynamics of the neighborhood context in order to explain deviant behavior fully. It appears that users are more socially active, are more likely to associate with older friends, and have a neighborhood rather than a school base for their friends.

Users reported being closer to their friends in terms of how much they confide in and trust them than did nonusers, suggesting that users find it more necessary to discuss problems with their friends. When the stability of friendship networks was assessed from one wave to the next (approximately a six-month time period), the friendship networks of users were found to be less stable than those of nonusers. Although users rely on their friends for social support, they are likely to acquire a different set of friends within a fairly short time period. This may suggest that the intimacy of friendship networks reflects more the immediate needs than the strength or quality of the relationship. This study is seen as a beginning step in the process of investigating differences in the social network structure of users and nonusers, but the results suggest that this may be a promising avenue to pursue.

Gangs and Delinquency

A type of social network that is particularly germane to the study of delinquent behavior is the adolescent street gang. At the beginning of the Rochester study, gangs were not a major problem in Rochester. However, within the first year that we were in the field, police and community leaders became concerned about a growing gang problem, and we began to assess the level of gang membership and the impact that such membership had on rates of delinquent behavior. Doing so has allowed us to examine the impact of a social network explicitly organized around deviant behavior on the life course of individual gang members.

Thornberry (1998) reported that slightly under one-third of the Rochester sample indicated that they had been in a street gang prior to the end of high school. These gang members, while accounting for slightly less than one-third of the population, accounted for two-thirds of the acts of general delinquency, 86% of the serious delinquency, 68% of the violent delinquency, and 70% of the drug sales that were reported. Bjerregaard and Smith (1993) compared female and male gang members in Rochester in terms of their delinquent behavior and found that female gang members, like male gang members, had elevated rates of serious and violent delinquency when compared with non-members. Bjerregaard and Lizotte (1995) found that gang members in Rochester were more than three times as likely as non-members to own a gun for protective reasons.

These results clearly demonstrate the strong relationship between gang membership and delinquent behavior, particularly serious and violent delinquency. Why do gang members have such high rates of delinquent behavior? Thornberry et al. (1993b) identified three models that could account for this relationship. A *selection model* suggests that gangs recruit or attract individuals who are already involved in delinquency and violence. If this is the case, then prior to periods of active gang membership, gang members should be more heavily involved in delinquency and violence than are non-members. In a *facilitation model*, the norms, group processes, and network characteristics of the gang are thought to facilitate involvement in delinquency and violence. If this model is accurate, then gang members would not be particularly different from non-members prior to or after their periods of active gang membership; during that period, however, they would be much more extensively involved in delinquency. The third model is a *mixed model*, suggesting that both selection and facilitation are at work.

By using the longitudinal design of the RYDS, Thornberry et al. (1993b) were able to examine the rates of different forms of delinquency before, during, and after gang membership for males. In addition, we could distinguish the impact of gang membership on delinquency rates for more stable gang members (those who remained in a gang for more than a year) as compared to short-term gang members (those who remained in a gang for a year or less). We found strong support for the facilitation model and virtually no support for the selection model. For example, gang members have higher rates of violent offenses only when they are active gang members. The rate of violent crime is about twice as large when they are in the gang compared to when they are not in the gang. The drop in violent crimes, once gang members leave the gang, was particularly evident. Support for the facilitation model was evident for both stable and short-term gang members, although there was some support for a mixed model for stable gang members. Using a similar technique to analyze rates of gun ownership, Bjerregaard and Lizotte (1995) also found strong support for the facilitating effect of gang membership. However, there was also a weak selection factor because future gang members were slightly more likely to own a gun prior to gang membership than were non-members.

It is possible that factors other than gang membership might have created what appears to be a facilitation effect. For example, gang members may have elevated rates of violence because of the accumulation of risk in their backgrounds. To examine this possibility, Thornberry (1998) grouped violent delinquency into the same three periods analyzed in Thornberry et al. (1993b) and then regressed self-reported violence on a dummy variable indicating whether the subject was a gang member during that year along with a variety of prior risk factors. The inclusion of the dummy variable allows for an assessment of the facilitative effect of active gang membership on violent behavior net of the impact of the other antecedent variables. The results indicate that the relationship between gang membership and violent delinquency is not spurious. Even when family poverty level, parental supervision, commitment to school, experiencing negative life events, prior involvement in violence, and associating with delinquent peers are held constant, gang membership exerts a strong impact on the incidence of violent behavior.

We began the discussion of gangs by suggesting that they are a form of peer social network. It is not clear, therefore, whether the effect of being a member of a gang simply reflects association with delinquent peers or if gang membership is qualitatively different. To examine this issue, Thornberry (1998) classified male respondents into five groups at each interview wave. One group consists of active gang members at that wave. Respondents who were not gang members were divided into quartiles based on their score on a scale measuring their association with delinquent peers. The most important comparison concerns the non-members in the highest quartile (those with the greatest number of delinquent peers) and the gang members. If gang members are qualitatively different, then they should have substantially higher rates of delinquency than the non-members who associate with highly delinquent peer groups. This is precisely what was found at all eight waves for which the data were analyzed. All of the differences between the gang members and the non-members in the highly delinquent peer group are statistically significant for violent delinquency. A similar analysis was conducted separately for males and females at age 15 (Battin-Pearson, Thornberry, Hawkins, & Krohn, 1998). For both males and females, gang members have significantly higher rates of general delinquency, violent delinquency, drug selling, and drug use than non-members in the highly delinquent peer group.

These earlier publications on gangs demonstrate that membership in street gangs has a very potent impact on adolescent life. We continued this line of research in *Gangs and Delinquency in Developmental Perspective* (Thornberry et al., in press). In this book we extended many of the analyses just summarized, with the same substantive results, and added several new analyses. Only the latter are summarized here.

While there are many studies of the correlates of gang membership, there are surprisingly few examinations of *prior* risk factors for gang membership or of the causal pathways that lead to gang membership. Thornberry et al. (in press, Chapters 4 and 5) examined both of these issues. Compared to adolescents who never joined a gang, gang members have multiple risk factors from multiple domains. Perhaps the strongest message, for both male and female gang members, concerns the accumulation of deficits in their backgrounds. We examined risk factors in seven developmental domains: area of residence, sociodemographic characteristics, parent-child relations, school, peers, individual factors, and earlier deviance. Of the youth who did not experience risk in any of these domains, none of the males or females became a gang member. At the other end of the continuum, of those with risk in all seven domains, however, 60% of the males and 40% of the females became gang members.

The Rochester data afford two ways of examining the question of why youth join street gangs. One is based on the perceptions of the gang members and the other on a path model derived from interactional theory (Thornberry, 1987). The two approaches offer complementary results. Results based on gang member reports focus on the positive pull of the street gang; the most frequent reasons provided were to be with friends and family and to take part in the fun and excitement of gang life. Results based on the causal analysis focus more on the push stemming from the youths' backgrounds; structural disadvantage, school failure, involvement in antisocial networks and behaviors, and high levels of stress are all interrelated to increase the chances of gang membership. These two stories are, of course, not inconsistent: youth may well see the gang as an oasis of relief from the consequences of growing up in these disadvantaged, urban settings.

Thornberry et al. also examined the interplay between gangs, guns, and crime (in press, Chapter 7). As with other forms of deviance, there is no evidence that gangs select members who already own and carry illegal guns. There is strong evidence, however, that street gangs facilitate both carrying guns that are owned and the carrying of guns whether or not they are owned. Indeed, it appears that gang membership greatly facilitates the ability of adolescents to rent or borrow guns that they carry, even if they do not own the gun. More gang members carry guns that they do not own than carry guns that they do own. Gang members who carry guns that they own and gang members who do not own the guns that they carry commit more crime than gang members who do not carry guns and those who are neither gun carriers nor gang members. For example, they commit ten times more violent crime than one would expect from their numbers in the population. In addition, gang members who own and carry their guns commit more crime than those gang members who borrow or rent the guns that they carry. All of this is especially true for violence and drug offenses. Finally, in early adolescence, carrying guns that are not owned leads to dramatically increased levels of illegal gun ownership and carrying among young adults.

Overall, our analyses of the impact of gang membership demonstrate that it has substantial short-term effects on adolescent behavior. Because of that, and based on the life-course focus of interactional theory, Thornberry et al. (in press, Chapter 9) investigated the impact of gang membership on life-course transitions from adolescence to adulthood. Independent of other predictors, gang membership generates considerable disorder later in the life course. For males, stable gang members are significantly more likely to drop out of school, impregnate a girl, become a teen father, have an unstable employment record, cohabit, and experience multiple disorderly transitions. For the females, gang membership is significantly related to pregnancy, early motherhood, unstable employment, and experiencing multiple transitions.

Overall our investigation indicates that membership in street gangs has pernicious consequences for these youths. Adolescents with multiple deficits are more likely to join the gang and gang membership certainly exacerbates these disadvantages, in the long-term as well as the short-term. Finally, we note that the pattern of relationships observed is quite similar for male and female gang members in the Rochester study. Although the girls are in the gang for shorter periods of time than are the boys (Thornberry et al., in press), their prevalence of joining a gang is almost as high (29% vs. 32%) and the impact of the gang on their behavior and life course is every bit as damaging.

Thornberry et al. (in press, Chapter 10) discuss the policy implications of these findings in light of the evidence that there are no gang prevention programs known to be effective (Klein, 1995; Spergel, 1995). We recommend that the safest course at the moment is to use gang membership as a marker variable to identify youth with increased need of services. The services themselves, however, should be based on the delinquency treatment literature that has identified effective programs.

Summary

A concern with the impact of peer influences and social networks is one of the hallmarks of the Rochester Youth Development Study. Our data indicate strong, systematic effects of these variables. Associations with deviant peers and peer reinforcement for deviance increases delinquency (Thornberry et al., 1994) and drug use (Krohn et al., 1996). These studies also demonstrate that delinquency and drug use both influence the selection of peer networks. Social network characteristics also influence patterns of deviance and, when attention is focused on perhaps the clearest type of deviant social network, the street gang, the impact on the life course is most evident. Embeddedness in deviant social networks interrupts the normal course of adolescent development, both in the short-term and in the long-term.

The Impact of Structural Position

Communities impact the individuals living in them in a variety of ways. Communities set the stage for and provide a context in which individual actors play out their lives. In addition, one's position in the social structure, especially in terms of social class, influences both life-course trajectories and the chances of delinquency. Interactional theory predicts that youngsters who grow up in poor families and in poor neighborhoods are more likely to be delinquent than are their counterparts, in large part because these structural conditions adversely impact process variables. Several papers from the Rochester study have examined the interplay between community characteristics, the individual's structural position in those communities, and the impact of these factors on delinquency.

In an early paper, Farnworth, Thornberry, Krohn, and Lizotte (1994) dispelled the notion that there is no direct relationship between social class and delinquency. We showed that when social class is measured in theoretically appropriate ways, for example, by using measures of continuing underclass status, there is a significant, consistent class-crime association. This is particularly the case for prolonged involvement in more serious forms of delinquency. Interestingly, when we correlated the more typical, yet theoretically less relevant measures of class based on status attainment theory and omnibus indices of delinquency, the relationship between class and delinquency vanishes. Theoretically-informed measures appear to be crucial to a fuller understanding of this association.

Two papers examined the impact of community structure. Stern and Smith (1995) studied the impact of living in disadvantaged neighborhoods on delinquency, as those neighborhood effects are mediated through basic family processes. Living in disadvantaged neighborhoods is correlated with economic hardship, life distress, social isolation, and lack of partner support. Together, these disadvantages lead to a lack of parent-child involvement, attachment, and control over adolescents. In turn, these parenting variables are significantly associated with increased delinquency. Overall, Stern and Smith found that disadvantaged neighborhoods have both direct and indirect effects on delinquency, the latter mediated through reduced parent involvement and control of adolescents.

Lizotte, Thornberry, Krohn, Chard-Wierschem, and McDowall (1994b) also found that neighborhood characteristics have an indirect impact on delinquency. For example, in places where poverty is high and where there are high levels of ethnic heterogeneity, parents are not well-integrated into their neighborhoods. In these neighborhoods, parents provide less supervision of adolescent peer groups and, when this occurs, the children are more likely to be delinquent. Once again, there is an indirect impact of neighborhood characteristics on parents' ability to control and monitor their children, which leads to delinquency.

Lanctot and Smith (2001) investigated the impact of a range of proximal and distal predictors on sexual activity, pregnancy, substance abuse, and status offenses among African American girls in the sample. Neighborhood characteristics affect sexual activity and pregnancy among African American girls, although they do not affect drug and alcohol use and status offenses. Girls who are exposed to disadvantaged neighborhoods are more likely than those in more affluent neighborhoods to make accelerated role transitions into early sexual activity (prior to age 16) and teen pregnancy.

Stern et al. (1999) also demonstrated that social and economic disadvantage impacts parent distress and adversely affects parenting, with negative effects on adolescent mental health, including internalizing and externalizing behaviors. Poverty, specifically, is linked with parent distress and with disrupted discipline. Disruptions in parenting are in turn directly associated with adolescent mental health problems.

Smith and Krohn (1995) showed how the impact of economic hardship and single-parent families on parent-child attachment and involvement lead to different delinquent outcomes for White, African American, and Hispanic subjects. That is, economic hardship and single-parent families produce different pathways to delinquency for different racial and ethnic groups. Adversity in African American families is less associated with parenting problems and delinquency than among White and Hispanic families. Structural disadvantage may have different effects in different cultural and community contexts.

In summary, the role of economic adversity and community disadvantage in generating delinquency has been studied mainly through its impact on parenting, which is itself a key proximal correlate of delinquency. Although some RYDS studies indicate that family economic and neighborhood disadvantage elevate the risk of adverse developmental outcomes such as teen pregnancy and parenting (Lanctot & Smith, 2001), other studies do not find a link between distal economic risk and outcomes such as gang membership (Bjerregaard & Smith, 1993) and fatherhood (Thornberry, Smith, & Howard, 1997). There are indications that the impact of structural position may be interwoven with single-parent status and race (Smith & Krohn, 1995). The impact of structural adversity on the next generation is now being investigated in the intergenerational sequel to RYDS.

Long-Term Developmental Effects

The life-course focus of interactional theory (Thornberry & Krohn, 2001) emphasizes the importance of examining involvement in antisocial behavior across the full lifespan and of examining the impact that delinquent behavior has on the life chances of the individual. Participation in deviant behavior can create schisms with prosocial influences and decrease chances of success in prosocial pursuits. In addition, those engaging in deviant behavior are more likely to engage in other risky behaviors that can further attenuate conventional life chances.

One of the central tenets of developmental criminology is that early onset offenders are likely to be particularly vulnerable to these processes and, as a result, to have longer, more serious criminal careers. Krohn et al. (2001) examined this issue using data not only from Rochester, but also from Pittsburgh and two Montreal cohorts. Unlike many previous studies of the consequences of early onset offending that used a rather high age cutoff (e.g., age 14), this analysis examined onset groups as young as 4 to 10 years of age. Although there were some differences across the four cohorts studied, the general hypothesis was supported: early onset offenders remain active offenders for longer periods of time than later onset offenders. For example, in Rochester 39% of those who began offending between the ages of 4 and 10 self-reported offending at ages 19 to 22, compared to 23% of those who started at ages 13 or 14.

Consistent with Thornberry and Krohn's (2001) hypothesis, the association between onset and duration, while statistically significant, is relatively modest. In the Rochester data, for example, of the youngsters who began offending at age 10 or less, 60% were *not* still involved in offending between ages 19 and 22.

Although there is general agreement in the literature that there is a link between early onset offending and the extensiveness of later careers (Krohn et al., 2001), there is less agreement about the processes that bring it about. Interactional theory hypothesizes that one fundamental reason centers on the adverse consequences that antisocial behavior has on human development. Given this hypothesis, we have examined the consequences of adolescent delinquency and drug use in a series of papers.

Having a child during adolescence can adversely affect the adolescent's chances of finishing school and getting a job, and that can result in long-term instability. Thornberry et al. (1997) examined the risk factors that predict teenage fatherhood among our male respondents. We identified ten general domains incorporating 39 risk factors and estimated their relationships to teenage fatherhood. We found a clear link between teenage fatherhood and other deviant behaviors. Gang membership and chronic drug use are particularly important in predicting who will father a child during adolescence. Thornberry et al. also found that the cumulation of risk factors is very important in predicting teen fatherhood. For example, of those with four risk factors, 12% are teenage fathers, whereas almost a third of those with five risk factors and about half of those with six or more risk factors become teenage fathers.

Teenage parenthood can be considered a premature or precocious transition to an adult role. Such precocious transitions can reduce the success of adult development. In turn, the timing, order, and success of transitions to adult statuses may affect the probability of the continuation and perhaps escalation of deviant behavior. Krohn, Lizotte, and Perez (1997) examined the impact of early drug use on precocious transitions and the effect of precocious transitions on drug use during early adulthood. In addition to parenthood, we included pregnancy, high school dropout, and living independently from one's parents during the teenage years, as precocious transitions.

Krohn et al. (1997) found that for males substance use prior to the age of 15 is significantly related to all four precocious transitions even when controlling for several potential correlates of use and precocious transitions. For females, early substance use is related to teenage parenthood and independent living, but not to pregnancy and dropout. We then examined the impact of these transitions on later alcohol and drug use. For males, all four precocious transitions are significantly related to later alcohol and drug use, even after controlling for a number of potential correlates including prior substance use. For females, all four precocious transitions predict later drug use, but only pregnancy predicts later alcohol use.

Accelerated role transitions are also the topic of a study exploring the predictors of early sexual activity and pregnancy among girls in the RYDS sample. Lanctot and Smith (2001), focusing on the African American girls in the sample, found that although both early sexual activity and teen pregnancy are associated with engaging in problem behaviors (status offenses and drug and alcohol use), early sexual activity is associated with non-conformity to a greater extent than is getting pregnant. Both proximal and distal risk factors are involved in sexual activity and pregnancy. The most salient early adolescent predictors of early sexual initiation include living in a disorganized neighborhood, having low school expectations, holding deviant values, and engaging in gang activity, status offenses, and substance use. Predictors of early pregnancy include living in disorganized neighborhoods, having low school expectations, having been maltreated as a child, and having a mother who gave birth at a young age. Predictors of early sexual activity are more similar to those of early deviance than are predictors of pregnancy.

Early sexual activity is both interwoven with deviant behavior and associated with further developmental difficulties. A study by Smith (1997) used lifespan and ecological frameworks to investigate the factors associated with early sexual activity among RYDS adolescents. A range of factors are associated with sexual activity under age 16, including early substance use and family risk. Some gender differences in risk were observed: child maltreatment is a risk factor for boys and low school aspirations is significant for girls. For both genders, early sexual activity (in contrast to engaging in sex in late adolescence) is associated with risky sexual activity and teen parenthood.

Another paper by Smith et al. (2000) examined the role of early deviance in relation to precocious transitions among male adolescents, not only in the Rochester sample but also using Denver and Pittsburgh data. Precocious transitions include causing a pregnancy, dropping out of school, and living independently, as well as a measure combining all three. Delinquency, as well as alcohol and drug use, is related to the number of precocious transitions across all sites, and the findings for the separate measures of transitions are generally replicated across sites.

Overall, these studies suggest that deviant behavior can increase the probability that youth exit adolescent roles early and without proper developmental preparation. The early adoption of adult roles, in turn, has long-term consequences, including the continued use of drugs.

Violence

Youth violence is one of the most serious problems facing American society today. All three studies in the Program of Research on the Causes and Correlates of Delinquency have been actively involved in researching this important area and much of this work has been collaborative across the three sites. Over the 10- to 19-year-old age range, we found high levels of youth violence in all three cities. For males, these rates continue to increase through age 19. For the females, we also found substantial amounts of violence, but those rates did begin to decline during the late teens (Kelley, Huizinga, Thornberry, & Loeber, 1997).

Thornberry, Huizinga, and Loeber (1995) focused particular attention on chronic, or high rate, violent offenders. As in other longitudinal studies, our data also identify a group of chronic violent offenders who are only a small proportion of the population (15%), but who account for the vast majority of violent crimes (75%). The chronic violent offenders are also those who are most heavily involved in other forms of delinquency, including property crimes, public disorder and status offenses, drug sales, and drug use (Thornberry et al.). The careers of chronic violent offenders also start earlier and end later, and follow a progression from minor aggression at younger ages to violent serious delinquencies at older ages.

This research found that chronic violent offenders experience many risk factors that do not exist in isolation from one another. These risk factors have additive and interactive effects compounding violent behavior. Particularly troubling risk factors for promoting violence among youth are maltreatment, partner violence among parents, and family hostility (Smith & Thornberry, 1995; Thornberry, 1994; Thornberry et al., 1995). Furthermore, experiencing multiple types of family violence significantly elevates self-reported violence by the subjects.

Youth and Guns

Over the course of the Rochester Youth Development Study, the United States experienced dramatic increases in firearm homicides among young males. Fortunately, we have consistently collected data on both legal and illegal gun ownership and use among our subjects, providing a unique opportunity to investigate how patterns of gun use unfold over the adolescent-young adult life course.[3] Lizotte, Tesoriero, Thornberry, and Krohn (1994a) showed that there are real differences between boys who own guns for legitimate sporting reasons and those who own for more troubling reasons. First, they own different types of

---

[3] Given the uneven gender distribution of gun carrying in our sample, these analyses are limited to the male subjects.

guns; those who own for sporting purposes own rifles and long guns, while those who own for "protection" own pistols, sawed-off rifles, and sawed-off shotguns. Second, and perhaps more importantly, they differ in their behaviors. In terms of their criminal activity, those who own guns for sport essentially look like those who do not own guns at all. However, boys who own guns for protection are much more likely to commit a wide array of criminal behaviors and they do so at high rates. Furthermore, we have found that socialization into sporting gun ownership comes from the family, while socialization into protective ownership comes from associating with peers who own and use illegal guns.

Bjerregaard and Lizotte (1995) and Thornberry et al. (in press, Chapter 7) found that gang membership has complex linkages to illegal gun ownership. Joining a gang increases the probability of illegal gun ownership dramatically. However, upon leaving the gang, the likelihood of gun ownership decreases. The same pattern holds for involvement in gun-related crimes before, during, and after gang membership.

While there is a relatively large literature on gun ownership, there are surprisingly few investigations of the determinants of gun *carrying*, an important step for many types of crimes. We investigated this issue by examining the impact of gang membership, drug selling, and friend's illegal gun ownership on the likelihood of gun carrying over the adolescent-young adult life course (Lizotte, Howard, Krohn, & Thornberry, 1997). We found that sizable percentages of adolescents carry guns (between 6% and 10%, depending upon age), but most of this illegal gun carrying is transient. More than half of the carriers carry for only six months or less. Illegal gun carrying is associated with peers who own illegal guns, gang membership, and drug selling. The impact of gang membership is larger when the boys are younger, while the effect of drug selling is greater when they are older (Lizotte, Krohn, Howell, Tobin, & Howard, 2000).

Typically studies of illegal gun ownership and use compare subjects who own or carry guns to those who do not. When doing this, one finds that gun carriers are much more active criminals than are non-carriers. The conclusion is that in some way guns are used to facilitate criminal behavior. However, this comparison blurs the distinction between gun use and the kind of a person who chooses to use a gun in a crime. Because the RYDS data are longitudinal, we have addressed this issue by comparing the amount of criminal activity that illegal gun carriers commit during periods when they carry guns to the amount that they commit when these same individuals do not carry guns (Lizotte, Bonsell, McDowall, Krohn, & Thornberry, 2002). When making these comparisons, we find that during periods of time when boys carry guns they commit about five times more serious, violent crimes compared to when they do not carry guns. Similarly, boys commit about 10 times more drug sales during periods of gun carrying than during periods when they do not carry. Over the period of time considered (4.5 years) this amounts to about 5000 more crimes associated with gun carrying for a relatively small number of boys (139). For property crimes there is no difference between the number of crimes committed during periods of gun carrying and no gun carrying.

Future Directions

The Rochester Youth Development Study has followed a sample of urban adolescents from ages 13 to 26—from the time they were in middle school until college and entry to work roles. The detailed information we have gathered through the tremendous cooperation we have received from these subjects and their parents has allowed us to investigate a number of substantive topics and this work has contributed to our understanding of the causes and consequences of delinquency. Although we feel we have learned a great deal, there is much left to be done. We will, of course, continue to analyze the data already collected and to refine the theoretical models that inform this study. In addition, current data collection is focused on continuing to follow these subjects across time to gain a fuller understanding of how delinquency unfolds over the life course. There are two interrelated projects underway at the present time.

Intergenerational Transmission of Antisocial Behavior

One project focuses on the intergenerational transmission of antisocial behavior. Past research indicates considerable behavioral continuity across adjacent generations. That is, antisocial parents often have antisocial children and prosocial parents often have prosocial children. But there are also substantial degrees of behavioral discontinuity. That is, many parents who were antisocial during adolescence have prosocial children and many parents who were prosocial during adolescence have antisocial children. This leads to an intriguing set of theoretical questions. One is simply estimating, in a fully prospective design, the levels of intergenerational continuity and discontinuity. In fact, surprisingly little is known about this issue. Other questions concern an attempt to explain why some families exhibit intergenerational continuity while others exhibit discontinuity in their patterns of behavior. Understanding the causal processes that bring about these varying outcomes is important for both theory and practice.

The Rochester Youth Development Study is ideally suited to investigate this issue. Approximately one-third of the sample members were teen parents and about half were parents by age 22. Thus, there is an abundant number of parents and young children to study. Indeed, we have already enrolled over 400 of the oldest biological children who are two years of age or older as the focal subjects of the new study.

The design and implementation of this project is complex because multiple developmental stages, multiple caregivers, and varying family structures are involved. Nevertheless, the potential payoff seems well worth the effort. By embedding a longitudinal study of these young children within the ongoing longitudinal investigation of their parents, we should be able not only to investigate the intergenerational transmission of antisocial behavior, but also to expand our understanding of the development of antisocial behavior beginning in childhood.

Adult Transitions

The other current project of the Rochester Youth Development Study focuses on the transition to adulthood by following the full sample of Rochester subjects up to age 30. This portion of the study is strongly focused on testing the life-course extension of interactional theory developed by Thornberry and Krohn (2001). This perspective views criminal activity and drug use as intricately interwoven with movement along basic life-course trajectories such as family, education, and work. The mid to late twenties is a particularly crucial time for understanding these relationships, since during these years transitions to adult statuses are made (or fail to be made), largely determining the course of adult development. Specifically, we are interested in the impact of adolescent development, including antisocial behavior, on the timing and success of transitions to adult roles and statuses and the effect of those transitions on the continuation of or desistance from criminal activity. We are also interested in examining the interplay of multiple problem behaviors, including delinquency, gang membership, risky sexual behavior, and drug use. A life-course perspective suggests that the best way to understand both the causes *and* consequences of these behaviors is to follow the same respondents across long portions of the life course, examining the reciprocal interplay among these variables.

We will capitalize on the rich body of data that the Rochester Youth Development Study has collected over the past 14 years. This will be supplemented by two additional waves of data collected at age 28 and age 30. These later data collection points will allow us to examine bidirectional relationships between problem behaviors and transitions to adult roles and statuses, focusing on this high-risk sample during a critical period in the life course. We are particularly interested in the impact that adolescent development has on continuity and change in problem behaviors for young adults. We will also study the impact of transitional life events on problem behaviors and how problem behaviors impact transitional life events. Finally, the adult transitions phase of the Rochester project will allow us to consider the dynamics of late initiation into, and desistance from, problem behaviors.

ACKNOWLEDGMENTS. This chapter was prepared under Grant 86-JN-CX-0007 (S-3) from the Office of Juvenile Justice and Delinquency Prevention, Office of Justice Programs, U.S. Department of Justice; Grant 5 R01 DA05512-02 from the National Institute on Drug Abuse; and Grant SBR09123299 from the National Science Foundation. Work on this project was also aided by grants to the Center for Social and Demographic Analysis at the University at Albany from NICHD (P30 HD32041) and NSF (SBR-9512290). Points of view or opinions in this document are those of the authors and do not necessarily represent the official position or policies of the funding agencies.

References

Battin-Pearson, S. R., Thornberry, T. P., Hawkins, J. D., & Krohn, M. D. (1998, October). Gang membership, delinquent peers, and delinquent behavior, *Juvenile Justice Bulletin.* Washington, DC: U.S. Department of Justice, Office of Juvenile Justice and Delinquency Prevention.

Bjerregaard, B., & Lizotte, A. J. (1995). Gun ownership and gang membership. *Journal of Criminal Law and Criminology, 86*, 37–58.

Bjerregaard, B., & Smith, C. A. (1993). Gender differences in gang participation, delinquency, and substance use. *Journal of Quantitative Criminology, 9*, 329–355.

Elder, G. H., Jr. (1985). Perspectives on the life course. In G. H. Elder, Jr. (Ed.), *Life course dynamics* (pp. 23–49). Ithaca, NY: Cornell University Press.

Elder, G. H., Jr. (1997). The life course and human development. In R. M. Lerner (Ed.), *Handbook of child psychology: Vol. 1. Theoretical models of human development* (pp. 939–991). New York: Wiley.

Farnworth, M., Thornberry, T. P., Krohn, M. D., & Lizotte, A. J. (1994). Measurement in the study of class and delinquency: Integrating theory and research. *Journal of Research in Crime and Delinquency, 31*, 32–61.

Fischer, C. S., Jackson, R. M., Stueve, C. A., Gerson, K., Jones, L. M., & Baldassare, M. (1977). *Networks and places: Social relations in the urban setting.* New York: Free Press.

Ireland, T. O., Smith, C. A., & Thornberry, T. P. (2002). Developmental issues in the impact of child maltreatment on later delinquency and drug use. *Criminology, 40*, 359–399.

Jang, S. J., & Krohn, M. D. (1995). Developmental patterns of sex differences in delinquency among African American adolescents: A test of the sex-invariance hypothesis. *Journal of Quantitative Criminology, 11*, 195–222.

Jang, S. J., & Smith, C. A. (1997). A test of reciprocal causal relationships among parental supervision, affective ties, and delinquency. *Journal of Research in Crime and Delinquency, 34*, 307–336.

Jang, S. J., & Thornberry, T. P. (1998). Self-esteem, delinquent peers, and delinquency: A test of the self-enhancement thesis. *American Sociological Review, 63*, 586–598.

Kelley, B. T., Huizinga, D., Thornberry, T. P., & Loeber, R. (1997, June). Epidemiology of serious violence, *Juvenile Justice Bulletin.* Washington, DC: U.S. Department of Justice, Office of Juvenile Justice and Delinquency Prevention.

Kelley, B. T., Thornberry, T. P., & Smith, C. A. (1997, August). In the wake of childhood maltreatment, *Juvenile Justice Bulletin.* Washington, DC: Office of Juvenile Justice and Delinquency Prevention, U.S. Department of Justice.

Klein, M. W. (1995). *The American street gang: Its nature, prevalence, and control.* New York: Oxford University Press.

Krohn, M. D. (1986). The web of conformity: A network approach to the explanation of delinquent behavior. *Social Problems, 33*, 581–593.

Krohn, M. D., & Thornberry, T. P. (1993). Network theory: A model for understanding drug abuse among African-American and Hispanic youth. In M. D. La Rosa & J. L. Recio Adrados (Eds.), *Drug abuse among minority youth: Advances in research methodology* (pp. 102–128) (NIDA Research Monograph 130). Rockville, MD: U.S. Department of Health and Human Services.

Krohn, M. D., & Thornberry, T. P. (1999). Retention of minority populations in panel studies of drug use. *Drugs & Society, 14*, 185–207.

Krohn, M. D., Stern, S. B., Thornberry, T. P., & Jang, S. J. (1992). The measurement of family process variables: An examination of adolescent and parent perceptions of family life on delinquent behavior. *Journal of Quantitative Criminology, 8*, 287–315.

Krohn, M. D., Thornberry, T. P., Collins-Hall, L., & Lizotte, A. J. (1995). School dropout, delinquent behavior, and drug use: An examination of the causes and consequences of dropping out of school. In H. B. Kaplan (Ed.), *Drugs, crime, and other deviant adaptations: Longitudinal studies* (pp. 163–183). New York: Plenum Press.

Krohn, M. D., Lizotte, A. J., Thornberry, T. P., Smith, C., & McDowall, D. (1996). Reciprocal causal relationships among drug use, peers, and beliefs: A five-wave panel model. *Journal of Drug Issues, 26*, 405–428.

Krohn, M. D., Lizotte, A. J., & Perez, C. M. (1997). The interrelationship between substance use and precocious transitions to adult statuses. *Journal of Health and Social Behavior, 38*, 87–103.

Krohn, M. D., Thornberry, T. P., Rivera, C., & LeBlanc, M. (2001). Later delinquency careers. In R. Loeber & D. P. Farrington (Eds.), *Child delinquents: Development, intervention, and service needs* (pp. 67–93). Thousand Oaks, CA: Sage.

Lanctot, N., & Smith, C. A. (2001). Sexual activity, pregnancy, and deviance in a representative urban sample of African American girls. *Journal of Youth and Adolescence, 30*, 349–372.

Lizotte, A. J., & Bordua, D. J. (1980). Firearms ownership for sport and protection: Two divergent models. *American Sociological Review, 45*, 229–244.

Lizotte, A. J., Tesoriero, J. M., Thornberry, T. P., & Krohn, M. D. (1994a). Patterns of adolescent firearms ownership and use. *Justice Quarterly, 11*, 51–74.

Lizotte, A. J., Thornberry, T. P., Krohn, M. D., Chard-Wierschem, D., & McDowall, D. (1994b). Neighborhood context and delinquency: A longitudinal analysis. In E. G. M. Weitekamp & H. J. Kerner (Eds.), *Cross-national longitudinal research on human development and criminal behaviour* (pp. 217–227). Dordrecht, The Netherlands: Kluwer Academic Publishers.

Lizotte, A. J., Howard, G. J., Krohn, M. D., & Thornberry, T. P. (1997). Patterns of illegal gun carrying among young urban males. *Valparaiso University Law Review, 31*, 375–393.

Lizotte, A. J., Krohn, M. D., Howell, J. C., Tobin, K., & Howard, G. J. (2000). Factors influencing gun carrying among young urban males over the adolescent-young adult life course. *Criminology, 38*, 811–834.

Lizotte, A. J., Bonsell, T. L., McDowall, D., Krohn, M. D., & Thornberry, T. P. (2002). Carrying guns and involvement in crime. In R. A. Silverman, T. P. Thornberry, B. Cohen, & B. Krisberg, (Eds.), *Crime and justice at the millennium: Essays by and in honor of Marvin E. Wolfgang* (pp. 153–167). Boston: Kluwer Academic Publishers.

McCluskey, C. P., Krohn, M. D., Lizotte, A. J., & Rodriguez, M. L. (in press). Early substance use and school achievement: An examination of Latino, White, and African American youth. *Journal of Drug Issues.*

Moffitt, T. E. (1993). "Life-course-persistent" and "adolescence-limited" antisocial behavior: A developmental taxonomy. *Psychological Review, 100*, 674–701.

Moffitt, T. E. (1997). Adolescence-limited and life-course-persistent offending: A complementary pair of developmental theories. In T. P. Thornberry (Ed.), *Developmental theories of crime and delinquency* (pp. 11–54). New Brunswick, NJ: Transaction Publishers.

Patterson, G. R., Capaldi, D., & Bank, L. (1991). An early starter model for predicting delinquency. In D. J. Pepler & K. H. Rubin (Eds.), *The development and treatment of childhood aggression* (pp. 139–168). Hillsdale, NJ: Erlbaum.

Smith, C. (1996). The link between childhood maltreatment and teenage pregnancy. *Social Work Research, 20*, 131–141.

Smith, C. A. (1997). Factors associated with early sexual activity among urban adolescents. *Social Work, 42*, 334–346.

Smith, C., & Krohn, M. D. (1995). Delinquency and family life among male adolescents: The role of ethnicity. *Journal of Youth and Adolescence, 24*, 69–93.

Smith, C., & Stern, S. B. (1997). Delinquency and antisocial behavior: A review of family process and intervention research. *Social Service Review, 71*, 382–420.

Smith, C., & Thornberry, T. P. (1995). The relationship between childhood maltreatment and adolescent involvement in delinquency. *Criminology, 33*, 451–481.

Smith, C., Lizotte, A. J., Thornberry, T. P., & Krohn, M. D. (1995). Resilient youth: Identifying factors that prevent high-risk youth from engaging in delinquency and drug use. In J. Hagan (Ed.), *Delinquency and disrepute in the life course* (pp. 217–247). Greenwich, CT: JAI Press.

Smith, C. A., Krohn, M. D., Lizotte, A. J., McCluskey, C. P., Stouthamer-Loeber, M., & Weiher, A. (2000). The effect of early delinquency and substance use on precocious transitions to adulthood among adolescent males. In G. L. Fox & M. L. Benson (Eds.), *Families, crime and criminal justice* (pp. 233–253). Amsterdam: JAI Press.

Spergel, I. A. (1995). *The youth gang problem.* New York: Oxford University Press.

Stern, S. B., & Smith, C. A. (1995). Family processes and delinquency in an ecological context. *Social Service Review, 69*, 703–731.

Stern, S. B., Smith, C. A., & Jang, S. J. (1999). Urban families and adolescent mental health. *Social Work Research, 23*, 15–27.

Thornberry, T. P. (1987). Toward an interactional theory of delinquency. *Criminology, 25*, 863–891.

Thornberry, T. P. (1994, December). *Violent families and youth violence* (Fact Sheet #21). Washington, DC: U.S. Department of Justice, Office of Juvenile Justice and Delinquency Prevention.

Thornberry, T. P. (1998). Membership in youth gangs and involvement in serious and violent offending. In R. Loeber & D. P. Farrington (Eds.), *Serious & violent juvenile offenders: Risk factors and successful interventions* (pp. 147–166). Thousand Oaks, CA: Sage.

Thornberry, T. P., & Krohn, M. D. (1997). Peers, drug use, and delinquency. In D. M. Stoff, J. Breiling, & J. D. Maser (Eds.), *Handbook of antisocial behavior* (pp. 218–233). New York: Wiley.

Thornberry, T. P., & Krohn, M. D. (2001). The development of delinquency: An interactional perspective. In S. O. White (Ed.), *Handbook of youth and justice* (pp. 289–305). New York: Plenum Publishers.

Thornberry, T. P., Lizotte, A. J., Krohn, M. D., Farnworth, M., & Jang, S. J. (1991). Testing interactional theory: An examination of reciprocal causal relationships among family, school, and delinquency. *Journal of Criminal Law and Criminology, 82*, 3–35.

Thornberry, T. P., Bjerregaard, B., & Miles, W. (1993a). The consequences of respondent attrition in panel studies: A simulation based on the Rochester Youth Development Study. *Journal of Quantitative Criminology, 9*, 127–158.

Thornberry, T. P., Krohn, M. D., Lizotte, A. J., & Chard-Wierschem, D. (1993b). The role of juvenile gangs in facilitating delinquent behavior. *Journal of Research in Crime and Delinquency, 30*, 55–87.

Thornberry, T. P., Lizotte, A. J., Krohn, M. D., Farnworth, M., & Jang, S. J. (1994). Delinquent peers, beliefs, and delinquent behavior: A longitudinal test of interactional theory. *Criminology, 32*, 47–83.

Thornberry, T. P., Huizinga, D., & Loeber, R. (1995). The prevention of serious delinquency and violence: Implications from the Program of Research on the Causes and Correlates of Delinquency. In J. C. Howell, B. Krisberg, J. D. Hawkins, & J. J. Wilson (Eds.), *Sourcebook on serious, violent, and chronic juvenile offenders* (pp. 213–237). Thousand Oaks, CA: Sage Publications.

Thornberry, T. P., Smith, C. A., & Howard, G. J. (1997). Risk factors for teenage fatherhood. *Journal of Marriage and the Family, 59*, 505–522.

Thornberry, T. P., Smith, C. A., Rivera, C., Huizinga, D., & Stouthamer-Loeber, M. (1999, September). Family disruption and delinquency, *Juvenile Justice Bulletin*. Washington, DC: U.S. Department of Justice, Office of Juvenile Justice and Delinquency Prevention.

Thornberry, T. P., Ireland, T. O., & Smith, C. A. (2001). The importance of timing: The varying impact of childhood and adolescent maltreatment on multiple problem outcomes. *Development and Psychopathology, 13*, 957–979.

Thornberry, T. P., Krohn, M. D., Lizotte, A. J., Smith, C. A., & Tobin, K. (in press). *Gangs and delinquency in developmental perspective*. New York: Cambridge University Press.

3

Delinquency and Crime

Some Highlights from the Denver Youth Survey

David Huizinga, Anne Wylie Weiher, Rachele Espiritu, and Finn Esbensen

Introduction

This chapter summarizes some of the findings over the past ten years from the Denver Youth Survey. This study is a prospective longitudinal study of delinquency, drug use, victimization, and mental health that focuses on both antisocial and successful development during childhood, adolescence, and young adulthood. The aim of the study is to identify social conditions, personal characteristics, and developmental patterns that are linked to sustained involvement in delinquency and drug use, and to examine the relationship of these developmental patterns and behaviors to mental health and victimization. The research project is thus focused on the identification of both risk and protective factors that may initiate, sustain, terminate, or, perhaps more importantly, prevent delinquency and problem drug use across the lifespan. The project includes extensive focus on female delinquency, neighborhoods, school environment, mental health issues, gang involvement, problem drug use, and victimization.

The Denver Youth Survey (DYS) is based on a probability sample of households in "high-risk" neighborhoods of Denver, Colorado. The neighborhoods were selected on the basis of a social ecology analysis of population and housing

Taking Stock of Delinquency: An Overview of Findings from Contemporary Longitudinal Studies, edited by Thornberry and Krohn. Kluwer Academic/Plenum Publishers, New York, 2003.

characteristics associated with delinquency. Only those socially disorganized neighborhoods that had high official crime rates (in the upper one third) were included. The survey respondents include 1,527 children and youth (806 boys and 721 girls) who were 7, 9, 11, 13, or 15 years old in 1987, and one of their parents, who lived in one of the more than 20,000 randomly selected households.

This sampling procedure resulted in the inclusion of a large number of African American, Hispanic, and other minority youth and includes both "in-school" and "drop-out" youth. Over 92% of the households originally sampled were successfully screened for the presence of eligible children. The screened households contained an estimated 1,794 eligible children of which 1,527 (85%) completed the first year's interview. Completion rates were 91–93% of the first year respondents for the second through fifth annual data collection periods (1989–1992), which is notably high by prevailing standards. Due to a gap in funding for data collection, there was a two-year gap in data collection that resulted in difficulties tracking the highly mobile survey respondents. As a result, the completion rate was a constant 80% for the 1995–1998 period, although the project has continued to interview over 90% of those located each year.

The DYS has, in most regards, met the requirements of the model research design developed by the NIJ-MacArthur Foundation program of research on crime and delinquency (Farrington, Ohlin, & Wilson, 1986; Tonry, Ohlin, & Farrington, 1991), including the use of a multi-cohort accelerated longitudinal design, the use of a household sample, the inclusion of both younger and older cohorts, and a large interdisciplinary measurement space. Each child or youth, and one of their parents, were interviewed annually from 1988 to 1992 and from 1995 to 1999, thus covering the ages from 7–26. Respondents who moved anywhere in the United States or overseas in the military and those in jails or prisons continued to be included in the survey.

The DYS is part of OJJDP's Program of Research on the Causes and Correlates of Delinquency involving three projects located in Denver, Pittsburgh, and Rochester, NY. In its initial stage, the three projects of the Program worked collaboratively in creating a sequence of core measures used in at least two and usually all three sites. This development served to enhance the overall measurement space of each project. In addition, each project developed measures specific to the individual site. For the DYS, this combination of core and specific measures resulted in a large measurement battery for child, youth, young adult and parent interview schedules. Some of the scales and measures are adaptations from previous studies, especially from our own previous survey work (e.g., the National Youth Survey, Elliott, Huizinga, & Ageton, 1985; Elliott, Huizinga, & Menard, 1989) and others were developed specifically for this survey.

Although the list of variables is large, it is not an eclectic list. The selection of variables is guided by the problem behaviors and by the rich mix of variables provided by a conceptual model that guides the study. This model is based in an integrated theoretical model, designed as an explanation for adolescent delinquency that synthesizes strain, social control, and social learning perspectives (Elliott et al., 1985). For the DYS, this model was expanded to incorporate effects of neighborhood social disorganization, biological history including perinatal events, childhood experience and socialization, personality and mental health, formal and informal secondary (external) controls, and rational choice.

Included among the measures are (1) measures of delinquency and drug use, as well as other problem behavior and psychopathology; (2) family demographics; (3) neighborhood social characteristics and family integration and support within these neighborhoods; (4) family variables, including parenting, the child's involvement in and attachment to the family, marital discord, parents' domestic violence, and self-reported parental drug use and criminality, as well as arrests of family members; (5) child/youth involvement in school, community activities, religious activities, and work; (6) personal and psychological characteristics of the child/youth; (7) personal and psychological characteristics of parents; (8) medical history, including birth trauma, family medical and behavioral problems, developmental and learning problems as well as current physical characteristics and nutrition; (9) involvement with and the delinquent/drug use orientation of peers, including a special section on gangs; (10) educational, occupational, and current social strain; (11) secondary controls and rewards for drug use and delinquency, including risk of arrest and juvenile justice system processing; and (12) use of drug treatment and mental health services by focal child/youth respondents and other family members.

Based on our prior experiences with the National Youth Survey, the project developed new self-report drug use and delinquency measures, which we believe are substantial improvements over earlier measures. The drug use measure includes items about the use of both prescription and illicit nonprescription drugs and collects information about frequency of use, amounts used, location of use, and other follow-up information. The delinquency measure attempts to eliminate reporting of trivial events and the potential double counting of events and obtains information about physical location, nature of offense, and other follow-up information. Based on our earlier work and in collaboration with the Pittsburgh project, the DYS developed child measures of delinquency and drug use that mirrored the adolescent measures but which were suitable for children as young as seven years of age. In addition to self-reports of delinquent behavior and drug use, official arrest data from the Denver Police Department for all respondents in the longitudinal survey were obtained, covering all arrests and contacts of survey respondents through 1992.

Over its twelve-year history, the Denver Youth Survey (DYS) has benefited from the combination of major funding for the project from the Office of Juvenile Justice and Delinquency Prevention (OJJDP) and the National Institute on Drug Abuse (NIDA). The DYS was originally funded as a study of the causes and correlates of delinquency over the 1986–1992 period by the Office of Juvenile Justice and Delinquency Prevention, which also supported analyses and other research efforts during the 1993–1994 period. Supplemental funding from NIDA was provided from 1988–1992 to increase the drug use focus of the study and to permit a special study of the peers of a sample of the child and youth respondents of the main survey. During the 1995–1999 period, support for the main survey was provided by NIDA, with OJJDP providing supplemental funding for analyses and other research efforts.

In addition, the MacArthur Foundation supported an increased focus on neighborhoods within the main survey and a separate survey of the full city of Denver, using similar and, for the most part, identical instrumentation to that of the main survey over the 1989–1991 period. Funds supporting a collaborative international study of the transition from school to work, as that transition affects delinquency and drug use, which is based on the sample of the DYS and a similar sample in Bremen, Germany, was funded by the German-American Academic Council for the 1997–1999 period with matching funds from OJJDP.

Given the breadth of the DYS, it is difficult to select specific important or key findings to include in a summary such as this, since what is important varies by the orientation of different audiences. Nevertheless, we hope that the selection provided includes topics of interest for many readers. The topics have been grouped into general sections about (1) the epidemiology of delinquency, drug use, and victimization, and the co-occurrence and interrelationship between these problem behaviors; (2) information about gangs and peers; (3) explanatory, risk, and protective factors; (4) the influence of arrest on subsequent behavior; and (5) help-seeking for youth.

Epidemiology of Delinquency, Drug Use, and Victimization

Over-Time Changes in Delinquency and Drug Use: The 1970s and the 1990s

Much has been said about the changing nature of delinquency and drug use over the past two decades. To examine these changes, equivalent measures of delinquency and drug use from the National Youth Survey in 1979 and from the DYS in 1991 were compared. The particular years examined were selected because both surveys were then in their fourth years and matching drug use data was available. The samples were matched on age (14–18), urbanicity, and social class (Huizinga, 1997a). Although these samples are not perfectly comparable, one being a subset of a national sample and the other a specific city sample, it would be expected that major trends or differences over time would be indicated in data from the two matching samples. Differences in delinquency rates, if any, would be expected to be higher in the Denver data given its high-risk sample.

The prevalence rates of various kinds of delinquency (percentage of persons involved in a given type of offense), for both males and females are given in Table 1. For status offenses, serious property offenses, and for serious violence, there are essentially no differences in the prevalence rates over the 13-year period. Public disorder, minor property, and drug sale offenses all show substantial decreases. However, for males, gang fights show a substantial increase over this period, with the rate doubling from 8% to 16%.

Although the prevalence rates for serious violence are similar across these years, changes in the seriousness of violent offenses, as indicated by the level of injury and use of weapons, is also of interest. Examination of level of injury from assaults indicated that the level of injury has changed over time, with the prevalence of victims of violence being left in need of hospitalization or unconscious almost doubling, from 33% to 58%, across the 1979 to 1991 period. Correspondingly, the prevalence of weapons use has changed. While in 1979, 31% of serious assaults involved a weapon, in 1991 this rate had risen to 82%; and for gang fights, the rate had risen from 42% to 58%.

In contrast to delinquency, and as reported in other research, the prevalence of drug use has decreased substantially over the 1979 to 1991 period. For both genders, the use of alcohol is lower in 1991 (from about 80% to about 53%); the use of marijuana has been reduced by about half, from around 40% to around 20%; and the use of hard drugs has dropped from about 19% to 4%. Given these findings of few changes in the rates of serious delinquency and substantial decreases in the rates of drug use, a question arises of whether the often-reported relationship between

Table 1. Prevalence of Delinquency and Drug Use By Type of Delinquency and Gender: 1979 and 1991

Delinquency	Total Sample		Males		Females	
	1979	1991	1979	1991	1979	1991
Status Offenses	58	59	63	62	52	57
Public Disorder	44	26	46	29	41	23
Minor Property	27	17	38	21	16	13
Serious Property	10	10	15	15	05	05
Serious Violence	12	12	16	17	07	06
Drug Sales	12	05	17	07	08	02
Gang Fights	07	11	08	16	06	05
Drug Use						
Alcohol	80	53	80	55	79	51
Marijuana	41	18	40	21	43	16
Hard Drugs	19	04	18	04	19	03

delinquency and drug use changed over this period. Findings indicated that the nature of the relationship has changed. For example, in 1991 a smaller proportion of serious delinquents are using drugs (71% in 1979; 47% in 1991). However, a greater proportion of drug users are serious offenders (28% in 1979; 42% in 1991).

In sum, for both male and female adolescents, it appears that there has been either little change or a decrease in the prevalence rates of delinquency, including serious delinquency and serious violence over the 1979 to 1991 period. The sole exception to this generalization is the prevalence of gang fights, which, for males, has doubled over this period. However, the level of injury from violent offenses has increased substantially, and this increase corresponds to an increase in the use of weapons. A combined focus on reducing not only the prevalence of violent offenders, but also factors that would reduce the severity of the violent offenses they commit, would seem appropriate.

In contrast to delinquency, for both genders the prevalence of alcohol, marijuana, and hard drug use all decreased substantially over the 1979 to 1991 period. While current levels of adolescent drug use remain unacceptably high, it seems informative to remember and compare them with the levels of drug use one or two decades ago, so that small changes in prevalence rates are evaluated in a historical context and are not exaggerated for particular purposes.

Epidemiology: Age, Gender, and Ethnicity

Much prior research has indicated that the commission of delinquency and drug use is not evenly distributed in our society. Levels of involvement have been shown to vary by age, gender, and ethnic group. Several reports about the epidemiology of delinquency, drug use, serious offending, and violence based on the DYS and the other projects of the Program of Research are in general agreement with this prior research (Espiritu, 1998; Espiritu & Huizinga, 1996; Huizinga, Loeber, & Thornberry, 1991a, 1995).

During adolescence, both males and females are involved in delinquency, serious delinquency, violence and drug use, and the level of involvement in serious and violent behavior indicates that concern about delinquency committed by both genders is clearly warranted. However, in general and across all ages, a larger proportion of males are engaged in serious and violent offenses and, on average, an active male offender commits these acts more often than a female offender. For example, in the Denver study, by age 16, 39% of males and 16% of females had been involved in serious violence.

One of the surprising findings of the DYS is that the developmental age curve for serious violence for males does not show a customary drop following mid-adolescence (see Figure 1). Females show an expected age curve, with prevalence rates peaking in the midteenage years and generally declining thereafter. In contrast,

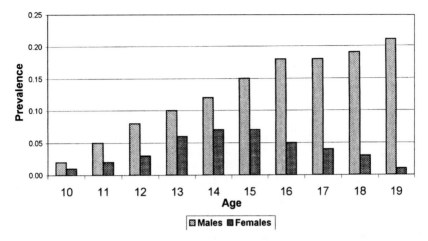

Figure 1. Prevalence of serious assault by age and gender.

for males there is no decline through age 19. This finding for males, replicated in the other sites of the Causes and Correlates Program of Research, is different from other studies. In Denver, the serious violence rate for males does begin to decline during the twenties, however.

With the exception of "street offenses" and serious violence that are of concern to the public, there are few consistent differences in the prevalence of delinquency across different ethnic groups. However, there is also a developmental factor; during childhood (ages 7–10) there are no consistent ethnic differences, but during adolescence, minority youth have significantly higher rates of involvement in "street offenses" and in serious violence. These rates, however, are sufficiently small (less than 15% annually for any group) that it is clear that, even during adolescence, the vast majority of all ethnic groups are not involved in serious or violent delinquency.

Age of Initiation and Subsequent Delinquency

Several DYS analyses have examined the relationship of age of initiation to later offending patterns. These analyses are based on self-reported data, and thus are not restricted to official discovery, processing, and record keeping that may not accurately reflect the true age when offending behavior began. In general, these findings indicate that early initiation is quite strongly related to later offending. For example, among males, the percent of different age of initiation groups who became serious offenders during the ages of 15–17 is given in Table 2. In this table, age of initiation is the age of first committing any delinquent offense, and serious offenders during late adolescence were defined as those committing three

**Table 2. Age of Initiation and Later Serious
Offending during Ages 15–17 for Males**

Age of Initiation	Percent Who Became Serious Offenders
Before Age 9	67%
Ages 9–11	63%
Ages 12–14	27%
Ages 15–17	29%

**Table 3. Age of Initiation and Later
Chronic Violent Behavior**

Age of Initiation	Percent Who Become Chronic Violent Offenders
Before Age 9	62%
Ages 9–11	48%
Ages 12–14	20%

or more relatively serious offenses, including serious assaults, robbery, arson, burglary, auto theft, other thefts over $5, and selling drugs, among other offenses. As can be seen in Table 2, the earlier the age of initiation, the higher the probability of becoming a serious offender in late adolescence. In fact, about two-thirds of those who initiated by age 11 became serious offenders during adolescence. Similar patterns held for females who became frequent offenders, although not necessarily serious offenders, in the 15–17 age period (Huizinga et al., 1994).

Another example is provided by the age of initiation of violence or fighting and later chronic violent offending, which is listed in Table 3 (Huizinga, Loeber, & Thornberry, 1995). This table is based on self-report information provided by the three oldest cohorts of the DYS. Age of initiation is the age of first-reported violent offense, including getting into fights with other youngsters as well as minor and serious assaultive offenses. Being a chronic violent offender is defined as being in the top one-quarter of the cumulative frequency distribution of self-reported violence over the first five years of the DYS. Although some youth engage in a few acts of violence while growing up, others engage in violence frequently and repetitively, and these latter are here identified as chronic offenders. As can be seen, the earlier the age of initiation in violent offenses, the greater is the probability that one will become a chronic violent offender. This finding is replicated by the other projects of the Program of Research (Huizinga et al., 1995).

As these two sets of findings quite clearly illustrate, age of initiation of delinquent behaviors is related to later serious offending patterns. Early initiators, those initiating before age 12, are a high-risk group.

The Intermittency of Serious and Violent Offending

It has been noted elsewhere that a small proportion of youth account for the majority of the serious and violent crime committed by adolescents and that there are relatively long developmental pathways leading to serious delinquent careers (e.g., Thornberry, Huizinga, & Loeber, 1995). These findings suggest a fair degree of stability in serious and violent offending. There is, however, an episodic or intermittent nature to serious and violent offending. That is, the majority of individuals engaged in these behaviors over time do not commit these behaviors regularly, not even every year. This can be illustrated by examining transitions in delinquency typologies that indicate that being a serious offender one year had little effect on being a serious offender in some specific year later on (Huizinga, Esbensen, & Weiher, 1994; Huizinga et al., 1995) and by examining the actual patterning of involvement in serious or violent offending across multiple years (Thornberry et al., 1995). For example, for well over 50% of those whose violent careers lasted three or more years, the patterning of violent and serious violent offenses was intermittent, i.e., there were years in which they committed no violent offenses. For those whose careers spanned five years, 75% had intermittent offending patterns.

This intermittent nature of serious offending and the subset of serious violent offending has important implications for research. First, cross-sectional surveys and longitudinal surveys with several years between data collections may fail to detect the serious or violent behavior of either intermittent offenders or those engaged in these behaviors only once, since they may be observed either before, after, or between periods in which they are active. Longitudinal designs with regular measurement are clearly needed. Second, even in longitudinal studies with regular measurement, it may be necessary to employ measures of offending patterns over several years to accurately identify serious or serious violent offenders. An example is provided by the previous age of initiation findings. The results reported there used delinquency involvement over a three-year period. If the same analyses were restricted to being a serious offender at the specific age of 17, the percent of those who initiated before age 9 and became serious offenders drops from 67% to 39%, and quite different conclusions might be drawn. Clearly, the intermittent patterning of serious offending is an issue that needs greater attention in our research designs and analyses.

Victimization

In addition to problem behavior, the DYS includes a major project component on victimization. Findings taken from several publications and reports (Esbensen & Huizinga, 1991a; Esbensen, Huizinga, & Menard, 1998;

Espiritu & Huizinga, 1996; Menard, 1997; Menard, Esbensen, & Huizinga, 1998; Menard and Huizinga, 2001) indicate a substantial level of victimization among the DYS sample. Over the five-year period 1987–1991, 85% to 87% of the DYS high-risk sample, aged 7–19, were victims of violent or theft offenses. About one-fourth of these youth were victims of serious violent offenses. Over the five-year period, the DYS sample experienced a total of 11,400 victimizations, including 731 robberies, 699 assaults with a weapon, 72 sexual assaults, 4,619 minor assaults, 824 nonaccidental injuries, and 4,495 thefts. Each year about 18% of respondents who had never previously been victimized experienced their first victimization, and about 3% who had never previously been victims of serious violence experienced their first violent victimization. Clearly, the youth in this high-risk sample are at high risk for victimization. However, victimization is to some extent concentrated among a smaller subgroup of respondents. Over one-third of all theft victimizations and over one-half of all violent victimizations were concentrated among 10% of the sample.

There is a temporal patterning to the reported victimization. Two-thirds of the respondents were *chronic multiple* victims. That is, they were *both* victims in more than one year *and also* victims of multiple offenses in at least one year. Most victims of crime experienced intermittent victimization; victimization in one year, followed by a year in which they were not a victim, followed by at least one year in which they were again a victim of crime.

There are substantial gender differences in the rates of victimization. Males were more likely victims of crime than were females, especially for serious violent victimization. However, in this high-risk sample ethnicity was largely unrelated to victimization.

As these findings attest, victimization is not an insignificant aspect of the lives of the DYS child and adolescent sample. Given the reported association between victimization and other problem behavior—including delinquency, violence, drug use, and school problems—and evidence that victimization frequently occurs first (Menard et al., 1998), there is more than ample reason for concern about the impact of victimization on the lives of these young individuals.

The Co-Occurrence or Overlap of Problem Behaviors

Several DYS reports have examined the overlap of various combinations of problem behaviors including delinquency, drug use, mental health problems, school problems, victimization, and sexual behavior and pregnancy (e.g., Espiritu, 1998; Huizinga & Jakob-Chien, 1998; Huizinga, Loeber, & Thornberry, 1993; Huizinga et al., 1995; Huizinga, Loeber, & Thornberry, 1997; Weiher, 1996). Some findings from these reports are summarized in the following section.

Delinquency and Drug Use

One of the most robust empirical findings over the last several decades is the relationship between drug use and other delinquent behaviors (see Huizinga & Jakob-Chien, 1998). Although the extent of overlap and strength of the relationship varies across studies by site, age, gender, types of drugs, and delinquencies measured, and decade of the 20th century considered, the drugs-delinquency relationship is an enduring finding that has been established by many researchers. Results from the DYS and from the Program of Research are consistent with these findings. For example, using a general delinquency measure, subjects were placed into one of four groups depending on their level of delinquent and drug-use involvement—a nondelinquent and nondrug using group, a delinquent but not drug using group, a drug using but not delinquent group, and a both delinquent and drug using group. The proportion of children and youth who fall into these groups is illustrated in Table 4. For children, drug use is measured by alcohol or marijuana use, and in Denver the largest proportion of these youngsters are neither delinquent nor drug using (65%). Among those involved in some form of delinquency, less than 20% are using alcohol or marijuana. However, 67% of those experimenting with these drugs are also delinquent.

A similar but even stronger finding holds for the adolescents, where drug use is measured by use of marijuana or other drugs. Overall, a little over one-third of the adolescents are not delinquent and do not use drugs, about one-quarter or less of the delinquents are using drugs, but almost all of the drug users are involved in some kind of delinquency. Thus, it appears that during the teen years most drug users are delinquent but that there are many delinquents who are not using drugs. These general findings are replicated in data from the Pittsburgh and Rochester projects (Huizinga et al., 1993).

Because many youth are involved in some form of minor delinquency other than drug use, it is also important to examine the drug-delinquency relationship

Table 4. Overlap of Delinquency and Drug Use for Children and Adolescents

Delinquency	Drug Use	Child Sample	Adolescent Sample
No	No	65%	36%
Yes	No	26%	48%
No	Yes	3%	1%
Yes	Yes	6%	15%
Percent of Delinquents Who Are Drug Users		20%	24%
Percent of Drug Users Who Are Delinquent		67%	94%

Table 5. Prevalence and Frequency of Drug Use Within Types of Offenders

Type of Offender	Alcohol		Marijuana		Other Drugs	
	%	Frequency	%	Frequency	%	Frequency*
Serious Violent (9%)	58	61	34	137	9	—
Serious Nonviolent (9%)	51	29	25	73	7	—
Minor (25%)	38	25	14	34	3	—
Nondelinquent (57%)	15	13	3	24	1	—

*Frequency of other drug use is not tabulated since a small number of users makes estimates unreliable.

for more serious forms of delinquency. Is drug use also related to more serious and violent offending? The prevalence and frequency of drug use among types of offenders is given in Table 5. In this table, serious violent offenders are those among adolescents (11–17 years of age) involved in aggravated assault, robbery, rape, and gang fights. Serious nonviolent offenders are *not* engaged in serious violence but are involved in other serious delinquencies such as thefts over $50, auto theft, burglary, etc. Nonserious offenders are those involved in only minor forms of property and assault offenses, and nondelinquents are involved in neither. As seen in Table 5, serious offenders are substantially more likely to be drug users and to use drugs more often than are less serious offenders, and nondelinquents are less likely to use drugs than offenders of any kind.

In addition to the contemporaneous relationship of drug use and delinquency, it is interesting that when the substance use/delinquency relationship is examined over time, prior increases in substance use are found to have a larger impact on subsequent increases in delinquency, while prior increases in delinquency have a somewhat smaller impact on subsequent increases in drug use. The reverse is also true—prior decreases in substance use have a greater impact on decreases in delinquency than prior decreases in delinquency have on decreases in drug use (Huizinga et al., 1993, 1995).

These various findings have several implications. First, although the drugs-delinquency relationship is robust, it would be incorrect to assume that all delinquents or all serious delinquents are drug users. And, conversely, it would be wrong to conclude that all drug users are serious delinquents. This observation calls into question the existence of a single problem-behavior syndrome that includes delinquency and drug use, or the assumption of a single underlying trait in structural equation models examining these behaviors. Second, it would be wrong to conclude that all delinquents are in need of drug use/abuse treatment. However, the sizeable proportion of delinquents that are using drugs and the observation that drug use is related to future increased levels of delinquent involvement does suggest that current interventions to monitor and reduce drug use among apprehended juveniles, such as drug courts and other multimodal treatments, are well founded.

Delinquency and Mental Health Problems

Criminal behavior, especially violence, committed by persons who are mentally ill is often of public fascination and concern, and mentally ill offenders are often assumed to be especially dangerous and feared. On the other hand, mental illness may be seen as an excusing condition for the commission of criminal behavior, and offenders are seen as less culpable or blameworthy for their criminal acts. Moreover, apprehended serious offenders with mental health problems may be in need of mental health services, but since screening and treatment options are often not available, these youth present special challenges to the juvenile justice system.

Given public and practical interest in the potential relationship between serious crime and mental health problems, it is surprising that there is very little empirical knowledge about the co-occurrence of serious and violent offending and mental health problems in juvenile populations, and most of that which does exist is based on unrepresentative captive or detained samples. Moreover, the few studies that include a juvenile focus often examine childhood and adolescent traits as predictors of future offending behavior, focus on conduct disorder or minor offending, or examine correlations or linear models between mental health problems and criminal behavior *variables*, none of which permit determination of the actual level of co-occurrence or overlap of serious offending and mental health problems.

How extensive is the overlap between serious violent and serious nonviolent offending and mental health problems? Given the paucity of information from general population studies, the answer is—we really don't know. Some illustration, however, is provided in data from the DYS (Huizinga & Jakob-Chien, 1998). Not surprisingly, serious violent offenders score significantly higher on externalizing symptoms and aggressive behavior. With this exception, however, differences in the prevalence of psychological problems are found between nondelinquents and delinquents (rather than between serious delinquents and other youth). For both genders, the prevalence of elevated levels of psychological problems is higher among both minor and serious delinquents and lower among nondelinquents. It should be noted, however, that less than half of delinquents of any kind display high levels of various psychological problems, so it would be incorrect to characterize delinquents as a group as having particular psychological problems.

Two variables related to mental health, *self-esteem* and *social isolation*, have sometimes been described as being associated with delinquency. There is a rather traditional view that low self-esteem causes or is an instigator of violence; that aggression or violence is one way of gaining prestige and esteem. This view is applied to youth and adults alike and has led to esteem-building activities in prevention and intervention programs. However, there is sufficient justification to question this view and to argue that it is high self-esteem and threats to this high esteem that lead to violence (Baumeister, Smart, & Bodin, 1996). Thus, the nature of the relationship between self-esteem and serious violence should not be considered as empirically demonstrated. Also, it is assumed that aggressive/violent individuals would be rejected by individuals around them and become socially isolated, and there is some evidence for this in childhood (Dishion, Patterson, Stoolmiller, & Skinner, 1991). However, whether this isolation extends into adolescence is perhaps questionable.

To contribute additional empirical information to these questions, DYS data were used to examine differences between various types of delinquents and non-delinquents in their feelings of self-esteem and social isolation (Huizinga et al., 1995). This examination revealed no differences between delinquents and non-delinquents on these variables. In fact, for both males and females, the mean scores were, in essence, substantively and statistically identical, with similar standard deviations and similar frequency distributions. The belief that serious violent or serious delinquent offenders feel isolated at school, at home, or with their peers, or that they are different from other youth in their level of self-esteem was not supported. Given these findings and the opposing views concerning the relationship of self-esteem and social isolation to delinquency and violence, there clearly is a need for further examination of the role of these variables in relation to serious delinquency. This is especially true since affecting levels of these variables is a goal of some delinquency prevention and intervention programs.

Delinquency and School Problems

There is a widely held belief and considerable empirical evidence that school problems (poor academic performance, truancy, and drop out) are related to delinquent behavior. The relationship of school problems and delinquent behavior has been demonstrated in many studies and over a long historical period. Given the relationship between school problems and delinquency, it is interesting that the actual level of co-occurrence of school problems and *serious* delinquency within the adolescent population is not often examined. As might be anticipated, data from the DYS indicates a substantial overlap of school problems with serious and serious violent delinquency (Huizinga & Jakob-Chien, 1998).

The greatest overlap of serious offending and school problems was found for truancy and school suspension, and substantially less overlap for school grades and for dropping out of school. While for *any one specific* school problem the overlap is not always extensive, when school problems are considered in total (i.e., having one or more school problems), the vast majority of serious violent offenders (87%) and serious nonviolent offenders (79%) had one or more school problems, most commonly truancy or school suspension. In contrast, 65% of minor offenders and 41% of nondelinquents had one or more school problems. The level of overlap of delinquency and school problems is sufficiently high that school problems can be seen as contemporaneous risk factors for serious delinquency and may provide targets for intervention strategies. However, it should be noted that although some kinds of school problems may be considered characteristic of serious delinquents, the majority of youth with school problems are not delinquent.

Delinquency and Victimization

There is reason to suppose that those involved in delinquency, especially assaultive behavior, are at risk for victimization. Those engaged in assaults may also be injured in defending themselves or by retaliation at a later date, and those who live in environments that support delinquent behavior may have a greater chance of being victimized. Thornberry and Figlio (1974) suggested that the juvenile years may be characterized by both the commission of and victimization by various property and violent offenses. Similar thoughts and empirical data to support the delinquency-victimization relationship have been provided by others (e.g., Sampson & Lauritsen, 1990; Singer, 1981, 1986). Findings from the DYS also indicate a substantial overlap of offending and victimization (Esbensen & Huizinga, 1991a; Esbensen, Huizinga, & Weiher, 1993a; Menard et al., 1998). For example, almost half (49%) of male serious violent offenders also report violent victimizations. However, it must be noted that only 20% of male victims of violence were serious violent offenders, so that being a victim does not necessarily imply that one is also an offender.

As might be anticipated, there are substantial gender differences in the strength of the relationship between victimization and delinquency. The relationship between violent and nonviolent victimization and delinquency is stronger for males.

The observation that many respondents were both victims and perpetrators of crime raises the question of which came first, victimization or prior offending. Is one a risk factor for the other? Examination of onset and temporal order indicated that victimization usually occurred first. However, later victimization and other problem behaviors appear to reciprocally influence each other. Injury victimization, in particular, appears to be a risk factor for other later problem behavior. That later victimization and offending often co-occur is further indicated by examining risk factors for victimization. The best predictors of annual prevalence and frequency of victimization were (1) the delinquent behavior of the victim's friends; (2) the victim's own delinquent behavior, especially injury-inflicting offenses; (3) being male; and (4) frequency of alcohol use.

Overall, these findings suggest that the reduction of adolescent victimization, particularly violent victimization, could help reduce the onset, prevalence, and frequency of other problem behaviors.

Multiple Problems

One of the consistent findings across several DYS reports is that the influence of several problems or risk factors greatly increases the probability of delinquent

Table 6. Level of Delinquency by Number of Other Problems for Males

Number of Problems	Serious Violent Offender	Serious Non-Violent Offender	Minor Delinquent	Non-Delinquent
0	2	5	10	83
1	9	10	24	57
2	16	19	30	36
3	32	21	27	20
4	54	31	10	5

behavior over the influence of a single problem or risk factor. As the number of problems across school, drug use, mental health and victimization increase, so does the probability of being a delinquent. This can be seen in Table 6 that indicates the level of delinquency among males for groups with different numbers of risk factors. As can be seen in the table, as the number of problems increases, the probability of being a serious offender steadily increases. Among those facing only one problem, 7% are serious offenders, but among those facing four problems, 85% are serious offenders. Similar findings hold for females, although, as the number of problems increases, the major distinction is between being a delinquent of any kind and being a nondelinquent.

Examination of combinations of problems also indicated the importance of an interactive effect of drug use. For males, the addition of drug use to any one or a combination of other problems generally doubled, and sometimes tripled, the proportion of serious delinquents.

It should also be noted that although having multiple problems is a strong risk factor for serious delinquency for males and a strong risk factor for delinquency for females, there are many youth with multiple problems who are not delinquent. On the other hand, most delinquents of both genders, and serious male delinquents, face multiple problems beyond their delinquency, and the need for multicomponent interventions seems clearly indicated.

Delinquency, Drug Use, Sexual Activity, and Pregnancy

There is a fairly high rate of sexual activity and pregnancy reported by the subjects of the DYS. The overlap of delinquency, alcohol/drug use, sexual intercourse, and pregnancy has been examined using data from subjects who were 13–17 years old in 1989 (Huizinga et al., 1993). To simplify presentation, alcohol and drug use have been combined into a single category. Table 7 gives data on the overlap of sexual activity, delinquency, and alcohol/drug use, listing the percentage of youth who are active in different combinations of these behaviors. For example, adding together the values for the total sample for the four rows that have a "yes" for sexual activity, 43% of the youth respondents are sexually active.

Table 7. Percent of Youth in Different Behavioral Groups for Total Sample, Males, and Females

Delinquency	Alcohol and/or Drug Use	Sexual Activity	Total Sample	Males	Not Pregnant Females	Pregnant Females
No	No	No	21	19	26	0
Yes	No	No	23	21	28	0
No	Yes	No	2	2	3	0
Yes	Yes	No	12	11	14	0
No	No	Yes	4	4	4	13
Yes	No	Yes	14	16	9	30
No	Yes	Yes	2	2	1	3
Yes	Yes	Yes	23	26	15	54

However, only 4% of youth are involved only in sexual activity and 23% are involved in all three kinds of behaviors.

In Table 7, females have been divided into not-pregnant and pregnant groups, so that the overlap of pregnancy with other behaviors can be examined. As can be seen, sexual activity is strongly related to involvement in both delinquency and drug use. Although there are many delinquents and alcohol/drug users who are not sexually active, the majority of both boys and girls who are sexually active are also involved in delinquency, alcohol/drug use, or both.

Similarly, the majority of girls who report being pregnant also report involvement in delinquency, alcohol/drug use, or both, and over half report alcohol/drug use. Although these data suggest there may be a fair amount of alcohol or drug use during pregnancy among these subjects, additional data about this specific issue was obtained in later waves of the DYS (Weiher, 1996). This data clearly indicated that the majority (over 70%) of girls who became pregnant discontinued their alcohol and other drug use when they became pregnant. However, the majority (approximately 70%) of those smoking tobacco continued their tobacco use during the pregnancy. This observation provides concern because of the possible health consequences for the children of these young mothers.

Peers and Delinquent Gangs

Delinquent Gangs

The DYS is one of the few large-scale survey projects examining delinquent gangs within a general sample of youth. The individual-level longitudinal data of the project provides the opportunity to examine personal characteristics, delinquent behavior, and developmental issues surrounding gang membership and to permit comparisons with other youth. Several DYS reports and publications have involved studies of delinquent gang members (Esbensen & Huizinga, 1993; Esbensen, Huizinga, & Weiher, 1993b; Huizinga, 1997b, 1998a,b). Some findings from these reports are summarized below.

General Findings

Only a small proportion of youth are involved in delinquent gangs. Roughly 5–6% of the high-risk youth are gang members in a given year, and, over the first five years of the survey, approximately 14% of the youth indicated that they were active gang members for some period of that time. However, membership in gangs is a transient phenomenon. Contrary to some popular conceptions, gang members are not gang members for life and most gang members are members for only one year (this finding is also found in our companion project in Rochester; Thornberry, Krohn, Lizotte, & Chard-Wierchem, 1993). Being a member of a gang is not restricted to males, and there is a substantial involvement of girls in gangs. Within the DYS, roughly 20–25% of gang members are girls, a finding consistent with other recent studies (Esbensen & Deschenes, 1998; Esbensen & Winfree, 1998; Miller, 2001).

In the period before joining a gang, future DYS gang members have a greater involvement in delinquency than do other youth or other delinquent youth, and they have a greater involvement with delinquent peers during this period. However, in comparison to other youth and to other serious delinquents, during the time youth are active gang members they are exceedingly delinquent. Their delinquency is substantially higher while in a gang than either before joining or after leaving the gang. The social processes of the gang clearly facilitate or enhance the delinquent behavior of its members. (This finding is also replicated in Rochester; Thornberry et al., 1993.)

Personal Characteristics of Gang Members

In many respects, gang members are not different from other youth. They are as likely as nongang members to attend school (although they are more likely to be truant or suspended from school for some period of time), to hold jobs, to be involved in school and community athletics and activities, and to attend religious activities.

On important social and psychological variables, gang members are also very similar to nongang members who are involved in serious delinquency. Yet, both of these groups are quite different from those youth who are not involved in serious delinquency. For example, gang members are not different from other serious delinquents in their commitment to their delinquent friends, their attitudes about the wrongfulness of delinquent behavior and drug use, or the need to violate rules and laws to achieve desired goals.

Also, gang members, other serious delinquents, and other minor or non-delinquent youth do not vary significantly on their feelings of self-esteem, their feelings of social isolation, or their feelings of opportunities for the future. Gang members do differ from other youth, however, in other important ways. They are less likely to feel guilty for committing delinquent acts, their teachers see and/or label them as being "bad" or "disturbed" kids, they spend a far greater amount of time in unsupervised settings (spending about two to three times as much as other youth), and their family situations are often more distressed than the family situations of other youth. Fewer gang members come from homes with two parents and over 20% are in living situations where there is no parent figure.

Gang Members Account for the Majority of Violent and Serious Property Crimes

What proportion of the total amount of crime is attributable to gang members? Is the attention given to gangs in the news media, in public perception, and in research justified? An examination of the total number of serious crimes that are committed by those youth who are or will be gang members suggests that the attention given to gangs is clearly justified. As noted above, gang members are particularly active offenders during the time they are active members of a gang. Thus, it might be expected that they would contribute disproportionately to the overall volume of crime.

Counting the total number of offenses committed by the DYS sample over the 1987–1991 period, the percentage of various types of crimes that can be attributed to the 14% of youth (18% of males, 9% of females) who were gang members during this period is given in Table 8. Quite obviously, gang members during this period account for the vast majority of all serious crime committed by the DYS sample over the five-year period and for a large and disproportionate amount of minor crime as well. Similar findings have been found in our companion project

Table 8. Proportion of Offenses Committed by Gang Members 1987–1991

Offense Type	Males		Females		Total	
	Nongang	Gang	Nongang	Gang	Nongang	Gang
Serious Violence						
Including gang fights	10%	90%	16%	84%	11%	89%
Excluding gang fights	26%	74%	13%	87%	21%	79%
Minor Violence	28%	72%	73%	27%	42%	58%
Property						
Serious	27%	73%	49%	51%	29%	71%
Minor	44%	56%	64%	36%	50%	50%
Drug Sales	13%	87%	9%	91%	13%	87%

in Rochester, and cross-nationally for groups who might be considered gangs, in our companion project in Bremen, Germany (Huizinga & Schumann, 2001).

Additional analyses indicated that a very large majority of the serious crimes committed by those who were gang members at some time during the period examined occurred while they were active gang members. For example, 85% of the serious violent offenses (excluding gang fights) committed by those who were gang members at some time were committed while they were active participating gang members. Similarly, 86% of all serious property crimes and 80% of all drug sales committed by those who became gang members were committed while they were active gang members.

Perhaps not surprisingly, gang membership appears to be exceedingly criminogenic. More surprising, perhaps, is the observation that the individuals who are or will become gang members account for the vast majority of all serious crimes committed by the DYS sample over a five-year period, and that the majority of the crimes were committed while they were active gang members. The attention given to gangs seems more than justified, and the need for gang prevention and intervention programs is clearly indicated.

Developmental Risk Factors for Gang Membership

Given the high volume of crime committed by gang members, it is important to consider what factors contribute to youth joining gangs. In the period before joining a gang, do future gang members share similar experiences or characteristics that put them at particular risk for becoming gang members? And, can such factors provide targets for risk-focused prevention and intervention programs?

When asked why they joined a gang, DYS gang members indicated several reasons. Although many reasons were idiosyncratic, the most common reason, given by almost half the gang members (46%), was that they joined the gang "to be a real part of things ... to be where the action is." Another 8% indicated that they joined for protection, and 4% indicated that they joined as a way to make money. When asked if anything would have happened to them if they hadn't joined, almost all the gang members indicated that nothing would have happened. It thus appears, at least in Denver, that there is little direct pressure or coercion to join gangs, but that a good number do so in order to be part of what is perceived to be where exciting things are happening.

To examine additional developmental risk factors for gang membership, groups of individuals were identified who joined gangs at ages 13–14, at ages 15–16, and at ages 17–18. Other groups in the same birth cohorts as the gang members were also identified and classified as being serious offenders (those committing four or more serious offenses over the prior two years), or as nonserious offenders. For each of the age groups, these three types of offending groups were compared on 36 different risk factors, including family, peer, school, neighborhood, and personal characteristics in the two years *preceding* the period in which the future gang members joined a gang. In general, it was found that the same risk factors were important at all three age periods.

These risk factors included (1) high levels of prior delinquency, including both minor and serious offending, *problem* use of alcohol and marijuana, and being arrested; (2) peer factors, with future gang members having higher levels of involvement with delinquent peers and lower levels of involvement with conventional peers; and (3) truancy and suspension from school (these school factors separated individuals who were not serious offenders from serious offenders and gang members).

Personal risk factors for future gang membership included (1) weak beliefs/attitudes about the wrongfulness of delinquent behavior, (2) willingness to use excuses for delinquent behavior (neutralization), and (3) psychological problems (externalizing behavior).

Most of the future gang members had multiple risk factors in the years preceding their joining a gang. Eighty-nine percent of the future gang members had high scores on four or more risk factors in the years preceding gang membership, compared to 61% of nongang serious offenders and 31% of nonserious or nondelinquent youth. However, it should be noted that gang members make up only 10% of youth who score high on four or more risk factors.

It is also interesting that gang members and serious delinquents were generally attached to school and were doing almost as well academically in school as other youth (although they were more often truant and more often suspended); were not strongly influenced by various family factors; had reasonable levels of self-esteem/self-efficacy; held conventional values about employment and success; and had feelings similar to other youth about opportunities for education, for future jobs, and general optimism about the future.

Overall, it appears that major risk factors for gang membership are similar to risk factors for other serious offenders, coupled with the perception that gangs will be an exciting place to be. However, in the years before joining a gang, for future gang members these risk factors are heightened to levels even above those affecting other serious offenders. Peer groups may be an important target for intervention since future gang members have higher involvement with delinquent peers and lower involvement with conventional peers than other delinquent youth, and it has been shown that conventional peers are a true protective factor for reducing gang membership (Elliott & Huizinga, 2000). Public portrayals of gangs as nonexciting and dangerous may also have some influence, since one of the main reasons given by DYS ex-gang members for leaving a gang is fear of death or serious injury. This latter belief is to some extent borne out empirically, since approximately 15% of the DYS gang members report serious injury victimization while being an active gang member, compared to 3% of nongang youth.

Peers, Gangs, and Co-Offending

The Influence of Peers

One of the strongest and most consistent findings from self-report studies of delinquency is the influence of delinquent peers on delinquent behavior. The relationship between delinquent peers and violence can be illustrated using data from the DYS. Youth aged 14–19 in 1991 were classified into four groups—those who had low, medium, and high involvement with delinquent friends, and those who were gang members. Not surprisingly, gang members have the highest average involvement with delinquent friends. The prevalence of involvement in serious assaults (aggravated assault, robbery, rape, gang fights) among these four groups is given in Table 9. The influence of delinquent peers is readily seen. For both males and females, as the level of involvement with delinquent peers increases, the proportion of youth engaged in assault increases substantially. The extreme influence of gang membership is also clearly seen, with nearly three-quarters of gang members involved in serious assault, compared to only 17% of other youth with a high involvement with delinquent peers.

The Role of Co-Offending

While the relationship between delinquent peers and delinquent behavior is well documented in self-report studies, it has been suggested that this finding results from co-offending. That is, the relationship between delinquent peers and delinquency may simply reflect the fact that many youth commit offenses primarily with their peers. Thus, individuals engaged in delinquency report they have friends engaged in delinquency simply because they do it together. If this is true, then peer groups may not be a particularly important causal factor in the development of delinquency. However, evidence from the DYS indicates that the relationship between the delinquency of one's peers and one's own behavior is not just a simple matter of co-offending. Using information provided by the DYS youth respondents, the relationship between the level of involvement with delinquent peers and group offending is given in Table 10.

Table 9. Prevalence of Serious Assault Among Groups with Different Levels of Involvement with Delinquent Peers

	Level of Involvement with Delinquent Peers			
	Low	Medium	High	Gang Member
Males	2%	8%	20%	72%
Females	0%	3%	13%	72%
Total	1%	6%	17%	72%

Table 10. Average % of Assault Offenses Committed in Groups by Level of Involvement with Delinquent Peers

	Level of Involvement With Delinquent Peers			
	Low	Medium	High	Gang Member
Males	100%	92%	77%	74%
Females	92%	100%	58%	55%
Total	91%	86%	70%	71%

Table 11. Percent of Males with High Proportion of Delinquent Friends Over Time

	1988	1989	1990	1991
1991 Delinquency Status				
Non- or Low-Delinquency in 1991	37%	29%	32%	34%
Initiating Serious Delinquency in 1991	67%	71%	68%	73%
Initiating Gang Membership in 1991	66%	61%	70%	87%

For both males and females, as the level of involvement with delinquent peers *increases*, the percentage of offenses committed in groups *decreases* and the number of offenses committed alone increases. Both those with high numbers of delinquent friends and gang members (who have the highest involvement with delinquent peers) have the lowest percentage of group offenses and the highest proportion of solo offenses. In fact, in data not presented, for these two more serious groups of offenders, over half (about 60%) of their serious assaults are committed solo. Also, it is those who have lower involvement with delinquent friends who report committing all or almost all of their offenses in groups. This raises the possibility of a developmental process, where delinquency is initiated in group behavior, but as it becomes more and more frequent and serious, it tends to become split between both solo and group offending. However, for the purpose here, what is important to note is that although the often-reported relationship between having delinquent peers and involvement in more frequent and serious offending may involve co-offending, the explanation for the relationship between delinquent peers and delinquency is not simply a matter of co-offending.

Delinquent Peers and Future Delinquency

Not only do delinquent friends have a concurrent influence on delinquent behavior, but they may also influence future involvement in serious delinquency and gang membership. The percentage of males who have a high proportion of delinquent friends is given in Table 11 across the 1988–1991 period for three separate groups: those who initiated serious delinquent involvement in 1991, those who initiated gang membership in 1991, and other youth. (Given the low number of female gang members in the sample, estimates for females were unreliable and are not presented.) As can be seen, a majority of those initiating serious offending or becoming gang members in 1991 already had a large proportion of delinquent friends in 1988 and, for gang members, the percentage is slightly increasing over time.

It is interesting to note that for those becoming gang members in 1991, their levels of group vs solo offending did not change over the years, but held relatively constant at 74–75% group offenses and 25–26% solo offenses over the 1988–1991 period. While the majority of their offenses occur in a group context, they are more likely than other youth, even in the pregang years, to also commit solo offenses.

Some Comments about Peer Groups

These findings point out the robust relationship between having delinquent peers and both current and future delinquency and violence. The consistency of these findings in the Program of Research and in other studies suggests that peer groups are an important target for prevention and intervention. Successful strategies that break up the social networks and cohesiveness of delinquent peer groups and gangs would be anticipated to have success in reducing future violence. In addition, early reduction of delinquent peer group involvement may reduce future gang involvement, and, given the disproportionate volume of crime attributable to gang members, reduce future levels of crime. On the other hand, prevention and intervention strategies that bring delinquent or predelinquent youth together for education and training, recreational activities, or other reasons may not be as effective. Such programs increase the risk of maintaining or increasing the delinquent peer networks of the youth involved, and as illustrated above, this may have quite deleterious effects.

Explanatory, Risk, and Protective Factors

Risk and Protective Factors for Successful Adolescence

Various reports of the DYS have examined risk and protective factors for delinquency, serious delinquency, and gang membership, as well as the influence of gang membership on these factors. These analyses have often revealed that it is the presence of several risk or protective factors in combination that have the greatest effect. As an example, an examination of some risk and protective factors for "successful adolescence" is presented (Huizinga, 1997c). Although several requirements could be specified for a successful adolescence, the criteria used included involvement in no more than two serious delinquencies; having problems resulting from drug use on no more than two occasions; being in an age-appropriate grade in school, or having graduated from high school and not being a dropout; and consistently having good self-esteem/self-efficacy.

Somewhat distressing was the finding that by the fifth year of the survey, when the three oldest cohorts were 15–19, less than half (39%) of these youth would be considered a success by these criteria. Clearly, if other criteria such as lack of mental health problems were added, the percentage of success cases would be even smaller.

There is some disagreement in the literature about what are called risk and protective factors. In some instances, variables that are considered to be unconventional or not prosocial are considered to be risk factors, while variables considered to be conventional or prosocial are considered protective factors. For example, poor parenting is considered a risk factor while good parenting is considered a protective factor. This means, however, that the same variable can be considered as either a risk or a protective factor (or both), depending on its particular use in a research investigation. Another use of these terms comes from the study of resilience (achieving success or well-being in the face of adversity). Here, the use of the term "protective factor" is more often reserved for variables that interact with known risk factors (variables that result in or correlate with a lack of success or well-being) and reduce the effect of these risk factors (see e.g., Tiet & Huizinga, 2002). For the purpose here, the former use of the terms "risk" and "protective factors" has been adopted, so that variables generally considered unconventional and not prosocial are considered as risk factors (e.g., having delinquent peers) and those generally considered conventional or prosocial (e.g., having conventional peers) are considered protective factors.

In addition, some variables identified as being true protective factors in resilience research are included and called resilience variables to distinguish them from other protective factors. The relation of various risk and protective factors to adolescent success is given in Table 12. The lengthy table is provided to show the breadth of variables related to adolescent success. The figures given are the conditional probability of success given the presence or absence of a risk/protective factor (expressed as a percentage). For example, for the total sample, within the group that had high levels of involvement with delinquent peers, only 21% were successful, while among those without delinquent peers, 55% were successful.

A discriminant analysis revealed that the best predictors of success were peer delinquency (negatively related to success), having conventional friends, having a stable family and good parental monitoring, and having expectations or perceived opportunities for the future. These and additional analyses clearly indicated, however, that there was no one "silver bullet" or variable that leads to success. Rather, there are combinations of risk and protective factors, and as the number of risk factors increases, the probability of success decreases; and as the

Table 12. Conditional Probability of Success Given the Presence or Absence of Risk, Protective, and Resilience Factors

	Total Sample Presence of Risk or Protective Factor		Males Presence of Risk or Protective Factor		Females Presence of Risk or Protective Factor	
	Yes	No	Yes	No	Yes	No
Peer Variables						
Peer Delinquency (R)	21	55***	19	56 ***	24	54 ***
Peer Drug Use (R)	24	51***	18	49 ***	32	54 ***
Conventional Friends (P)	53	22***	50	13 ***	56	30 ***
Problem Behavior						
Gang Member (R)	11	42***	11	37 ***	13	46 **
Arrest (Arrest not ticket -R)	27	43***	27	38 **	27	47 **
School Problems (Truancy, Suspension, Poor grades-R)	28	58***	25	52 ***	31	64 ***
Family Variables						
Stable 2-Parent Family (P)	53	33***	53	26***	54	40*
Multiple Family Changes (R)	28	43***	21	39***	36	47***
Family on Welfare (R)	32	43**	27	39**	39	47 ns
Parental Monitoring (P)	54	20***	51	19***	55	22***
Home Curfew Rules (P)	53	22***	56	48 ns	68	52**
Parental Discipline (P)	41	36 ns	36	30 ns	47	41 ns
Family Crime (R)	35	41*	27	37*	42	45 ns
Parental Drug Use (R)	27	38 ns	11	34*	40	43 ns
Resilience Variables						
Being Popular/Well-Liked	52	33***	46	28***	60	38***
Above Average School Grades	58	30***	56	27***	59	34***
Support of Significant Other	41	25***	37	20***	45	32 ns
Aspirations, Expectations, and Optimism for the Future						
Educational Aspirations (P)	49	27***	42	25***	57	30***
Educational Expectations(P)	52	22***	46	18***	58	26***
Future Educational Strain(R)	34	47**	28	45**	42	49 ns
General Opportunities (P)	54	16***	50	13***	58	20***
Educational Optimism (P)	50	13***	45	13***	55	15***
General Optimism (P)	46	18***	40	18***	53	19***
Job Expectations (P)	45	18***	40	16***	51	21***

*** Statistically significant at .001 level, ** at .010 level, * at .050 level.
R = Risk Factor, P = Protective Factor.

Table 13. Successful Adolescence by Counts of Risk and Protective Factors

Number of Protective Factors Minus the Number of Risk Factors	−8	−7	−6	−5	−4	−3	−2
Percent Having a Successful Adolescence	0%	0%	0%	0%	5%	12%	9%
Number of Protective Factors Minus the Number of Risk Factors	−1	0	1	2	3	4	5
Percent Having a Successful Adolescence	12%	13%	19%	26%	32%	43%	43%
Number of Protective Factors Minus the Number of Risk Factors	6	7	8	9	10+		
Percent Having a Successful Adolescence	61%	58%	85%	87%	90%		

number of protective factors increases, the probability of success increases. This is illustrated in Table 13 which provides the arithmetic difference between counts of the number of protective factors and the number of risk factors. For any individual, a negative score indicates that the number of risk factors exceeds the number of protective factors and a positive score that the number of protective factors exceeds the number of risk factors. As can be seen, if the number of risk factors exceeds the number of protective factors, there is a very small chance of a successful adolescence. And, the chance of a successful adolescence is not high until the number of protective factors far exceeds the number of risk factors.

These findings indicate that many of the youth in the DYS sample are not having a very successful adolescence, at least as defined here. They also suggest that interventions need to be multi-faceted and affect multiple risk and/or multiple protective factors. Focusing on just one factor probably will not be too successful.

Multiple Etiological Pathways to Delinquency

The idea that there are multiple pathways to delinquency is not new. The notion that the underlying causes leading to participation in delinquent behavior may be different for different types of individuals has been expressed many times. Some youth run away from home because of a poor family environment, some run away because they are pushed out from their homes, while still others run away for fun and excitement and others because they are "over-bonded" and over-protected at home. Similarly, it might be anticipated, and there is some empirical evidence, that some youth steal for different reasons, that some youth engage in violent behavior for different reasons, and that some youth use drugs for different reasons.

Although there is a history of interest in the notion of multiple etiological pathways leading to delinquency, there has been little major theoretical or empirical work exploring this possibility. Most theoretical presentations seem to suggest that the effects of the causal variables work more or less the same for everyone. These presentations rarely attempt to consider the possibility that there may be multiple types of offenders with quite different developmental sequences associated with the onset, maintenance, or termination of involvement in delinquent behavior. An important theoretical concern thus arises. Is there one underlying constellation of variables leading to delinquency that works more or less the same for everybody, or are there subsets of individuals, each subset having a common background and experience, for which the variables work differently? That is, are there different pathways to delinquent behavior?

A preliminary examination of the existence of multiple pathways to delinquency was made using the DYS (Huizinga, Esbensen, & Weiher, 1991b). This examination used empirical numerical taxonomy or cluster analytic methods but was not atheoretical. The analysis, being structured in DYS data, reflects a general developmental model. The taxonomic approach employed three separate typologies of children and youth based on (1) their delinquent behavior at Time 1; (2) a set of theoretical factors that include both personal and environmental characteristics (family and parent variables, youth attitudes and beliefs, impulsivity and hyperactivity, and the delinquent and conventional behavior of friends); and (3) their delinquent behavior at Time 2.

The cross tabulation of these typologies (Delinquency at Time 1 × Personal Environment × Delinquency at Time 2) allows examination of potentially complex nonlinear interactions in etiological variables as influences on the onset as well as on increases or decreases in delinquent behavior. The basic question addressed is whether there are relatively distinct types of etiological environments that lead to initiation or changes in delinquent involvement.

The cluster analyses identified several different child and youth "personal environments" that varied on nature of parenting, personal beliefs about delinquency, impulsivity/hyperactivity, and friends' behavior. There were differences in the "personal environments" of these children and youth that were related to their level of delinquent behavior and to the year-to-year transitions between delinquency types. Of interest in both the child and youth samples, personal environments appeared to provide both protective and risk factors. For example, having a personal environment that includes a positive home and conventional attitudes appears to reduce delinquency involvement, while having a personal environment that involves delinquent friends and/or being impulsive leads to initiation, maintenance, or increases in delinquency.

Although there is a relationship between the personal and delinquency typologies and transitions between delinquency types, it is important that there were a substantial number of children and youth in each personal environment type who were classified as nondelinquent, low-level delinquent, and as higher level delinquent. Delinquent involvement was not unique to any one personal environment type. Youth with quite different personal characteristics and life experiences were delinquent. There clearly are multiple paths leading to initiation and to increased involvement in delinquency.

Potential differences by sex in the child and youth samples indicated that, although there were some differences, in general, the same pattern of findings held for both genders. A substantial number of males and females were contained in each delinquency cluster. Although the personal environment typology shows some relationship to sex (boys more likely to be classified as impulsive/hyperactive and girls more likely to be classified as having a positive home and a conventional orientation), none of the differences was large, and the relationship of personal environment to transitions in delinquency over time is generally similar for both child and youth samples for both genders.

In summary, the findings indicated the following:

(1) There is typological diversity among the child and youth samples in etiological or explanatory variables, and there is a differential relationship between these types and involvement in delinquent behavior and over-time transitions in levels of involvement in delinquency.

(2) Those classified as delinquent, even those classified as very high delinquents, include individuals from most of the different personal environment types. Other variables not included in these preliminary analyses may account for why some of the children and youth in particular types engage in delinquency. However, it seems clear that individuals with quite different personal environments and prior levels of delinquency are later classified as delinquent. That is, there do appear to be multiple etiological paths to delinquency.

(3) The findings suggest that in both theory and practice it may be appropriate, and perhaps necessary, to pay greater attention to typological diversity. Intervention programs need to be designed with this diversity in mind. Not all children or youth are the same or engage in delinquency for the same reasons, and identifying and treating different types of individuals is necessary. The same shoe in theory, or practice, does not fit everyone.

Developmental and Gender Differences in Explanatory Models

Several reports of the DYS have examined developmental and gender differences in patterns of delinquency and victimization over the child through adolescent age span. And, given the wide range of individual, family, peer, school, and social context measures included in the DYS that are presumed causal factors or risk factors for delinquency, these reports have also examined developmental and gender differences in theoretical explanations for delinquency (Espiritu, 1998; Espiritu & Huizinga, 1996; Menard, 1996). It might be anticipated that the influence of various risk, protective, and predictive factors varies over different parts of the life span and may differ by gender.

In analyses examining gender differences, males and females were found to be more similar than different in models examining the influence of individual, family, school, and peer factors on delinquency. The influence of these factors was similar across genders during childhood and early adolescence, although, with increasing age, some significant gender differences were found during middle adolescence and young adulthood. For example, the influence of delinquent peers, weak prosocial beliefs, and use of neutralization techniques (excuses for delinquent behavior) were stronger for males. However, the single most important predictor of delinquent behavior across both genders and all age groups was having friends who are engaged in delinquency. (A finding common in previous research.) A second major predictor was having school problems (cheating on tests, truancy, suspension). The presence of psychological problems was also related to delinquency during adolescence for both genders. However, the relationship was not absolute; many of the youth with psychological problems were not delinquent.

Various age-graded models indicated that our ability to explain delinquent involvement increases with age, being greatest during early and midadolescence. This may suggest that early delinquent involvement may be experimental behavior during childhood and not strongly linked to the explanatory or risk factors often examined. However, it may also indicate that explanations for delinquent offending during childhood and late adolescent/young adulthood are in need of greater development. As recent interest in the very young offender and in the transition to adulthood is increasing, a reconsideration and focus on age-graded risk, protective, and explanatory factors for the child and young adult offender seems needed, and such reconsideration is part of the planned future work of the DYS.

Intergenerational Transmission of Delinquency and Drug Use

There has been recent interest in the apparent relationship of delinquency and drug use across generations. Using data from the "high-risk" sample of the Denver Youth Survey, the influence of past and current parental problem behavior (criminality and drug use) on the delinquency and drug-use behavior of their children was explored (Huizinga, Esbensen, & Weiher, 1992).

Using a composite measure of parental problem behavior, a clear relationship between parental problem behavior and serious delinquency was found. As the seriousness of parental problem behavior increased, so did the likelihood of serious delinquency on the part of their children. About 11% of the children of parents with no problem behavior were frequently involved in serious delinquency, while 24% of the children of parents who report more serious problem behavior are involved in serious delinquency. Also, among more serious delinquent offenders, 40% have parents with more serious problem behavior. It should be carefully noted, however, that over half the children of parents with serious problem behavior are not seriously delinquent. Having "problem parents" is a risk factor for, but no sure indicator of, delinquency.

Similar results also hold for minor delinquent offending, alcohol use, marijuana use, and other illicit drug use, although the relationship of parental problem behavior to these various adolescent behaviors is not as strong.

Analyses examining the relative influence of parents and peers on delinquency and drug use clearly indicate the overwhelming importance of peers. As long as a youth did not have a delinquent/drug-using peer group, they were not particularly delinquent/drug using themselves, regardless of parental problem behavior. However, the combination of parental problem behavior coupled with delinquent/drug-using peers resulted in the highest levels of involvement in delinquency and/or drug use.

Overall, there appears to be some relationship between parental criminality and drug use and the delinquency and drug use of their children. However, this influence is largely mitigated by the kind of friends that the children have. Finding ways to build and maintain prosocial peer networks thus appears to be a potentially viable strategy in developing protective factors for children and youth.

Neighborhoods and Problem Behavior

The role of community factors in explaining delinquency has a long history, perhaps most notably through the work of social disorganization theorists who have identified community characteristics such as poverty, mobility, housing density, family structure, occupational status, and ethnic mix as factors associated with higher rates of problem behavior. At its inception, the DYS had a major objective of investigating the impact of living in "high risk" neighborhoods on problem behavior, and extensive measurement of both neighborhood ecology and of variables that theoretically mediate between social disorganization factors and problem behavior was included. This emphasis on neighborhoods reflects the project's goal of identifying interventions at the neighborhood level that may reduce problem behavior. The DYS also acted as a "host" study for the initial study of neighborhood effects by the MacArthur Foundation Program on Successful Adolescence, and DYS staff were later involved in a city-wide study of neighborhoods sponsored by the MacArthur Program. This role expanded the project's neighborhood measurement of potential mediating factors such as limited institutional resources, levels of community cohesion and informal social control, and consensus on values and norms, which in turn impacts more directly upon families and residents.

Several DYS reports and publications have provided findings about neighborhoods (Elliott & Huizinga, 1993; Elliott, Wilson, Huizinga, Sampson, Elliott, & Rankin, 1996; Esbensen & Huizinga, 1991b; Huizinga, Esbensen, & Elliott, 1990). To examine neighborhood effects, a first necessary question is, "What is a neighborhood?" Although study findings suggested a census block group was not inappropriate as a definition of a neighborhood, it was found that there was a good deal of individual variation in the definition of one's neighborhood and that the size and location of a neighborhood may vary by the type of question asked a resident. For example, questions about knowing your neighbors or having a grocery store in your neighborhood may result in reports about different-sized neighborhoods from the same resident. Clearly some care is needed in defining "neighborhoods" in survey research.

Although the DYS is based on a sample from "high-risk" neighborhoods, we have found that there are different types of "high-risk" or "disorganized" neighborhoods. The neighborhoods included in the sample were selected on the basis of a cluster analysis that identified seven types of neighborhoods, three of which would be considered disorganized. One cluster was economically disadvantaged and had high rates of unemployment, racial mix (Anglo, Hispanic, and African American), single-parent households, persons per room, and school dropouts. The second was economically disadvantaged and contained many unmarried persons and a highly mobile population with many multiple-unit dwellings. The third was also economically disadvantaged and was predominantly a minority (African American) cluster with high rates of single parent and unmarried person households and high rates of persons per room.

Much prior research has considered all socially disorganized areas as being the same. However, the DYS sampling and research findings suggest that greater attention may need to be given to the diversity of neighborhoods called disorganized. Although differences in delinquency rates across different kinds of disorganized neighborhoods were not large, differences in youths' perceptions of the opportunities to succeed (economic and educational success) did vary by type of disorganized neighborhood, as did the reasons for and locations of drug use. Thus, explanatory or risk variables may vary across different types of disorganized neighborhoods.

Examination of mediating variables (variables affected by neighborhood disorganization which in turn affect problem behavior) indicated that at the macro-neighborhood level, the effects of social disorganization (poverty, mobility, single parent families, ethnic diversity) were mediated by neighborhood social control, social bonding, and normative consensus on values and behavior. This is as would be expected on the basis of social disorganization theory. At the individual level, however, the explanation of problem behavior by neighborhood disorganization and mediating variables is not very accurate. This finding of good explanation for macro-neighborhood rates of problem behavior but poor explanation of the problem behavior of individuals on the basis of these neighborhood variables is not unique to the DYS (see e.g., Jencks & Mayer, 1990). Clearly, further work is needed to understand how neighborhoods affect individual behavior, and this issue continues to be examined within the DYS.

Arrest and Imprisonment

The Impact of Arrest

The impact of arrest on future behavior can be viewed from various theoretical orientations, including deterrence theory, labeling and the amplification of deviance, and social learning theory. From these views the impact of arrest can be seen as (1) a deterrent to future delinquency, (2) an event that facilitates or results in increased levels of delinquent involvement, or (3) an event that may either increase or decrease future delinquent involvement, depending on the nature of warning and punishment provided by the juvenile justice system and the rewards and negative reinforcements provided by family, peers, and community in which the individual lives. In the context that may follow arrest, an arrestee may find support and encouragement and learn additional delinquent orientations and skills by a justice-system-enforced differential association with other officially identified delinquent youth.

These theoretical views are not without political and practical consequences. A "labelling" perspective may lead to a policy of "nonintervention" for most youth and development of diversion programs, as occurred in the 1970s. A deterrence perspective may lead to a "get-tough and lock them up" strategy, as experienced in the 1980s and 90s. A learning perspective may say neither extreme is correct, but rather the outcome of arrest depends on the individual and the nature of the reinforcements provided by the justice system and the environment in which the individual lives. In this latter case, the effect of arrest may be quite different for different types of youth.

Several DYS reports have examined factors surrounding arrest and the influence of arrest on subsequent delinquent behavior (Esbensen, Thornberry, & Huizinga, 1991; Huizinga & Esbensen, 1992; Huizinga, Esbensen, & Weiher, 1996). Included are examinations of who gets arrested—the demographic characteristics and prior delinquent behavior of arrestees—and the impact of arrest on future delinquency. Several summary statements of the findings can be made. First, many high-risk youth are arrested and have contact with the juvenile justice system. In the DYS, 44% of the youth aged 11–15 in 1987 had an arrest for a delinquent offense (excluding traffic offenses) sometime in the next five years. Both males and females have high arrest rates, over half of males (55%) and one-third of females (33%), so there is ample reason for concern about both genders in the juvenile justice system.

The age distribution of arrestees can be seen in Table 14. Since 10 is the age of criminal responsibility in Colorado, counts of police contacts (that are not formally an arrest) for a delinquent behavior are used for youth aged 9 and under. As might be anticipated, very few youth under the age of 10 have a police contact for a delinquent offense. Over the 11–18 year old ages, there is a steady increase in the percentage of youths who are arrested, and this pattern is observed for both genders. At the older ages, slightly over one-third of the males and almost one-fifth of the females are arrested for delinquent behavior.

Although a large proportion of youths are arrested, the presenting offense of an arrest is not a very good indicator of offending behavior. For example, in a given year, only about one-third of active serious offenders are arrested, and of those arrested most are arrested for a status or minor offense. This is illustrated in Table 15. Although the relationship between seriousness of offender type and seriousness of presenting offense can be seen in the table, serious offenders are most likely to be arrested for a status or minor offense. Also, regardless of offender type, whether serious or not, the majority of each type are not arrested. Thus, the delinquent behavior of individuals does not appear to be well described by their arrests. This is not a particularly unusual observation and it provides the major impetus for the development of self-report measures in the study of crime and delinquency.

Several DYS reports have examined the impact of arrest on subsequent delinquent behavior. Although a substantial number of youth are arrested, for

Table 14. Percent of Age Group Arrested

	Age					
	7–8	9–10	11–12	13–14	15–16	17–18
Total Sample	1.6%	3.0%	6.7%	17.9%	28.0%	28.0%
Males	2.9%	3.9%	8.7%	21.7%	38.1%	37.3%
Females	0.0%	1.9%	4.6%	13.5%	17.2%	18.6%

Table 15. Most Serious Arrest Among Different Types of Offenders

		Most Serious Arrest		
	None	Status Offense	Minor Offense	Serious Offense
Type of Offender				
Nonoffender	0%	0%	0%	0%
Status Offender	88%	8%	4%	0%
Minor Offender	84%	7%	8%	1%
Serious Offender	68%	9%	15%	8%
Gang Member	39%	15%	15%	31%

many arrestees, arrest and juvenile justice system processing does not seem to have the desired effect. For example, the delinquent behavior in the year following arrest of about three-fourths of first-time arrestees was no different or was higher than that of a matched control who was not arrested. In fact, in only 8% of the cases was the serious offending rate of the arrested juvenile less than the matched control. These and other findings suggest that being arrested is not a very strong deterrent against future delinquent behavior. Similar findings have also been found in comparing those individuals placed and not placed on formal probation (Huizinga & Espiritu, 1999).

Theoretically, these findings are most consistent with an amplification of deviance hypothesis. However, additional work on the impact of arrest is underway within the DYS, and in a cross-national investigation of the impact of arrest with our companion project in Bremen, and within the Program of Research on the Causes and Correlates of Delinquency. This further research will help understand the reasons underlying these findings about the effect of an arrest, and perhaps provide some guidance for policy and interventions.

Initiation of Violent Offending and Age at First Arrest

Youths involved in chronic and serious violent offending often begin their offending careers at an early age. However, for most of these youths, there is either no contact with the juvenile justice system in terms of arrest, or arrest follows the initiation of offending by several years. This finding was consistent across all three Causes and Correlates projects (Huizinga et al., 1994). Restricting attention to the first commission of serious violent acts that resulted in the victim being left bleeding, hospitalized, or unconscious provides additional information. During the first five years of the DYS, among these serious violent offenders, 26% were never arrested, 51% had an arrest before, or in the same year as, their first serious violent offense, and 24% were arrested after initiating their serious violent offending. Almost all of these arrests, however, were for nonviolent or minor violent offenses, and only 6% were arrested for a serious violent offense.

The first of these findings about early initiation indicates the need for prevention programming outside the formal juvenile justice system, since offending careers begin early, before official recognition of the offending career occurs. The second finding, however, suggests that if serious violent offenders could be recognized at the time of their first arrest and effective intervention strategies put in place, a substantial reduction in serious violent offending might be possible. As noted, however, identification of such offenders cannot be accurately based simply on the presenting offense of the arrest.

Adolescent Precursors to Young Adult Imprisonment

Given the high-risk nature of the DYS sample and the current political and social orientation toward incarceration of offenders, it is perhaps not too surprising that a fair number of DYS respondents are in prison during the early-adult period. Given that a substantial number are in prison, the questions of who goes to prison and what were they like as younger adolescents can be examined. In the DYS, by 1999, 14% of males and 1% of females of the three oldest cohorts, who were by that time young adults, were confined in prison. This includes those incarcerated for at least one year, although most are serving multiyear sentences, and does *not* include those held in local jails or other short-term facilities (Huizinga, 2000). Minorities, especially African American males, are overrepresented in the prisoner population. For example, African Americans comprise 33% of the largely minority DYS sample, but account for 48% of young adult prisoners. With this higher rate of imprisonment, 19% of African American males are in prison, compared to 12% of Hispanic males, 7% of other minorities, and 3% of Whites. The most common offenses resulting in imprisonment were violent offenses (murder, assault, robbery), accounting for 58% of prisoners, followed by drug offenses (18%), burglary and theft offenses (16%), and other offenses (8%).

What were these young adult prisoners like as adolescents? Because of the very low imprisonment rate among females, only summary data for males are reliable, and examination of adolescent precursors to young adult imprisonment is restricted to males. Table 16 presents the prevalence of most serious delinquency, arrest, and incarceration as a juvenile for the young-adult prisoners and for the remainder of the male sample. Perhaps not surprisingly, the vast majority of male young-adult prisoners were active delinquents during adolescence. As can be seen in Table 16, 77% of the prisoners were violent offenders (serious or minor) during adolescence, compared to 44% of other individuals; 82% of

Table 16. Juvenile Delinquency and Juvenile Justice Experience among Young Adult Male Prisoners and Nonprisoners

	Prisoners	*Nonprisoners*
Adolescent Delinquency		
Serious Violence	64%	34%
Serious Nonviolence	14%	22%
Minor Violence	13%	10%
Minor Nonviolent	5%	12%
Status & Public Disorder	5%	23%
Nondelinquent	0%	0%
Adolescent Arrest	82%	39%
Adolescent Incarceration	39%	8%

Table 17. The Influence of the Juvenile Justice System on Life-Course Patterns of Serious Juvenile Offenders

Adolescent Delinquent Type	Juvenile Justice Experience	Prevalence of Imprisonment as a Young Adult
Serious Violent	Never Arrested	9%
	Arrested but Not Incarcerated	19%
	Arrested and Incarcerated	51%
Serious Non-Violent	Never Arrested	4%
	Arrested but Not Incarcerated	15%
	Arrested and Incarcerated	20%

prisoners had a juvenile arrest, compared to 39% of others; and 39% had been incarcerated as a juvenile, in comparison to 8% of others. Certain adolescent risk factors also distinguished those who were sent to prison. These included having school problems as an adolescent (92% of prisoners, 66% of others), having parents who were involved in crime (51% of prisoners, 35% of others), problem drug use (50% of prisoners, 30% of others), and being a gang member (41% of prisoners, 12% of others).

The influence of the juvenile justice system on the life-course patterns of serious juvenile offenders is given in Table 17. As can be seen in the table, even controlling for type of offender, the further the penetration into the juvenile justice system, the more likely one is to be convicted of a crime and become a prisoner as a young adult. Similar findings hold for minor offenders, although very few individuals who were minor offenders during adolescence were incarcerated as juveniles. There are different possible explanations for these findings. First, persons on a particularly problematic life course in terms of delinquent/criminal offending may be receiving increased sanctions as juveniles and as young adults. Second, juvenile justice system processing may be criminogenic, increasing association among active offenders and increasing labeling, stigmatization, and changes in self-identity. Third, both of these explanations may be correct when applied to different individuals. Additional work is underway within the DYS to examine these alternatives. In either case, however, the findings are consistent with the notion of using the least restrictive confinement of juvenile offenders within the limits of public safety.

Help-Seeking for Psychological Behavior Problems

Several DYS reports have examined the help-seeking of parents for their children with mental health, delinquency, and drug-use problems, as well as help-seeking for the parents and other family members (Espiritu, 1996; Huizinga,

Bashinski, & Lizotte, 1991c; Huizinga & Jakob-Chien, 1998). Data about the frequency of help-seeking, source of help, and satisfaction with help obtained has been collected throughout the life of the DYS.

The most frequently given reasons for seeking help for either children or adolescents are for school and behavioral problems, followed by family and emotional problems. A greater proportion of parents of delinquent adolescents have sought help than have parents of nondelinquents. However, only a small proportion of parents of delinquent youth, roughly 30% for adolescents and 20% for children, report seeking help for their children. For adolescents, the prevalence of help-seeking increases with increasing seriousness of delinquency and with increasing levels of psychological problems.

In general, for both youth and child samples, the most common places or service providers where parents sought help were professionals (MDs, psychiatrists, counselors) in mental health clinics or in private practice, schools, and religious mentors (ministers, rabbis, and priests). Some parents of adolescents and children with behavioral problems or in trouble with the law and *not* experiencing school problems, still listed the school as a place where help for their children was sought. There is thus a suggestion that schools may be seen as a central service provider for many problems outside usual school issues.

A majority (about two-thirds) of parents who sought help reported that they received a great deal of help from the various resources used. However, an examination was also made of whether the youth and children for whom help had been sought changed their level of delinquent behavior in the following year. These analyses indicated that controlling for original-year delinquency level, there were no statistically significant differences in the subsequent year delinquency classification between those for whom help was sought and other youth and children for whom no help was sought. The magnitude of the differences suggests, if anything, that those for whom help was sought had equal, if not higher, delinquency levels in the following year than other youth and children. This does not mean that help-seeking was not beneficial, since parents who sought help may have been seeking help for the most troublesome youth. Neither does it demonstrate, however, that the help sought has been, in general, particularly successful.

Two observations might be drawn from these findings. First, for the majority of delinquent and serious delinquent youth, help has not been sought for their problem behavior. Given a presumed long developmental history of these problem behaviors, there is the opportunity for the earlier provision of services that might reduce this later behavior. Ongoing work in the DYS is examining blockages to service and why services are not more frequently used. Second, many parents approached schools for assistance with their child's nonschool problem behavior as well as other problems. Although schools may not be prepared and may lack the resources to help parents with these problems, perhaps schools could be funded to have resources or to provide referrals to parents for nonschool problems.

Some Final Comments and Plans for the Future

The original paper which initiated this chapter was titled "Some Not So Boring Findings From the Denver Youth Survey", and we hope that readers have found some of the findings reported interesting or informative. There are some themes running through the various findings.

First, there is indication that rates of involvement in nondrug serious delinquencies have not changed much over the last few decades, while rates of drug use are substantially lower. This finding is based on self-reported delinquency data that should more accurately reflect behavior than do official statistics. Official statistics are influenced by many factors other than involvement in delinquent behavior, such as the percentage of offenders apprehended, changes in operating procedures of police departments, and changes in laws. For example, as illustrated in the analyses presented, many serious offenders are either unknown to the justice system or are only known as minor offenders. However, even with these differences, official offending rates from the 1970s to the 1990s also show little change for violent crime (see e.g., Howell, Krisberg, & Jones, 1995). The observation of only small changes in rates of violence over longer periods of time in both self-report and official data is important, since it calls into question reports covering shorter time periods that overly emphasize increases (or decreases) in serious crime to create exciting news or for political purposes. What has changed over time is the use of weapons and the seriousness of victim injuries.

The finding of little change in the rates of serious crime over time applies to females as well as males. Examination of more recent epidemiology also indicated the well-known difference in offending rates between genders, with females having substantially lower delinquency rates than males. However, substantial numbers of females are involved in delinquency and become involved in the juvenile justice system, and there is ample reason for concern about the delinquency and juvenile justice system involvement of both genders.

Second, many serious offenders start their offending careers early and long before they have any contact with the juvenile justice system. Prevention programs that can divert these youngsters from later more serious delinquency involvement are clearly needed. Following the old adage, it may be easier to prevent involvement in serious delinquency than to attempt to intervene in later years when delinquency and other problem behavior are more entrenched. It is fortunate that there are some successful early prevention programs (see e.g., Muller & Mihalic, 1999). However, at the current time these programs are not widespread throughout the country, and prevention activities are often given a lower priority.

Although there is a need for prevention programs, a note of caution about their development and implementation seems in order. Many children displaying problem and aggressive, violent behavior discontinue this behavior on their own in later childhood or early adolescence (Espiritu, Huizinga, Loeber, & Crawford, 2001).

As a result, identifying future serious delinquents at an early age is likely to be inaccurate. Thus, targeting problematic children for various "treatments," although done with the best of motives and intentions, may through labeling and other processes, be counterproductive and potentially increase the number of future serious delinquents. Universal interventions applied to all children in a classroom or group and that are beneficial to both at-risk and not-at-risk youth, or interventions where the targeted youth cannot be identified by themselves or by others as being a select or problem group, seem more promising. Most of the empirically demonstrated successful early interventions seem to have followed this prescription (see e.g., the successful programs described in Muller & Mihalic, 1999).

Third, delinquency, especially serious delinquency, does not often occur in isolation but occurs with other problem behaviors and is preceded by, or occurs in the presence of, combinations of other risk factors. Common among these are drug use and problem drug use, school problems, family and parenting factors (e.g., economic disadvantage, lack of supervision, criminal parents), and personal factors (e.g., having weak beliefs about the wrongfulness of delinquent behavior, willingness to use excuses for engaging in delinquent behavior).

Two risk factors are particularly salient, delinquent peers and membership in delinquent gangs. Consistent with much past research, the strong influence of delinquent peers on involvement in delinquency was evidenced in several sections of this chapter. Gang membership in particular was identified as being particularly criminogenic. Although the findings indicated that delinquency is widespread in the population, that the relatively small group of gang members accounts for the vast majority of all serious crimes committed by the DYS sample clearly indicates their current importance.

Several comments follow these observations. Prevention and intervention programs need to be comprehensive and have multiple components. Delinquent youth often face multiple problems beyond their delinquent behavior, and these problems are interwoven and lie across different social settings of family, school, and neighborhood, as well as in their own personal characteristics. In creating such programs, it is important to remember the large influence of delinquent peers. This influence suggests that programs that bring delinquent or predelinquent youth together for "treatment," social activities, or athletics may actually contribute to future delinquency by increasing exposure and bonding among current and new delinquent friends. The need for the development of effective gang prevention and intervention programs is also clear.

Given these observations, it is also important to note that there is good evidence that not all youth are involved in delinquency for the same reasons, nor do all delinquents face the same combination of risk factors. There are different developmental sequences or pathways leading to delinquency. Thus, it should not be concluded that all delinquents have troubled families, use drugs, have mental health problems, have school problems, and so on; nor should it be concluded that youths with a particular combination of problems are necessarily delinquent. Rather, it is necessary to discover and understand the combination of needs and problems of individual youth in designing appropriate interventions. In this regard, it is also worth noting that many scholars find it exciting to create, examine, and argue about grand omnibus theories of crime and delinquency. Commonly, however, these theories are described as applying equally to all youth, and it would seem that greater attention to individual differences may be needed in theory as well as in intervention.

Fourth, in considering "risk" and "protective" factors, very few *true* protective factors for delinquency have been identified, that is, factors that actually interact with known risk factors to reduce undesirable outcomes. The concept of resilience, i.e., success or adaptation in the face of risk and adversity, suggests there may be such variables. However, most examinations of resilience to risk factors leading to delinquency have simply defined protective factors as the absence or low levels of known risk factors (including some findings reported in this chapter). The identification of true protective factors is extremely important, however, since they may provide significant information and avenues for the development of successful intervention strategies, and it is clear that substantial research work is needed for this purpose.

Finally, it was found that arrest and juvenile justice system experiences did not seem to have the desired effect. The delinquent behavior of approximately three-quarters of arrestees was no different or was higher than that of similar youth who were not arrested. It is uncertain what meaning should be given to these findings, and the interpretation may depend on the political or social leanings of particular individuals. For example, it might be concluded that the juvenile justice system is simply a "paper tiger" and that sanctions are not sufficiently strong to deter future delinquent behavior. On the other hand, it might also be concluded that the juvenile justice system by its practices is criminogenic, and actually exacerbates the delinquent behavior of offenders; or that those in the juvenile justice system are on a different life trajectory than others. Or, perhaps different explanations are correct when applied to particular juvenile offenders. In any case, further research efforts are clearly needed to understand factors underlying the apparent lack of effectiveness of the juvenile justice system. Also, although the DYS is based on a high-risk sample, it is disconcerting that a reasonably large proportion of males end up in prison by their early twenties. In addition to being involved in delinquency and arrested as a juvenile, adolescent risk factors for such later incarceration included school problems, problem drug use, having parents involved in crime, and gang membership. For some youth and for society, these adolescent risks have very serious long-term consequences.

Although there are many interesting and useful findings stemming from the DYS, there is much left to do. In many ways, the DYS is only now on the threshold of being able to conduct the research originally envisioned at its inception.

With the collection of data from the 1999 survey and using the accelerated longitudinal design, the DYS will have prospective longitudinal data spanning the ages of 7 through 26. The project will thus be in a position to begin the research analyses originally conceived many years ago. The identification and examination of developmental pathways from childhood through adolescence to young adulthood, pathways that lead to successful and to deviant and criminal adaptations, still lies ahead. We look forward to the challenge of the life-course developmental research that awaits.

ACKNOWLEDGMENTS.   The research reported here was supported by grants from the Office of Juvenile Justice and Delinquency Prevention (96-MU-FX-0017) and the National Institute on Drug Abuse (R01-DA09409). Opinions or points of view expressed in the paper are those of the authors and do not represent the official positions or policies of these agencies. Portions of this report were presented at the 1998 Annual Meetings of the American Society of Criminology, Washington, DC.

A project such as the Denver Youth Survey requires the goodwill of many individuals and the hard work and dedication of project staff over an extended period. Major credit for the success of the project must be given to the study respondents who have endured our endless probing of their personal lives for more than a decade, and their long-term cooperation is most gratefully acknowledged.

This report and the reports on which it is based would not have been possible without the considerable long-term efforts of the survey, data processing, and research analysis staff of the DYS, who thus deserve the credit for this report, but none of a reader's critical comments. These individuals include Field Supervisors Judy Armstrong-Laurie and Linda Kuhn; Survey Assistants Linda Cunningham, Julie VanSpriel, Linda Zittleman, Meg Dyer, and Judy Perry; Research Assistants Joanne Dunbar, Sylvia Portillo, Karen Montz-Duran; and Data Analysts Amanda Elliott, Bertha Thomas, and Deborah Hopkins.

We are also indebted to our collaborators from Bremen, Germany, Karl Schumann and Beate Ehret, for their support and efforts in our cross-national projects, and to the directors, Rolf Loeber and Terence Thornberry, and the staffs of the Pittsburgh Youth Survey and Rochester Youth Development Study, for their collegiality and help since the inception of the project. Irving Pilliavin and Ross Matsueda provided invaluable support and collegiality at the inception of the project, especially in the conceptualization and measurement of rational choice measures.

The support and encouragement of our federal grant monitors who helped sustain and guide the project, James Howell, Betty Chemers, Katherine Browning, Donnie LeBoeuf, Joan Hurley, Pam Swain and Barbara Tatem-Kelley of OJJDP; and Jagjitsing Khalsa and Andrea Kopstein of NIDA, is also gratefully recognized.

References

Baumeister, R. F., Smart, L., & Boden, J. M. (1996). Relation of threatened egoism to violence and aggression: The dark side of high self-esteem. *Psychological Review, 103*, 5–33.

Dishion, T., Patterson, G. R., Stoolmiller, M., & Skinner, M. L. (1991). Family, school, and behavioral antecedents to early adolescent involvement with antisocial peers. *Developmental Psychology, 5*, 311–319.

Elliott, A. E., & Huizinga, D. (2000). *Risk and protective factors for gang membership: Is there a difference.* Paper presented at the annual meeting of the American Society of Criminology, San Francisco, CA.

Elliott, D. S., & Huizinga, D. (1993). *The mediating effects of social structure in high risk neighborhoods* (Denver Youth Survey, Project Rep. No. 10). Boulder, CO: University of Colorado.

Elliott, D. S., Huizinga, D., & Ageton, S. (1985). *Explaining delinquency and drug use.* Beverly Hills, CA: Sage Publications.

Elliott, D. S., Huizinga, D., & Menard, S. (1989). *Multiple problem youth: Delinquency, drugs and mental health.* New York: Springer-Verlag.

Elliott, D. S., Wilson, W. J., Huizinga, D., Sampson, R. J., Elliott, A., & Rankin, B. (1996). The effects of neighborhood disadvantage on adolescent development. *Journal of Research in Crime and Delinquency, 33*(4), 389–426.

Esbensen, F. A., & Deschenes, E. (1998). A multi-site examination of gang membership: Does gender matter? *Criminology, 36*, 799.

Esbensen, F. A., & Huizinga, D. (1991a). Community structure and drug use from a social disorganization perspective, *Justice Quarterly, 7*(4), 691–709.

Esbensen, F. A., & Huizinga, D. (1991b). Victimization and delinquency. *Youth and Society, 23*(2), 202–228.

Esbensen, F. A., & Huizinga, D. (1993). Gangs, drugs, and delinquency in a survey of urban youth. *Criminology, 31*(4), 565–589.

Esbensen, F. A., & Winfree, T. (1998). Race and gender differences between gang and non-gang youth: Results from a multi-site survey. *Justice Quarterly, 15*, 505–526.

Esbensen, F. A., Thornberry, T. P., & Huizinga, D. (1991). Arrest and delinquency. In D. Huizinga, R. Loeber, & T. P. Thornberry (Eds.), *Urban delinquency and substance abuse* (pp. 4.1–4.27). Washington, DC: Office of Juvenile Justice and Delinquency Prevention.

Esbensen, F. A., Huizinga, D., & Weiher, A. W. (1993a). Gang and non-gang youth: Differences in explanatory factors. *Journal of Contemporary Criminal Justice, 9*(2), 94–116.

Esbensen, F. A., Huizinga, D., & Weiher, A. W. (1993b). *Violent crime—violent victimization.* Paper presented at the Annual Meeting of the American Society of Criminology, Phoenix, AZ.

Esbensen, F. A., Huizinga, D., & Menard, S. (1998). *Family context and victimization.* (A report of the Denver Youth Survey).

Esbensen, F. A., Huizinga, D., & Menard, S. (1999). Family context and criminal victimization. *Youth and Society, 26*, 23–53.

Espiritu, R. (1996). *Help-seeking patterns of parents of high-risk youth.* (Research Report of the Denver Youth Survey). Boulder, CO: University of Colorado.

Espiritu, R. (1998) *Are girls different?: An examination of developmental gender differences in pathways to delinquency.* (Unpublished doctoral dissertation, University of Colorado).

Espiritu, R., & Huizinga, D. (1996). Developmental gender differences in delinquency and victimization. In R. Loeber, D. Huizinga, & T. P. Thornberry (Eds.), *Annual report of the Program of Research on the Causes and Correlates of Delinquency* (pp. 153–166). Washington, DC: Office of Juvenile Justice and Delinquency Prevention.

Espiritu, R., Huizinga, D., Loeber, R., & Crawford, A. (2001). Epidemiology of self-reported delinquency. In R. Loeber & D. F. Farrington (Eds.), *Child Delinquents* (pp. 47–66). Thousand Oaks, CA: Sage Publications, Inc.

Farrington, D. P., Ohlin, L. O., & Wilson, J. Q. (1986). *Understanding and controlling crime: Toward a new research strategy*. New York: Springer-Verlag.

Howell, J. C, Krisberg, B., & Jones, M. (1995). Trends in juvenile crime and youth violence. In J. C. Howell, B. Krisberg, J. D. Hawkins, & J. J. Wilson (Eds.), *A sourcebook: Serious and violent juvenile offenders* (pp. 1–35). Thousand Oaks, CA: Sage Publications.

Huizinga, D. (1997a). *Overtime changes in delinquency and drug use: The 1970's to the 1990's*. Paper prepared for the Office of Juvenile Justice and Delinquency Prevention, Washington, DC.

Huizinga, D. (1997b). *Gangs and the volume of crime*. Paper presented at the 1997 Annual Meeting of the Western Society of Criminology, Honolulu, HI.

Huizinga, D. (1997c). *Risk and protective factors for successful adolescence*. Paper presented at the National Institute of Justice Conference on Evaluation and Research, Washington, DC.

Huizinga, D. (1998a). *Influence of gangs on male and female gang members and non-gang youth*. Paper presented at the 1998 Annual Meeting of the American Sociological Association, San Francisco.

Huizinga, D. (1998b). *Developmental risk factors for gang membership*. Paper presented at the 1998 Annual Meeting of the Western Society of Criminology, Newport Beach, CA.

Huizinga, D. (2000). *Who goes to prison?* Paper presented at the Annual Conference on Criminal Justice Research and Evaluation, Washington, DC.

Huizinga, D., & Esbensen, F. A. (1992). An arresting view of justice. *School Safety, 3*, 15–17.

Huizinga, D., & Espiritu, R. (1999). *Delinquent behavior of youth in the juvenile justice system: Before, during, and after different court dispositions*. Report prepared for the National Center for Juvenile Justice, National Juvenile Court Judges Association, Pittsburgh, PA.

Huizinga, D., & Jakob-Chien, C. (1998). The contemporaneous co-occurrence of serious and violent juvenile offending and other problem behaviors. In R. Loeber & D. Farrington (Eds.), *Serious and violent juvenile offenders: Risk factors and successful interventions* (pp. 47–67). Beverly Hills, CA: Sage Publications.

Huizinga, D., & Schumann, K. (2001). Gang membership in Bremen and Denver: Comparative longitudinal data. In M. W. Klein, H.-J. Kerner, C. Mason & E. G. M. Weitekamp (Eds.), *The eurogang paradox* (pp. 231–246). London: Kluwer Academic Publishers.

Huizinga, D., Esbensen, F. A., & Elliott, D. S. (1990). *Community structure, perceived limited opportunity, delinquency, and drug use*. (Denver Youth Survey, Project Rep. No. 9) Boulder, CO: University of Colorado.

Huizinga, D., Loeber, R., & Thornberry, T. P. (Eds.) (1991a). *Urban delinquency and drug use*. Report prepared for the Office of Juvenile Justice and Delinquency Prevention, Washington, DC.

Huizinga, D., Esbensen, F. A., & Weiher, A. W. (1991b). Are there multiple paths to delinquency? *Journal of Criminal Law & Criminology, 82*, 83–118.

Huizinga, D, Bashinski, H., & Lizotte, A. J. (1991c). Adolescent employment and delinquency. In D. Huizinga, R. Loeber, & T. P. Thornberry (Eds.), *Urban delinquency and substance abuse* (pp. 16.1–16.14). Office of Juvenile Justice and Delinquency Prevention.

Huizinga, D., Esbensen, F. A., & Weiher, A. W. (1992). *Intergenerational transmission of delinquency and drug use*. Paper presented at the 1992 meeting of the Society for Research on Adolescence, Washington, DC.

Huizinga, D., Loeber, R., & Thornberry, T. P. (1993). Delinquency, drug use, sex, and pregnancy among urban youth. *Public Health Reports, 108* (Suppl.), 90–96.

Huizinga, D., Esbensen, F. A., & Weiher, A. W. (1994). Examining developmental trajectories in delinquency using accelerated longitudinal designs. In H.-J. Kerner & E. G. M. Weitekamp (Eds.), *Cross-national longitudinal research on human development and criminal behavior* (pp. 203–216). New York: Kluwer Academic Publishers.

Huizinga, D., Loeber, R., & Thornberry, T. P. (1995). *Recent findings from the Program of Research on the Causes and Correlates of Delinquency.* Report prepared for the Office of Juvenile Justice and Delinquency Prevention, Washington, DC.

Huizinga, D., Esbensen, F. A., & Weiher, A. W. (1996). The impact of arrest on subsequent delinquent behavior. In R. Loeber, D. Huizinga, & T. P. Thornberry (Eds.), *Annual report of the Program of Research on the Causes and Correlates of Delinquency* (pp. 82–101). Office of Juvenile Justice and Delinquency Prevention, Washington, DC.

Huizinga, D., Loeber, R., & Thornberry, T. P. (1997). *The co-occurrence of persistent problem behavior.* Report prepared for the Office of Juvenile Justice and Delinquency Prevention, Washington, DC.

Jencks, C., & Mayer, S. B. (1990). The social consequences of growing up in a poor neighborhood. In L. E. Lynn, Jr. & M. G. H. McGeary (Eds.), *Inner city poverty in the United States* (pp. 111–186). Washington, DC: National Academy Press.

Menard, S. (1996). Age and the impact of family, school, and friends on selected forms of delinquent behavior. In R. Loeber, D. Huizinga, & T. P. Thornberry (Eds.), *Annual report of the Program of Research on the Causes and Correlates of Delinquency* (pp. 102–125). Office of Juvenile Justice and Delinquency Prevention, Washington, DC.

Menard, S. (1997). *Victimization from pre-adolescence to early adulthood.* Report prepared for the Office of Juvenile Justice and Delinquency Prevention, Washington, DC.

Menard, S., & Huizinga, D. (2001). Repeat victimization in a high-risk sample of adolescents. *Youth and Society, 32*(4), 447–472.

Menard, S., Esbensen, F. A., & Huizinga, D. (1998). *Victimization, delinquency, drug use, and school problems.* Report prepared for the Office of Juvenile Justice and Delinquency Prevention, Washington, DC.

Miller, J. (2001). *One of the guys.* New York: Oxford University Press.

Muller, J., & Mihalic, S. (1999). *Blueprints for violence prevention.* Factsheet, Office of Juvenile Justice and Delinquency Prevention, Washington, DC.

Sampson, R. J., & Lauritsen, J. L. (1990). Deviant lifestyles, proximity to crime, and the offender-victim link in personal violence. *Journal of Research in Crime and Delinquency, 27,* 110–139.

Singer, S. I. (1981). Homogeneous victim-offender populations: A review and some research implications. *Journal of Criminal Law and Criminology, 72,* 779–788.

Singer, S. I. (1986). Victims of serious violence and their criminal behavior: Subcultural theory and beyond. *Violence and Victims, 1*(1), 61–70.

Thornberry, T. P., & Figlio, R. M. (1974). Victimization and criminal behavior in a birth cohort. In T. P. Thornberry & E. Sagrin (Eds.), *Images of crime: Offenders and victims* (pp. 102–112). New York: Praeger.

Thornberry, T. P., Krohn, M., Lizotte, A., & Chard-Wierchem, D. (1993). The role of juvenile gangs in facilitating delinquent behavior. *Journal of Research in Crime and Delinquency, 30,* 55–87.

Thornberry, T. P., Huizinga, D., Loeber, R. (1995). The prevention of serious delinquency and violence. In J. Howell, B. Krisberg, & D. J. Hawkins (Eds.), *Sourcebook on serious, chronic, and violent offenders* (pp. 213–237). Thousand Oaks, CA: Sage.

Tiet, Q., & Huizinga, D. (2002). Dimensions of the construct of resilience and adaptation among inner-city youth. *Journal of Adolescent Research, 17*(3), 260–276.

Tonry, M., Ohlin, L. E., & Farrington, D. P. (1991). *Human development and criminal behavior: New ways of advancing knowledge.* New York: Springer-Verlag.

Weiher, A. W. (1996). Precipitating factors for and outcomes of teen pregnancy. In R. Loeber, D. Huizinga, & T. P. Thornberry (Eds.), *Annual report of the Program of Research on the Causes and Correlates of Delinquency* (pp. 126–152). Washington, DC: Office of Juvenile Justice and Delinquency Prevention.

4

The Development of Male Offending

Key Findings From Fourteen Years of The Pittsburgh Youth Study

Rolf Loeber, David P. Farrington,
Magda Stouthamer-Loeber, Terrie E. Moffitt,
Avshalom Caspi, Helene Raskin White,
Evelyn H. Wei, and Jennifer M. Beyers

Introduction

Although there are a plethora of longitudinal studies on the development of anti-social and delinquent behavior (see Loeber & Farrington, 1998, 2001; Loeber, Farrington, Stouthamer-Loeber, & Van Kammen, 1998a), many of them have serious limitations. First, although it has long been known that an early onset of offending during the elementary school period predicts later chronic offending (Loeber, 1982), few studies started with preadolescent samples. Second, few studies started by measuring life-time delinquent behavior at the first assessment; as a result, it is often impossible to gauge whether the measured onset of delinquent acts (e.g., in the previous year) was truly an onset or a mere repetition of earlier behavior. Third, many studies had relatively small samples, making it difficult to trace the antecedents and causes of relatively serious delinquency. Fourth, attrition in longitudinal studies is often relatively high (Capaldi & Patterson, 1987), which by necessity affects statistical power and casts doubts on the validity of

Taking Stock of Delinquency: An Overview of Findings from Contemporary Longitudinal Studies, edited by Thornberry and Krohn. Kluwer Academic/Plenum Publishers, New York, 2003.

conclusions drawn from the data. Lastly, many studies have only a small number of assessments spaced over many years. This makes it impossible to trace the development of deviancy and the duration of exposure to risk factors, which can only be achieved by regular assessments of risk factors *and* outcomes at frequent intervals (e.g., yearly).

These were the main reasons for starting the Pittsburgh Youth Study, which is a prospective longitudinal survey of the development of juvenile offending, mental health problems, drug use, and their risk factors in three samples of inner-city boys. The principal investigator for the main study is Rolf Loeber, with Magda Stouthamer-Loeber and David P. Farrington as coinvestigators, who were joined by Helene Raskin White in recent years. The current chapter concentrates on the development of delinquency (for a companion paper that deals with findings on boys' mental health, see Loeber, Farrington, Stouthamer-Loeber, Moffitt, Caspi, & Lynam, 2001a). Participants in the study included preadolescent and adolescent boys. Further, the first assessment included life-time measurements up to that point; subsequent assessments were carried out at half-yearly intervals (later changed to yearly intervals) without interruption in data collection (Table 1). Moreover, the sample size was large, and attrition has been low. Also, the study measured risk and protective factors as well as antisocial behavior in all follow-up assessments. These and other features of the Pittsburgh Youth Study will be discussed later. Importantly, the Pittsburgh Youth Study is one of three coordinated studies which all started in the late 1980s. The other two studies are overseen by David Huizinga (Denver Youth Survey) and Terence P. Thornberry (Rochester Youth Development Study).

The key aims of the Pittsburgh Youth Study are to investigate and describe developmental pathways to serious delinquency, the risk and protective factors that influence the development of serious offending, and the prevalence and pattern of help seeking for youth with disruptive and delinquent behavior.

A crucial activity over the past fourteen years has been to accomplish these goals by ensuring long-term funding for the study. It was originally funded by the Office of Juvenile Justice and Delinquency Prevention (OJJDP), and data collection began in 1987–88. Since that time, the participants have been followed up regularly, and two books (Loeber, Farrington, Stouthamer-Loeber, & Van Kammen, 1998b; Stouthamer-Loeber & Van Kammen, 1995) and 85 papers have been published or are in press. The study is currently supported by the Office of Juvenile Justice and Delinquency Prevention (OJJDP), the National Institute of Mental Health (NIMH), and the National Institute of Drug Abuse (NIDA). Since not all publications are easily accessible to readers, this chapter summarizes the major findings from the first fourteen years of the study with reference to our original publications.

Table 1. Design and Sequence of Assessments in the Pittsburgh Youth Study

C1	1987		1988		1989		1990		1991		1992		1993		1994		1995		1996		1997		1998		1999	
C2	1988		1989		1990		1991		1992		1993		1994		1995		1996		1997		1998		1999		2000	
	Sp	Fa	Sp	Fa	Sp	Fa	Sp	Fa	Sp	Fa	Sp	Fa	Sp	Fa	Sp	Fa	Sp	Fa	Sp	Fa	Sp	Fa	Sp	Fa	Sp	Fa
Youngest Sample																										
Age	7	7.5	8	8.5	9	9.5	10	10.5	11		12		13		14		15		16		17		18		19	
Assm.	S	A	B	C	D	E	F	G	H		J		L		N		P		R		T		V		Y	
Middle Sample																										
Age	10	10.5	11	11.5	12	12.5	13											follow-up at age 22 in 2001–2002								
Assm.	S	A	B	C	D	E	F																			
Oldest Sample																										
Age	13	13.5	14	14.5	15	15.5		16.5		17.5		18.5		19.5		20.5		21.5		22.5		23.5		24.5		25.5
Assm.	S	A	B	C	D	E		G		I		K		M		O		Q		SS		U		W		Z

C1 = Cohort 1 assessments (oldest third of sample); C2 = Cohort 2 assessments (other two-thirds of sample); Sp = Spring; Fa = Fall; Assm. = Assessment.

Design and Methods

Participants

Boys attending the first, fourth, and seventh grades in the public school system in inner-city Pittsburgh (called the youngest, middle, and oldest samples) were randomly selected for participation in a longitudinal study of the development of disruptive and delinquent behaviors. Participant selection and methods have been described in detail elsewhere (Loeber, Stouthamer-Loeber, Van Kammen, & Farrington, 1991; Loeber et al., 1998a) and are summarized only briefly here. Of those families contacted (about 1,000 in each grade), 85% of the boys and their parents agreed to participate. An initial screening (S) assessment then followed to identify high-risk participants. About 850 boys were screened in each grade. Boys in the youngest and middle samples were given the Self-Reported Antisocial Behavior (SRA) questionnaire (Loeber, Stouthamer-Loeber, Van Kammen, & Farrington, 1989), while those in the oldest sample completed the Self-Reported Delinquency (SRD) questionnaire (adapted from the National Youth Survey, see Loeber et al., 1998a). Parents and teachers were given the respective forms of the Child Behavior Checklist.

The information from this screening assessment was used to identify approximately 30% of the boys with the most severe disruptive behavior problems (approximately 250 boys in each of the three samples). Additionally, a random selection of boys from the remaining 70% of each sample was made (approximately another 250 boys in each sample). This selection process resulted in approximately 500 boys in each follow-up sample (503, 508, 506, in the youngest, middle, and oldest samples, respectively), half being high risk and half average or low risk. It is possible to weight results from these samples back to the original population. Just over half of the follow-up samples were African American boys, and just under half were Caucasian boys, reflecting the racial composition of Pittsburgh Public Schools at the time.

The boys in the follow-up samples, as well as their parents and teachers, were initially followed up at half-yearly intervals (9 assessments for the youngest sample, 7 for the middle sample, and 6 for the oldest sample), after which only the youngest and oldest samples were followed up at yearly intervals (see Table 1). The middle sample was discontinued when the youngest sample began to overlap it in age. However, a single follow-up of the middle sample is currently under way at age 22 (principal investigator: Don Lynam).

In addition to the main study, several substudies have been executed to examine specific issues in more detail. Two should be mentioned in particular: In the summer of 1990, boys from the middle sample were intensively assessed on neuropsychological, impulsivity, and personality measures (principal investigator: Terrie E. Moffitt). Also, a study of psychophysiological and biological risk factors for violence was undertaken in 1996 through 1998 on the youngest sample (principal investigator: Adrian Raine). The results are currently being analyzed.

In total, the youngest and oldest samples probably constitute the most extensively uninterrupted followed-up sample in the United States, spanning late childhood, adolescence, and early adulthood with information about delinquency, substance use, and mental health problems. The youngest sample has now been followed up a total of 18 times (from age 7 to 20). The oldest sample has been followed up 16 times (from age 13 to 25). There are no gaps in missed assessments at the follow-ups of these samples, which makes it possible to reconstruct the boys' lives in a cumulative manner. We are planning to undertake further follow-ups but at intervals of several years rather than yearly.

Measures

The aim was to measure key constructs that were thought to be causes or correlates of delinquency. When possible, we used existing measures; however, a large number of measures had to be developed specially or modified to contain language suitable for an urban, generally low socioeconomic status sample. Some of these new measures were derived from earlier work at the Oregon Social Learning Center, and we are greatly indebted to the input from staff there. In addition, several measures resulted from collaboration among investigators of the OJJDP Program of Research on the Causes and Correlates of Delinquency (Terence P. Thornberry, Alan J. Lizotte, Margaret Farnworth, and Susan B. Stern in Rochester; David Huizinga, Finn Esbensen, and Delbert S. Elliott in Denver). A listing of the measures can be found in Loeber et al. (1998a). That source also contains a detailed description of many of the constructs used in analyses to date and their psychometrics.

Official records of offending were searched in the Juvenile Court of Allegheny County (which includes the city of Pittsburgh and the surrounding area), covering the period up to the date of the first follow-up assessment (A) for participants in that county and prospectively for a period of about six years subsequent to that assessment up to 1994. We also recently obtained state and F.B.I. records of delinquency during adulthood, but these records were not yet available for this report. In addition, California Achievement Test scores on reading, language, and mathematics were collected yearly from the schools (see Loeber et al., 1998a for details), and records from the Child and Youth Services have been extracted and coded (Stouthamer-Loeber, Loeber, Homish, & Wei, 2001).

The Interviewing Process

Practical aspects of data collection and management in the Pittsburgh Youth Study have been described in several publications (Stouthamer-Loeber, 1993;

Stouthamer-Loeber & Van Kammen, 1995; Stouthamer-Loeber, Van Kammen, & Loeber, 1992; Van Kammen & Stouthamer-Loeber, 1997). Many longitudinal studies show that the most elusive and uncooperative respondents tend to be disproportionately delinquent and antisocial (e.g., Farrington, Gallagher, Morley, St. Ledger, & West, 1990). Hence, the loss of respondents is especially serious and likely to produce misleading and invalid results in studies focusing on delinquent and antisocial behavior. Methods of dealing with missing data (e.g., by imputation) are a very poor substitute for collecting as complete data as possible. Therefore, we felt it was essential to maximize the initial response rate, as well as the rate of retaining participants subsequently in the study.

As mentioned, the initial response rate in the screening assessment (S) in the Pittsburgh Youth Study, which required cooperation from *both* the parent and the boy, was 85%. Subsequent retention rates were high, with 82% of the youngest sample participating at the 18th assessment, and 83% of the oldest sample participating at the 16th assessment.

For each participating boy, every year a teacher was requested to complete a questionnaire booklet. The school district administration did not allow us to pay teachers. It was, therefore, very important that our contacts with the schools were positive, and we took several steps to make the cooperation of the schools more rewarding for school personnel. Principals were visited first, and the procedure for the data collection was discussed with them. Then a letter was sent to the teachers to let them know that a study involving students from their school was in progress and that we would be in touch with them at a later point. An appointment was set up with the teachers and the study was explained, the questionnaire booklets were distributed, and a date was set to pick them up. In general, principals and secretaries proved vital in achieving the data collection in schools. Teacher participation was high up to age 16, averaging 89% for the youngest sample from Waves S through P, 89% for the middle sample from Waves S through F, and 88% for the oldest sample from Waves S through D. After age 16, teacher participation rates fell in the youngest and oldest sample to 51–73%, largely because teachers had become less familiar with their students by that age.

Data collection in the Pittsburgh Youth Study was organized and controlled in-house (Stouthamer-Loeber & Van Kammen, 1995). We believe that the quality and completeness of data would have been lower if the interviewing process had been contracted to an agency. It seems unlikely that any data collection agency—however experienced, reputable, and professional—could be as passionately concerned as we have been about the quality and completeness of the data and the well-being of our participants. Furthermore, we believe that it is important for principal investigators and analysts to have close and continuing contact with the data collection process in order to be fully aware of all the decisions made at key choice points, as well as the strengths and weaknesses in the data.

The data collection process, especially in the early years, was a daunting and very labor-intensive task. Each year there were 9,000 assessments (500 boys × 3 samples × 2 assessments × 3 informants), each containing several different questionnaires and hundreds of variables. By the beginning of 2001, we had accomplished over 50,000 assessments.

It was necessary to coordinate about 30–40 part-time interviewers and 10 data-entry staff in addition to other staff involved in data checking, construct development, and documentation. Staff were organized into teams headed by three supervisors, and ultimately by Magda Stouthamer-Loeber and Welmoet Van Kammen (more recently, Rose Jarosz). Beginning from 1994–95, interviewers carried laptop computers and entered the information from participants directly, but the transition from paper-based to fully computerized data collection was a painstaking process that consumed many more person-hours than anticipated.

Interviewers and Staff

Much time and effort was dedicated to training interviewers and staff to ensure high quality data collection. Details of these procedures, scheduling, and quality control during data collection have been published in several publications and the reader is referred to these (e.g., Stouthamer-Loeber & Van Kammen, 1995). Over the years, a cadre of reliable interviewers was gradually assembled who were used repeatedly for several waves of data collection. In order to minimize interviewer bias, however, interviewers did not contact the same participants at consecutive assessments and, therefore, our group of interviewers needed constant replenishment.

Boys and parents were paid for each interview, and we believe that this was important in maximizing the response rate. The parents were initially paid $12.50, with an additional $5 for boys in the oldest sample, and these fees were increased gradually. In the last assessment, we paid the parent $60 and the boy $85.

Many of the more delinquent boys were difficult to locate because their living circumstances were not stable. Interviewers were required to search diligently for participants and were trained in techniques to overcome the participants' reluctance to cooperate. When participants moved long distances away from Pittsburgh, interviews were accomplished by telephone. Fortunately, Pittsburgh is a relatively stable city, but sometimes the tracking processes were long and frustrating. Nevertheless, we have been highly successful in retaining participants in the study.

Overall, in an atmosphere where accuracy and completeness of the data were emphasized and highly valued, staff took great pride in going to extraordinary lengths to do the best possible job. We are very grateful to both interviewers and participants for their invaluable efforts.

Development of Offending

Prevalence, Frequency, and Onset

Several of our publications contain information about the prevalence, frequency, and onset of delinquency (e.g., Farrington, Loeber, Stouthamer-Loeber, & Van Kammen, 1996; Farrington, Loeber, Stouthamer-Loeber, Van Kammen & Schmidt, 1996; Huizinga, Loeber, & Thornberry, 1993; Loeber et al., 1998a). We will first highlight the findings from boys', parents', and teachers' information on delinquency as reported by Farrington, Loeber, and Van Kammen (1996) since they are the most extensive. It should be kept in mind that, because of their young age, boys in the youngest and middle samples responded to the Self-Reported Antisocial Behavior questionnaire up to age 10, after which they were given the Self-Reported Delinquency questionnaire. Since the two questionnaires are only partly overlapping, the results for ages 6 to 10 are only partly comparable to those for ages 11 to 16.

Figure 1 shows the yearly, weighted prevalence of serious delinquency (the percentage committing acts at each age) between ages 6 to 23 for the three samples. Serious delinquency includes car theft, breaking and entering, strongarming, attacking to seriously hurt or kill, or forced sex (but excludes drug dealing). The prevalence increased from 5% at age 6 to a peak of 18% at age 15 (oldest sample), returning to about 5% at age 21. Thus, between ages 6 and 21, there are 15 years in which more than 5% of the sample engage in seriously delinquent acts. As the prevalence increased, so did the mean frequency of serious offending (Figure 2), peaking at ages 17 and 20, thus later than the peak prevalence of serious offending (calculated for active offenders only). Figure 3 shows the cumulative onset of serious delinquency up to age 22, indicating that one out of five of

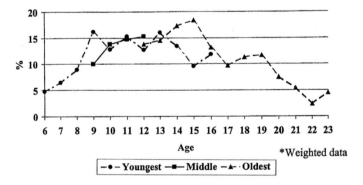

Figure 1.   Weighted prevalence of serious delinquency between ages 6 and 23.

Note: Based on parent, teacher & child self-report (SRD) youngest sample up to age 10 based on SRA.

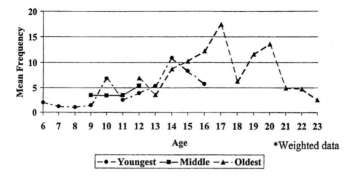

Figure 2.   Mean frequency of seriously delinquent acts (active offenders only) between ages 6 and 23.
Note: Based on child self-report (SRD) youngest sample up to age 10 based on SRA.

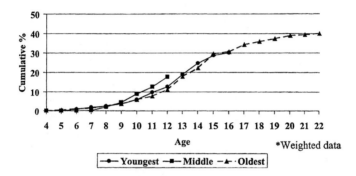

Figure 3.   Cumulative age of onset of serious delinquency between ages 4 and 22.
Note: Based on child self-report (SRD) youngest sample up to age 10 based on SRA.

the serious delinquents in the oldest sample had emerged by age 12, and four-fifths of the serious delinquents had emerged by age 15.

Serious delinquency may or may not take place repeatedly. For that reason, we also focused on persistent serious offending (defined as recurrent offending over at least two waves). Recent analyses (Stouthamer-Loeber, Loeber, Wei, Farrington, & Wikström, 2002) found that the weighted prevalence of persistent serious offending (which included drug selling) was 22% for boys in the youngest sample by age 13 and 37% of boys in the oldest sample by age 19.

An important question is when the eventual serious offenders had their onset of offending. Given that many serious offenders tend to have an early onset of offending (Loeber & Farrington, 2001), we expect that almost all of them will have experienced an onset by mid-adolescence. This is confirmed by the analyses: by age 14, over 80% of the eventual persistent serious offenders in the oldest sample already had emerged (Loeber & Farrington, 1998). Thus, although the frequency of serious offending peaks in the period between late adolescence and early adulthood (Figure 2), the onset of this category of delinquency takes place much earlier. Moreover, if we include less serious forms of delinquency as well, the onset of such acts tends to take place even earlier, well before the onset of serious forms of offending (Loeber, Wung, Keenan, Giroux, Stouthamer-Loeber, Van Kammen, & Maughan, 1993).

Prevalence and onset of juvenile delinquency vary across different neighborhoods. First, Wikström and Loeber (2000) found that the prevalence of serious offending was twice as high in the disadvantaged public housing areas compared to the advantaged neighborhoods (64% versus 31%). The same applies to persistent serious offending. Stouthamer-Loeber et al. (2002) found that 69% of the boys in the oldest sample living in public housing areas had engaged in persistent serious offending by age 19, compared to 18% of boys living in high socioeconomic neighborhoods.

Second, Wikström and Loeber (2000) reported that an early onset of offending prior to age 13 is more common in disadvantaged compared to the other neighborhoods. Also, disadvantaged neighborhoods see more late-onset offenders, which are particularly more common in public housing areas than in advantaged neighborhoods (13% vs. 34%). In conclusion, it appears that the risk window for male juveniles starting their serious delinquent careers is longer for those living in disadvantaged areas compared to those living in better-off areas.

Several publications focused on the prevalence of violence (Farrington & Loeber, in press; Loeber et al., 1993). For example, Farrington and Loeber (in press), using a combination of reports by the boy, his parent, and teacher, reported that between ages 14 and 16, 40% of the African American boys and 12% of the Caucasian boys in the middle sample had committed index violence as young as age 13. Since it could be argued that some forms of violence are common, we also computed the prevalence of repeated violence. In the oldest sample, the weighted prevalence of repeated violence between ages 13.5 and 19.5 was 14%, and it was almost twice as high in disadvantaged compared to advantaged neighborhoods (17% vs. 10%; Beyers, Loeber, Wikström, & Stouthamer-Loeber, 2001).

Prevalence of Delinquency in Court Records

Court records were searched for the period between each boy's 10th birthday and about age 16 for the middle sample, and between the boy's 10th and 18th birthday in the oldest sample (Farrington, Loeber, Stouthamer-Loeber, Van Kammen, & Schmidt, 1996; Loeber et al., 1998a). In the middle sample, 30% of the boys had been petitioned to the court for a delinquent offense, compared to 45% of the boys in the oldest sample. Boys in the youngest sample were too young in 1994 for many of them to be petitioned to the court; their records are currently being searched and scored. Comparable figures for court petitions for index offenses in the middle and oldest samples were 22% and 34%, respectively, and for index violence were 12% and 15%, respectively.

The prevalence of court petitions for violence varied by ethnicity. By age 16, 21% of the African American boys compared to only 1% of the Caucasian boys in the middle sample had a court petition for index violence (Farrington & Loeber, in press).

The prevalence of homicide by young males in the study samples was surprisingly high (Loeber, Crawford, Farrington, Stouthamer-Loeber, Creemers, & Rosenfeld, 2001b). By the summer of 2001, 26 males out of the 1,517 participants had been convicted of homicide, with another 10 having been accused but not convicted. The search and verification of homicide offenders is still underway, and for that reason is not further reported here. Most of the known homicides were committed by guns and occurred in the mid-1990s during a rise in crime in the worst areas of the city.

Victimization

The high rate of delinquency in the sample was matched by a high rate of criminal victimization. By age 19, about one in eleven boys in the oldest sample (9%, weighted data) had been seriously wounded or killed; 7 had been killed by guns, another 3 died by other causes, and 28 had been wounded by guns but did not die (Loeber, DeLamatre, Tita, Cohen, Stouthamer-Loeber, & Farrington, 1999a). Longitudinal analyses showed that the majority of the homicide victims had been highly delinquent themselves and had engaged in gang fights and in drug selling. Also, 61% of the victims carried a gun, compared to 24% of the controls. Victims, compared to controls, tended to have had a long history of problems, including poor academic performance and externalizing behavior problems. Also, victims tended to have been poorly supervised by their parent(s) and have poor communication with them. In summary, many of these inner-city victims of violence had several characteristics in common with serious offenders and appeared to live in circles engaged in illegal behavior.

Concentration of Offending in Families

It has been long known that some families produce more delinquents within and across generations. This was also observed in the Pittsburgh Youth Study (Farrington, Jolliffe, Loeber, Stouthamer-Loeber & Kalb, 2001) based on mothers' reports of arrests of family members at the third assessment. Altogether, 10% of the boys, 10% of their brothers, 3% of sisters, 33% of fathers, 7% of mothers, 13% of uncles, 3% of aunts, 5% of grandfathers, and 2% of grandmothers had ever been arrested. Overall, 44% of families included at least one arrested person. Delinquency was concentrated in some families: 5% of the families contained 30% of the offenders, and, more broadly, 12% of the families contained almost half (44%) of the offenders. These figures did not vary markedly by ethnicity. Arrests of family members predicted arrests of the study boys, with the arrests of the father predicting his son's delinquency independently of all other arrested relatives. Although it is possible that there is a direct link between delinquency of the father and his son (e.g., through modeling, poor parenting, or genetic factors), indirect processes may be associated with criminal fathers' living with a young and/or deviant mother or their residence in a disadvantaged neighborhood.

Development of Delinquency, Aggression, and Violence

Stability of Delinquency and Aggression

Although the stability of antisocial and delinquent behavior has been documented in many studies (e.g., Loeber, 1982; Loeber & Farrington, 1998), relatively little is known about the stability of types of delinquent acts and changes in stability with age. Zhang, Loeber, and Stouthamer-Loeber (1997) examined the stability of minor and serious forms of theft and violence over eight assessment waves covering a period of four years. They found that over three years, the year-to-year odds ratios for the stability of minor theft offenses in the youngest sample amounted to 4.9, 7.6, and 7.1, while the odds ratios for the stability of serious violence were 5.4, 7.0, and 6.7 (the odds ratio expresses the likelihood that those with minor offenses at Time 1 also display such offenses at Time 2). Similar odds ratios were observed for other delinquent behaviors, also in the middle sample. Thus, the continuity of delinquent involvement across different forms and severity levels of delinquency was substantial.

Loeber and Hay (1997) showed that the prevalence of physical fighting decreased in adolescence, especially between ages 12 and 17. They also found some indication that the stability of physical fighting increased between ages 6–7 and 9–10. Year-to-year odds ratios in the youngest sample increased from 10.6 to 18.6. Likewise, Zhang et al. (1997) found that year-to-year odds ratios for minor violence increased with age from 5.6 to 8.2; serious violent offenses occurred at a rate too low to compute stability estimates (see also Farrington & Loeber, in press).

Against the backdrop of stability of delinquency, however, we should accept that there are substantial changes as well. The first source of change is that the levels of severity of offending increase with age (Loeber et al., 1993). The second source of change is the fact that year-to-year fluctuations in offending are distinct. For example, Huizinga, Loeber, Thornberry, and Cothern (2000) found that over three years one quarter (28%) of the boys in the Pittsburgh Youth Study engaged in serious delinquency for just one year, one fifth (20%) for two years, and one tenth (10%) for all three years. Also, violence in the older samples was often intermittent from year-to-year for most of the active violent offenders (Huizinga et al., 1993).

Developmental Pathways

We were interested in specifying the age at which nonviolent boys engaged in violent acts for the first time and in establishing when less serious forms of aggression first emerged. As shown in Loeber and Hay (1997), the onset of minor aggression (e.g., arguing, bullying) tended to occur first, followed by the onset of physical fighting (including gang fighting), and then by the onset of violence. These results were replicated across the three samples. Further, the age of onset curves based on prospective information from the youngest sample largely overlapped with data collected retrospectively in the middle and oldest samples. We also created onset curves for minor delinquency, moderate delinquency, and serious delinquency (Loeber et al., 1998a; Loeber, DeLamatre, Keenan, & Zhang, 1998b; Loeber, Wei, Stouthamer-Loeber, Huizinga, & Thornberry, 1999b), which showed that minor delinquency emerged first, followed by moderate delinquency, which in turn was followed by serious delinquency. Again, the results applied to all three samples.

The above findings on the onset of various levels of delinquency seriousness suggested that individuals' development toward serious forms of delinquency may be orderly. We investigated whether a single or a multiple pathway model would best represent delinquent development and, if a multiple pathway model was best, what would be the dimensions on which to distinguish different pathways. The rationale for identifying dimensions of overt and covert antisocial acts and, to a lesser extent, conflict with authority figures was supported by meta-analyses of parent and teacher ratings from many other studies (e.g., Loeber & Schmaling, 1985; Frick et al., 1993).

After initial research comparing single and multiple pathways (Loeber et al., 1993), a model of three pathways (Figure 4) was found to fit the data in the oldest sample, using retrospective data collected at the beginning of the study and six waves of prospective assessments covering three years. The pathways were as follows: (1) An Authority Conflict Pathway prior to the age of 12 that starts with stubborn behavior, has defiance as a second stage, and authority avoidance (e.g., truancy) as a third stage; (2) a Covert Pathway prior to age 15 which starts with minor covert acts, has property damage as a second stage, and moderate to serious delinquency as a third stage; and (3) an Overt Pathway that starts with minor aggression, has physical fighting as a second stage, and more severe violence as a third stage.

Each of the three pathways represents different developmental tasks and processes. The Overt Pathway represents aggression as opposed to positive problem solving; the Covert Pathway represents lying, vandalism, and theft versus

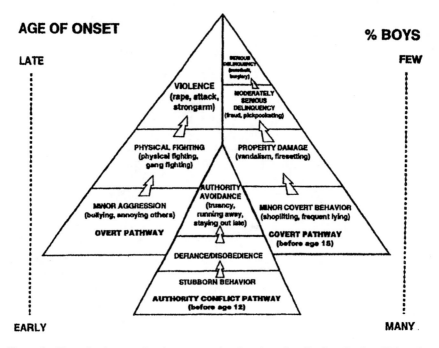

Figure 4.   Three developmental pathways toward serious juvenile offending (Loeber, Wei et al., 1999b).

honesty and respect for property; the Authority Conflict Pathway represents conflict with and avoidance of authority figures versus respect for authority figures. This conceptualization implies that if a juvenile achieves one developmental task (such as honesty), it does not necessarily mean that he will achieve another developmental task (such as nonaggressive problem solving). Therefore, the pathway model can help to explain the development of single and multi-problem boys.

We were able to replicate the pathway findings on the middle and youngest samples using data collected over six and eight assessments, respectively (Loeber, et al., 1998b; Loeber et al., 1993). A refinement was to distinguish boys whose antisocial behavior was temporary (called experimenters) from those who persisted in their antisocial acts. Research showed that persisters fit the pathways better than experimenters (Loeber et al., 1997). The majority of those who escalated to the highest stage in a pathway tended to begin by committing less serious behaviors in the hypothesized order. The pathway analyses were replicated for African American and Caucasian boys.

Recently, Tolan, Gorman-Smith, and Loeber (2000) have replicated the pathway findings in a sample of African American and Hispanic adolescents in Chicago and in a nationally representative U.S. sample of adolescents (also see

Elliott, 1994, and Le Blanc, 1997, for similar evidence for developmental sequences toward violence). Replications have also been undertaken in the two sister studies: The Denver Youth Survey and the Rochester Youth Development Study (Loeber et al., 1999b). These analyses from ages 4 to 19 showed that the Covert Pathway applied best to boys younger than age 15. In summary, there is substantial evidence for developmental pathways starting with disruptive behaviors and leading to serious forms of delinquency, and that these pathways are similar for different ethnic groups (see summary in Loeber & Stouthamer-Loeber, 1998). Developmental pathways to serious offending in girls still remain to be documented.

The pathway model allowed several conceptualizations of development toward increasing seriousness of antisocial and delinquent behavior: (1) escalation within a pathway; (2) persistence of problem behavior over time; (3) escalation in multiple pathways; and (4) age of onset of behaviors in each step of the pathways. The results showed that with age, boys progressed on two or three pathways, indicating an increasing variety of problem behavior over time (Kelley, Loeber, Keenan, & DeLamatre, 1997; Loeber et al., 1993; Loeber et al., 1997). We found some evidence that development in more than one pathway was orderly, in that boys who were escalating in the overt pathway were more likely to escalate in the covert pathway as well, compared to a lower probability of boys in the covert pathway escalating in the overt pathway. Thus, aggressive boys were particularly at risk of also committing covert acts but not vice versa. Further, escalation in either the overt or covert pathway was often preceded by boys' escalation in the authority conflict pathway (Loeber et al., 1993). In other words, conflict with authority figures was either a precursor or a concomitant of boys' escalation in overt or covert acts. Also, an early age of onset of problem behavior or delinquency, compared to an onset at a later age, is more strongly associated with boys' escalation to more serious behaviors in the pathways (Tolan et al., 2000). The pathway model accounted for the majority of the most seriously affected boys, that is, the self-reported high rate offenders (Loeber et al., 1993; Loeber et al., 1997) and court-reported delinquents (Loeber et al., 1997).

In summary, the pathway model that we developed for boys shows that the warning signs of early onset of disruptive behavior must not be dismissed with a "this soon will pass" attitude (Kelley et al., 1997). However, we cannot yet distinguish accurately between those boys whose problem behavior will get worse over time and those who will improve. We see the pathway model as a way to help identify youth at risk and optimize early interventions before problem behavior becomes more stable and worse over time.

Dynamic Typology of Offenders

The study of developmental pathways is only one method to link the development of successive problem behavior and delinquency to the development of individuals. In addition, we studied typologies of offenders on the basis of their onset, escalation, stability, and desistance of offending over four waves of data (Loeber et al., 1991). We made a distinction between four levels of delinquency seriousness: nondelinquency, minor delinquency, moderate delinquency, and serious delinquency. On the basis of the seriousness classification at four data points, seven types of offenders were identified: stable nondelinquents, starters, stable moderates, escalators, stable highs, de-escalators, and desisters. We found substantial differences among the three samples in the most common types, with the nondelinquents and starters the most prevalent in the youngest sample (ages 7–10), the nondelinquents and escalators most prevalent in the middle sample (ages 10–13), and the stable moderates, escalators, and de-escalators most prevalent in the oldest sample (ages 13–16). The shifts in the most common types with age represent the beginning, worsening, and decreasing of delinquent activities from middle childhood to adolescence (see also Loeber & Le Blanc, 1990).

Risk and Protective Factors

It is well known that juvenile delinquency is multidetermined rather than caused by a single risk factor. Also, it is now generally accepted that risk factors are situated within the individual child, in the family, in the peer group, and in macrolevel factors, such as neighborhoods. Further, it is now more recognized that risk factors operate in the context of protective factors. We will briefly review our findings for each.

Child Risk Factors

Impulsivity

A detailed multisource, multimethod battery of impulsivity measures was administered to the boys in the middle sample in the summer of 1990 when they averaged 12 to 13 years of age (White et al., 1994). The goals of this project were (1) to examine the interrelations among a variety of different measures of impulsivity, (2) to identify different possible underlying dimensions of impulsivity tapped by a variety of different impulsivity measures, and (3) to determine if different measures of impulsivity are differentially related to self-reported delinquency. The boys were invited to come to our laboratory, along with a parent, for a testing session. We collected data using 11 different measures of impulsivity, representing the most reliable and valid published measures to date (for details, see Loeber, Farrington, Stouthamer-Loeber, & Van Kammen, 1998c).

In general, the correlations among the 11 impulsivity measures were low, ranging from $-.08$ to $.33$, suggesting that the construct of impulsivity is not uni-dimensional. However, certain subsets of impulsivity measures were more highly interrelated than others. Exploratory and confirmatory factor-analysis techniques pointed to two correlated but distinct forms of impulsivity. The first factor, labeled Behavioral Impulsivity, appeared to measure impulsivity that was associated with lack of behavioral control. This interpretation is consistent with the finding that the variables with the highest loadings on this factor were those that tapped disinhibited, undercontrolled behavior, such as parent-reported undercontrol, observer-rated motor restlessness, teacher-reported impulsivity, self-reported impulsivity, and observer-rated impatience/impersistence. The second factor, labeled Cognitive Impulsivity, appeared to measure impulsivity that was the converse of effortful and planful cognitive performance. The variables with the highest loadings on this factor were variables that tapped mental control and the mental effort required to switch adaptively between mental sets, such as performance on the Trail Making Test time, Stroop errors, time perception, number of cards played on the Card Playing Computer Task, circle tracing, and delay of gratification.

Both cognitive and behavioral impulsivity were significantly and positively related to delinquency. However, the links between behavioral impulsivity and the self-reported delinquency outcome measures (average $r = .43$, $p < .001$) were stronger than those between cognitive impulsivity and the delinquency outcome measures (average $r = .18$, $p < .01$). To assess the unique contribution of impulsivity to the variance in delinquency, we also statistically controlled for effects of individual differences in SES and IQ and found that cognitive and behavioral impulsivity together accounted for 16% of the variance in delinquency. However, cognitive impulsivity was not related to delinquency independently of IQ, whereas individual differences in behavioral impulsivity were significantly related to delinquency above and beyond individual differences in IQ.

Because it has been hypothesized that stable and severe antisocial behavior is especially associated with poor impulse control, we compared the impulsivity of three groups of boys: (1) stable nondelinquents, (2) stable, serious delinquents, and (3) all other delinquent boys (i.e., delinquent boys who did not meet criteria for the stable, serious delinquency group). Stable serious delinquents showed the highest levels of cognitive and behavioral impulsivity. Indeed, they were nearly 1 standard deviation above the sample norm and almost 2 standard deviations more impulsive than were the boys who had never been delinquent. Stable nondelinquents had the lowest mean scores, and the impulsivity of the nonserious delinquent group fell in between the scores of the two other delinquent groups.

Further follow-up research revealed that impulsivity interacts with neighborhood context to influence juvenile offending (Lynam et al., 2000). Impulsive boys were at greatest risk for juvenile offending in Pittsburgh's disadvantaged neighborhoods. The effects of impulsivity may be amplified in disadvantaged neighborhoods because these neighborhoods may be characterized by lower levels of informal social controls. Another possibility is that impulsive boys in these disadvantaged neighborhoods may encounter and take advantage of more opportunities to commit delinquent acts than impulsive boys in better-off neighborhoods. These results emphasize that explanations of antisocial behavior that rely on trait explanations alone are incomplete. Although impulsivity has emerged as one of the strongest individual-level predictors of antisocial behavior in our research, its effects on offending are clearly shaped by the social context of development.

Lack of Guilt, ADHD, and Child Risk Factors

We examined the cross-sectional relationship between several other risk factors and serious delinquents in the middle and the oldest samples, and moderate and serious delinquents in the youngest sample (Loeber et al., 1998a). We found that the following child factors were related to delinquency: boy's lack of guilt feelings, being old for the grade (being held back because of low academic achievement), high Attention Deficit-Hyperactivity Disorder (ADHD) score, low achievement (ratings by boy, parent, and teacher), and depressed mood. In hierarchical multiple regressions, the most important child predictor was lack of guilt, a finding which was consistent across samples. Also, among the next most important predictors were being old for the grade (all samples) and depressed mood (youngest and oldest samples). In addition, a high ADHD-score contributed in the youngest and middle samples, and HIA problems (hyperactivity, impulsivity, and attention problems as rated by parents and teachers) in the middle and the oldest samples. Low (academic) achievement entered only for the oldest sample.

Intelligence

A robust finding in many studies is that delinquents score 8–10 IQ points lower than nondelinquents (Wilson & Herrnstein, 1985), but researchers have disagreed about the correct interpretation of this finding and its possible implications for prevention. Data from the middle sample of boys shed light on this issue (Lynam, Moffitt, & Stouthamer-Loeber, 1993). In the summer of 1990, when the boys were aged 12–13, they were given the WISC-R, which is a standardized intelligence test. An initial analysis showed that the self-reported delinquent boys scored on average 8 points lower than the nondelinquent boys, and the most serious delinquents scored 11 points lower.

Some critics who are skeptical of the link between IQ and delinquency have objected that the observed relation between IQ and delinquency could be an artifact of social class or race. In this study, a measure of social class was entered as a control in the analysis of the relationship between IQ scores and self-reported delinquency scores, but this control reduced the mean difference between delinquents and nondelinquents by only one IQ point. Race was addressed by analyzing the data separately for African American and Caucasian boys, which revealed that delinquents scored 8 points below nondelinquents within *both* ethnic groups.

Critics have also argued that delinquents score poorly on IQ tests because they are not interested in doing well, they are oppositional to the tester, or they come from a subculture that values intellectual performance differently. In this study, the boys were videotaped while taking the IQ test, and later, research assistants who were blind to the nature of the study watched the videos and rated each boy on interest, effort, boredom, impatience, and impersistence during the test. For example, raters watched for boys who laid their heads on the table, yawned often, or refused to attempt parts of the test. Although there was quite a range of scores on this rating, entering it as a control reduced the difference between delinquents and nondelinquents by only 2 IQ points.

A further study addressed the question of whether the relationship between IQ and delinquency depended on the boys' neighborhood (Moffitt, Caspi, Silva, & Stouthamer-Loeber, 1995). However, the relation was the same in disadvantaged and advantaged Pittsburgh neighborhoods. A further artifactual possibility that was also checked was whether impulsivity mediated the association between IQ and delinquency. Many measures of impulsive self-control are known to correlate with IQ scores, and thus perhaps a delinquent boy's impulsiveness is an important link between his IQ score and his delinquency. However, analyses showed that only about one fifth of the effect of IQ on delinquency operated via impulsivity.

Critics have argued that the subset of delinquents who get caught for their delinquent acts (and thus complete an IQ test in jail) may have lower IQ scores than boys who are just as delinquent but who more intelligently evade detection. In other words, IQ is related to getting caught but not to offending. The study proved that this was not the sole explanation of the IQ-delinquency link by showing that IQ relates to self-reports of delinquency (Lynam et al., 1993), as well as to mothers' and teachers' reports of delinquent acts (Moffitt et al., 1995).

These analyses appeared to rule out the current major artifactual explanations of the relation between IQ and delinquency. Having ruled out the alternatives, this study turned to testing a causal explanation. A plausible theory is that low IQ leads to frustration, failure, and humiliation at school, and that these alienating experiences prompt youth to engage in delinquency. Using cross-sectional data, Lynam et al. (1993) found evidence that this correlational pathway is at least partially true, primarily for the African American boys. For these boys, 75% of the relation between IQ and delinquency was mediated through the boys' school achievement, as reported by their teachers. Boys with high IQ may enjoy favor from teachers and may find that the rewards school has to offer are more attractive than delinquency. Research has shown that it is not easy to improve children's IQ scores permanently, but these findings suggest that the refractory nature of IQ need not be a source of pessimism. It is not necessary to change IQ if it is feasible to improve the reception that low IQ children experience in schools. If all children found school as rewarding as the brightest children do, schools could be a more powerful delinquency-prevention tool.

Personality

Studying the middle sample, we developed an assessment instrument to describe the personalities of the boys. In the summer of 1990, the parents completed the "Common Language" version of the California Child Q-Sort (CCQ), a language-simplified, personality assessment procedure intended for use with lay observers (Caspi et al., 1992). The CCQ contains 100 statements written on individual cards that describe a wide range of personality attributes. The boys' parents (primarily mothers) were asked to sort these item-cards into a forced nine-category distribution along a continuum ranging from "most like this boy" to "not at all like this boy."

The CCQ can be used to obtain scores for children on three "superfactors" of personality: Constraint, Negative Emotionality, and Positive Emotionality (Tellegen et al., 1988). Individuals high on Constraint endorse conventional social norms, avoid thrills, and act in a cautious and restrained manner. Individuals high on Negative Emotionality have a low general threshold for the experience of negative emotions such as fear, anxiety, and anger and tend to break down under stress. Individuals high on Positive Emotionality have a low threshold for the experience of positive emotions and for positive engagement in their social environments, and view life as essentially a pleasurable experience. The results revealed robust personality correlates of delinquency. Whether delinquency was measured using self-, parent-, or teacher-reports, and whether delinquency was assessed among African American or Caucasian boys, greater delinquent participation was associated with greater negative emotionality and less constraint (Caspi et al., 1994; Moffitt et al., 1995). Also, the personality correlates of delinquency in Pittsburgh were similar to those found in a New Zealand study.

Related work on personality and delinquency has focused on psychopathy. Borrowing from the adult literature, Lynam (1997) operationalized psychopathy using extensive data collected on the middle sample. The results showed that psychopathy had a childhood manifestation that could be measured reliably by focusing on indicators such as low empathy and lack of guilt. Psychopathic children, like their adult counterparts, were the most frequent, severe, aggressive, and temporally stable offenders. Psychopathic children were also impulsive, as assessed with a multimethod, multisource battery of measures. They were prone to externalizing behavior disorders and comparatively immune to internalizing disorders. Most important, childhood psychopathy predicted serious stable antisocial behavior in adolescence over and above other known predictors and other classification approaches. This work provides clear support to the growing body of evidence attesting to the importance of personality as a contributor to delinquency.

Attitudes

It is well known that delinquents tend to have attitudes favorable to delinquency. It is less clear, however, to what extent attitudes favorable to delinquency predict later delinquent acts, to what extent delinquent acts predict favorable attitudes, whether both delinquent acts and attitudes are symptoms of the same underlying construct, and whether relationships vary for violent compared to nonviolent delinquents. Zhang et al. (1997) showed that in most cases delinquent attitudes predicted delinquency as well as the reverse. However, attitudes predicted delinquency better with advancing age. The findings also showed some specificity: on average, a delinquent attitude had a stronger concurrent association with its counterpart behavior than with other behaviors (e.g., tolerance of minor violence was more strongly related to minor violence than to minor theft).

Poor Reading

The relationship between poor academic performance and delinquency was examined further in several papers (Maguin & Loeber, 1996; Maguin, Loeber, & LeMahieu, 1993). For example, Maguin et al. (1993) in cross-sectional analyses showed that the likelihood of delinquency for boys with poor reading performance was similar for African Americans and Caucasians, even though African Americans had a higher prevalence of delinquency and had been repeating grades more often. The worse the reading performance in any ethnic group, the more serious the delinquency. However, further analyses showed that the relationship between poor reading performance and delinquency could be explained by the presence of attention problems as rated by parents and teachers. This was further confirmed in a large meta-analysis (Maguin & Loeber, 1996).

Drug Dealing

We examined drug dealing by boys in the oldest sample over a period of three years. Drug dealing was defined independently from drug use, as dealing in marijuana or hard drugs (Van Kammen & Loeber, 1994; Van Kammen, Maguin, & Loeber, 1994). At the age of about 15, 13% of the boys had initiated drug dealing, with the typical age of onset being later than the onset of illicit drug use and serious delinquency. Having friends involved in drug dealing increased the risk of boys' drug dealing by a factor of 10.

Event history analyses showed that prior repeated property or violent offenses and repeated drug use increased the risk of onset of drug dealing. Once initiated, drug dealing was associated with an increase in violent offenses and carrying a concealed weapon. Further, initiation of drug dealing was uniquely related to an increased frequency of property offenses, particularly car-related theft and fraud. Discontinuation of drug dealing was associated with a decrease in delinquent activities. In summary, results show the reciprocal relations between delinquency and drug dealing, with one being a risk factor for the other.

Family Factors

Of the family variables, Loeber et al. (1998a) found in cross-sectional analyses that poor supervision was the best explanatory variable for delinquency, increasing the risk of delinquency by a factor of 2.6 for the oldest sample, but somewhat less for the other samples (Odds Ratios (OR): 1.9 and 1.5). Next came poor parent-boy communication, which increased the risk of delinquency by a factor of 2.4 in the middle sample and 1.5 in the oldest sample (this was not measured in the youngest sample). Physical punishment by the mother increased the risk of delinquency by a factor of about 2 in each of the three samples. Interestingly, physical punishment predicted delinquency for Caucasian boys but not for African American boys (Farrington & Loeber, in press). Several other parent variables increased the risk of delinquency, but only for the youngest and the middle samples, such as the mother's high stress, substance use problems, and anxiety/depression.

In hierarchical regression analyses, physical punishment predicted delinquency for the middle and oldest samples, while poor supervision predicted for the oldest sample only. Parent anxiety/depression predicted delinquency, but for the middle sample only, while unhappy parents were most relevant for the youngest sample. Remarkably, no other parent variable predicted delinquency in the youngest sample; other parent variables only predicted delinquency for older children.

Child-parent interactions change quite a lot from childhood through adolescence. Using data from the three samples covering the age 6- to 18-year-old span, Loeber et al., (2000) found a relatively high stability of child-parent interactions in such areas as physical punishment, communication, supervision, positive parenting, and bad parent-child relationship quality. Growth-curve analyses, however, showed that absolute scores changed for some forms of child-parent interactions, but not for others. Physical punishment decreased, while poor supervision and low-level positive parenting increased. In contrast, poor communication and a disadvantaged relationship between the parent and child did not materially change between ages 6 and 18. Some categories of parents experienced significantly worse interactions with their sons over time: single parents and teenage mothers. These developmental analyses are important because they show that: (1) child-parent interactions typically can change over time, especially in certain categories of parents; and (2) the strength of associations between child-parent interactions and outcomes such as delinquency probably are not constant because both the independent and dependent variables change with development.

Not all family factors usually associated with delinquency were found in the Pittsburgh Youth Study. For example, although the number of family transitions (e.g., following a divorce or parental separation) was related to delinquency in Denver and Rochester, in the Pittsburgh Youth Study the trend was nonsignificant for boys in the oldest sample (Thornberry, Smith, Rivera, Huizinga, & Stouthamer-Loeber, 1999).

Teenage Fatherhood

Teenage parenthood has been studied mostly from the mother's perspective, but we were able to address this from the father's point of view (Stouthamer-Loeber & Wei, 1998; Thornberry, Wei, Stouthamer-Loeber, & Van Dyke, 2000; Wei, 1999). The prevalence of teenage fatherhood is quite high in the oldest sample: 22% of the oldest sample had fathered a child by age 19 (34% of the African Americans and 13% of the Caucasians). About a third of teenage fathers (31%) had fathered more than one child (103 males fathered a total of 152 children). Levels of father involvement were fairly low, as only 28% of teenage fathers lived with their children, less than half saw their children on a daily basis, and 12% never saw their children.

Compared to nonfathers, teenage fathers at age 19 were significantly more likely to be gang members, to engage in serious violent delinquency (assault, but not rape or robbery), and to have been arrested during the past year. Teenage fathers were also significantly more likely to commit moderately serious delinquent acts such as carrying weapons, fencing stolen goods, gang fighting, and joyriding. More than a third of teenage fathers (38%) were classified as serious delinquents who had committed more than one kind of serious act, compared to 19% of nonfathers. In order to investigate the impact of fatherhood on subsequent delinquent acts, Stouthamer-Loeber and Wei (1998) compared 62 teenage fathers to controls matched on age, race, and neighborhood. Fatherhood was associated with a great increase in delinquent behavior. In the same year that these young men reported becoming fathers, they were 7.5 times more likely to commit a serious delinquent act, and in the year after they became fathers, the odds ratio for serious delinquency remained high (odds ratio = 4.2).

Peer Factors

Peer factors are highly correlated with delinquency because of the high rate of co-offending of juveniles and their peers, and because peer reports of offending are often based on reports of respondents about their peers' involvement. Thus, arguably, peer delinquency could simply be an indicator of the boy's own delinquency. However, Keenan, Loeber, Zhang, Stouthamer-Loeber, and Van Kammen (1995) examined the temporal relations between boys' exposure to deviant peer behavior and the boys' own initiation of disruptive and delinquent behavior. The results showed that exposure to deviant peers was significantly followed by initiation of disruptive/delinquent behaviors characteristic of the overt and covert pathways.

Lahey, Gordon, Loeber, Stouthamer-Loeber, and Farrington (1999) investigated gang membership and gang activity in the oldest sample over ten waves. Almost all gang activity was engaged in by African American boys (54 African American vs. 8 Caucasian boys). By age 19, a third (34%) of the African American and less than one-tenth (8%) of the Caucasian boys had joined a gang. Prospective analyses showed that Conduct Disorder, increasing levels of conduct problems, and self-reports of crimes against persons predicted first gang entry. In addition, having friends who engaged in aggressive forms of delinquency further increased the risk of gang entry, but only during early adolescence. The results show how important it is to examine gang activity within delinquency careers, particularly as a step in the escalation towards serious offending.

Macro Factors

In cross-sectional analyses, Loeber et al. (1998a) found that of the socioeconomic factors, the family being on welfare was associated with the highest risk of delinquency in all three samples ($ORs = 2.1$, 2.5, and 2.4), followed by low socioeconomic status of the family (1.5, 2.2, and 1.5). Other variables that increased the risk of delinquency in two out of the three samples were family living in a small house, an unemployed father, and a poorly-educated mother. Among the demographic variables, the most strongly related to delinquency were a broken family (2.0, 2.9, and 2.8), and African American ethnicity (1.9, 2.5, and 2.3). A young mother (under age 20 at the time of the boy's birth) about doubled the risk of delinquency, but only for the middle and oldest samples. Finally, living in a disadvantaged neighborhood, either measured through census data or by means of the mother's report, doubled the risk for delinquency in all three samples.

Hierarchical regression analyses showed that having a young mother, an unemployed father, and living in a disadvantaged neighborhood were significant independent predictors of delinquency in two of the three samples. African American ethnicity was a less consistent predictor (middle sample only). The relative unimportance of ethnicity in the explanation of delinquency was remarkable, especially since African American boys tended to commit more serious acts. However, Peeples and Loeber (1994), reporting on the oldest sample, demonstrated that when African American boys did not live in underclass neighborhoods, their delinquent behavior was similar to that of Caucasian boys. Once individually measured factors (such as a single-parent family and poverty/welfare dependence) were included in hierarchical regression analyses predicting serious delinquency, residence in an underclass neighborhood was still significantly related to serious delinquent behavior, but ethnicity was not.

Neighborhoods

To investigate whether offending and risk factors differed across neighborhoods, 1980 census data were used to distinguish between low, medium, and high socioeconomic status neighborhoods (Loeber & Wikström, 1993). We wanted to investigate to what extent boys' advancement on the overt and covert pathways was different in different neighborhoods. The results for the middle and oldest samples showed that more boys in low than in high SES areas, especially at younger ages, were involved in overt behavior. Moreover, a higher proportion of boys living in low SES areas tended to advance on the overt pathway and engage in violence than those living in high SES neighborhoods. More boys in the low SES areas had been involved in covert behaviors, and more boys in those areas, compared to boys in high SES areas, had reached the highest step in the covert pathway (especially for the middle sample). Thus, deviant development, known to be associated with later serious delinquency, tended to occur more quickly in the worse neighborhoods and, in the case of overt behaviors, tended to occur at a relatively young age in those areas. We will return to neighborhood effects when reviewing findings on the relative impact of risk and protective factors.

A Final Note on Risk Factors

Most of the cross-sectional findings on explanatory factors for delinquency observed in one sample of the Pittsburgh Youth Study were replicated in the other two samples. This applied both to univariate relationships and to multivariate logistic regression results (Loeber et al., 1998a). Further, many of the longitudinal predictors of delinquency and violence in the middle sample of the Pittsburgh Youth Study were similar to predictors of the same outcomes in the Cambridge Study on Delinquent Development, despite differences in time and place (Farrington, 1998; Farrington & Loeber, 1999). For example, Farrington and Loeber (1999) found that several risk factors were replicated across the two studies: hyperactivity and impulsivity, low school achievement, poor parental supervision, parental conflict, an antisocial parent, a young mother, large family size, low family income, and a broken family. Many of these predictors were also apparent in multiple regression analyses. Risk factors were generally similar for African American and Caucasian boys (Farrington & Loeber, in press; see also, Stouthamer-Loeber et al., 2002). Also, many of the risk factors identified in the Pittsburgh Youth Study are corroborated in the existing literature on risk factors (see reviews by Farrington, 1996; Loeber & Farrington, 1998; Loeber et al., 1998a).

Protective Factors

Protective factors are often conceptualized as those factors that buffer the impact of risk factors in reducing the probability of a negative outcome, implying that a protective factor interacts with one or more risk factors in the prediction of a negative outcome (Rutter, 1985; 1990). However, we argue that, along with the study of main effects of risk factors, we need to study the *main effects of protective factors* before investigating the interaction effects between protective and risk factors. Here, we will use the term *promotive factors* when examining the main effects of "protective" factors.

To that end, we examined the effects of promotive and risk factors as represented by opposite poles of the same variable (Stouthamer-Loeber et al., 1993). All variables were trichotomized as closely as possible at the 25th and 75th percentiles within each sample. In the case of the delinquency classification, groups of nondelinquents, minor delinquents, and serious delinquents were formed. Similarly, the independent variables were trichotomized into positive (potentially protective), neutral, and negative (potentially risk) sections of the score distribution. This made it possible to study promotive effects (versus the neutral category) and risk effects (versus the neutral category) separately.

The results showed that promotive and risk effects often co-occurred in the same variables, that few variables had risk effects only, and none had protective effects only. Overall, protective effects were as likely to promote nondelinquency as to suppress serious delinquency. Also, risk effects were as likely to suppress nondelinquency as to promote serious delinquency. Several variables differentiated between nondelinquency and minor delinquency rather than between minor and serious delinquency. Examples are parental stress, parental supervision, parent-child communication, peer delinquency, and boys' attitude toward antisocial behavior. Only two variables (age of the mother at the birth of the child and mother's education) exclusively differentiated between minor and serious delinquency. All of the externalizing behaviors (e.g., accountability, oppositional defiant behavior, attention deficit/hyperactivity, and the ability to feel guilt) were about equally associated with the lower *and* the upper ends of the delinquency categorization. The results also showed that the magnitude of protective and risk effects, as judged from the contingency coefficients and number of significant odds ratios, increased with age.

Recently, Stouthamer-Loeber et al. (2002) examined the predictive association between risk/ protective factors and persistent serious offending over a period of seven years. Examples of promotive effects with an odds ratio of 3 or higher in the youngest sample were: high accountability, trustworthiness, ability to feel guilt, school motivation, and residence in a nondisadvantaged neighborhood. The authors found that the number of risk and promotive domains predicted persistent serious offending in a similar way in disadvantaged and advantaged neighborhoods. However, these rather broad set of analyses do not preclude that specific risk and promotive factors operate differently in different settings. For example, Wikström and Loeber (2000) found that neighborhoods differed more in terms of protective factors (by a factor of 4) than in terms of risk factors (by a factor of 2.5).

The Prevalence of Risk and Protective Factors in Different Neighborhoods

The ecology of offending should be examined in the context of the ecology of risk and protective factors. If some neighborhoods compared to other neighborhoods are characterized by high levels of juvenile delinquency, then it is likely that the high-crime neighborhoods have a higher prevalence of factors contributing to delinquency (i.e., risk factors) and a lower prevalence of factors that inhibit offending (i.e., protective factors). Stouthamer-Loeber et al. (2002) examined this for the youngest and oldest samples and found that, with increasing neighborhood disadvantage (defined by census variables), there was an increase in the prevalence of risk factors known to be relevant for serious offending. Likewise, with increasing neighborhood advantage, there was an increase in the prevalence of protective factors. Specifically, disadvantaged neighborhoods, including public housing, were characterized by a low prevalence of protective factors and a high prevalence of risk factors.

In Pittsburgh, African Americans predominantly inhabit the most disadvantaged neighborhoods. For that reason, we expected that African American compared to Caucasian youth would be more exposed to risk factors. This was indeed found in analyses undertaken by Farrington & Loeber (in press) for the middle sample: 62% of the African American boys lived in families on welfare compared to 20% of the Caucasian boys. On average, African American boys experienced 7.3 of 21 risk factors, almost twice as many as the Caucasian boys (4.4).

Since it is well known that family factors play an important role in the development of juvenile delinquency, Stouthamer-Loeber, Drinkwater, and Loeber (1999) investigated whether certain patterns of family disadvantage were concentrated in certain types of neighborhoods. Using a cluster analysis technique, they distinguished between four family functioning profiles. Of these profiles, families with a punishment profile (a pattern of poor supervision, physical punishment, but little parental deviance) were over-represented in disadvantaged neighborhoods. These findings are highly relevant for preventive interventions, and there is a need to extend these analyses into other domains of risk factors to better understand which configurations of risk factors are the most prevalent in which types of neighborhoods.

Differences in Risk and Promotive Factors with Age

Loeber et al. (1991) in their investigation of predictors of initiation, escalation, and desistance, found several shifts in risk factors over four data waves. For example, they found that physical aggression and social withdrawal decreased with age in their strength of prediction of delinquency, while school problem behaviors, peer deviance, and boys' positive attitude to deviancy increased in predictive efficiency. Some factors were especially associated with the early initiation of offending before age 12, including social withdrawal and depression, a positive attitude to problem behavior, association with deviant peers, and family problems. In contrast, the later onset of offending (between ages 13–14) was associated with low school motivation. Nearly all (90%) of the stable high offenders in the youngest sample scored high on physical aggression, compared to 51% and 44% in the middle and oldest samples, respectively. In the middle and oldest samples, predictors of escalation were: poor school functioning, disruptive behaviors, a positive attitude to deviant behavior, and some aspects of family functioning. In summary, the results indicate some common risk factors at different ages, but also some risk factors whose impact becomes more pronounced at an early compared to a later age.

In predictive analyses, Stouthamer-Loeber et al. (2002) identified more promotive effects for the oldest (19) compared to the youngest sample (9). The comparable numbers of risk factors were 19 and 13, respectively. These findings suggest that as children age, they become exposed to increasing domains of risk (and promotive) effects. This accords with the notion that, from childhood to adolescence, children are introduced to factors in their peer group and neighborhood, which for most did not exist in their early childhood.

Against this backdrop of shifts in risk and promotive factors with age, Stouthamer-Loeber et al. (2002) noted that the association between the number of risk domains (and the number of promotive domains) and subsequent persistent serious offending was basically the same for children in the youngest and oldest samples. Thus, increased exposure to risk domains and reduced access to promotive domains bodes ill for children of different ages.

It can be argued that neighborhood context affects the age of onset of juvenile offending. Wikström and Loeber (2000) classified neighborhoods based on the 1990 census. They then examined risk and protective factors as predictors of serious offending, and came to the following conclusions: (1) The overwhelming majority of boys with a high risk score were involved in serious offending regardless of the socioeconomic context of their neighborhood. Also, "there were no significant differences in the rate of serious offending for those living in disadvantaged public housing areas regardless of whether they had high protective scores, high risk scores, or a balanced score ..." (p. 1131); (2) however, "for those with a balanced score in risk and protective factors, their socioeconomic neighborhood context clearly mattered for serious offending" (p. 1131); (3) late onset, which is more common in the disadvantaged neighborhoods, was more common among those with high scores of protective factors and for those with balanced scores. Wikström and Loeber (2000) concluded that "neighborhood context appears predominantly to have a direct impact on the rate of late onsets for those with high protective or balanced scores..." In contrast, "the prevalence of early onsets is predominantly a function of individual risk-protective characteristics rather than any direct effect of neighborhood context" (pp. 1131–1132).

Cumulative Effects of Risk and Protective (Promotive) Factors

Although many lay people still think that there is a single cause to delinquency, the evidence points to juvenile offending becoming more probable the higher the number of risk factors to which youth are exposed. To support this, Loeber et al. (1998a) first examined the impact of accumulation of risk factors on serious delinquency. The risk score was based on 12 key explanatory variables: lack of guilt, old for grade, low achievement (parent, boy, teacher ratings), ADHD-score, depressed mood, poor supervision, physical punishment, ethnicity, broken family, low SES, family on welfare, and disadvantaged neighborhood (mother rating). Especially in the oldest sample, there was a linear relation between the number of risk factors and the concurrent probability of serious delinquency.

Although it is important to know how many risk factors individuals are exposed to, it is even more important to know what the balance is of individuals' exposure to risk and protective factors over time. Analyses by Stouthamer-Loeber et al. (2002) focused on risk and promotive factors in the youngest and oldest samples associated with persistent serious offending over seven years. The results show that for each sample the sum of risk and promotive domains was linearly associated with the risk of persistent offending (see Figure 5). The distribution of scores for the oldest sample was from −6 (predominately promotive effects) to +6 (predominantly risk effects).

Three quarters of the boys with a risk/promotive score of +4 or higher were classified as persistent serious offenders, compared with none of those who had a risk/promotive score of −5 or −6. Similar results were found for the youngest sample. Regression analyses confirmed that promotive and risk domains each contributed independently to the prediction of persistent serious offending, and promotive domains tended to buffer the impact of risk domains. Further, Stouthamer-Loeber et al. (2002) found a linear association between risk/promotive effects and later persistent serious offending, which was similar across different neighborhood contexts. Thus, the thesis is rather general that an accumulation of risk domains over promotive domains is associated with persistent serious juvenile offending.

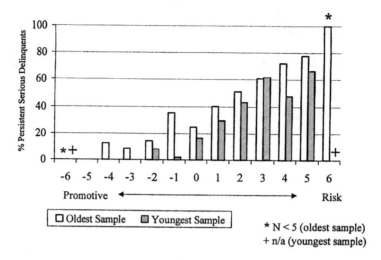

Figure 5. The predictive association between risk and promotive domains and later persistent serious delinquency (Stouthamer-Loeber et al., 2002).

Predictors of Violence

All too often, studies on delinquency have not examined whether risk factors predict all types of delinquency equally well. For instance, if predictors of violence are different than predictors of property offenses, this has considerable practical and theoretical implications. We addressed three questions in this context. First, what are the predictors of violence? Second, what predicts violence in advantaged neighborhoods? Third, are there predictors that are specific to violence and do not apply to property crime? To address the first question, Farrington and Loeber (in press) investigated the extent to which factors measured at the first follow-up (at age 10) predicted reported violence (i.e., by the boy, parent, or teacher) up to age 13 and court reports of violence up to age 16. Twenty-four out of 40 factors examined predicted reported violence, and a subset of these factors (15 in total) predicted court reports of violence. Multivariate analyses showed that low academic achievement, lack of guilt, being old for the grade, the parents disagreeing on discipline, and African American ethnicity predicted later reported violence. Multivariate analyses showed that the following factors predicted court reports of violence: being old for grade, the family on welfare, large family, and African American ethnicity. It is likely that African American ethnicity only predicted violence because it was associated with a large number of risk factors (see earlier findings).

Separate analyses were undertaken by White, Loeber, Stouthamer-Loeber, and Farrington (1999) to investigate over a period of six years (ages 13 to 18) the concurrent and longitudinal association between alcohol/marijuana use and violence in the oldest sample. The results showed that ORs between concurrent frequent alcohol and marijuana use and violence ranged from 3.5 to 10.5. With one exception (age 13.5), there was not a significant difference between minor and serious delinquents in terms of the frequency of alcohol use, which means that there was no linear or dose-response relationship between frequency of alcohol use and seriousness of violence. Longitudinal analyses showed a reciprocal association between alcohol and violence: the ORs between the frequency of alcohol use and the later frequency of violence were similar to those for violence to later alcohol use (the effects for marijuana became weaker when earlier violence was taken into account). Overall, changes in alcohol consumption, compared to changes in marijuana use, were a much stronger predictor of changes in violence. These results confirm earlier research showing a dynamic, and often very proximal, confluence between alcohol consumption and violence.

A key question is whether different predictors apply to violence occurring in disadvantaged compared to advantaged neighborhoods. On the one hand, we would expect that, given different distributions of risk factors across neighborhoods, violence in the most disadvantaged neighborhoods would be caused by different sets of risk factors than violence in the better neighborhoods. On the other hand, it is also possible that there are sets of risk factors that are generically associated with violence independently of neighborhood setting. These questions were addressed by Beyers, Loeber, Wikström, and Stouthamer-Loeber (2001) for repeated violence in the oldest sample between ages 13.5 and 19.5. In regression analyses, the best predictor of repeated violence for boys in advantaged neighborhoods was physical aggression, while the following predictors of repeated violence were found for boys in disadvantaged neighborhoods: lack of guilt, having early sex, carried a hidden weapon, and poor parent-adolescent communication. These findings need replication, but they suggest that violence in advantaged neighborhoods may be driven more by individual factors such as aggression, while violence in disadvantaged neighborhoods is more a function of social and context-dependent factors.

Few studies have addressed whether certain factors are specific to violence rather than to property crime. Stouthamer-Loeber et al. (2001) investigated the impact of child abuse on later offending. About 10% of the boys up to age 18 in the oldest sample had been abused, based on substantiated investigation by Children and Youth Services. Child abuse victims and controls were compared on the extent that they exhibited behavior characteristic of the Overt and Covert Pathways. Victims scored higher than controls on all three steps and on the total score of the Overt Pathway. For example, whereas 77% of the victims engaged in physical fighting, this was the case for only 43% of the controls ($OR = 4.5$). In comparison, victims did not differ from controls on three out of the five comparisons for the Covert Pathway. Turning to delinquency as recorded in the juvenile court records, slightly over half of the victims (54%) had at least one petition to the juvenile court, compared to just over one third of the controls (39%; $OR = 1.9$). Victims were more likely than controls to have a petition for index property offenses ($OR = 2.1$), but not for index violence. The results indicate that child abuse is associated more with parents' and boys' reports of aggression than covert acts.

Predictors of Desistance

Desistance in offending has been little investigated, despite the fact that knowledge about the factors which are associated with the cessation of delinquency are obviously relevant to interventions. In separate analyses over four data waves, Loeber et al. (1991) found the following correlates of short-term desistance: low social withdrawal, low disruptive behavior, and positive motivational and attitudinal factors. However, it is highly important to investigate longer-term desistance, especially between adolescence and adulthood when desistance becomes more common. We expect to do this in the future.

Co-Occurrence of Problem Behaviors and Delinquency

It is important to investigate to what extent different types of problem behavior are interrelated and hence the degree to which they are all symptoms of the same underlying syndrome. Another important topic is to what extent risk factors are the same for all types of problem behavior. To the extent that different types of problem behavior are interrelated, it is useful to study risk factors for multiple-problem boys.

The first question is, what is the overlap between mental health problems and persistent serious delinquency? Mental health problems were defined if the boy scored in the top 10% of the distribution of internalizing or externalizing symptoms on the CBCL (Huizinga et al., 2000). Over the three samples, 14% of the persistent serious delinquents had mental health problems, while almost half of those with mental health problems (46%) also engaged in persistent serious delinquency. The results show the high overlap between mental health problems and serious delinquency at a young age. However, these results did not address which specific mental health problems were related to serious offending.

To address this, Loeber et al. (1998a) studied eight problem behaviors in the youngest, middle, and oldest samples in the screening and first follow-up assessments (Loeber et al., 1998a): delinquency, substance use, attention deficit, conduct problems, physical aggression, covert behavior, depressed mood, and shy/withdrawn behavior. All risk factors and problem behaviors were dichotomized. The eight problem behaviors were significantly interrelated in most cases, and there was no tendency for the strength of relationships to vary with age. In a factor analysis, all eight problem behaviors had substantial weightings on the first factor. These results support the idea that all eight behaviors are symptoms of the same underlying syndrome. However, it was noticeable that depressed mood, shy/withdrawn behavior, and substance use had the lowest correlations with the other five problem behaviors, which were highly interrelated. Also, weightings on the second factor distinguished delinquency and physical aggression at one extreme from depressed mood and shy/withdrawn behavior at the other. Therefore, the results also supported the idea of distinct (but interrelated) internalizing and externalizing syndromes.

When 40 key explanatory risk factors were studied (selected because of their predictive validity in earlier studies), there was no indication that the strength of relationships between risk factors and problem behaviors varied with age. Delinquency and conduct problems were related to the largest number of risk factors (over 50%), while shy/withdrawn behavior and substance use were related to the smallest number (less than 40%). Generally, the child and family risk factors were related to a variety of different problem behaviors: low achievement, lack of guilt, hyperactivity-impulsivity-attention deficit (HIA) problems, poor parent-boy communication, and poor parental supervision were related to almost all problem behaviors at all ages. The macro risk factors tended to be more specific: African American ethnicity, disadvantaged neighborhood, and young mother were especially related to delinquency.

Boys with four or more problem behaviors (20–25% of boys) were identified as multiple-problem boys. In general, these boys were characterized more by externalizing problems than by depressed mood, shy/withdrawn behavior, or substance use. They were predicted especially by lack of guilt, HIA problems, low achievement, poor parent-boy communication, and parental stress. Macro factors did not predict being a multiproblem boy independently of child and family factors, suggesting that any effect of macro factors in producing multiple-problem boys operated indirectly through child and family factors. When the multiple-problem boys were excluded from the analysis, relationships between single risk factors and single problem behaviors were attenuated but not eliminated. Uniquely, the strength of the relationship between African American ethnicity and delinquency was *greater* among boys who did *not* have multiple problems, suggesting that delinquent Caucasian boys were *more* likely to have multiple problems than delinquent African American boys.

Delinquency, conduct problems, physical aggression, attention deficit, and covert behavior were particularly closely interrelated. These five externalizing behaviors were predicted by a variety of child and family risk factors, and they were particularly characteristic of the multiple-problem boys. These results should be investigated longitudinally, to see how much risk factors predict *later* multiple-problem behaviors.

Substance Use

It has been long known that certain substances, such as alcohol, may activate delinquency, especially violence (see above). Huizinga et al. (2000) investigated drug use in combination with and in the context of other problems that often co-occur with delinquency, including school and mental health problems. First, more than a third (36%) of the delinquents were also drug users, while more than two thirds (70%) of the drug users were also delinquents. When the overlap between delinquency, drug use, school problems, and mental health problems was examined, persistent drug use was the common element among the persistent serious delinquents with multiple co-occurring problems. Loeber, Stouthamer-Loeber, and White (1999c) explored the intersection between persistent substance use, persistent delinquency, and internalizing problems. The best predictors of the co-occurrence of persistent substance use and persistent delinquency were Oppositional Defiant Disorder (ORS = 3.7 and 3.9 for the youngest and oldest samples, respectively), and persistent internalizing problems (ORS = 2.4, and 3.9 for the youngest and middle samples, respectively). These findings indicate the importance of internalizing problems in the etiology of serious delinquency, but the results do not specify which types of internalizing problems interact most with earlier behavior problems to increase the risk of persistent serious delinquency later.

Help Seeking

We investigated the extent to which parents of delinquent boys received help for dealing with their problems (Stouthamer-Loeber, Loeber & Thomas, 1992; Stouthamer-Loeber, Loeber, Van Kammen, & Zhang, 1995). We considered help received from anyone (including lay people) and from professionals (especially mental health professionals). In addition, delinquents are often referred to the juvenile court, and the question is to what extent parents have received help to deal with the behavior problems of their boys. In general, help seeking for behavior problems was twice as common for the oldest compared to the youngest boys (21% vs. 11%). However, help seeking very often resulted in only one contact with a help provider.

Delinquency Seriousness

The percentage of parents who had sought any help, help for behavior problems, or help from mental health professionals increased with increasing seriousness of delinquency. Less than half of the parents of seriously delinquent boys had received help, and only one quarter of the parents of these boys had received help from a mental health professional. Thus, three quarters of the parents of seriously delinquent boys had never sought help from a mental health professional (Stouthamer-Loeber, Loeber et al., 1992).

Stouthamer-Loeber et al. (1995) examined which behaviors of the developmental pathways model (Loeber et al., 1993) distinguished between those who received help and those who did not. In general, the higher the advancement in multiple pathways, the higher the frequency of help seeking. The age of onset of any disruptive behavior or serious disruptive behavior was inversely related to the frequency of help seeking. This finding indicates that early-onset problem behavior, even of a serious nature, in general does not trigger help seeking or the provision of professional services.

Court Contact

A comparison between boys with and without court contact showed that court-involved delinquents received more intensive help than no-court delinquents. It may well be possible that court intervention brought the necessity for help to the parents' attention. Only 17% of the boys' parents sought help *before* the year in which their boy was referred to the juvenile court. The average age of onset for any disruptive behavior was 7.4 and the average age at which the first help was sought was 9.9, which shows that there was a two-and-a-half year gap between when the problems first appeared and when help was sought.

We also examined how long disruptive behaviors had been apparent in boys who eventually were referred to the juvenile court for an index offense (Office of Juvenile Justice and Delinquency Prevention, 1998). The results showed that the average onset of the first step in any of the pathways tended to take place at age 7.0, of moderately serious problem behavior at age 9.5, of serious delinquency at age 12.0, while the average age of first contact with the juvenile court was 14.5. This analysis showed that about seven-and-a-half years on average elapsed between the earliest emerging disruptive behavior and the first contact with the juvenile court. It should be noted that delinquent boys who were not referred to the juvenile court also tended to have a long history of problem behaviors.

In summary, the development of disruptive and delinquent behaviors was largely left unchecked by parents and helping agencies. These findings have important implications for planners of preventive interventions and policy makers. Preventive interventions should take place in the relatively long time window between the onset of early problem behaviors of a minor kind and the first contact with the juvenile court. Policy makers should realize that eventual index offenders have often had the unchecked opportunity to commit delinquent acts for many years.

Conclusions and Future Priorities

The Pittsburgh Youth Study has a unique combination of features. Three different samples of boys have been followed up at frequent intervals (six months or one year), making it possible to assess how far results are replicable. The youngest and oldest samples have so far been followed up for fourteen years with no gaps in data collection (18 and 16 assessments, respectively). The middle sample was followed up for three years (7 assessments) and is now being followed up at age 22. Information has been collected from different sources (the boy, mother, and teacher) about explanatory variables from different domains (boy, family, peer, school, neighborhood) and many different types of outcome variables (not only delinquency but also substance use, sexual behavior, and externalizing and internalizing mental health problems). Over time, the attrition rate has been very low.

Theoretical Considerations

When we started the Pittsburgh Youth Study, we were aware of key criminological theories (Elliott, Huizinga, & Ageton, 1985; Gottfredson & Hirschi, 1990; Wilson & Herrnstein, 1985), and many constructs from such theories have been incorporated in the measurements of our study. At the same time, we realized that none of the existing theories covered all important risk factors but, instead, usually focused on a small subset of such factors. Our approach has been to measure a wide variety of known and potential risk factors, to permit the testing of a wide variety of current and future theories. Our conceptualization takes into account that offending has both long-term and immediate antecedents, and that both are necessary for persisting delinquency. Examples of long-term antecedents are poor parental monitoring over extended periods of time and low birth weight. Examples of more immediate antecedents to offending are the use of drugs prior to the commission of a delinquent act, and provocation by others prior to a violent act.

With the exception of a few theories (Catalano & Hawkins, 1996; Farrington, 1996; Le Blanc & Fréchette, 1989), most theories tend to be adevelopmental, and do not view serious offending as caused by the accumulation of risk processes from childhood through adulthood. Our own conceptualization has added several important theoretical aspects. First, we developed and expanded the concept of developmental criminology (Farrington, 1997; Le Blanc & Loeber, 1998; Loeber & Le Blanc, 1990; Thornberry & Krohn, 2001), in which we laid out key developmental aspects of offending and how to operationalize them. Second, we conceptualized developmental criminology as an interdisciplinary effort to integrate knowledge about the development of predelinquent problem behavior and knowledge of the development of offending. In that way, we expanded the inquiry to better account for the slow but steady growth in deviancy in some but not in other youth. Our findings support the notion that a dichotomy between early- and late-onset offenders can be defended, but at the same time it constitutes a simplification of a gradual entry of youth into delinquent offending between childhood and adolescence. As a corollary of the developmental approach to offending, we want to document different causal processes for the onset, escalation, and desistance of deviance.

A basic premise that organizes our research is that offending by most juveniles results from forces within the individual and forces in the individual's social environment (parents, siblings, and peers) in different social contexts (family, home, school, neighborhood). Proximal individual factors (such as impulsivity, lack of guilt), but also distal individual factors (such as birth complications), are known to affect later functioning. Examples of family risk factors include parental pathology and parents' child-rearing practices. Examples of peer risk factors are rejection by peers and association with deviant peers. These social factors operate differently in different settings. The life-course/social context approach to juvenile delinquency takes into account that social interactions relevant to the development of offending initially take place within the family, but are subsequently broadened to include the school and the neighborhood as youth become more mobile and face different problems of adaptation in each setting. We are interested not only in the impact of early risk factors on delinquency in childhood and adolescence, but also in how later risk factors influence offending through the life course into adulthood.

Whereas several theories of juvenile offending appear to imply that causes are invariant with age, we assumed that causes are likely to differ for those with different ages of onset of offending. Specifically, we believe that similar risk factors may affect all youth, but that causal processes represented by risk factors vary by age of onset of offending. Thus, we expect that individual factors may dominate causal processes affecting early onset offenders, but psychosocial factors may affect late-onset offenders.

Most theories are correlational in nature and tend to use data from all juveniles in a sample, while not distinguishing between those who engage in serious versus less serious forms of offending. As a result, most of these theories emphasize relationships between risk factors and delinquency (usually indicated by low correlations), but do not yield information about the causes that differentiate why some juveniles and not others escalate to serious offending. Our approach is not to construct a single theory attempting to explain offending in all juveniles. Instead, we attempt to explain why some youth escalate to serious offending after an early onset, why others reach such behaviors while starting later in life, and why some youth desist from offending. Thus, in the best of circumstances, we will eventually produce specific explanations for developmentally-defined subgroups of offenders. Our conceptualization of developmental pathways in offending constitutes a first step in this process toward specific rather than general theoretical explanations. Our approach is based on the assumption that empirical knowledge relevant for interventions and sanctions has to be based on the life course of *individuals* rather than the usually weak relationships between *variables*, while recognizing that knowledge about relationships between variables can inform knowledge about types of individuals.

Eventually, juvenile justice personnel, therapists, and public health planners need to know what the main causes are that apply to specific groups of juveniles. This brings us to the last point relevant to theories. We see our empirical efforts as part of an attempt to intervene in delinquency processes *prior to* juveniles getting arrested or brought before the court. Advances in the prevention of serious juvenile delinquency are predicated upon improving our knowledge of causes for youth at risk for serious delinquency, especially those causes that are potentially modifiable.

Future Research

Key priorities for future research in the Pittsburgh Youth Study include the following. First, we need to better address the development of serious offending as a function of the persistence and change in risk and protective factors from childhood to adolescence. Second, we will examine the consequences of delinquent offending and address the relationship between self-reports and court petitions at different ages to estimate the probability of an offense leading to a court petition and factors related to this probability. Third, we need to investigate why some boys develop patterns of multiple problems and others do not, and see to what extent multiple-problem boys can be predicted at an early age. Fourth, we need to examine factors that influence boys' successful transition from adolescence to adulthood, including desistance from delinquency. Also, we aim to study the effect of gangs by measuring delinquency before, during, and after gang membership. In addition, we can study the impact of gun carrying on later violence and the precursors and consequences of partner violence. Lastly, we have started a major study on the development of antisocial and delinquent behavior in girls (the Pittsburgh Girls Study). In due course, it should be possible to establish, while using the same measurements, to what degree risk factors for boys are similar to those for girls.

The following are examples of high priority areas for future analyses using data from the Pittsburgh Youth Study. Several of these topics are included in the next book on the study (Loeber, Farrington, Stouthamer-Loeber, & White, 2001c):

- The epidemiology of serious and violent offending (onset, prevalence, frequency, and persistence) and its relation to drug use, drug dealing, gang membership, and mental health problems;

- Psychophysiological and neurohormonal factors of serious and violent offending;
- Within-subject change in risk factors over time;
- Homicide offenders and homicide victims in more detail;
- Protective factors against offending, particularly among nondelinquent boys from disadvantaged neighborhoods;
- Types of offenders;
- Screening assessment devices for teachers and court personnel;
- Prediction of desistance in offending;
- Cost/burden on society of different types of delinquent boys;
- Late-onset offenders;
- Effects of life events on delinquency, such as residential mobility, parental divorce, and association with a prosocial partner;
- Cross-validate findings against the Denver Youth Survey and the Rochester Youth Development Study;
- One of the greatest challenges for us in the future is to translate research findings into practice that is relevant to juvenile justice, mental and public health, and public policy. Along that line, challenges include the generation of information relevant for preventive interventions and the dissemination of easily understandable results in that area to policy makers and practitioners.

ACKNOWLEDGMENTS.   This chapter is an update of an earlier summary paper on research findings from the Pittsburgh Youth Study: "The Development of Male Offending: Key Findings from the First Decade of the Pittsburgh Youth Study" (Loeber, Farrington, Stouthamer-Loeber, Moffitt & Caspi, 1998d). The present chapter extends these findings to the first fourteen years of the Pittsburgh Youth Study. Because of space limitations, this chapter does not review several methodological issues investigated in the Pittsburgh Youth Study, such as the validity of self-reports and adults' reports of juvenile delinquency (Farrington, Loeber, Stouthamer-Loeber, Van Kammen, & Schmidt, 1996), and the advantages of dichotomization of data (Farrington & Loeber, 2000).

We are greatly indebted to present and past interviewers, data staff, and other staff members working on the Pittsburgh Youth Study. Without their dedication and hard work, the study would not have been possible. We are also much indebted to many colleagues who collaborated on the papers, including Stewart Anderson, Jacqueline Cohen, Anne Crawford, Judith Creemers, Bruce Giroux, Mary DeLamatre, Matthew Drinkwater, Doni Lynn Homish, Derek Jolliffe, Larry Kalb, Barbara Tatem Kelley, Kate Keenan, Benjamin Lahey, Don Lynam, Barbara Maughan, Eugene Maguin, Faith Peeples, Laura Schmidt, Chris Thomas, Welmoet B. Van Kammen, P.-O. Wikström, Phen Wung, Yanming Yin, and Quan Zhang. We are particularly grateful to David Huizinga and his colleagues and staff on the

Denver Youth Survey, and to Terence Thornberry and his colleagues and staff on the Rochester Youth Development Study for their inspiration and enthusiasm over the past fourteen years.

The paper was prepared with financial assistance from grants No. 86-JN-CX0009 and 96-JN-CX-0003 from the Office of Juvenile Justice and Delinquency Prevention (OJJDP), and grants Nos. MH48890 and MH50778 from the National Institute of Mental Health (NIMH). Points of view or opinions in this document are those of the authors and do not necessarily represent the official position of OJJDP, the Department of Justice, or NIMH.

References

Beyers, J. M., Loeber, R., Wikström, P-O. & Stouthamer-Loeber, M. (2001). Predictors of adolescent violence by neighborhood. *Journal of Abnormal Child Psychology, 29*(5), 369–381.

Capaldi, D., & Patterson, G. R. (1987). An approach to the problem of recruitment and retention rates for longitudinal research. *Behavioral Assessment, 9*, 169–177.

Caspi, A., Black, J., Block, J. H., Klopp, B., Lynam, D., Moffitt, T. E. & Stouthamer-Loeber, M. A. (1992). A "common-language" version of the California Child Q-Set for personality assessment. *Psychological Assessment, 4*, 512–523.

Caspi, A., Moffitt, T. E., Silva, P. A., Stouthamer-Loeber, M., Krueger, R. F., & Schmutte, P. S. (1994). Are some people crime-prone? Replications of the personality-crime relationship across countries, genders, races, and methods. *Criminology, 32*, 163–195.

Catalano, R. F., & Hawkins, J. D. (1996). The social development model: A theory of antisocial behavior. In J. D. Hawkins (Ed.), *Delinquency and crime: Current theories* (pp. 149–197). New York: Cambridge University Press.

Elliott, D. S. (1994). Serious violent offenders: Onset, developmental course, and termination. The American Society of Criminology 1993 presidential address. *Criminology, 32*, 1–21.

Elliott, D. S., Huizinga, D., & Ageton, S. S. (1985). *Explaining delinquency and drug use*. Beverly Hills: Sage Publications.

Farrington, D. P. (1996). The explanation and prevention of youthful offending. In J. D. Hawkins (Ed.), *Delinquency and crime: Current theories* (pp. 64–148). New York: Cambridge University Press.

Farrington, D. P. (1997). Human development and criminal careers. In M. Maguire, R. Morgan & R. Reiner (Eds.), *The Oxford handbook of criminology*. (2nd ed., pp. 511–584). Oxford, UK: Clarendon Press.

Farrington, D. P. (1998). Predictors, causes and correlates of male youth violence. In M. Tonry & M. Moore (Eds.), *Youth and Violence: Vol. 24. Crime and justice* (pp. 421–475). Chicago: University of Chicago Press.

Farrington, D. P., & Loeber, R. (1999). Transatlantic replicability of risk factors in the development of delinquency. In P. Cohen, C. Slomkowski, & L. N. Robins (Eds.), *Historical and geographical influences on psychopathology* (pp. 299–329). Mahwah, NJ: Lawrence Erlbaum.

Farrington, D. P., & Loeber, R. (2000). Some benefits of dichotomization in psychiatric and criminological research. *Criminal Behaviour and Mental Health, 10*, 102–122.

Farrington, D. P., & Loeber, R. (in press). How can the relationship between race and violence be explained? In D. F. Hawkins (Ed.), *Violent crimes: The nexus of ethnicity, race and class*. New York: Cambridge University Press.

Farrington, D. P., Gallagher, B., Morley, L., St. Ledger, R., & West, D. J. (1990). Minimizing attrition in longitudinal research: Methods of tracing and securing cooperation in a 24-year follow-up study. In D. Magnusson, & L. Bergman (Eds.), *Data quality in longitudinal research* (pp. 122–147). Cambridge: Cambridge University Press.

Farrington, D. P., Loeber, R., Stouthamer-Loeber, M., & Van Kammen, W. B. (1996, November). *Prevalence of delinquent acts between ages 6 and 16*. Paper presented at the annual meeting of the American Society of Criminology, Chicago.

Farrington, D. P., Loeber, R., Stouthamer-Loeber, M., Van Kammen, W.B., & Schmidt, L. (1996). Self-reported delinquency and a combined delinquency seriousness scale based on boys, mothers, and teachers: Concurrent and predictive validity for African Americans and Caucasians. *Criminology, 34*, 493–517.

Farrington, D. P., Jolliffe, D., Loeber, R., Stouthamer-Loeber, M., & Kalb, L. (2001). The concentration of offenders in families, and family criminality in the prediction of boys' delinquency. *Journal of Adolescence*, 24(5), 479–596.

Frick, P. J., Lahey, B. B., Loeber, R., Tannenbaum, L., Van Horn, Y., Christ, M. A. G., Hart, E. A. & Hanson, K. (1993). Oppositional defiant disorder and conduct disorder: A meta-analytic review of factor analyses and cross-validation in a clinic sample. *Clinical Psychology Review, 13*, 319–340.

Gottfredson, M., & Hirschi, T. (1990). *A general theory of crime*. Stanford, CA: Stanford University Press.

Huizinga, D., Loeber, R. & Thornberry, T. (1993). Longitudinal study of delinquency, drug use, sexual activity, and pregnancy among children and youth in three cities. *Public Health Reports: Journal of the U.S. Public Health Service, 108*, Supplement 1 (pp. 90–96).

Huizinga, D., Loeber, R., Thornberry, T., & Cothern, L. (2000, November). Co-occurrence of delinquency and other problem behaviors. *OJJDP Juvenile Justice Bulletin*.

Keenan, K., Loeber, R., Zhang, Q., Stouthamer-Loeber, M. & Van Kammen, W. B. (1995). The influence of deviant peers on the development of boys' disruptive and delinquency behavior: A temporal analysis. *Development and Psychopathology, 7*, 715–726.

Kelley, B. T., Loeber, R., Keenan, K., & DeLamatre, M. (1997, November). Developmental pathways in disruptive and delinquent behavior. *Juvenile Justice Bulletin, Office of Juvenile Justice and Delinquency Prevention*.

Lahey, B. B., Gordon, R. A., Loeber, R., Stouthamer-Loeber, M., & Farrington, D. P. (1999). Boys who join gangs: A prospective study of predictors of gang entry. *Journal of Abnormal Child Psychology, 27*, 261–276.

Le Blanc, M. (1997, November). *The development of interpersonal violence: Gradation in relation to other problem behavior and delinquency and the social and personal characteristics of various trajectories of violent behavior*. Paper presented at the annual meeting of the American Society of Criminology, San Diego.

Le Blanc, M., & Fréchette, M. (1989). *Male offending from latency to adulthood*. New York: Springer-Verlag.

Le Blanc, M., & Loeber, R. (1998). Developmental criminology updated. In M. Tonry (Ed.), *Crime and justice:* Vol. 23, pp. 115–197. Chicago: Chicago University Press.

Loeber, R. (1982). The stability of antisocial and delinquent child behavior. *Child Development, 53*, 1431–1446.

Loeber, R., & Farrington, D. P. (Eds.) (1998), *Serious and violent juvenile offenders: Risk factors and successful interventions*. Thousand Oaks, CA: Sage.

Loeber, R., & Farrington, D. P. (Eds.) (2001). *Child delinquents: Development, intervention and service needs*. Thousand Oaks, CA: Sage.

Loeber R., & Hay, D. F. (1997). Key issues in the development of aggression and violence from childhood to early adulthood. *Annual Review of Psychology, 48*, 371–410.

Loeber, R., & Le Blanc, M. (1990). Toward a developmental criminology. In M. Tonry & N. Morris (Eds.), *Crime and justice* (Vol. 12, pp. 375–473). Chicago: University of Chicago Press.

Loeber, R., & Schmaling, K. (1985). Empirical evidence for overt and covert patterns of antisocial conduct problems. *Journal of Abnormal Child Psychology, 13*, 337–352.

Loeber, R., & Stouthamer-Loeber, M. (1998). The development of juvenile aggression and violence: Some common misconceptions and controversies. *American Psychologist, 53*, 242–259.

Loeber, R., & Wikström, P-O. (1993). Individual pathways to crime in different types of neighborhood. In D. P. Farrington, R. J. Sampson, & P. O. Wikström (Eds.), *Integrating individual and ecological aspects of crime* (pp. 169–204). Stockholm, Sweden: National Council on Crime Prevention.

Loeber, R., Stouthamer-Loeber, M., Van Kammen, W. B., & Farrington, D. P. (1989). Development of a new measure of self-reported antisocial behavior for young children: Prevalence and reliability. In M. W. Klein (Ed.), *Cross-national research in self-reported crime and delinquency*, (pp. 203–225). Dordrecht, Netherlands: Kluwer.

Loeber, R., Stouthamer-Loeber, M., Van Kammen, W. B., & Farrington, D. P. (1991). Initiation, escalation and desistance in juvenile offending and their correlates. *Journal of Criminal Law and Criminology, 82*, 36–82.

Loeber, R., Wung, P., Keenan, K., Giroux, B., Stouthamer-Loeber, M., Van Kammen, W. B., & Maughan, B. (1993). Developmental pathways in disruptive child behavior. *Development and Psychopathology, 5*, 101–132.

Loeber, R., Keenan, K., & Zhang, Q. (1997). Boys' experimentation and persistence in developmental pathways toward serious delinquency. *Journal of Child and Family Studies, 6*, 321–357.

Loeber, R., Farrington, D. P., Stouthamer-Loeber, M., & Van Kammen, W. B. (1998a). *Antisocial behavior and mental health problems: Explanatory factors in childhood and adolescence.* Mahwah, NJ: Lawrence Erlbaum.

Loeber, R., DeLamatre, M., Keenan, K., & Zhang, Q. (1998b). A prospective replication of developmental pathways in disruptive and delinquent behavior. In R. Cairns (Ed.), *The individual as a focus in developmental research* (pp. 185–215). Thousand Oaks, CA: Sage.

Loeber, R., Farrington, D. P., Stouthamer-Loeber, M., & Van Kammen, W. B. (1998c). Multiple risk factors for multi-problem boys: Co-occurrence of delinquency, substance use, attention deficit, conduct problems, physical aggression, covert behavior, depressed mood, and shy/withdrawn behavior. In R. Jessor (Ed.). *New perspectives on adolescent risk behavior* (pp. 90–149). Cambridge: Cambridge University Press.

Loeber, R., Farrington, D. P., Stouthamer-Loeber, M., Moffitt, T. E., & Caspi, A. (1998d). The development of male offending: Key findings from the first decade of the Pittsburgh Youth Study. *Studies in Crime and Crime Prevention, 7*, 141–172.

Loeber, R., DeLamatre, M., Tita, G., Cohen, J., Stouthamer-Loeber, M., & Farrington, D. P. (1999a). Gun injury and mortality: The delinquent backgrounds of juvenile victims. *Violence and Victims, 14*, 339–352.

Loeber, R., Wei, E., Stouthamer-Loeber, M., Huizinga, D., & Thornberry, T. (1999b). Behavioral antecedents to serious and violent juvenile offending: Joint analyses from the Denver Youth Survey, Pittsburgh Youth Study, and the Rochester Development Study. *Studies on Crime and Crime Prevention, 8*, 245–263.

Loeber, R., Stouthamer-Loeber, M., & White, H. R. (1999c). Developmental aspects of delinquency and internalizing problems and their association with persistent juvenile substance use between ages 7 and 18. *Journal of Clinical Child Psychology, 28*, 322–332.

Loeber, R., Drinkwater, M., Yin, Y., Anderson, S. J., Schmidt, L. C., Crawford, A. (2000). Stability of family interactions from ages 6 to 18. *Journal of Abnormal Child Psychology, 28*, 353–369.

Loeber, R., Farrington, D. P., Stouthamer-Loeber, M., Moffitt, T. E., Caspi, A., & Lynam, D. (2001a). *Mental health problems, psychopathology and personality traits: Key findings from the first fourteen years of the Pittsburgh Youth Study.* Pittsburgh, PA: Western Psychiatric Institute and Clinic.

Loeber, R., Crawford, A., Farrington, D. P., Stouthamer-Loeber, M., Creemers, J., & Rosenfeld, R. (2001b). *The prediction of male homicide.* Manuscript in preparation.

Loeber, R., Farrington, D. P., Stouthamer-Loeber, M., & White, H. R. (2001c). *Serious and violent juvenile delinquency: Developmental course and origins from childhood to early adulthood.* Pittsburgh, PA: Western Psychiatric Institute and Clinic. Manuscript in preparation.

Lynam, D. R. (1997). Pursuing the psychopath: Capturing the fledgling psychopath in a nomological net. *Journal of Abnormal Psychology, 106*, 425–438.

Lynam, D. R., Moffitt, T. E., & Stouthamer-Loeber, M. (1993). Explaining the relation between IQ and delinquency: Class, race, test motivation, school failure, or self-control? *Journal of Abnormal Psychology, 102*, 187–196.

Lynam, D. R., Caspi, A., Moffitt, T., Wikström, P-O., Loeber, R., & Novak, S. (2000). The interaction between impulsivity and neighborhood context on offending: The effects of impulsivity are stronger in poorer neighborhoods. *Journal of Abnormal Psychology, 109*, 563–574.

Maguin, E., & Loeber, R. (1996). Academic performance and delinquency. In M. Tonry (Ed.), *Crime and Justice* (Vol. 20, pp. 145–264). Chicago: University of Chicago Press.

Maguin, E., Loeber, R., & LeMahieu, P. (1993). Does the relationship between poor reading and delinquency hold for different age and ethnic groups? *Journal of Emotional and Behavioral Disorders, 1*, 88–100.

Moffitt, T. E., Caspi, A., Silva, P. A., & Stouthamer-Loeber, M. (1995). Individual differences in personality and intelligence are linked to crime: Cross-context evidence from nations, neighborhoods, genders, races, and age-cohorts. In J. Hagan (Ed.), *Current perspectives on aging and the life cycle: Vol. 4. Delinquency and disrepute in the life course* (pp. 1–34). Greenwich, CT: JAI Press.

Office of Juvenile Justice and Delinquency Prevention (1998). Serious and violent juvenile offenders. *Juvenile Justice Bulletin.* (U.S. Department of Justice, Office of Juvenile Justice and Delinquency Prevention).

Peeples, F., & Loeber, R. (1994). Do individual factors and neighborhood context explain ethnic differences in juvenile delinquency? *Journal of Quantitative Criminology, 10*, 141–157.

Rutter, M. (1985). Resilience in the face of adversity: Protective factors and resistance to psychiatric disorder. *British Journal of Psychiatry, 147*, 598–611.

Rutter, M. (1990). Psychosocial resilience and protective mechanisms. In J. E. Rolf, A. S. Masten, D. Cicchetti, K. H. Nuechterlein, & S. Weintraub (Eds.), *Risk and protective factors in the development of psychopathology* (pp. 181–124). New York, NY: Cambridge University Press.

Stouthamer-Loeber, M. (1993). Optimizing data quality of individual and community sources in longitudinal research. In D. P. Farrington, R. J. Sampson, & P. O. Wikström (Eds.), *Integrating individual and ecological aspects of crime* (pp. 259–277). Stockholm, Sweden: National Council on Crime Prevention.

Stouthamer-Loeber, M., & Van Kammen, W. B. (1995). *Data collection and management: A practical guide.* Newbury Park, CA: Sage.

Stouthamer-Loeber, M., & Wei, E. (1998). The precursors of young fatherhood and its effect on the delinquency career of teenage males. *Journal of Adolescent Health, 22*, 56–65.

Stouthamer-Loeber, M., Loeber, R., & Thomas, C. (1992). Caretakers seeking help for boys with disruptive delinquent behavior. *Comprehensive Mental Health Care, 2*, 159–178.

Stouthamer-Loeber, M., Van Kammen, W. B., & Loeber, R. (1992). The nuts and bolts of implementing large-scale longitudinal studies. *Violence and Victims, 7*, 63–78.

Stouthamer-Loeber, M., Loeber, R., Farrington, D. P., Zhang, Q., Van Kammen, W. B., & Maguin, E. (1993). The double edge of protective and risk factors for delinquency: Interrelations and developmental patterns. *Development and Psychopathology, 5*, 683–701.

Stouthamer-Loeber, M., Loeber, R., Van Kammen, W. B., & Zhang, Q. (1995). Uninterrupted delinquent careers: The timing of parental helpseeking and juvenile court contact. *Studies on Crime and Crime Prevention, 4*, 236–251.

Stouthamer-Loeber, M., Drinkwater, M., & Loeber, R. (1999). Family functioning profiles, early onset offending, and disadvantaged neighborhoods. *International Journal of Child and Family Welfare, 4*, 247–256.

Stouthamer-Loeber, M., Loeber, R., Homish, D. L., & Wei, E. (2001). Maltreatment of boys and the development of disruptive and delinquent behavior. *Development and Psychopathology, 13*(4), 941–955.

Stouthamer-Loeber, M., Loeber, R., Wei, E., Farrington, D. P., & Wikström, P-O. (2002). Risk and promotive effects in the explanation of persistent serious delinquency in boys. *Journal of Clinical and Consulting Psychology, 70*, 111–123.

Tellegen, A., Lykken, D., Bouchard, T. J., Wilcox, K. J., Segal, N. L., & Rich, S. (1988). Personality similarity in twins reared apart and together. *Journal of Personality and Social Psychology, 54*, 1031–1039.

Thornberry, T. P., & Krohn, M. D. (2001). The development of delinquency: An interactional perspective. In S. O. White (Ed.), *Handbook of youth and justice* (pp. 289–305). New York: Plenum.

Thornberry. T. P., Smith, C. A., Rivera, C., Huizinga, D., & Stouthamer-Loeber, M. (1999, September). Family disruption and delinquency. OJJDP Juvenile Justice Bulletin.

Thornberry, T. P., Wei, E. H., Stouthamer-Loeber, M., & Van Dyke, J. (2000, January). Teenage fatherhood and delinquent behavior, *OJJDP Juvenile Justice Bulletin*.

Tolan, P. H., Gorman-Smith, D., & Loeber, R. (2000). Developmental timing of onsets of disruptive behaviors and later delinquency of inner-city youth. *Journal of Child and Family Studies, 9*, 203–230.

Van Kammen, W. B., & Loeber, R. (1994). Are fluctuations in delinquent activities related to the onset and offset of juvenile illegal drug use and drug dealing? *Journal of Drug Issues, 24*, 9–24.

Van Kammen, W. B., & Stouthamer-Loeber, M. (1997). Practical aspects of data collection and data management. In L. Bickman & D. Rog (Eds.), *Handbook of applied social research methods* (pp. 375–397). Thousand Oaks, CA: Sage.

Van Kammen, W. B., Maguin, E., & Loeber, R. (1994). Initiation of drug selling and its relationship with illicit drug use and serious delinquency in adolescent boys. In E. G. M. Weitekamp & H. J. Kerner (Eds.), *Cross-national longitudinal research on human development and criminal behavior* (pp. 229–241). Dordrecht, The Netherlands: Kluwer.

Wei, E. H. (1999). *Teenage fatherhood and pregnancy involvement among urban, adolescent males: Risk factors and consequences.* Unpublished Ph.D. dissertation. School of Public Health, University of Pittsburgh.

White, J., Moffitt, T. E., Caspi, A., Bartusch, D. J., Needles, D., & Stouthamer-Loeber, M. (1994). The measurement of impulsivity and its relationship to delinquency. *Journal of Abnormal Psychology, 103*, 192–205.

White, H. R., Loeber, R., Stouthamer-Loeber, M., & Farrington, D. P. (1999). Developmental associations between substance use and violence. *Development and Psychopathology, 11*, 785–803.

Wikström, P-O., & Loeber, R. (2000). Do disadvantaged neighborhoods cause well-adjusted children to become adolescent delinquents? A study of male juvenile serious offending, risk and protective factors, and neighborhood context. *Criminology, 38*, 1109–1142.

Wilson, J. Q., & Herrnstein, R. J. (1985). *Crime and human nature.* New York: Simon & Schuster.

Zhang, Q., Loeber, R., & Stouthamer-Loeber, M. (1997). Developmental trends of delinquency attitudes and delinquency: Replication and synthesis across time and samples. *Journal of Quantitative Criminology, 13*, 181–216.

5

Key Results from the First Forty Years of the Cambridge Study in Delinquent Development

David P. Farrington

Introduction

The Cambridge Study in Delinquent Development is a prospective longitudinal survey of the development of offending and antisocial behavior in 411 South London boys, mostly born in 1953. These males have been followed up by personal interviews from age 8 to age 46. The Study began in 1961, and for the first 20 years was directed by Donald West. I joined him to work on it in 1969, and I have directed the Study for the past 20 years. It has been funded primarily by the Home Office and secondly by the Department of Health. Results of the Study have been described in four books (West, 1969, 1982; West & Farrington, 1973, 1977), and in nearly 120 articles: see Farrington and West (1990) and Farrington (1995b). This chapter focuses particularly on the most recently obtained results.

Methods

Aims

The original aim of the Study was to describe the development of delinquent and criminal behavior in inner-city males, to investigate how far it could be

Taking Stock of Delinquency: An Overview of Findings from Contemporary Longitudinal Studies, edited by Thornberry and Krohn. Kluwer Academic/Plenum Publishers, New York, 2003.

predicted in advance, and to explain why juvenile delinquency began, why it did or did not continue into adult crime, and why adult crime often ended as men reached their twenties. The main focus was on continuity or discontinuity in behavioral development, on the effects of life events on development, and on predicting future behavior. The Study was not designed to test any one particular theory about delinquency but to test many different hypotheses about the causes and correlates of offending, and many different mechanisms and processes linking risk factors and antisocial behavior.

One reason for casting the net wide at the start and measuring many different variables was the belief that theoretical fashions changed over time and that it was important to try to measure as many variables as possible in which future researchers might be interested. Another important reason was that, in testing hypotheses about the causes of offending, it was essential to investigate how far one risk factor predicted delinquency independently of all other plausible explanatory factors. Another reason for measuring a wide range of variables was the fact that long-term longitudinal surveys were very uncommon, and that the value of this particular one would be enhanced if it yielded information of use not only to criminological researchers but also to those interested in alcohol and drug use, educational difficulties, poverty and poor housing, unemployment, sexual behavior, aggression, other social problems, and human development generally.

Characteristics of the Sample

At the time they were first contacted in 1961–62, the boys were all living in a working-class area of South London. The vast majority of the sample was chosen by taking all the boys who were then aged 8–9 and on the registers of 6 state primary schools within a one-mile radius of a research office which had been established. In addition to 399 boys from these 6 schools, 12 boys from a local school for the educationally subnormal were included in the sample in an attempt to make it more representative of the population of boys living in the area. Hence, the boys were not a probability sample drawn from a population, but rather a complete population of boys of that age in state schools in that area at that time.

Most of the boys (357, or 87%) were White in appearance and of British origin, in the sense that they were being brought up by parents who had themselves been brought up in England, Scotland, or Wales. Of the remaining 54 boys, 12 were Black, having at least one parent of West Indian (usually) or African origin. Of the remaining 42 boys of non-British origin, 14 had at least one parent from the North or South of Ireland, 12 had parents from Cyprus, and the other 16 boys had at least one parent from another country (Poland, Malta, Germany, France, Australia, Spain, Sweden, and Portugal). On the basis of their fathers' occupations when they were aged 8, 94% of the boys could be described as working-class (categories III, IV, or V on the Registrar General's scale, describing skilled, semi-skilled, or unskilled manual workers), in comparison with the national figure of 78% at that time. The majority of the boys were living in conventional two-parent families with both a father and a mother figure; at age 8–9, only 6% of the boys had no operative father and only 1% had no operative mother. This was, therefore, overwhelmingly a traditional White, urban, working class sample of British origin.

Data Collected at Different Ages

A major aim in this survey was to measure as many factors as possible that were considered (at that time) to be causes or correlates of offending. The boys were interviewed and tested in their schools when they were aged about 8–9, 10–11, and 14–15, by male or female psychologists. For simplicity, these tests are referred to as the tests at ages 8, 10, and 14. The males were interviewed in our research office at about 16, 18, and 21, and in their homes at about 25 and 32, by young male social science graduates. A ninth interview at age 46 is currently under way (see pp. 172–173).

At all ages except 21 and 25 (when subsamples were interviewed), the aim was to interview the whole sample, and it was always possible to trace and interview a high proportion; 389 out of 410 still alive at age 18 (95%) and 378 out of 403 still alive at age 32 (94%), for example. The tests in schools measured individual characteristics such as intelligence, attainment, personality, and psychomotor impulsivity, while information was collected in the interviews about such topics as living circumstances, employment histories, relationships with females, children, illnesses and injuries, leisure activities such as drinking, drug use, physical fighting, and offending behavior.

In addition to interviews and tests with the boys, interviews with their parents were carried out by female psychiatric social workers who visited their homes. These took place about once a year from when the boy was about 8 until when he was aged 14–15 and was in his last year of compulsory education. The primary informant was the mother, although many fathers were also seen. The parents provided details about such matters as the boy's daring or nervousness, family income, family size, their employment histories, their history of psychiatric treatment, their child-rearing practices (including attitudes, discipline, and parental disharmony), their closeness of supervision of the boy, and his temporary or permanent separations from them. Obstetric records were obtained for boys born in hospitals. Also, when the boy was aged 12, the parents completed questionnaires about their child-rearing attitudes and about his leisure activities.

The teachers completed questionnaires when the boys were aged about 8, 10, 12, and 14. These furnished data about their troublesome and aggressive school behavior, their restlessness and poor concentration, their school achieve-ment and their truancy. Delinquency rates of secondary schools were obtained from the local education authority. Ratings were also obtained from the boys' peers when they were in the primary schools, about such topics as their daring, dishonesty, troublesomeness, and popularity. Searches were also carried out in the central Criminal Record Office in London to try to locate findings of guilt of the males, of their biological mothers, fathers, brothers and sisters, of their wives and female partners, and of people who offended with them (their co-offenders). The minimum age of criminal responsibility in England is 10. The Criminal Record Office contains records of all relatively serious offenses committed in Great Britain or Ireland. In the case of 18 males who had emigrated outside Great Britain and Ireland by age 32, applications were made to search their criminal records in the 8 countries where they had settled, and searches were actually carried out in five countries. Since most males did not emigrate until their twenties, and since the emigrants had rarely been convicted in England, it is likely that the criminal records are quite complete.

The latest search of conviction records took place in the summer of 1994, when most of the males were aged 40. Between ages 10 and 16 inclusive (the years of juvenile delinquency in England at that time), 85 males (21%) were convicted. Altogether, up to age 40, 164 males (40%) were convicted (Farrington, Barnes, & Lambert, 1996; Farrington, Lambert, & West, 1998). Convictions were only counted if they were for offenses normally recorded in the Criminal Record Office, thereby excluding minor crimes such as common assault, traffic infractions, and drunkenness. The most common offenses included were thefts, burglaries, and unauthorized takings of vehicles, although there were also quite a few offenses of violence, vandalism, fraud, and drug abuse. In order to supplement official records information about delinquency and crime, self-reports of offending were obtained from the males at every age from 14 onwards (Farrington, 1989c).

Tracing and Securing Cooperation

Tremendous efforts were made to secure interviews, because of our belief (based in part on previous results obtained in this survey) that the most interest-ing subjects in any research on offending tended to be the hardest to locate and the most uncooperative. Surveys in which less than 75% of the target sample is interviewed may produce results that seriously underestimate the true level of criminal behavior (see Capaldi & Patterson, 1987, for a review of response rates in longitudinal surveys). Generally, an increase in the percentage interviewed from 75% to 95% leads to a disproportionate increase in the validity of the results; for example, at age 18, 36% of the one-sixth of the sample who were the most diffi-cult to interview were convicted, compared with only 22% of the majority who were interviewed more easily, a statistically significant difference (West & Farrington, 1977).

At age 32, after a great deal of detective work, every one of our men was located. Up to this age, 8 of the men had died, and 20 had emigrated permanently. Of the remaining 383 who were alive and in the United Kingdom, 360 were interviewed personally (94%). Seven of the 20 emigrated men were also interviewed, either abroad or during a temporary return visit that they made to the United Kingdom, giving a total number interviewed of 367. In addition, 9 emigrated men filled in questionnaires, and two cooperative wives of refusers filled in questionnaires on behalf of their husbands, in at least one case with the husband's collaboration and assistance. Therefore, interviews or questionnaires were obtained for 378 of the 403 men still alive (94%).

In general, success in tracing the men was achieved by persistence and by using a wide variety of different methods (Farrington, Gallagher, Morley, St. Ledger, & West, 1990a). Searching in electoral registers and telephone directories, and visits to a man's presumed address, were the most successful tracing methods for the men who were not particularly elusive. Searches in the Criminal Record Office, National Health Service records, and leads from other men were the most useful for the more elusive persons. The key factor in obtaining the men's cooperation was probably the pleasantness of the interviewer in the first face-to-face meeting.

Summarizing, the Cambridge Study in Delinquent Development has a unique combination of features. Nine face-to-face interviews have been completed with the males over a 40-year period, from 1961 to 2002. The attrition rate has been unusually low for such a long-term survey. The main focus of interest is on crime and delinquency, but the survey also provides information about alcohol and drug abuse, educational difficulties, poverty and poor housing, sexual behavior, unemployment, and other social problems. The sample size of about 400 is large enough for many statistical analyses, but small enough to permit detailed case histories of the males and their families.

Information has been obtained from multiple sources, including the males themselves, their parents, teachers, peers, and official (criminal, hospital, and school) records. Generally, the data came from parents, teachers, peers, or tests completed by the males between ages 8 and 14, but primarily from interviews with the males between ages 16 and 46. Information has been collected about a wide variety of theoretical constructs at different ages, including biological (e.g., heart rate, height, weight), psychological (e.g., intelligence, impulsivity), family (e.g., parental supervision and discipline), and social (e.g., poor housing, socioeconomic status) factors. Hence, the relative importance of these different factors as predictors and correlates of offending can be investigated. So far, analyses of interview data extend up to age 32, while analyses of criminal records extend up to age 40. As mentioned, the interviews at age 46 are currently (in 2002) under way.

Criminal Careers

Natural History of Offending

As mentioned, 40% of the Study males were convicted of criminal offenses up to age 40. The comparable national prevalence of convictions of males in England and Wales born in 1953 up to age 40 is 31% (Prime, White, Liriano, & Patel, 2001). The prevalence of offending increased up to age 17 and then decreased. Many other projects show a similar age-crime curve for prevalence (Farrington, 1986a). While the peak age for the number of offenders was 17, the mean age of convictions was 21, showing the skewness of the age-crime curve (Farrington et al., 1998).

The peak age of increase in the prevalence of offending was 14, while the peak age of decrease was 23 (Farrington, 1990a). These times of maximum acceleration and deceleration in prevalence draw attention to periods in male lives when important life changes may be occurring that influence offending. Perhaps the most important social influence changes from parents to male peers around age 14 and from male peers to female partners around age 23.

Up to age 40, the mean age of onset (the first conviction) was 18.6, while the mean age of desistance (the last conviction) was 25.7. Hence, the average duration of criminal careers was 7.1 years. The average frequency of offending (per offender) was 4.6 crimes. Excluding one-time offenders, whose duration was zero, the average duration of criminal careers was 10.4 years (Farrington et al., 1998). The average time interval between convictions was 3.3 years. The distribution of average time intervals was highly skewed, with about half of the Study males having an average time interval of less than 2 years.

Offending by Family Members

Farrington et al. (1998) summarized the conviction careers not only of the Study males but also of their brothers, sisters, fathers, mothers, and wives or female partners. Generally, criminal careers of the Study males' generation (all followed up to age 39–40) were quite similar, although females incurred fewer convictions (average convictions per offender 2.3 for wives, 2.8 for sisters, 4.4 for brothers, 4.6 for Study males). The average age of conviction was similar (21–22) for Study males, brothers, sisters, and wives. The peak age of conviction was 2–3 years later for sisters and wives (19–20) than for Study males and brothers (17). The average age of onset was about 2 years later for sisters and wives (20–21) than for Study males and brothers (18–19). The average age of desistance was about one year earlier for sisters and wives (24–25) than for Study males and brothers (25–26). Excluding one-time offenders, the average duration of criminal careers was 2–3 years longer for Study males and brothers (10–11 years) than for sisters and wives (8 years).

The conviction careers of fathers and mothers (up to an average age of 70) were very different, however (Farrington et al., 1998). Contrary to the view that offending is heavily concentrated in the teenage years, the average age of conviction was 30 for fathers and 35 for mothers. Contrary to the view that most people who are going to offend begin before age 20, the average age of onset was 27 for fathers and 33 for mothers. One quarter of convicted fathers did not start offending until after age 35, and one quarter of convicted mothers did not start offending until after age 42. Contrary to the view that most offenders "grow out" of crime in their twenties, the average age of desistance was 36 for convicted fathers and 38 for convicted mothers. One quarter of convicted fathers did not stop offending until after age 45, and one quarter of convicted mothers did not stop offending until after age 48. Contrary to the view that criminal careers are relatively short, their average duration (excluding one-time offenders) was 16 years for fathers and 15 years for mothers. Hence, when complete criminal careers are studied, officially recorded offending is far more persistent than previously thought.

Persistence in Offending

There was significant continuity between offending in one age range and offending in another. For example, nearly three quarters (73%) of males convicted as juveniles at age 10–16 were reconvicted between ages 17 and 24, in comparison with only 16% of those not convicted as juveniles (Farrington, 1992a). Nearly half (45%) of the juvenile offenders were convicted between ages 25 and 32, in comparison with only 8% of those not convicted as juveniles. Other studies show similar continuity in offending (e.g., Krohn, Thornberry, Rivera, & LeBlanc, 2001; Stattin & Magnusson, 1991).

While offenders were persistent, there was little specialization in offending. For example, 55 of the 65 males with a conviction for violence also had a conviction for a nonviolent crime (Farrington, 1997c). To a large extent, the frequent offenders were versatile and sooner or later committed a violent offense. The probability of committing a violent offense increased steadily with the number of offenses committed, from 18% of one-time offenders to 82% of those with 12 or more convictions (Farrington, 1997c). The data fitted a model specifying that violent crimes occurred at random in criminal careers (Farrington, 1991b).

The probability of persistence in offending increased steadily after each conviction. For the Study males, this probability was .68 after the first conviction, and it increased to .91 after the eighth conviction (Farrington et al., 1998). These results have been replicated in many other studies (e.g., Blumstein, Farrington, & Moitra, 1985; Tarling, 1993; Wolfgang, Figlio, & Sellin, 1972). National English data for males born in 1953 shows that the probability of persistence increased from .51 after the first conviction to .87 after the eighth (Prime et al., 2001). These national probabilities are lower than those in the Cambridge Study because of differences in the definition of what was a conviction. In the Cambridge Study, each offense committed on a different day counted as a conviction, whereas in the national study (where dates of offenses were not recorded) each conviction referred to one court appearance.

The "chronic offenders" at age 32 were defined as the 24 men (6% of the sample) who committed half of all officially recorded offenses (Farrington & West, 1993). Many other projects have reported a similar proportion of chronic offenders (e.g., Tracy, Wolfgang, & Figlio, 1990). The chronics had each committed at least 9 officially recorded offenses, and they had especially long criminal careers characterized by high rates of offending. They were versatile rather than specialized offenders; 16 of the 24 committed at least five different types of offenses (out of 10 types altogether). They also accounted for substantial proportions of the self-reported offenses (discussed later). For example, between ages 15 and 18, the chronic offenders committed 53% of all self-reported burglaries and 48% of all self-reported thefts of vehicles. Because they are so few and account for so much of the crime problem, the chronics are important targets for prevention and treatment.

The males first convicted at the earliest ages tended to become the most persistent offenders, in committing large numbers of offenses at high rates over long time periods. For example, the 35 males first convicted at age 10–13 averaged 8.8 convictions each up to age 40, with an average career duration of 11.6 years (Farrington et al., 1998). Similar results were obtained for other family members and by many other researchers (e.g., LeBlanc & Frechette, 1989; Tolan & Thomas, 1995). Moffitt (1993) suggested that the "life-course-persistent" offenders, who began early, were different in kind from the "adolescence-limited" offenders who began later and had short criminal careers. These groups were identified using conviction records in the Cambridge Study (Nagin, Farrington, & Moffitt, 1995). However, according to self-reports, the apparent reformation of the adolescence-limited offenders was less than complete. At age 32, they continued to drink heavily, use drugs, get into fights, and commit undetected offenses.

Replication of Criminal Career Results

Farrington and Wikström (1994) investigated how far the criminal career results (up to age 25) in the Cambridge Study were replicated in Project Metropolitan in Stockholm (focusing on working class boys). Convictions in London were compared with police-recorded offenses in Stockholm. Nevertheless, the cumulative prevalence curves were remarkably similar, as were the age of onset curves, average career durations, measures of continuity in offending, and the growth in recidivism probabilities after each offense. In both London and Stockholm, an early onset predicted a long criminal career.

The main differences between the results occurred because there were many more offenses per offender in Stockholm. Whereas 6% of London boys accounted for half of all crimes, only 2% of Stockholm boys accounted for half of all crimes. Also, whereas the average offenses per offender did not vary with age in London, the average offenses per offender increased to a peak in the teenage years and then decreased in Stockholm.

Another replication study, of offending up to age 33, was conducted by Farrington and Maughan (1999). This was a comparison of the Cambridge Study boys with 310 boys born 7 years later and living in the same small area of South London at age 14. The younger birth cohort of London boys was more ethnically diverse. Unlike the Cambridge Study boys, they were subject to police cautioning during their juvenile years, which was intended to divert young people away from court. Nevertheless, the cumulative prevalence of convictions was almost identical in the two studies. Since an additional number of the younger boys had been cautioned, it was concluded that cautioning had widened the net of recorded offenders.

Including cautions, the younger cohort had an earlier age of onset of offending but shorter and less prolific criminal careers. This is understandable if cautioning was bringing in more occasional, less committed offenders. In agreement with this, there was more continuity in offending in the Cambridge Study sample and more chronic offenders.

Co-Offending and Motives

Most juvenile and young adult offenses leading to convictions were committed with others, but the incidence of co-offending declined steadily with age (Reiss & Farrington, 1991). This was not because co-offenders dropped out but because the males changed from co-offending in their teenage years to lone offending in their twenties. Burglary, robbery, and theft from vehicles were particularly likely to involve co-offenders.

Generally, there was some consistency in co-offending or lone offending between one offense and the next. Co-offenders tended to be similar in age, gender and race to Study males and lived close to their addresses and to the locations of the offenses. It was rare for Study males to offend with their fathers, mothers, sisters or wives, or with unrelated females. Co-offending with brothers was most likely when a Study male had brothers who were close in age to him.

About one third of the most persistent offenders continually offended with less criminally experienced co-offenders, and hence appeared to be repeatedly recruiting others into a life of crime. Recruiting was especially common for burglary offenses. The recruiters are prime targets for intervention to reduce offending.

The most common reasons given for property offenses were utilitarian, rational, or economic: offenses were committed for material gain (Farrington, 1993c).

The next most common category of reasons were hedonistic: for excitement, for enjoyment, or to relieve boredom. Vandalism and joy-riding were mainly committed for these reasons. Similar results were reported in Montreal by LeBlanc and Frechette (1989). Other reasons were designed to minimize the offender's responsibility (e.g., I was young; I was drunk) or to blame peers. Offenses at younger ages (under 17) were relatively more likely to be committed for hedonistic reasons, while offenses at older ages (17 or over) were relatively more likely to be committed for utilitarian reasons.

Reasons for physical fighting depended on whether the boy was alone or in a group (Farrington, Berkowitz, & West, 1982a). In individual fights, the boy was usually provoked, became angry, and hit out to hurt his opponent. In group fights, the boy often said that he became involved to help a friend or because he was attacked. The group fights were more serious, occurring in bars or streets, and they were more likely to involve weapons, produce injuries, and lead to police intervention. Fights often occurred when minor incidents escalated, because both sides wanted to demonstrate their toughness and masculinity and were unwilling to react in a conciliatory way.

Self-Reported Offending

Most criminal career results reported so far were based on convictions. However, as mentioned, self-reports of offending were obtained at every age from 14 onwards. Compared with convictions, it is to be expected that self-reports will indicate a higher prevalence and frequency of offending, an earlier age of onset, and a later age of desistance. The cumulative prevalence of self-reported offending was very high; up to age 32, 96% of males admitted committing at least one crime that could, in theory, have led to a conviction. Hence, at least in this sample of urban working-class males, offending was not statistically deviant, although it was less common to commit relatively serious offenses such as burglary. Only 22% of males admitted burglary, and only 14% were convicted of burglary, up to age 32 (Farrington, 1989c).

According to repeated self-reports, the most common crimes of burglary, shoplifting, theft of and from vehicles, and vandalism declined in prevalence from the teenage years to the twenties and thirties, but the same decreases were not found for theft from work, assault, drug abuse, and fraud (Farrington, 1989c). Interestingly, the degree of continuity and specialization in offending was very similar according to self-reports and convictions. To a considerable extent, the self-reports and official records identified the same people as the worst offenders, as other researchers have also found (e.g., Huizinga & Elliott, 1986). The 80 boys who admitted the highest number of delinquent acts when seen at ages 14 and 16 overlapped significantly with the 85 convicted juvenile delinquents, since 41 boys were in both groups (West & Farrington, 1973). Consequently, conclusions about characteristics of offenders based on convictions were generally similar to conclusions based on self-reported offending.

The relationship between self-reported offending and convictions was strongest for burglary and for theft of and from vehicles, but it was also significant for shoplifting, theft from machines, assault, and drug use (Farrington, 1989c). The two measures were not significantly related for theft from work, vandalism, and fraud, because of the low probability of an offender being convicted for these offenses. When data were cumulated over the whole period between ages 10 and 32, the probability of an offender being convicted (sooner or later) was quite high for several types of offenses: over 50% for burglary and theft of vehicles, and 25% for theft from vehicles. The probability of an offender being convicted increased with age.

Several methodological studies of self-reported delinquency were carried out. In particular, the first demonstration of predictive validity—that self-reported delinquency by unconvicted boys predicted later convictions—was published by Farrington (1973). A later test (Farrington, 1989c) showed that this was true for particular types of offenses: burglary, theft of and from vehicles, and drug use (but not for shoplifting).

Another important comparison was between prospective self-reports of offending (at ages 14, 18, 21, and 25) and long-term retrospective self-reports of offending at age 32 (in response to the question, "Have you ever done X?"). About half of all offenses admitted prospectively were denied retrospectively (Farrington, 1989c). This suggests that valid self-report information about criminal careers requires repeated questions in prospective longitudinal surveys and cannot be obtained retrospectively in a cross-sectional survey.

Mathematical Models of Criminal Careers

Barnett, Blumstein, and Farrington (1987) tested several mathematical models of the conviction careers of the Study males, restricting the analysis to those with two or more convictions. They found that models assuming that all offenders had the same frequency of offending were inadequate. In order to fit the data, they assumed that there were two categories of offenders, termed "frequents" and "occasionals," who differed both in their rates of offending and in their probabilities of desistance after each conviction. Both types incurred convictions at a constant (but different) rate during their criminal careers. The two types had a similar average career duration.

Barnett, Blumstein, and Farrington (1989) also carried out a predictive test of this model. The model was developed on conviction data between the 10th and 25th birthdays and aimed to predict reconviction data between the 25th and 30th birthdays. Generally, the model performed well, but it was necessary to assume that there was some intermittency (desisting and later restarting) of criminal careers. Some of the frequents ceased offending at an average age of 19 but then restarted after a period of 7–10 years with no convictions. This restarting may be connected to life changes such as losing a job or separating from a spouse (see later).

Nagin and Farrington (1992b) articulated two alternative reasons for the continuity between past and future offending. The first is that it reflects a stable underlying construct such as criminal potential; this was termed the "persistent heterogeneity" explanation. The second is that the commission of one crime leads to an increase in the probability of committing future crimes, perhaps because of reinforcement or stigmatization; this was termed the "state dependence" explanation. Because past convictions did not predict future convictions independently of age and background factors, the persistent heterogeneity argument was supported. In other words, the continuity between past and future convictions reflected continuity in an underlying criminal potential. Similar conclusions were reached by Paternoster, Brame, & Farrington (2001), arguing that later life events have minimal effects on this continuity.

Nagin and Farrington (1992a) tested similar explanations of why an early age of onset predicts a long criminal career and a large number of offenses. This can occur either because an early age of onset is one symptom of a high criminal potential, which later shows itself in persistent offending, or because an early age of onset in some way facilitates later offending (e.g., because of early reinforcement or early stigmatization). The data showed that the inverse relationship between age of onset and persistence of offending was entirely attributable to the persistence of a previously existing criminal potential, and that an early age of onset had no additional impact on persistence.

Risk Factors for Offending

Childhood Risk Factors

Before anyone was convicted, at age 8–10, the future convicted juvenile delinquents differed significantly from the nondelinquents in many respects (self-reported delinquency will be discussed later). For example, the future convicted juvenile delinquents were more likely than nondelinquents to have been rated troublesome and dishonest in their primary schools. Convicted delinquents tended to be from poorer families, from larger-sized families, living in poor houses with neglected interiors, supported by social agencies, and physically neglected (in clothing, hygiene, or food) by their parents. However, they did not significantly tend to come from low socioeconomic status families (as measured by the occupational prestige of the family breadwinner) or to have working mothers. The delinquents were more likely to have convicted parents and delinquent older siblings (see pp. 150–151). They tended to be receiving poor parental child-rearing behavior, characterized by harsh or erratic parental discipline, cruel, passive, or neglecting parental attitude, and parental conflict. Their parents tended to supervise them poorly, being lax in enforcing rules or undervigilant (West & Farrington, 1973; Farrington, 1992c).

Up to the 10th birthday, the future juvenile delinquents were more likely to have experienced broken homes or separations from their parents for reasons other than death or hospitalization. Their parents tended to be uncooperative towards the research, endorsed authoritarian child-rearing attitudes on question-naires, and were uninterested in the boy's education. Their mothers tended to be nervous or in poor physical health, while their fathers tended to have erratic job histories, including periods of unemployment. The boys who became delinquents were more likely to have low intelligence and low school achievement and to be rated as daring (taking many risks) by parents and peers. The boys' teachers said that they were hyperactive and had poor concentration. Interestingly, hyperactiv-ity at age 8–10 predicted juvenile convictions independently of conduct problems at age 8–10 (Farrington, Loeber, & van Kammen, 1990b). Delinquents tended to be impulsive on psychomotor tests and personality questionnaires and unpopular with their peers, but they were not nervous. They were likely to have below-average height and average weight (Farrington, 1992c; West & Farrington, 1973).

Similar results have been reported by many other researchers (see e.g., Farrington, 1999a, 2001b). It seems likely that early risk factors for offending are largely replicable over time and place. Farrington and Loeber (1999) systemati-cally compared childhood risk factors for court delinquency in the Cambridge Study and in the Pittsburgh Youth Study (see Chapter 4 by Loeber et al.). Replicable risk factors included hyperactivity, impulsivity, and poor concentra-tion; low school achievement; poor parental supervision; parental conflict; an antisocial parent; a young mother; large family size; low family income; and coming from a broken family. It was interesting that these risk factors were replic-able despite considerable social differences between London in the early 1960s and Pittsburgh in the late 1980s. For example, family size was greater in London and broken families and young mothers were more prevalent in Pittsburgh.

Where there were differences in results, these seemed largely attributable to different meanings of the risk factors. For example, maternal physical punishment was more important as a risk factor for delinquency in London, and socioeco-nomic status was more important in Pittsburgh. However, maternal physical pun-ishment included a cold, rejecting attitude in London, but it could be given in the context of a loving relationship in Pittsburgh; and socioeconomic status in Pittsburgh included parental education, whereas in London it reflected only occu-pational prestige. (An earlier comparison of personality factors in the Cambridge Study and in a Montreal longitudinal study of adolescents was also completed by Farrington, Biron, & LeBlanc, 1982b.)

At age 14, when the boys were in their last year of compulsory schooling, the differences between juvenile delinquents and nondelinquents were similar in many respects to those found at age 8–10. For example, the convicted delinquents still tended to have cruel, passive, or neglecting parents who were in conflict with each other, and they were still significantly low on measures of intelligence and attainment. They were described by their teachers as frequent liars, truants, daring, lacking in concentration or restless, and they left school at the earliest possible age of 15. Special efforts were made at age 14 to measure aggressiveness, and the delinquents proved to be significantly aggressive according to self-reports, teacher ratings, and a semantic differential test. Also, the delinquents were likely to have relatively many delinquent friends (Farrington, 1992c; West & Farrington, 1973), as other researchers have found (e.g., Elliott, Huizinga, & Ageton, 1985).

Mechanisms and Processes

Several attempts have been made to go beyond the identification of risk factors in multivariate analyses and to test alternative theories about mechanisms and processes relating risk factors and offending. For example, the concentration of offending in a small number of families was remarkable in the Cambridge Study. Less than 6% of the families were responsible for half of the convictions of all family members (fathers, mothers, sons, and daughters) of all 400 families (Farrington et al., 1996). Having a convicted father, mother, brother, or sister significantly predicted a boy's own convictions. In fact, having a convicted parent before the 10th birthday was usually the best explanatory predictor of the boy's later offending and antisocial behavior, and it continued to be predictive after controlling for all other explanatory variables.

The design of the Cambridge Study does not permit any disentangling of genetic and environmental transmission of antisocial behavior from parents to children. However, West and Farrington (1977) did test various hypotheses about the link between convicted fathers and convicted sons. For example, the percentage of males who were convicted did not vary according to whether the father was last convicted before or after the boy's birth, suggesting that there was no direct behavioral influence of criminal fathers on delinquent sons. There was no evidence that convicted fathers directly encouraged their sons to commit crimes or taught them criminal techniques. On the contrary, convicted fathers condemned their sons' offending. Hardly any convicted fathers co-offended with any of the Study males (Reiss & Farrington, 1991).

Convicted fathers were significantly likely to be married to convicted mothers, but a convicted father predicted the boy's offending even when no other family member was convicted. The influence of a convicted father did not vary according to the extent of his criminal record. Convicted fathers had no more effect on older sons than on younger sons, again casting doubt on the importance of direct environmental influence (on the assumption that the older sons, on average, would have spent more time with their fathers).

Convicted fathers also predicted self-reported offending by the Study male. However, at all levels of self-reported offending (even at low levels), a convicted father predicted an increased likelihood of the boy being convicted. This suggests that a boy from a known criminal family who was apprehended for offending might have been more likely to be convicted than an equally delinquent boy from a noncriminal family. A convicted father was especially associated with poor parental supervision, and this was not because of imprisonment (which was rare). Poor parental supervision may be one link in the causal chain between convicted fathers and convicted sons.

As another example, Juby and Farrington (2001) tested different explanations of the relationship between disrupted families and delinquency. Trauma theories suggest that the loss of a parent has a damaging effect on a child, most commonly because of the effect on attachment to the parent. Life-course theories focus on separation as a sequence of stressful experiences, and on the effects of multiple stressors such as parental conflict, parental loss, reduced economic circumstances, changes in parent figures, and poor child-rearing methods. Selection theories argue that disrupted families produce delinquent children because of pre-existing differences from other families in risk factors such as parental conflict, criminal or antisocial parents, low family income, or poor child-rearing methods.

Juby and Farrington (2001) concluded that the results favored life-course theories rather than trauma or selection theories. While boys from broken homes (permanently disrupted families) were more delinquent than boys from intact homes, they were not more delinquent than boys from intact high conflict families. Overall, the most important factor was the postdisruption trajectory. Boys who remained with their mother after the separation had the same delinquency rate as boys from intact low conflict families. Boys who remained with their father, with relatives or with others (e.g., foster parents) had high delinquency rates. The results were similar whether convictions or self-reported delinquency were studied.

Independent Predictors

In order to draw conclusions about possible causal effects, a risk factor should precede the outcome variable of offending, it should significantly predict the outcome variable, and it should predict the outcome variable after controlling for other possible explanatory variables. These considerations drove most of the multivariate analyses, which usually involved regression techniques to investigate the independent predictive effects of risk factors on outcomes. Sometimes, successive regressions were carried out. For example, in building up a model of stepping stones to adult criminal careers, Farrington (1986b) studied the independent predictors of (a) troublesomeness at 8–10, (b) convictions at 10–13, (c) convictions at 14–16, (d) convictions at 17–20, and (e) convictions at 21–24. In other cases, hierarchical regressions were carried out, entering variables in different categories as blocks (e.g., Farrington & Loeber, 1999).

A fundamental distinction was made between explanatory and nonexplanatory risk factors. An explanatory risk factor was one that measured some underlying theoretical construct that was clearly different from the construct measured by the outcome variable. Thus, the construct measured by poor parental supervision is clearly different from the construct measured by offending, and it is plausible to suggest that poor parental supervision could cause child offending. A nonexplanatory risk factor was one that arguably measured the same underlying construct as offending. Thus, it was considered that troublesome child behavior probably predicted later offending because both were measuring an underlying antisocial personality that persisted from childhood to adulthood with different behavioral manifestations at different ages (e.g., truancy, bullying, heavy drinking, drug use). It would not be sensible to suggest that troublesome child behavior caused offending. Heavy drinking may be an immediate situational trigger to offending, but it is not an explanatory risk factor in the sense that this term is used here.

A major problem of interpretation centers on delinquent friends. Having delinquent friends at age 14 (when it was first measured) clearly predicted later offending of the Study male. However, because most offenses under age 17 were committed with other young males, if a Study male offended then in most cases he inevitably had to have delinquent friends. Amdur (1989, p. 51) argued that delinquent friends and delinquency could be measuring the same underlying construct. Arguably, having delinquent friends was merely another indicator of offending and hence should not be treated as an explanatory predictor; delinquent friends may have predicted offending because of the continuity in offending over time. Explanatory analyses were based only on clearly explanatory risk factors, whereas analyses to investigate the accuracy of prediction were based on all (explanatory and nonexplanatory) risk factors.

In the analyses, the large number of possible explanatory variables was reduced to a small number (about 20 at age 8–10) that each seemed to measure a distinct theoretical construct and that were not highly correlated. Further reduction would have required the combination of different constructs. For example, a global measure of poor parenting could have been derived including discipline, supervision, conflict, disrupted families, and convicted parents, but it was thought that each of these constructs was potentially important and that a combined scale would be less meaningful. In general, all explanatory risk factors were always included in explanatory analyses, as it was considered problematic to demonstrate (for example) that X predicted offending independently of three possible confounders A, B, and C, when there are so many more plausible explanatory variables measured in the Study. Results may differ in neat modelling exercises based on a few variables compared with regression analyses based on many variables (e.g., Rowe & Farrington, 1997).

In many analyses, explanatory variables were dichotomized. Dichotomized variables are more concordant with the idea of "risk factors," make it very easy to communicate results to policy makers and practitioners, can be easily added to produce risk scores and identify multiple problem youth, and make it easy to study interactions between variables (see p. 164). Dichotomization makes it possible to use the odds ratio, which is a more meaningful, interpretable, and realistic measure of strength of association than the product-moment correlation and the percentage of variance explained. Dichotomization equates the sensitivity of measurement of all variables and hence makes it possible to compare their predictive efficiency, and also makes it possible to study nonlinear relationships (e.g., where there is a large increase in delinquency in the "worst" category of an explanatory variable). The main disadvantage with dichotomization is that information is lost, because cases below the threshold are treated as equivalent. Overall, however, it was considered that the advantages outweighed the disadvantages for many analyses (see Farrington & Loeber, 2000).

The most important predictors, at age 8–10, of later offending (whether measured by convictions or by self-reports) fell into 6 categories of theoretical constructs:

1. Antisocial child behavior, including troublesomeness, dishonesty and aggressiveness;
2. Hyperactivity-impulsivity-attention deficit, including poor concentration, restlessness, high daring (risk-taking), and psychomotor impulsivity;
3. Low intelligence and low school achievement;
4. Family criminality, including convicted parents, delinquent older siblings, and siblings with behavior problems;
5. Family poverty, including low family income, large family size, and poor housing;
6. Poor parenting, including harsh and authoritarian discipline, poor supervision, parental conflict, and separation from parents.

In regression analyses, it was often found that one factor from each of these categories predicted offending independently of all the other categories.

At age 8–10, the best independent predictors of official juvenile delinquency (convictions between ages 10 and 16) were troublesomeness, high daring, dishonesty, a behavior problem sibling, a convicted parent, and poor parental child-rearing behavior (Farrington, 1996a). When measures of antisocial child behavior were excluded from the regression analysis in order to investigate explanatory factors only, the best independent predictors were high daring, low school achievement, a convicted parent, harsh discipline, low nonverbal intelligence, and separation from a parent (Farrington & Loeber, 1999).

The best independent predictors of convictions up to age 32 were troublesomeness, a convicted parent, high daring, low junior school achievement, poor housing, and separation from a parent (Farrington, 1990b). Excluding measures of antisocial child behavior, the best independent predictors of convictions up to age 32 were large family size, a convicted parent, high daring, poor housing, separation from a parent, low school achievement, and not having few friends (Farrington, 1993a); social isolation seemed to act as a protective factor against delinquency (see p. 164). The best explanatory predictors at age 8–10 of adult convictions between ages 21 and 40 were low school achievement, a convicted parent, separation from a parent, and large family size (Farrington, 2000b).

Generally, the best predictors of convictions tended also to be the best predictors of the worst self-reported offenders (those who admitted the most acts). For example, of 39 key risk factors measured between ages 8 and 18, 35 were significantly related to both official and self-reported delinquency (Farrington, 1992c, Table 6.1). The only exceptions were that official (but not self-reported) delinquents were attending high delinquency rate schools and were relatively small at ages 8–10 and 18, while self-reported (but not official) delinquents tended to come from low socioeconomic status families at age 8–10.

Predicting Persisters

Farrington (1999b) compared the predictors at age 8–10 of persistent young offenders (those with 3 or more convictions between ages 10 and 18) and of occasional offenders (those with one or two convictions). The best independent predictors of occasional offenders (compared with unconvicted boys) were a convicted parent, high daring, unpopularity, and poor housing. The best predictors of persistent offenders (compared with occasional offenders) were different: low family income, poor concentration, low involvement of the father in the boy's leisure activities, low socioeconomic status, and a delinquent sibling. Therefore, predictors of persistence may be different from predictors of onset.

Persistence in crime after the 21st birthday, as opposed to desistance, was predicted especially by heavy drinking at age 18 and by having a father who rarely joined in the boy's leisure activities at age 12, as well as by unemployment at age 16, low verbal intelligence at age 8–10, and not trying to do well at school (Farrington & Hawkins, 1991). Convicted teenagers who were both unemployed and heavy drinkers had an exceptionally high probability of persistence (nearly 90%). Again, the predictors of persistence were different from the predictors of early onset, as other researchers have found (e.g., Loeber, Stouthamer-Loeber, van Kammen, & Farrington, 1991). The best independent predictors at age 8–10 of the chronic offenders up to age 32 were troublesomeness, a delinquent sibling, high daring, and a convicted parent (Farrington & West, 1993).

Offending and Antisocial Behavior

Antisocial Behavior at Age 18

The Cambridge Study shows that offending is only one element of a much larger syndrome of antisocial behavior that tends to persist over time, as Robins (1986) has persuasively argued. For example, the boys who were convicted up to age 18 (most commonly for offenses of dishonesty, such as burglary and theft) were significantly more deviant than the nonoffenders on almost every factor that was investigated at that age (West & Farrington, 1977). The convicted delinquents drank more beer, they got drunk more often, and they were more likely to say that drinking made them violent. They smoked more cigarettes, they had started smoking at an earlier age, and they were more likely to be heavy gamblers. They were more likely to have been convicted for minor motoring offenses, to have driven after drinking at least 10 units of alcohol (e.g., 5 pints of beer), and to have been injured in road accidents. The delinquents were more likely to have taken prohibited drugs such as marijuana or LSD, although few of them had convictions for drug offenses. Also, they were more likely to have had sexual intercourse, especially with a variety of different girls, and especially beginning at an early age, but they were less likely to use contraceptives.

The convicted delinquents at age 18 tended to hold relatively well-paid but low-status jobs, and they were more likely to have erratic work histories including periods of unemployment. They were more likely to be living away from home, and they tended not to get on well with their parents. They were more likely to be tattooed, and they had significantly low heart rates. The delinquents were more likely to go out in the evenings, and were especially likely to spend time hanging about on the street. They tended to go around in groups of four or more, and were more likely to be involved in group violence or vandalism. They were much more likely to have been involved in physical fights, to have started fights, to have carried weapons, and to have used weapons in fights. They were also more likely to express aggressive and anti-establishment attitudes on a questionnaire (negative to police, school, rich people, and civil servants).

It was interesting that the peak age of offending, at 17–18, coincided with the peak age of affluence for many convicted males. Convicted males tended to come from low-income families at age 8 and later tended to have low incomes themselves at age 32. However, at age 18, they were relatively well-paid in comparison with nondelinquents; whereas convicted delinquents might be working as unskilled laborers on building sites and getting the full adult wage for this job, nondelinquents might be in poorly paid jobs with prospects, such as bank clerks, or might still be students. These results show that the link between income and offending is quite complex.

Antisocial Behavior at Age 32

Generally, the Study males were less antisocial at age 32 than at age 18. Most types of offending declined with age, although binge drinking, drunk driving, and the use of hard drugs (heroin and cocaine) increased (Farrington, 1990a). While the Study males became less deviant in absolute terms, those who were relatively more deviant at age 18 still tended to be relatively more deviant at age 32. Therefore, there was relative stability but absolute change. Between ages 18 and 32, there was a decrease in aggressive and anti-establishment attitudes and in self-reported impulsivity. Most of the men (76%) were living with a wife or female partner at age 32, and their job records had become much more stable. These two factors of settling down with female partners and being in stable jobs seemed most plausible in explaining the decrease in offending (see p. 173).

Convicted men differed significantly from unconvicted ones at age 32 in most aspects of their lives (Farrington, 1989b). Convicted men were less likely to be home owners and more likely to be renting (usually from the local council), more likely to have moved home frequently, more likely to be divorced or separated, to be in conflict with their wife or female partner and to have assaulted her, and more likely to be separated from a child. Convicted men were more likely to be unemployed, to have had low take-home pay, to have spent more evenings out per week, to be involved in physical fights, and to be heavy smokers, heavy drinkers, drunk drivers, drug users, and self-reported offenders. Also, convicted men were more likely to be identified as probable psychiatric cases on the General Health Questionnaire (Goldberg, 1978), which detects anxiety-depressive types of mental illness, but this was a relatively weak relationship.

Generally, the convicted men who were persisters (those convicted both before and after their 21st birthdays) were more deviant than desistors (those convicted only before their 21st birthdays) or late-comers to crime (those convicted only after their 21st birthdays). For example, adult social dysfunction at age 32 was assessed on a 9-point scale including quality of accommodation, cohabitation history, success with children, employment history, physical fighting, substance abuse, psychiatric disorder, and self-reported and official offending in the previous five years (Farrington, Gallagher, Morley, St. Ledger, & West, 1988b). A similar composite measure was developed by Zoccolillo, Pickles, Quinton, and Rutter (1992). While 87% of unconvicted men were living quite successful lives according to this composite measure, this was true of 67% of desistors, 59% of late-comers and only 44% of persisters (Farrington, 1989b). Even at age 32, the persisters tended to be significantly deviant in a variety of ways.

The Antisocial Personality Syndrome

In order to investigate the syndrome of antisocial behavior, composite measures of "antisocial personality" were devised at ages 10, 14, 18, and 32, based on indicators of deviant behavior at each age (Farrington, 1991a). For example, the measure of antisocial personality at age 18 included conviction, self-reported delinquency, self-reported violence, antisocial group behavior, taking a prohibited drug, heavy smoking, heavy drinking, drunk driving, irresponsible sex (having intercourse without using contraceptives), heavy gambling, an unstable job record, anti-establishment attitudes, being tattooed, and self-reported impulsivity (all referring to the 15–18 age range).

The antisociality scales at the four ages were all significantly intercorrelated, showing the continuity in antisocial behavior over time. For example, the scales at ages 18 and 32 correlated at .55, despite the dramatic environmental changes in men's lives between these ages, as they left the parental home, went through a period of residential instability and then typically settled down with a wife or female cohabitee. Hence, the high correlation probably reflects individual rather than environmental stability. Over half (60%) of the most antisocial males at age 18 were still antisocial at age 32, compared with only 14% of the remainder at age 18 who became antisocial at age 32.

The most important predictors of antisocial personality at each age were investigated (Farrington, 1996b, 2000b). For example, the best explanatory predictors at age 8–10 of antisociality at age 18 were a convicted parent, large family size, a nervous mother, high neuroticism, poor child-rearing, and low school achievement. The best explanatory predictors of antisociality at age 32 were a convicted parent, large family size, a young mother, and low nonverbal intelligence. Since low school achievement and low nonverbal intelligence were highly correlated, the best predictors of antisociality at ages 18 and 32 were very similar.

Numerous factors predicted adult social dysfunction at age 32, but the best independent predictors were a poor relationship with the parents at age 18, an unskilled manual job at age 18, no examinations taken by age 18, nervous-withdrawn at age 8, small at age 14, hospital treatment for illness at age 16–18, poor concentration or restlessness at age 12–14, and high neuroticism at age 14 (Farrington, 1993a). Nervousness seemed to be negatively related to offending but positively related to other types of social dysfunction.

Truancy and Physical Health

Research on truancy (Farrington, 1980, 1996a) showed that primary school truants at age 8–10 tended to become secondary school truants at age 12–14. The best independent predictors at age 8–10 of secondary school truancy were troublesomeness, a behavior problem sibling, a nervous or psychiatrically treated father, low nonverbal intelligence, separation from a parent, low parental interest in the boy's education, low school attainment, and daring. Generally, truants and delinquents were similar in childhood, adolescent, and adult features, but the most important difference was that nervousness was positively related to truancy but negatively related to delinquency. This suggested that, for some children, truancy was a behavioral symptom of a nervous-withdrawn temperament rather than of an antisocial personality, thus confirming the distinction between truancy and school refusal (Bools, Foster, Brown, & Berg, 1990).

Convicted males significantly tended to have accidents and injuries at ages 18 and 32 (Farrington, 1995a). However, convictions were only weakly related to hospital treatment for illness. Generally, convictions and self-reported offending predicted hospital treatment for injury and illness more than the reverse. All these predictive relationships held independently of antisocial personality and childhood risk factors. It was concluded that offending could lead to poor health.

Aggression and Violence

Continuity in Aggression

There was significant continuity between childhood aggression and adult violence (Farrington, 1989a, 1991b), as other researchers have also reported (e.g., Eron & Huesmann, 1990). Boys who were aggressive in childhood or adolescence tended to be more deviant in adulthood: living in worse home circumstances, more in conflict with and violent towards their wife or female partner, more likely to be unemployed, heavier smokers and drinkers, more likely to be drunk drivers and drug takers, and committing more offenses (including violence). This continuity, however, was probably not specific to aggression and violence but was part of the general continuity in antisocial and deviant behavior from childhood to adulthood. This was why aggressive children had deviant life styles 20 years later as adults.

Research on bullying (Farrington, 1993d) shows continuity both within and between generations. There was a significant tendency for the males who reported that they were bullies at age 14 also to report that they were bullies at age 32 and that their children were bullies when the males were at age 32. In addition to being bullies themselves, the men who had children who were bullies tended to be poor readers, heavy gamblers, and unpopular in their teenage years, and they tended to have authoritarian parents. The men were also asked at age 32 about whether their children were victims of bullying. Those who had children who were victims tended to be those who had been unpopular and had few friends at age 8–10, and those who were nervous and regular smokers at age 14. Knowing that these factors are associated with being bullied, it seemed likely that there was intergenerational continuity in being bullied as well as in bullying (see also Olweus, 1994).

Predictors of Aggression and Violence

The most important predictors of adolescent aggression and adult violence tended to fall into the categories listed earlier (Farrington, 1978, 1989a, 1998, 2000a, 2001a). For example, the best explanatory predictors at age 8–10 of convictions and self-reported violence up to age 20 were high daring, poor parental supervision, low family income, large family size, physical neglect, and a convicted parent. The best predictors of violence after age 21 were a convicted parent, separation from a parent, low socioeconomic status, low family income, and a young mother.

Conclusions drawn from these predictive analyses of aggression and violence were similar to those drawn about the prediction of delinquency and frequent offending. This further confirmed the argument put forward by West and Farrington (1977) that aggression was merely one element of a more general antisocial tendency, which arose in childhood and continued through the teenage and adult years. Violent offenders were very similar to nonviolent frequent offenders in childhood, adolescent, and adult features (Farrington, 1991b), suggesting that the causes of aggression and violence were essentially the same as the causes of persistent and extreme antisocial, delinquent, and criminal behavior. These results were replicated by Capaldi and Patterson (1996).

The predictors of soccer violence at age 18 and violence against spouses and female partners at age 32 were also investigated (Farrington, 1994a). The best predictors at age 15 of soccer violence were being relatively small, having a father who was not interested in the boy, not attending church, not being nervous, leaving school early, and having authoritarian parents. The best predictors at age 15 of spouse assault were a convicted parent, unpopularity, high daring, and separation from a parent. There seemed to be a link between experiencing parental disharmony and early separation from a parent in childhood, difficulties in relationships with peers and parents, and later difficulties in relationships with spouses and female partners. Teenage violence tended to develop into later spouse assault, but particularly for those aggressive males who had long-lasting difficulties in their relationships with other people.

Farrington et al. (1982a) analyzed physical fights reported by the males at age 15–18 (most occurring in bars or streets). As mentioned, group fights were more serious than individual fights, in involving weapons, injuries, and police intervention. A category of aggressive frequent group fighters was identified, and the best predictors at age 8–10 of these boys were low family income, large family size, low verbal intelligence, high daring, and low school achievement. The best childhood predictors of bullying were physical neglect, the father not joining in the boy's leisure activities, low school achievement, and a convicted parent, while having few friends predicted low rates of bullying (Farrington, 1993d). As mentioned, boys with few friends tend to be victims of bullying, not bullies.

According to Raine (1993, pp. 166–172), one of the most replicable findings in the literature is that antisocial and violent youth tend to have low heart rates. This may be because a low heart rate reflects autonomic underarousal, which leads to sensation-seeking, risk-taking, and aggression to increase arousal. Alternatively, a high heart rate may be associated with anxiety, behavioral inhibition, and a fearful temperament, and fearful people are unlikely to commit violent acts. Farrington (1997c) carried out extensive analyses on low heart rate as a predictor and correlate of official and self-reported violence and teacher-reported aggression. The relationship between low heart rate and these outcome variables held up after controlling for all other risk factors.

Accuracy of Prediction

Numerous studies of the accuracy of prediction of offending were carried out. For example, Farrington (1997a) investigated how far the "vulnerability" score at age 8–10 predicted violent and nonviolent convictions and self-reported offending up to age 20. This score was derived at an early stage (West & Farrington, 1973, p. 131) and was the number of risk factors out of five (low family income, large family size, a convicted parent, poor parental child-rearing behavior, and low nonverbal intelligence). The percentage who became offenders increased with the risk score. For example, the percentage convicted of violence increased from 3% (score 0) to 31% (score 4–5) and the percentage convicted of nonviolent offenses increased from 20% (score 0) to 70% (score 4–5).

Different risk scores were used in predicting convictions for violence and nonviolent offenses and self-reported violence after age 21 (Farrington, 2001a) and in predicting adult convictions after age 21 and antisocial personality at ages 18 and 32 (Farrington, 2000b). For example, 14% of males with no risk factors were convicted after age 21, compared with 64% of males with three or four risk factors at age 8–10 (low school achievement, a convicted parent, separation from a parent, large family size). Farrington (2002) also investigated the prediction at age 8–10 of boys who both had multiple problems and were violent between ages 10 and 20. The percentage who became multiple-problem violent boys increased from 1% (score 0) to 83% (score 7–8). These figures overestimate the extent to which multiple-problem violent boys could be predicted in a different sample. Nevertheless, it was generally true that the degree of predictability of later outcomes at age 8–10 was remarkable (even when behavioral predictors such as troublesomeness were excluded).

It was also surprising how accurately chronic offenders (the small number of men who accounted for half of all convictions) could be predicted. For example, a prediction scale was developed at age 8–10 based on troublesome child behavior, economic deprivation, low nonverbal intelligence, a convicted parent, and poor parental child-rearing behavior (Farrington, 1985). Of the 55 boys with the highest scores on this scale, 15 became chronic offenders before the 25th birthday (out of only 23 in the whole sample), 22 others were convicted, and only 18 were unconvicted at that time. Hence, there were few "false positives."

Life Events and Protective Factors

Effects of Life Events

An advantage of a longitudinal survey is that it is possible to investigate the effects of specific life events on the development of delinquency by comparing before and after measures of offending and carrying out quasi-experimental analyses using each subject as his own control (Farrington, 1988). For example, the effects on delinquent behavior of being found guilty in court were studied. If convictions have a deterrent or reformative effect, a boy's delinquent behavior should decline after he is convicted. On the other hand, if convictions have stigmatizing or contaminating effects, a boy's delinquent behavior should increase after he is convicted.

These hypotheses were tested by studying self-reports of delinquency before and after a boy was first convicted. It was found that boys who were first convicted between ages 14 and 18 increased their self-reported delinquency afterwards, both in comparison with the level before and in comparison with the offending of a carefully matched group of unconvicted boys (Farrington, 1977). The same result was obtained in studying the effect of first convictions occurring between ages 18 and 21 (Farrington, Osborn, & West, 1978). These results are concordant with Gold's (1970) findings in Michigan. However, self-reported delinquency decreased after later convictions, especially if they were followed by noncustodial sentences.

The effect on delinquency of going to different secondary schools was also investigated (Farrington, 1972). At age 11, most of the boys went to one of 13 secondary schools. These schools differed dramatically in their official delinquency rates, from one that had 20 court appearances per 100 boys per year to another where the corresponding figure was only 0.3. The key issue was whether the boys who went to high-delinquency-rate secondary schools became more likely to offend as a result, or whether the differing delinquency rates of the different secondary schools merely reflected differences in their intakes of boys at age 11.

As already mentioned, the best predictor of official juvenile delinquency in this survey was the rating of troublesomeness at age 8–10 by teachers and peers. Generally, the continuity between troublesomeness and delinquency was not greatly affected by the kind of school to which a boy went. There was a marked tendency for the more troublesome boys to go to the high delinquency rate secondary schools, and the delinquency rates of different secondary schools largely reflected their different intakes. In contrast to Rutter, Maughan, Mortimore, and Ouston (1979), who found somewhat greater school effects, it was concluded that these secondary schools had little effect on delinquency.

Another investigation of the effect of a specific event on offending focused on unemployment (Farrington, Gallagher, Morley, St. Ledger, & West, 1986a). The complete job history of each boy between leaving school at an average age of 15 and the interview at age 18 was obtained, including all periods of unemployment. The key question was whether the boys committed more offenses (according to official records) during their periods of unemployment than during their periods of employment.

The results showed that the boys did indeed commit more offenses while unemployed than while employed. Furthermore, the difference was restricted to offenses involving financial gain, such as theft, burglary, robbery, and fraud. There was no effect of unemployment on other offenses, such as violence, vandalism, and drug use, suggesting that the boys committed more offenses while they were unemployed because they lacked money at these times. Furthermore, the effect of unemployment only applied to those with the highest prediction scores for crime, suggesting that unemployment had a criminogenic effect especially on those boys with the greatest prior potential for offending.

Factors Encouraging Desistance

An important life event that encouraged desistance was moving out of London (West, 1982). Most families who moved out were upwardly mobile families who were moving to prosperous suburban areas in the Home Counties, often buying their own houses rather than renting in London. It was clear that both official and self-reported offending of the men decreased after they and their families moved out of London, possibly because of the effect of the move in breaking up delinquent groups.

It is often believed that marriage to a good woman is one of the best treatments for male offending. When we asked the males in their twenties why they had stopped offending, they often mentioned marriage and the influence of women, as well as the fact that they did not hang around so much with delinquent friends. The Study males were growing up in a time period when men and women who wanted to live together usually got married. The effects of marriage were initially studied by following both convictions and self-reported offending before and after early marriages (up to age 22). While the numbers were small, there was some suggestion that marriage led to a decrease in offending during the following two years, but only for offenders who married unconvicted women. Those who married convicted women continued to offend at the same rate after marriage as matched unmarried offenders (West, 1982). Similarly, the men's fathers who married convicted women incurred more convictions after marriage than those who married unconvicted women, irrespective of their own conviction records before marriage.

A more detailed study of marriage up to age 32 (Farrington & West, 1995) showed that, while convicted offenders were no more or less likely than nonoffenders to get married, offenders were more likely to separate from their wife and to conceive a child while unmarried. Regression analyses showed that separation from a wife predicted later self-reported and official offending (between ages 27 and 32) independently of all other variables, while an enduring marriage was negatively related to offending and seemed to act as a protective factor. Before-and-after matching analyses showed that getting married led to a decrease in conviction rates compared with remaining single (irrespective of whether a man married a convicted or unconvicted woman), whereas separation from a wife led to an increase in conviction rates compared with staying married. These results are concordant with those reported by Sampson and Laub (1993) in Massachusetts.

Protective Factors

Many of the findings of this survey are probably not surprising to people who work with offenders. Often, people are less interested in the continuity in offending and antisocial behavior than in discontinuity. For example, why do some boys from criminogenic backgrounds nevertheless become successful nonoffenders, and why do some boys from favorable backgrounds nevertheless become antisocial offenders? We investigated good boys from bad backgrounds and searched for protective factors against delinquency.

About one sixth of the boys (63) were identified as vulnerable at age 8–10, because they scored at least three out of five on the "vulnerability" measure discussed earlier. Three quarters of these vulnerable males were convicted of criminal offenses up to age 32, and the vulnerable males were also likely to be identified as having adult social dysfunction at age 32 on the combined measure of living circumstances and behavior. We investigated whether the unconvicted quarter of these boys were affected by any protective factors that might have helped them to achieve successful life outcomes (Farrington et al., 1988b).

Our earlier research suggested that being nervous and withdrawn might act as a protective factor in insulating vulnerable boys against juvenile delinquency (West & Farrington, 1973). Similar tendencies were apparent in the latest analyses up to age 32, but the effects were relatively weak. The most important results were that boys with few or no friends at age 8, and those without convicted parents or behavior problem siblings at age 10, tended to remain unconvicted; and that boys who were rated favorably by their mothers at age 10 tended to be leading relatively successful lives at age 32. Of course, it may be that the mothers accurately perceived who were the good boys at age 10, rather than that an approving mother had a positive effect on a boy's self-concept. There was some evidence that shyness acted as a protective factor for nonaggressive boys and as an aggravating factor for aggressive boys.

One problem with these analyses was that the unconvicted boys at age 32 were not necessarily leading the most successful lives. We studied the characteristics of unconvicted vulnerable men, convicted vulnerable men, unconvicted nonvulnerable men, and convicted nonvulnerable men at age 32 (Farrington, Gallagher, Morley, St. Ledger, & West, 1988a). Surprisingly, the unconvicted vulnerable men were often the most unsuccessful, for example in not being home owners, in living in dirty home conditions, in having large debts, and in having low status, lowly paid jobs. They were also the most likely of these four groups to have never married, to have no wife or cohabitee, and to be living alone. Also, they were the most likely to be in conflict with their parents. However, they were generally well-behaved, for example in not taking drugs other than marijuana and in being least likely to commit offenses. Their good behavior may be connected with the fact they were also the most likely to stay in every night.

The search for protective factors often involves the search for interaction effects, for example where a risk factor X predicts offending in the absence of a protective factor Y but not in the presence of a protective factor Y. Interaction effects of various types were reviewed and classified by Farrington (1997b). For example, the most significant interaction effect in predicting early convictions (at age 10–14) was between low family income and separation from a parent: boys who were both separated and from low income families had relatively low conviction rates, compared with boys who were separated only or boys from low income families only. This interaction effect, like others, was significantly predictive independently of all main effects (Farrington, 1994c).

Explaining the Development of Delinquency

As mentioned, many attempts were made to test hypotheses about intervening causal mechanisms and processes between risk factors and offending, as in the analysis of disrupted families by Juby and Farrington (2001), for example.

Also, some attempts were made to test larger theories in specific analyses, such as in the tests of labelling theory by Farrington (1977) and Farrington et al. (1978). However, there was also an attempt to propose a larger all-embracing theory that might explain most of the main findings on criminal careers and risk factors for offending.

There is far more agreement about risk factors than about their theoretical interpretation. The major risk factors for offending include poverty, poor housing, and living in public housing in inner city, socially disorganized communities (Farrington, 1999a, 2001b). They also include poor parental child-rearing techniques, such as poor supervision, harsh or erratic discipline, parental conflict, and separation from a biological parent. They also include impulsivity and low intelligence or attainment (which may reflect a poor ability to manipulate abstract concepts and deficits in the "executive functions" of the brain). It seems likely that communities influence parenting, and that parenting influences the development of impulsivity and low intelligence, which in turn are conducive to offending (Farrington, 1993b).

Other risk factors may be linked to poverty, poor parenting, impulsivity, or intelligence. For example, teenage mothers tend to live in poverty, with poor housing, unemployed fathers, poor parental supervision, and large families, and tend to have impulsive children (Morash & Rucker, 1989; Nagin, Pogarsky, & Farrington, 1997). Large family size may lead to poor parenting, because of the problem of dividing attention between several children at once. Convicted parents may be poor supervisors of children and disproportionally separated from their spouses, or alternatively there may be genetic transmission of a biological factor linked to offending (Rowe, 1994). The links between delinquent friends, delinquent schools, and offending are less clear, but may involve learning from deviant models. It is also likely that the occurrence of offenses depends on situational factors such as perceived costs, benefits, and opportunities (Clarke & Cornish, 1985).

As mentioned, it is important to establish which factors predict offending independently of other factors. Based on the independent predictors in the Cambridge Study, it might be suggested that impulsivity, low intelligence or attainment, poor parenting, an antisocial family, and poverty, despite their interrelations, all contribute in some way to the development of offending. In addition, of course, there is significant continuity in offending and antisocial behavior from childhood to adulthood, even though the prevalence of offending peaks in the teenage years. Any theory needs to give priority to explaining these results.

The Farrington Theory

The theory I have developed (Farrington, 1986b, 1992b, 1996c, 1998) was designed to explain offending and antisocial behavior by working-class males.

It distinguishes explicitly between the long-term development of antisocial tendency and the immediate occurrence of offenses and other antisocial acts (Figure 1). The long-term level of antisocial tendency depends on long-term risk factors and on energizing, directing, and inhibiting processes. The occurrence of offenses and other antisocial acts depends on the interaction between the individual (with a certain degree of antisocial tendency) and the social environment, and on a decision-making process in criminal opportunities.

It is proposed that the main energizing factors that ultimately lead to long-term, between-individual variations in antisocial tendency are desires for material

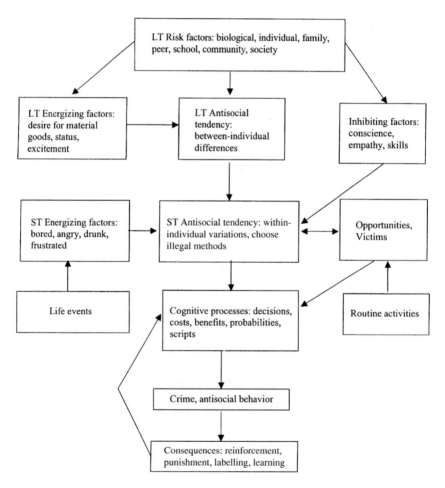

Figure 1. The Farrington Theory.

goods, status among intimates, and excitement. Risk factors influence both long-term antisocial tendency and these desires. For example, the desire for excitement may be greater among children from poorer families, perhaps because excitement is more highly valued by lower-class people than by middle-class ones, because poorer children think they lead more boring lives, or because poorer children are less able to postpone immediate gratification in favor of long-term goals (which could be linked to the emphasis in lower-class culture on the concrete and present as opposed to the abstract and future). The main energizing factors that lead to short-term, within-individual variations in antisocial tendency are boredom, frustration, anger, and alcohol consumption, which are influenced by life events.

In the directing stage, these motivations lead to an increase in antisocial tendency if socially disapproved methods of satisfying them are habitually chosen. The methods chosen depend on maturation and behavioral skills; for example, a five-year-old would have difficulty stealing a car. They also depend on risk factors. Some people (e.g., children from poorer families) are less able to satisfy their desires for material goods, excitement, and social status by legal or socially approved methods, and so tend to choose illegal or socially disapproved methods. The relative inability of poorer children to achieve their goals by legitimate methods could be because they tend to fail in school and tend to have erratic, low status employment histories. School failure in turn may often be a consequence of the less stimulating intellectual environment that lower-class parents tend to provide for their children, and their lack of emphasis on abstract concepts.

In the inhibiting stage, antisocial tendencies can be reduced by internalized beliefs and attitudes that have been built up in a social learning process as a result of a history of rewards and punishments. The belief that offending is wrong, or a strong conscience, tends to be built up if parents are in favor of legal norms, if they exercise close supervision over their children, and if they punish socially disapproved behavior using love-oriented discipline. Antisocial tendency can also be inhibited by empathy, which may develop as a result of parental warmth and loving relationships. There are individual differences in the development of these internal inhibitions. Perhaps because of associated neurological dysfunctions, children with high impulsivity and low intelligence are less able to build up internal inhibitions against offending, and therefore tend to have a high level of antisocial tendency.

The decision-making stage specifies how the individual interacts with the environment to commit crimes and other antisocial acts. In general, crimes require opportunities and victims, and these are influenced by routine activities. Encountering a tempting opportunity may cause a short-term increase in antisocial tendency, just as a short-term increase in antisocial tendency may motivate a person to seek out a criminal opportunity. Whether a person with a certain degree of antisocial tendency commits an antisocial act in a given situation depends on cognitive processes, including considering the costs, benefits, and probabilities of the different outcomes and stored behavioral repertoires or scripts. The costs and benefits include immediate situational factors such as the material goods that can be stolen and the likelihood and consequences of being caught by the police, as perceived by the individual. They also include social factors such as likely disapproval by parents or spouses and encouragement or reinforcement from peers. In general, people tend to make rational decisions. However, more impulsive people are less likely to consider the possible consequences of their actions, especially consequences that are likely to be long delayed.

The consequences of offending may, as a result of a learning process, lead to changes in antisocial tendency or in the cost-benefit calculation. This is especially likely if the consequences are reinforcing (e.g., gaining material goods or peer approval) or punishing (e.g., legal sanctions or parental disapproval). Also, if the consequences involve labelling or stigmatizing the offender, this may make it more difficult for him to achieve his aims legally, and hence there may be an increase in his antisocial tendency. In other words, events that occur after offending may lead to changes in energizing, directing, inhibiting, or decision-making processes in a dynamic system.

Applying the theory to explain some of the results reviewed here, children from poorer families may be likely to offend because they are less able to achieve their goals legally and because they value some goals (e.g, excitement) especially highly. Children with low intelligence may be more likely to offend because they tend to fail in school and hence cannot achieve their goals legally. Impulsive children, and those with a poor ability to manipulate abstract concepts, may be more likely to offend because they do not give sufficient consideration and weight to the possible consequences of offending. Also, children with low intelligence and high impulsivity are less able to build up internal inhibitions against offending.

Children who are exposed to poor parental child rearing behavior, disharmony, or separation may be more likely to offend because they do not build up internal inhibitions against socially disapproved behavior, while children from criminal families and those with delinquent friends tend to build up anti-establishment attitudes and the belief that offending is justifiable. The whole process is self-perpetuating in that poverty, low intelligence, and early school failure lead to truancy and a lack of educational qualifications, which in turn lead to low status jobs and periods of unemployment, both of which make it harder to achieve goals legitimately.

Other Issues

Limitations of the Study

The Cambridge Study provides information about the development of offending and antisocial behavior in an inner-city, working-class British White male sample born about 1953. How far the same results would be obtained with females, Black or Asian children, suburban or rural children, middle or upper class children, children born more recently, or children born in other countries are interesting empirical questions. Generally, results obtained with the Cambridge Study are similar to those obtained with comparable male samples from Sweden (Farrington & Wikström, 1994), Finland (Pulkkinen, 1988) and from other Western industrialized countries, but more replications would be desirable. In particular, new longitudinal studies should be mounted in England, to investigate the effect of social changes such as the increased number of single-parent families and delinquent development in different ethnic groups. No new English studies on the development of delinquency have been mounted for many years (although one began in the 1990s in Scotland).

The Cambridge Study has the usual methodological problems of longitudinal surveys. While the problem of attrition was largely overcome, the problem of testing effects (the effects on the subjects of repeated interviews) was not investigated. In retrospect, other boys from the same schools, who were not interviewed, should have been followed up in records to control for testing effects, but this was not a feature of the initial design (Farrington & West, 1981). More frequent data collection would have allowed better tracing of individual development over time, but, on the other hand, the gaps between data collection efforts gave time to analyze the data and write up the results.

Inevitably, some of the initial measures now appear rather old-fashioned. For example, the method of measuring parenting variables (relying on psychiatric social workers interviewing parents) caused problems, and great efforts had to be made to try to achieve consistency and objectivity. No pilot work was carried out at the beginning of the Study, because of the pressure to begin data collection as soon as possible. While the main aim was to measure all relevant variables, the measurements of biological and neighborhood variables were clearly inadequate, and the measurement of individual factors also left a lot to be desired in retrospect. It is unfortunately not possible in the Cambridge Study to investigate the interaction between individual development and neighborhood context.

Because we did not include a behavior-genetic design (e.g., studying twins or adopted children), we cannot investigate how much of the link between poor parenting and behavior was mediated by genetic factors. Because of the focus on English personality questionnaires, key constructs such as empathy, egocentricity, guilt, and depression were not measured. The attempts to study protective factors may have been inadequate, because far more was known about risk factors, and hence the measurement and analyses focused on risk factors. There should have been more emphasis on resilience, strengths, and successful outcomes of disadvantaged males.

Validity checks were made where possible to compare interview data with external information from records. For example, admissions of convictions were compared with criminal records of convictions, and the mother's report of the boy's birth weight was compared with hospital records. Reliability checks were also made. For example, information about the same topic (e.g., school leaving age) from different interviews was compared, as was information about the same topic from different parts of the same interview. Generally, the men were randomly allocated between our two or three interviewers in each wave in order to study interviewer effects, but fortunately these were rare. Sometimes, information could be tested for predictive validity, and the self-reported delinquency tests have already been mentioned. As another example, more than twice as many of those who said that they had sexual intercourse without using contraceptives at age 18 subsequently conceived a child outside marriage as of the remainder (Farrington & West, 1995). All of these checks suggested that our males were genuinely trying to tell the truth. Of course, more validity checks would have been desirable, but these would have required more types of external records than we could obtain.

The sample was too small to study rare events, such as sex offenders or perinatal complications, effectively. The interviews were too infrequent to establish the exact or relative timing of many life events, and hence to establish developmental sequences between presumed causes and observed effects. The lack of experimental interventions made it difficult to test causal models effectively. The single cohort design made it difficult to distinguish between aging and period effects; for example, between ages 14 and 18 the percentage who had taken drugs increased from less than 1% to 31%, but this was probably a function of the time period (from 1967 to 1971).

In order to overcome these kinds of problems, it would be highly desirable in future longitudinal studies of delinquency to include multiple age cohorts and experimental interventions, to begin prenatally with one cohort, and to have more frequent interviews and larger samples (Farrington, 1991c; Farrington, Ohlin, & Wilson, 1986b; Tonry, Ohlin, & Farrington, 1991). This kind of design has actually been implemented in Chicago (Harvard University, 2000). However, because ideal designs cost a great deal of money, more limited compromise designs like the Cambridge Study are likely to predominate in the foreseeable future (see Endnote).

Policy Implications

The main policy implications of the Cambridge Study are relevant to risk assessment and risk-focused prevention. Risk assessment tools such as the EARL-20B (Augimeri, Webster, Koegl, & Levene, 1998), which aims to identify children who are at risk of reoffending, are based on longitudinal surveys that have discovered the most important risk factors for offending. As mentioned, the predictive efficiency of various risk scores has been investigated in the Cambridge

Study (e.g., Farrington, 2000a, 2001a, 2002). While risk assessment and risk-focused prevention are relevant to the onset and persistence of offending, the Cambridge Study also has policy implications for desistance (e.g., in showing the beneficial effects of employment, marriage, and moving house).

Risk-focused prevention suggests that, in order to reduce offending, the key risk factors should be identified and programs should be implemented to tackle these risk factors (Farrington, 2001b; Hawkins & Catalano, 1992; Loeber & Farrington, 1998, 2001). Based on the Cambridge Study, it might be suggested that early prevention experiments are especially needed that target four important risk factors: low intelligence/attainment, poor parental child-rearing behavior, impulsivity, and poverty (Farrington, 1990b, 1994b, 2000a). To the extent that these experiments lead to reductions in offending, this will increase our confidence that these risk factors have causal effects or are part of causal chains leading to offending (Robins, 1992).

It is difficult to know how and when it is best to intervene, because of the lack of knowledge about developmental sequences, ages at which causal factors are most salient, and influences on onset, persistence, and desistance. For example, if truancy leads to delinquency in a developmental sequence, intervening successfully to decrease truancy should lead to a decrease in delinquency. On the other hand, if truancy and delinquency are merely different behavioral manifestations of the same underlying construct, tackling one symptom would not necessarily change the underlying construct. Experiments are useful in distinguishing between developmental sequences and symptoms, and indeed, Berg, Hullin, and McGuire (1979) found experimentally that decreases in truancy were followed by decreases in delinquency.

There is not space here to review effective intervention programs. Briefly, low intelligence and attainment can be targeted in preschool intellectual enrichment programs such as the Perry study (Schweinhart, Barnes, & Weikart, 1993). Poor parental child-rearing behavior can be targeted in general parent education programs in pregnancy and the first few years of life of the child (e.g., Olds et al., 1998) or in more specific parent management training programs (e.g., Patterson, 1982). Impulsivity can be targeted in cognitive-behavioral skills training programs (e.g., Ross & Ross, 1995). Poverty has been targeted in income maintenance experiments, but there is no evidence of any effect on children's delinquency (e.g., Groeneveld, Short, & Thoits, 1979). Combined programs that target several risk factors, using both parent training and child skills training for example, are often the most effective (Hawkins, Catalano, Kosterman, Abbott, & Hill, 1999; Tremblay, Pagani-Kurtz, Masse, Vitaro, & Pihl, 1995; Wasserman & Miller, 1998).

The Cambridge Study has influenced the thinking of the British government about crime policy. Certainly, between 1990 and 1992, it influenced Home Secretary Kenneth Baker and his junior minister John Patten, who drafted a Green Paper on early prevention in 1992 that drew on the Study's conclusions. In 1989, John Patten stated that:

> This important study has been influential both in this country and in the United States. It bears out much of the Home Office's current thinking about juvenile crime. It is an excellent example of how academic work, funded by government, can help in policy-making. I will be examining Dr. Farrington's conclusions, and their pointers toward future action, very fully indeed. (Rock, 1994, p. 153)

In documenting the development of early prevention ideas in the Home Office in 1990–92, Rock (1994) reported that:

> There was one article [Farrington & West, 1990] that circulated about the [Home] Office at just that time, an article that had again made out the case for using longitudinal studies to predict and control delinquency, and for social prevention experiments to prevent the development of crime and anti-social behaviour... An official remarked of Farrington's influence: "There is a theory for a particular time and maybe what he is saying is just one of the things that particularly suit at the moment." (p. 150)

From 1997 onwards, the new Labour government became more enthusiastic about risk-focused prevention, and it has been implemented in numerous places by the Rowntree Foundation in its "Communities That Care" program (Farrington, 1996c; Communities That Care, 1997). Especially taking account of more than 120 publications on the Cambridge Study, I would argue that the benefits of this project in advancing knowledge have greatly outweighed its costs.

Current Research and Future Plans

The males are now (in 2000–02) being given a social interview at about age 46 to assess their current and recent self-reported offending and their current success in different aspects of their lives (accommodation, employment, debts, illnesses and injuries, relationships, children, drinking, smoking, drug use, aggressive behavior and attitudes, and current personality). Questions are also asked about the use of health and social services, to permit an economic analysis of costs to society, and about problems of the men's children such as lying, stealing, truancy, disobedience, bullying, and restlessness. Many of the questions to the males are the same as those given at ages 18 and 32; the same attitude questionnaire is being given at ages 18, 32, and 46. The General Health Questionnaire is given at ages 32 and 46, and the Eysenck Personality Inventory at ages 16 and 46. The "Big Five" Personality Inventory is given at age 46.

The men are also being given a medical interview (using the Structural Clinical Interview for DSM (SCID)) to assess their current mental health and their life-time history of psychiatric disorders. Questions in both interviews, together with file data, make it possible to score each man on the Psychopathy Checklist. At the end of the medical interview, biological data are collected; saliva to measure testosterone, height, weight, waist circumference, pulse rate, blood pressure, and respiratory function. Questions on physical health and illnesses are also included, and medical records are being collected.

In addition, the men's female partners are being personally interviewed to collect information on household income, children, her child-rearing attitudes, relationships with the man, family violence, her physical and mental health, her antisocial behavior (including debts, offending, drinking and drug use), his antisocial behavior, his personality (on the "Big Five" Inventory), characteristics of the neighborhood, and household victimization. At age 46, the partner completes the same General Health Questionnaire as the man, and the same child-rearing attitude questionnaire as his partner completed at his age 32 and his mother completed when he was age 12.

The current follow-up project is very much a collaborative effort, directed by a steering committee consisting of myself (Chair), Jeremy Coid, John Gunn, Clive Meux, Terri Moffitt, and Donald West. The main aims are to investigate offending in the mid-40s, characteristics of late-onset offenders, and how far men who have stopped getting convicted are still involved in antisocial behavior. In addition, the social interview will establish how former juvenile delinquents, and former chronic offenders, are living successful lives in their 40s, in such areas as accommodation, employment, relationships, drinking, smoking, and drug use, so that protective factors can be studied. The medical interview will establish the relationship between offending and adult mental health problems, including antisocial personality disorder. The partner interview will establish the prevalence of different types of family violence and how far it can be predicted by risk factors in childhood and adolescence.

Regarding future data collection plans, it is hoped to obtain funding to interview up to 500 children of the Study males aged 13–30 in 2002–04. This Third Generation Follow-up would establish how far risk factors discovered years ago are still important in modern times and how far the relative importance of risk factors has changed. It would also provide unique data on the transmission of offending, antisocial behavior, and mental health problems between three generations, and also on why children from criminal families are particularly at risk of offending themselves. Perhaps even more important, the new project would suggest reasons why children from criminogenic backgrounds do not become offenders.

Because of the extensive data on the Study males, the Third Generation Follow-Up would provide detailed information about the importance of the father in relation to child offending and antisocial behavior. Many studies of family factors focus on the mother and neglect the father, because fathers are often more elusive than mothers. Also, the new project would make it possible to compare risk factors for offending and antisocial behavior for male children with those for female children. It is important to know whether the risk factors for offending are similar or different for males and females (see Moffitt, Caspi, Rutter, & Silva, 2001).

As indicated, there are many planned analyses, including studies of the development of and risk factors for alcohol and drug use. Currently, one fruitful collaboration is with Carolyn Smith in investigating parental child rearing versus child antisocial behavior in two successive generations. High priority analyses for the future include a more extensive analysis of the onset, frequency, and desistance of self-reported offending up to age 32, in comparison with convictions; and a study of the financial costs of offending. It would also be desirable to investigate late-comers to crime and to do more research on protective factors and on successful men from deprived backgrounds.

Conclusion

The Cambridge Study shows that the types of acts that lead to convictions (principally, crimes of dishonesty) are components of a larger syndrome of antisocial behavior. Generally, working class males are versatile rather than specialized in their offending and antisocial behavior. The high degree of continuity between ages 18 and 32, during a period of enormous environmental change, suggests that stability lies in the individual rather than in the environment. Our conclusion is that there are individual differences between people in some general underlying theoretical construct which might be termed "antisocial tendency," which is relatively stable from childhood to adulthood.

Importantly, there is relative stability but absolute change in antisocial behavior. Offending may increase or decrease over time, but the worst offenders at one age still tend to be the worst at another age. While the relative position of individuals on this underlying dimension is sufficiently stable to allow significant prediction from age 8 to age 32, the stability should not be exaggerated. Significant predictability does not mean that outcomes are inevitable or that people cannot and do not change. The good news is that most juvenile delinquents were leading quite successful lives by age 32.

The Cambridge Study also shows how far self-reported and official offending can be predicted in advance, in childhood. Previous projects did not measure such a wide range of theoretical constructs in advance of offending, and so they were not able to show so effectively which variables predicted offending independently of others or the relative importance of different variables. The most important independent childhood predictors of offending in this research could be grouped under the headings of antisocial child behavior, impulsivity, low intelligence or attainment, family criminality, poverty, and poor parental child-rearing behavior. Many of these findings have been replicated in other countries.

The Study also shows how far convicted offenders and unconvicted males were significantly different in numerous respects before, during, and after their criminal careers. Furthermore, differences between convicted offenders and unconvicted males were similar to differences between high and low self-reported delinquents, where boys in the high category were more frequent, serious, and versatile offenders. Previously, it has been argued that everyone committed offenses and that differences between convicted and unconvicted males largely reflected police or court biases, but this view can be firmly rejected. The concordance between official records and self-reports, and the ability of self-reports to predict future convictions, shows that both measures are validly detecting the worst offenders.

The Study provides detailed information about criminal careers and co-offending and shows how far offending is concentrated in certain persons and certain families. The study of conviction careers of fathers and mothers shows that offending is more persistent than previously believed. A small number of chronic offenders, usually coming from multiproblem families, accounted for substantial proportions of all official and self-reported offenses, and they were to a considerable extent predictable in advance. The fact that a large proportion of the crime problem is attributable to a small number of persons and families who are identifiable is potentially good news for prevention and treatment.

The Study also shows the importance of within-individual analyses, in documenting the effects of life events on the course of development of offending. In particular, it provides perhaps the most detailed quantitative information about factors influencing desistance: being employed as opposed to unemployed, getting married and staying married, and moving out of London. It also shows that desistance from offending generally coincides with an improvement in other life circumstances.

The main policy implication of the Cambridge Study is that, in order to reduce offending and antisocial behavior, early prevention experiments are needed targeting four important predictors that may be both causal and modifiable: low achievement, poor parental child-rearing behavior, impulsivity, and poverty. Because of the link between offending and numerous other social problems, any measure that succeeds in reducing crime will probably have benefits that go far beyond this. Early prevention that reduces offending would probably also reduce drinking, drunk driving, drug use, sexual promiscuity, and family violence, and perhaps also school failure, unemployment, and marital disharmony.

Social problems are undoubtedly influenced by environmental as well as individual factors. However, to the extent that all of these problems reflect an underlying antisocial tendency, they could all decrease together. It is clear from our research that antisocial children tend to grow up into antisocial adults, and that antisocial adults tend to produce antisocial children. Major intervention efforts, firmly grounded on empirical research results, such as those obtained in the Cambridge Study, need to be made to break this cycle.

Endnote

I am very grateful to the Home Office and the Department of Health for funding the Cambridge Study intermittently since 1961. However, the Study has never had the generous level of funding enjoyed by major American longitudinal surveys, and neither has it ever had a guarantee of continued funding for more than three years at a time. In general, funds have been provided only for data collection, not for data analysis. This has meant that, certainly in the last 20 years, the main burden of directing the study and doing most of the data manipulation and analysis has fallen on me. There are advantages in the principal investigator having intimate day-to-day contact with the data collection effort and doing most of the analyses himself, but there are obvious limitations on what one person can achieve.

It is easier to plan analyses than to carry them out, and of course it takes even longer to shepherd papers through the typically tortuous process of publication in major journals. Several years ago, I developed a master plan of desirable analyses, and I keep a careful record of all analyses completed and of the contents of all publications, which is necessary in order to write summary chapters like this one. However, the data has never been exploited to study less central topics such as the development of and risk factors for smoking, drinking, drug use, and sexual behavior, for example. In Great Britain, we have not generally had the tradition of Ph.D. students working with a professor on data collected in a major study. Rather, the British Ph.D. student typically designs his or her own study and single-handedly carries it through all the stages from conception to completion, including data collection, analysis, and writing up. Not surprisingly, British Ph.D. theses in criminology tend to be small-scale, cross-sectional surveys of no more than 200 persons.

Of course, one way of increasing the number of publications from a Study is to collaborate with other researchers, and I have enjoyed many collaborations. Another way is to deposit data in a data archive, and anonymized Cambridge Study data from age 8 to age 25 were deposited in the University of Michigan ICPSR archive in 1984, and later in the University of Essex data archive in England. While this has stimulated wider use of the data (e.g., Hagan, 1993; Hagan & Palloni, 1990; Paternoster & Brame, 1998; Polakowski, 1994), one disadvantage is that data users rarely contact the principal investigator, except when they want more data. Hence, it is largely a matter of chance whether the principal investigator finds out about publications based on the data, and there is no communication in practice about how the data are being used.

ACKNOWLEDGEMENTS. I am very grateful to Professor Donald West for his comments and for his inspiring work on the Cambridge Study. I am also grateful to Marvin Krohn, Chris Lewis, and Patrick Collier for helpful comments on an earlier draft. I am indebted to the Home Office and the Department of Health for continued financial support of this project and to Maureen Brown for her speedy and accurate typing of this chapter.

References

Amdur, R. L. (1989). Testing causal models of delinquency: A methodological critique. *Criminal Justice and Behavior, 16*, 35–62.

Augimeri, L. K., Webster, C. D., Koegl, C. J., & Levene, K. S. (1998). *Early assessment risk list for boys (EARL-20B)*. Toronto, Canada: Earlscourt Child and Family Centre.

Barnett, A., Blumstein, A., & Farrington, D. P. (1987). Probabilistic models of youthful criminal careers. *Criminology, 25*, 83–107.

Barnett, A., Blumstein, A., & Farrington, D. P. (1989). A prospective test of a criminal career model. *Criminology, 27*, 373–388.

Berg, I., Hullin, R., & McGuire, R. (1979). A randomly controlled trial of two court procedures in truancy. In D. P. Farrington, K. Hawkins & L. Lloyd-Bostock (Eds.), *Psychology, law and legal processes* (pp. 143–51). London: MacMillan.

Blumstein, A., Farrington, D. P., & Moitra, S. (1985). Delinquency careers: Innocents, desistors and persisters. In M. Tonry & N. Morris (Eds.), *Crime and justice* (Vol. 6, pp. 187–219). Chicago: University of Chicago Press.

Bools, C., Foster, J., Brown, J., & Berg, I. (1990). The identification of psychiatric disorders in children who fail to attend school: A cluster analysis of a nonclinical population. *Psychological Medicine, 20*, 171–181.

Capaldi, D. M., & Patterson, G. R. (1987). An approach to the problem of recruitment and retention rates for longitudinal research. *Behavioral Assessment, 9*, 169–177.

Capaldi, D. M., & Patterson, G. R. (1996). Can violent offenders be distinguished from frequent offenders? Prediction from childhood to adolescence. *Journal of Research in Crime and Delinquency, 33*, 206–31.

Clarke, R. V., & Cornish. D. B. (1985), Modelling offenders' decisions: A framework for research and policy. In M. Tonry & N. Morris (Eds.), *Crime and justice* (Vol. 6, pp. 147–85). Chicago: University of Chicago Press.

Communities That Care (1997). *Communities that Care (UK): A new kind of prevention program.* London: Communities that Care (UK).

Elliott, D. S., Huizinga, D., & Ageton, S. S. (1985). *Explaining delinquency and drug use.* Beverly Hills, CA: Sage.

Eron, L. D., & Huesmann, L. R. (1990). The stability of aggressive behavior—even unto the third generation. In M. Lewis & S. M. Miller (Eds.), *Handbook of developmental psychopathology* (pp. 147–156). New York: Plenum.

Farrington, D. P. (1972). Delinquency begins at home. *New Society, 21*, 495–497.

Farrington, D. P. (1973). Self-reports of deviant behavior: Predictive and stable? *Journal of Criminal Law and Criminology, 64*, 99–110.

Farrington, D. P. (1977). The effects of public labelling. *British Journal of Criminology, 17*, 122–135.

Farrington, D. P. (1978). The family backgrounds of aggressive youths. In L. Hersov, M. Berger & D. Shaffer (Eds.), *Aggression and antisocial behavior in childhood and adolescence* (pp. 73–93). Oxford: Pergamon.

Farrington, D. P. (1980). Truancy, delinquency, the home and the school. In L. Hersov & I. Berg (Eds.), *Out of school* (pp. 49–63). Chichester: Wiley.

Farrington, D. P. (1985). Predicting self-reported and official delinquency. In D. P. Farrington & R. Tarling (Eds.), *Prediction in criminology* (pp. 150–173). Albany, NY: State University of New York Press.

Farrington, D. P. (1986a). Age and crime. In M. Tonry & N. Morris (Eds.), *Crime and justice* (Vol. 7, pp. 189–250). Chicago: University of Chicago Press.

Farrington, D. P. (1986b). Stepping stones to adult criminal careers. In D. Olweus, J. Block & M. R. Yarrow (Eds.), *Development of antisocial and prosocial behavior* (pp. 359–384). New York: Academic Press.

Farrington, D. P. (1988). Studying changes within individuals: The causes of offending. In M. Rutter (Ed.), *Studies of psychosocial risk* (pp. 158–183). Cambridge: Cambridge University Press.

Farrington, D. P. (1989a). Early predictors of adolescent aggression and adult violence. *Violence and Victims, 4*, 79–100.

Farrington, D. P. (1989b). Later adult life outcomes of offenders and non-offenders. In M. Brambring, F. Losel & H. Skowronek (Eds.), *Children at risk: Assessment, longitudinal research, and intervention* (pp. 220–244). Berlin: De Gruyter.

Farrington, D. P. (1989c). Self-reported and official offending from adolescence to adulthood. In M. W. Klein (Ed.), *Cross-national research in self-reported crime and delinquency* (pp. 399–423). Dordrecht, Netherlands: Kluwer.

Farrington, D. P. (1990a). Age, period, cohort, and offending. In D. M. Gottfredson & R. V. Clarke (Eds.), *Policy and theory in criminal justice* (pp. 51–75). Aldershot, England: Gower.

Farrington, D. P. (1990b). Implications of criminal career research for the prevention of offending. *Journal of Adolescence, 13*, 93–113.

Farrington, D. P. (1991a). Antisocial personality from childhood to adulthood. *The Psychologist, 4*, 389–394.

Farrington, D. P. (1991b). Childhood aggression and adult violence: Early precursors and later life outcomes. In D. J. Pepler & K. H. Rubin (Eds.), *The development and treatment of childhood aggression* (pp. 5–29). Hillsdale, NJ: Lawrence Erlbaum.

Farrington, D. P. (1991c). Longitudinal research strategies: Advantages, problems and prospects. *Journal of the American Academy of Child and Adolescent Psychiatry, 30*, 369–374.

Farrington, D. P. (1992a). Criminal career research in the United Kingdom. *British Journal of Criminology, 32*, 521–536.

Farrington, D. P. (1992b). Explaining the beginning, progress and ending of antisocial behavior from birth to adulthood. In J. McCord (Ed.), *Advances in criminological theory: Vol. 3. Facts, frameworks and forecasts* (pp. 253–286). New Brunswick, NJ: Transaction.

Farrington, D. P. (1992c). Juvenile delinquency. In J. C. Coleman (Ed.), *The school years* (2nd ed., pp. 123–163). London: Routledge.

Farrington, D. P. (1993a). Childhood origins of teenage antisocial behavior and adult social dysfunction. *Journal of the Royal Society of Medicine, 86*, 13–17.

Farrington, D. P. (1993b). Have any individual, family or neighborhood influences on offending been demonstrated conclusively? In D. P. Farrington, R. J. Sampson & P-O. Wikström (Eds.), *Integrating individual and ecological aspects of crime* (pp. 3–37). Stockholm: National Council for Crime Prevention.

Farrington, D. P. (1993c). Motivations for conduct disorder and delinquency. *Development and Psychopathology, 5*, 225–241.

Farrington, D. P. (1993d). Understanding and preventing bullying. In M. Tonry (Ed.), *Crime and justice* (Vol. 17, pp. 381–458). Chicago: University of Chicago Press.

Farrington, D. P. (1994a). Childhood, adolescent and adult features of violent males. In L. R. Huesmann (Ed.), *Aggressive behavior: Current perspectives* (pp. 215–240). New York: Plenum.

Farrington, D. P. (1994b). Early developmental prevention of juvenile delinquency. *Criminal Behavior and Mental Health, 4*, 209–227.

Farrington, D P. (1994c). Interactions between individual and contextual factors in the development of offending. In R. K. Silbereisen & E. Todt (Eds.), *Adolescence in context* (pp. 366–389). New York: Springer-Verlag.

Farrington, D. P. (1995a). Crime and physical health: Illnesses, injuries, accidents and offending in the Cambridge Study. *Criminal Behavior and Mental Health, 5,* 261–278.

Farrington, D. P. (1995b). The development of offending and antisocial behavior from childhood: Key findings from the Cambridge Study in Delinquent Development. *Journal of Child Psychology and Psychiatry, 36,* 929–964.

Farrington, D. P. (1996a). Later life outcomes of truants in the Cambridge Study. In I. Berg & J. Nursten (Eds.), *Unwilling to school* (4th ed., pp. 96–118). London: Gaskell.

Farrington, D. P. (1996b). Psychosocial influences on the development of antisocial personality. In G. Davies, S. Lloyd-Bostock, M. McMurran & C. Wilson (Eds.), *Psychology, law and criminal justice: International developments in research and practice* (pp. 424–444). Berlin: de Gruyter.

Farrington, D. P. (1996c). *Understanding and preventing youth crime.* York, England: Joseph Rowntree Foundation.

Farrington, D. P. (1997a). Early prediction of violent and nonviolent youthful offending. *European Journal on Criminal Policy and Research, 5*(2), 51–66.

Farrington, D. P. (1997b). Key issues in studying the biosocial bases of violence. In A. Raine, P. A. Brennan, D. P. Farrington & S. A. Mednick (Eds.), *Biosocial bases of violence* (pp. 293–300). New York: Plenum.

Farrington, D. P. (1997c). The relationship between low resting heart rate and violence. In A. Raine, P. A. Brennan, D. P. Farrington & S. A. Mednick (Eds.), *Biosocial bases of violence* (pp. 89–105). New York: Plenum.

Farrington, D. P. (1998). Predictors, causes and correlates of male youth violence. In M. Tonry & M. H. Moore (Eds.), *Youth violence* (pp. 421–475). Chicago: University of Chicago Press.

Farrington, D. P. (1999a). Conduct disorder and delinquency. In H.-C. Steinhausen & F. C. Verhulst (Eds.), *Risk and outcomes in developmental psychopathology* (pp. 165–192). Oxford: Oxford University Press.

Farrington, D. P. (1999b). Predicting persistent young offenders. In G. L. McDowell & J. S. Smith (Eds.), *Juvenile delinquency in the United States and the United Kingdom* (pp. 3–21). London: Macmillan.

Farrington, D. P. (2000a). Adolescent violence: Findings and implications from the Cambridge Study. In G. Boswell (Ed.), *Violent children and adolescents* (pp. 19–35). London: Whurr.

Farrington, D. P. (2000b). Psychosocial predictors of adult antisocial personality and adult convictions. *Behavioral Sciences and the Law, 18,* 605–622.

Farrington, D. P. (2001a). Predicting adult official and self-reported violence. In G.-F. Pinard & L. Pagani (Eds.), *Clinical assessment of dangerousness* (pp. 66–88). Cambridge: Cambridge University Press.

Farrington, D. P. (2001b). The causes and prevention of violence. In J. Shepherd (Ed.), *Violence in health care* (2nd ed., pp. 1–27). Oxford: Oxford University Press.

Farrington, D. P. (2002). Multiple risk factors for multiple problem violent boys. In R. R. Corrado, R. Roesch, S. D. Hart & J. K. Gierowski (Eds.), *Multiproblem violent youth* (pp. 90–149). Amsterdam: IOS Press.

Farrington, D. P., & Hawkins, J. D. (1991). Predicting participation, early onset, and later persistence in officially recorded offending. *Criminal Behavior and Mental Health, 1,* 1–33.

Farrington, D. P., & Loeber, R. (1999). Transatlantic replicability of risk factors in the development of delinquency. In P. Cohen, C. Slomkowski & L. N. Robins (Eds.), *Historical and geographical influences on psychopathology* (pp. 299–329). Mahwah, NJ: Lawrence Erlbaum.

Farrington, D. P., & Loeber, R. (2000). Some benefits of dichotomization in psychiatric and criminological research. *Criminal Behavior and Mental Health, 10,* 100–122.

Farrington, D. P., & Maughan B. (1999). Criminal careers of two London cohorts. *Criminal Behavior and Mental Health, 9,* 91–106.

Farrington, D. P., & West, D. J. (1981). The Cambridge Study in Delinquent Development (United Kingdom). In S. A. Mednick & A. E. Baert (Eds.), *Prospective longitudinal research* (pp. 137–145). Oxford: Oxford University Press.

Farrington, D. P., & West, D. J. (1990). The Cambridge Study in Delinquent Development: A long-term follow-up of 411 London males. In H.-J. Kerner & G. Kaiser (Eds.) *Kriminalitat: Personlichkeit, lebensgeschichte und verhalten (Criminality: Personality, behavior and life history)* (pp. 115–38). Berlin: Springer-Verlag.

Farrington, D. P., & West, D. J. (1993). Criminal, penal and life histories of chronic offenders: Risk and protective factors and early identification. *Criminal Behavior and Mental Health, 3*, 492–523.

Farrington, D. P., & West, D. J. (1995). Effects of marriage, separation and children on offending by adult males. In Z. S. Blau & J. Hagan (Eds.), *Current perspectives on aging and the life cycle: Vol. 4. Delinquency and disrepute in the life course* (pp. 249–281). Greenwich, CT: JAI Press.

Farrington, D. P., & Wikström, P-O. H. (1994). Criminal careers in London and Stockholm: A cross-national comparative study. In E. G. M. Weitekamp & H-J. Kerner (Eds.), *Cross-national longitudinal research on human development and criminal behavior* (pp. 65–89). Dordrecht, Netherlands: Kluwer.

Farrington, D. P., Osborn, S. G., & West, D. J. (1978). The persistence of labelling effects. *British Journal of Criminology, 18*, 277–284.

Farrington, D. P., Berkowitz, L., & West, D. J. (1982a). Differences between individual and group fights. *British Journal of Social Psychology, 21*, 323–333.

Farrington, D. P., Biron, L., & LeBlanc, M. (1982b). Personality and delinquency in London and Montreal. In J. Gunn & D. P. Farrington (Eds.), *Abnormal offenders, delinquency, and the criminal justice system* (pp. 153–201). Chichester, England: Wiley.

Farrington, D. P., Gallagher, B., Morley, L., St. Ledger, R. J., & West, D. J. (1986a). Unemployment, school leaving, and crime. *British Journal of Criminology, 26*, 335–356.

Farrington, D. P., Ohlin, L. E., & Wilson, J. Q. (1986b). *Understanding and controlling crime.* New York: Springer-Verlag.

Farrington, D. P., Gallagher, B., Morley, L., St. Ledger, R. J., & West, D. J. (1988a). A 24-year follow-up of men from vulnerable backgrounds. In R. L. Jenkins & W. K. Brown (Eds.), *The abandonment of delinquent behavior* (pp. 155–173). New York: Praeger.

Farrington, D. P., Gallagher, B., Morley, L., St. Ledger, R. J., & West, D. J. (1988b). Are there any successful men from criminogenic backgrounds? *Psychiatry, 51*, 116–130.

Farrington, D. P., Gallagher, B., Morley, L., St. Ledger, R. J., & West, D. J. (1990a). Minimizing attrition in longitudinal research: Methods of tracing and securing cooperation in a 24-year follow-up study. In D. Magnusson & L. Bergman (Eds.), *Data quality in longitudinal research* (pp. 122–47). Cambridge: Cambridge University Press.

Farrington, D. P., Loeber, R., & van Kammen, W. B. (1990b). Long-term criminal outcomes of hyperactivity-impulsivity-attention deficit and conduct problems in childhood. In L. N. Robins & M. Rutter (Eds.), *Straight and devious pathways from childhood to adulthood* (pp. 62–81). Cambridge: Cambridge University Press.

Farrington, D. P., Barnes, G. C., & Lambert, S. (1996). The concentration of offending in families. *Legal and Criminological Psychology, 1*, 47–63.

Farrington, D. P., Lambert, S., & West, D. J. (1998). Criminal careers of two generations of family members in the Cambridge Study in Delinquent Development. *Studies on Crime and Crime Prevention, 7*, 85–106.

Gold, M. (1970). *Delinquent behavior in an American city.* Belmont, CA: Brooks/Cole.

Goldberg, D. (1978). *Manual of the general health questionnaire.* Windsor, England: NFER-Nelson.

Groeneveld, L. P., Short, J. F., & Thoits, P. (1979). *Design of a study to assess the impact of income maintenance on delinquency.* Washington, DC: National Institute of Juvenile Justice and Delinquency Prevention.

Hagan, J. (1993). The social embeddedness of crime and unemployment. *Criminology, 31*, 465–491.

Hagan, J., & Palloni, A. (1990). The social reproduction of a criminal class in working-class London, circa 1950–1980. *American Journal of Sociology, 96*, 265–299.

Harvard University (2000). *Project on human development in Chicago neighborhoods: 2000 annual report.* Cambridge, MA: Harvard University.

Hawkins, J. D., & Catalano, R. F. (1992). *Communities that Care.* San Francisco: Jossey-Bass.

Hawkins, J. D., Catalano, R. F., Kosterman, R., Abbott, R., & Hill, K. G. (1999). Preventing adolescent health-risk behaviors by strengthening protection during childhood. *Archives of Pediatrics and Adolescent Medicine, 153*, 226–234.

Huizinga, D., & Elliott, D. S. (1986). Reassessing the reliability and validity of self-report measures. *Journal of Quantitative Criminology, 2*, 293–327.

Juby, H., & Farrington, D. P. (2001). Disentangling the link between disrupted families and delinquency. *British Journal of Criminology, 41*, 22–40.

Krohn, M. D., Thornberry, T. P., Rivera, C., & LeBlanc, M. (2001). Later delinquency careers. In R. Loeber & D. P. Farrington (Eds.), *Child delinquents: Development, intervention, and service needs* (pp. 67–93). Thousand Oaks, CA: Sage.

LeBlanc, M., & Frechette, M. (1989). *Male criminal activity from childhood through youth.* New York: Springer-Verlag.

Loeber, R., & Farrington, D. P. (1998, Eds.), *Serious and violent juvenile offenders; Risk factors and successful interventions.* Thousand Oaks, CA: Sage.

Loeber, R., & Farrington, D. P. (2001, Eds.), *Child delinquents: Development, intervention and service needs.* Thousand Oaks, CA: Sage.

Loeber, R., Stouthamer-Loeber, M. S., van Kammen, W., & Farrington, D. P. (1991). Initiation, escalation, and desistance in juvenile offending and their correlates. *Journal of Criminal Law and Criminology, 82*, 36–82.

Moffitt, T. E. (1993). Adolescence-limited and life-course-persistent antisocial behavior: A developmental taxonomy. *Psychological Review, 100*, 674–701.

Moffitt, T. E., Caspi, A., Rutter, M., & Silva, P. A. (2001). *Sex differences in antisocial behavior.* Cambridge: Cambridge University Press.

Morash, M., & Rucker, I. (1989). An exploratory study of the connection of mother's age at childbearing to her children's delinquency in four data sets. *Crime and Delinquency, 35*, 45–93.

Nagin, D. S., & Farrington, D. P. (1992a). The onset and persistence of offending. *Criminology, 30*, 501–523.

Nagin, D. S., & Farrington, D. P. (1992b). The stability of criminal potential from childhood to adulthood. *Criminology, 30*, 235–260.

Nagin, D. S., Farrington, D. P., & Moffitt, T. E. (1995). Life-course trajectories of different types of offenders. *Criminology, 33*, 111–139.

Nagin, D. S., Pogarsky, G., & Farrington, D. P. (1997). Adolescent mothers and the criminal behavior of their children. *Law and Society Review, 31*, 137–162.

Olds, D. L., Henderson, C. R., Cole, R., Eckenrode, J., Kitzman, H., Luckey, D., Pettitt, L., Sidora, K., Morris, P., & Powers, J. (1998). Long-term effects of nurse home visitation on children's criminal and antisocial behavior: 15-year follow-up of a randomized controlled trial. *Journal of the American Medical Association, 280*, 1238–1244.

Olweus, D. (1994). Bullying at school: Basic facts and effects of a school based intervention programme. *Journal of Child Psychology and Psychiatry, 35*, 1171–1190.

Paternoster, R., & Brame, R. (1998). The structural similarity of processes generating criminal and analogous behaviors. *Criminology, 36*, 633–669.

Paternoster, R., Brame, R., & Farrington, D. P. (2001). On the relationship between adolescent and adult offending frequencies. *Journal of Quantitative Criminology, 17*, 201–225.

Patterson, G. R. (1982). *Coercive family process.* Eugene, OR: Castalia.

Polakowski, M. (1994). Linking self and social control with deviance: Illuminating the structure underlying a general theory of crime and its relation to deviant activity. *Journal of Quantitative Criminology, 10*, 41–78.

Prime, J., White, S., Liriano, S., & Patel, K. (2001). *Criminal careers of those born between 1953 and 1978*. London: Home Office (Statistical Bulletin 4/01).

Pulkkinen, L. (1988). Delinquent development: Theoretical and empirical considerations. In M. Rutter (Ed.), *Studies of psychosocial risk* (pp. 184–199). Cambridge: Cambridge University Press.

Raine, A. (1993). *The psychopathology of crime*. San Diego, CA: Academic Press.

Reiss, A. J., & Farrington, D. P. (1991). Advancing knowledge about co-offending: Results from a prospective longitudinal survey of London males. *Journal of Criminal Law and Criminology, 82*, 360–395.

Robins, L. N. (1986). Changes in conduct disorder over time. In D. C. Farran & J. D. McKinney (Eds.), *Risk in intellectual and social development* (pp. 227–259). New York: Academic Press.

Robins, L. N. (1992). The role of prevention experiments in discovering causes of children's antisocial behavior. In J. McCord & R. E. Tremblay (Eds.), *Preventing antisocial behavior* (pp. 3–18). New York: Guilford.

Rock, P. (1994). The social organization of a Home Office initiative. *European Journal of Crime, Criminal Law and Criminal Justice, 2*, 141–167.

Ross, R. R., & Ross, R. D. (Eds.) (1995). *Thinking straight: The reasoning and rehabilitation program for delinquency prevention and offender rehabilitation*. Ottawa, Canada: Air Training and Publications.

Rowe, D. C. (1994). *The limits of family influence*. New York: Guilford.

Rowe, D. C., & Farrington, D. P. (1997). The familial transmission of criminal convictions. *Criminology, 35*, 177–201.

Rutter, M., Maughan, B., Mortimore, P., & Ouston, J. (1979). *Fifteen thousand hours*. London: Open Books.

Sampson, R. J., & Laub, J. H. (1993). *Crime in the making*. Cambridge, MA: Harvard University Press.

Schweinhart, L. J., Barnes, H. V., & Weikart, D. P. (1993). *Significant benefits*. Ypsilanti, MI: High/Scope.

Stattin, H., & Magnusson, D. (1991). Stability and change in criminal behavior up to age 30. *British Journal of Criminology, 31*, 327–346.

Tarling, R. (1993). *Analyzing offending: Data, models and interpretations*. London: Her Majesty's Stationery Office.

Tolan, P. H., & Thomas, P. (1995). The implications of age of onset for delinquency risk. II. Longitudinal data. *Journal of Abnormal Child Psychology, 23*, 157–181.

Tonry, M., Ohlin, L. E., & Farrington, D. P. (1991). *Human development and criminal behavior*. New York: Springer-Verlag.

Tracy, P. E., Wolfgang, M. E., & Figlio, R. M. (1990). *Delinquency careers in two birth cohorts*. New York: Plenum.

Tremblay, R. E., Pagani-Kurtz, L., Masse, L. C., Vitaro, F., & Pihl, R. O. (1995). A bimodal preventive intervention for disruptive kindergarten boys: Its impact through mid-adolescence. *Journal of Consulting and Clinical Psychology, 63*, 560–568.

Wasserman, G. A., & Miller, L. S. (1998). The prevention of serious and violent juvenile offending. In R. Loeber & D. P. Farrington (Eds.), *Serious and violent juvenile offenders: Risk factors and successful interventions* (pp. 197–247). Thousand Oaks, CA: Sage.

West, D. J. (1969). *Present conduct and future delinquency*. London: Heinemann.

West, D. J. (1982). *Delinquency: Its roots, careers and prospects*. London: Heinemann.

West, D. J., & Farrington, D. P. (1973). *Who becomes delinquent?* London: Heinemann.

West, D. J., & Farrington, D. P. (1977). *The delinquent way of life*. London: Heinemann.
Wolfgang, M. E., Figlio, R. M., & Sellin, T. (1972). *Delinquency in a birth cohort*. Chicago: University of Chicago Press.
Zoccolillo, M., Pickles, A., Quinton, D., & Rutter, M. (1992). The outcome of childhood conduct disorder: Implications for defining adult personality disorder and conduct disorder. *Psychological Medicine, 22*, 971–986.

6

Testing an Integrative Theory of Deviant Behavior

Theory-Syntonic Findings from a Long-Term Multi-Generation Study

Howard B. Kaplan

Introduction

Over the past three decades, I, along with several colleagues, have conducted a systematic series of analyses designed to test the validity of an integrative theory of deviant behavior using data from a long-term study of (1) a cohort of adolescents followed over thirty years and (2) the children of the cohort who had reached the age of twelve, some of whom were also followed up after the initial interview. In the following pages I outline the integrative theory of deviance and evaluate the compatibility of our findings with the theory.

An Integrative Theory of Deviant Behavior

The theory addresses the general construct of deviance rather than more narrowly construed deviant patterns such as drug use or violence. Deviance refers to behaviors or attributes manifested by specified kinds of people in specified circumstances that are judged to violate the normative expectations of a specified group. Shared normative expectations refer to group evaluations regarding the

Taking Stock of Delinquency: An Overview of Findings from Contemporary Longitudinal Studies, edited by Thornberry and Krohn. Kluwer Academic/Plenum Publishers, New York, 2003.

appropriateness or inappropriateness of certain attributes or behaviors when manifested by certain kinds of people in certain situations. A group that shares a normative system may evaluate the behaviors or attributes even of individuals who do not belong to the group and may apply negative sanctions for the behaviors or attributes that are judged to deviate from the normative expectations that are believed to be incumbent on even nongroup members. Depending on the group's access to sanctions that are meaningful to the nongroup members, the application of negative sanctions may have a great adverse impact on the outcomes of nongroup members.

The history of the study of deviant behavior has witnessed the proposal of general theories that were interpreted as competing explanations of deviant behavior. The interpretation of diverse theories of deviant behavior as offering competing rather than complementary explanations has continued, to some extent, to the present. More recently, however, it has been recognized increasingly that the "competing" theories address different questions (why individuals initiate deviant behavior vs. why individuals continue to engage in deviant behavior once they have initiated the pattern) or focus on different explanatory factors that do not gainsay (but rather complement) the explanatory value of the other factors. Some theories focus on the opportunities to learn the deviant patterns; other theories focus on social or personal constraints on acting out the deviant behaviors. Recognition of these different foci has led to the offering of integrative theories that combine several different approaches (Akers, 2000; Kaplan, 1984; Messner, Krohn, & Liska, 1989; Shoemaker, 1990).

Although some commentators place our guiding theoretical framework under the rubric of control theory in particular (Gibbons & Krohn, 1991; Shoemaker, 1990), more often the theory is regarded as integrative in nature. Thus, Wells (1978, p. 194) cites Kaplan's (1975b) orientation as a major example of the synthesis of structural interaction analyses and socialization-control analysis:

> The fundamental propositions tying deviance and self-concept to the social structure are: (1) that commitment to the legitimate social order is a positive function of the adequacy of self-esteem level, and (2) that self-esteem is a cumulative product of socialization experiences which may be distributed across different social sectors or different kinds of interpersonal associations...
> When the situational structure of contingencies works against self-esteem maintenance, then the theory predicts a tendency to seek behavioral alternatives, either individual or collective, which are outside the conventional order and which provide more positive experiences...

Akers (2000, p. 248) also characterizes the theoretical approach in terms of the integration of several traditional frameworks:

> Howard B. Kaplan (1975b) proposed a self-esteem/derogation theory of adolescent deviance that brings together deviant peer influences (social learning theory), family and school factors (control theory), dealing with failure

to live up to conventional expectations (strain theory), and self-concept (symbolic interactionism and labeling theory).

The guiding theory is integrative in effect rather than in a purposive sense. The theory did not develop by purposely incorporating the separate ideas contained in diverse theoretical frameworks. Rather, the theory evolved by developing the implications of central theoretical premises. In so doing, it was inevitable that ideas developed piecemeal in one or another of the diverse theoretical frameworks would become relevant as part of the explanation of deviant behavior.

The integrative theory has been described in detail in a number of places from the perspectives of self-theory and stress-theory as well as from the perspective of deviant behavior (Kaplan, 1972, 1975b, 1980, 1982, 1983, 1984, 1986, 1995, 1996). Only a brief outline will be presented here.

The performance of acts that are defined as deviant relative to a particular normative framework are regarded as adaptations, either to the expectations of groups that define the acts as deviant or to the expectations of groups that define the acts as normative. Where the person is committed to the normative system that defines the acts as deviant but has consistently failed to do or be what was expected, the person loses motivation to conform and becomes motivated to deviate as a way of satisfying unresolved needs. In the course of the normal socialization process, one learns to value the possession of particular attributes, the performance of certain behaviors, and the particular experiences that are the outcome of the purposive or accidental responses of others toward one. These attributes, behaviors, and experiences are the basis for the individual's feelings of self-worth. If the person is unable to evaluate himself or herself positively, then the person will be motivated to behave in ways that will gain the attributes, enable the performance of the behaviors, and increase the likelihood of the experiences that will increase feelings of self-worth and decrease the feelings of psychological distress that are associated with self-rejecting attitudes. If a person perceives an inability to achieve the attributes, perform the behaviors, and enjoy the experiences he or she has been taught to value as the basis for overall positive self-evaluation through conventional behavior, then that person will be motivated to behave in deviant ways that offer promise of gaining attributes, facilitating behaviors, and enjoying experiences that will permit the person to gain a feeling of self-worth. The deviant behavior may involve using illegal means to achieve what the person has learned to value or engaging in deviant activities as a way of rejecting or avoiding the conventional standards by which the person failed and substituting deviant standards by which he or she could more easily succeed and earn feelings of self-worth.

Failure to approximate self-evaluative standards of membership groups results from misunderstandings of the expectations, conflicting expectations imposed upon the person, or the absence of instrumentally or intrinsically valued resources due to (1) congenital inadequacies, as in strength, dexterity, or intelligence; (2) the failure to acquire the skills and experience necessary for adapting to or coping with the environment as a result of faulty socialization experiences, or the disruption of already acquired adaptive/coping patterns by various life events; (3) placement in inadequate social support systems; (4) the occurrence of life events that impose legitimate requirements on an individual that cannot be met by his or her heretofore adequate resources; and (5) deviant attributions by other social systems.

Where the person is committed to a normative system that endorses the behavior in question, the need to approximate self-evaluative standards motivates performance of the act. The person internalizes the standards either by being born into and reared in a group that shares a deviant subculture or by later becoming attracted to such a group and becoming emotionally committed to the subcultural standards shared by the group. The person may become attracted to the group originally because of the deviant activities that promise gratification. Alternatively, the person may become attracted to the group independent of the deviant activities but adopt the deviant subculture as a means of evoking continued identification with the group whose approval he or she needs.

People act out or constrain their motives to perform deviant acts depending upon (1) the presence of counteracting motives not to perform the act, and (2) the situational context and other opportunities to perform the act. Counteracting motives encompass those needs ordinarily included under the rubric of social controls. The effectiveness of counteracting motives in forestalling the acting out of deviant dispositions is moderated by two general conditions. These conditions relate to emotional attraction to the conventional order and to the ability to define the deviant act as compatible with the conventional order. The opportunity to perform the act includes physical, personal, and interpersonal resources as well as the situational context that provides the occasions and the stimulus for the deviant behavior.

Once a person has performed deviant acts, what circumstances will lead to the continuation, repetition, or escalation of the person's degree of involvement in deviant activity? The first set of circumstances includes those that provide positive reinforcement of the need to perform deviant acts. The second set includes those circumstances that weaken the effects of motives that previously deterred the individual from performing deviant acts. The third set of circumstances increases or establishes ongoing opportunities for the performance of deviant behavior.

Deviant behavior is self-reinforcing in two ways. First, the performance of deviant behavior may satisfy important needs for the person. Because the behavior satisfies the needs, as the needs continue or recur, the deviant behavior will continue or be repeated in the expectation that the need will still or once again be satisfied. Second, regardless of the motivation for the initial performance of deviant behavior, the deviant behavior creates a need (specifically a need for self-justification) that is satisfied by continuation or repetition of the deviant act or by the structuring of the social environment in ways that facilitate the continuation or repetition of the deviant act.

Social controls are weakened by circumstances that either decrease expectations of adverse consequences or decrease attraction to conventional values. Decreased expectation of adverse consequences is accounted for directly by observation that few adverse consequences of initial deviance occurred and indirectly by the circumstances surrounding stigmatization of the deviant actor following initial deviance. In the latter case, when the initial deviance is observed and harshly responded to, the person effectively is expelled from conventional society and the interaction between the individual and representatives of conventional society is thereby markedly reduced. The attraction to the values of conventional society and to membership in conventional groups as a basis for positive self-evaluation is weakened both by the very same processes that influenced the person's initial motivation to perform deviant acts and by the responses of society to the initial deviance. The person's inability to succeed by conventional standards leads to negative self-attitudes and to the disposition to perform deviant acts that might lead to more positive self-feelings. At the same time, the person's association, in his own mind, between the distressful self-rejecting attitudes and the conventional standards that are the measure of his failure decreases his attraction to these standards. The self-rejection is increased by the negative sanctions applied in response to the initial deviance.

The early performance of deviant acts frequently has consequences that increase the individual's opportunity to perform deviant acts. As a result of the person's rejection of and by the conventional society, the person becomes increasingly attracted to deviant associates and increases the amount of social interaction with other deviants. With increasing interaction comes the motivation to conform to the expectations of deviant associates on whom the person depends for satisfaction of his or her day-to-day needs.

Data Sources

Aspects of the general theory of deviant behavior were tested using data from a long-term, two-generation study. The first generation sample included all of the seventh-grade students in a random half of the junior high schools in the Houston Independent School District as of March 1971. Students responded to a self-administered questionnaire (Time 1 data). Of the 9,335 students, 7,618 (81.6%) returned questionnaires that were usable in the longitudinal study. Students were also tested in the eighth (Time 2) and ninth (Time 3) grades. Of those subjects providing usable first administration questionnaires, 61.6% provided data at Time 2, and 41.3% provided data at both the second and third administrations.

In the 1980s we attempted to trace and reinterview all of the target sample from the first administration, including those who were not interviewed at Time 1. Of the subjects who were in the original target sample, 6,074 subjects were interviewed at Time 4 when the subjects were in the third decade of life. Close to one thousand of these subjects were not tested at Time 1.

Most recently, the first-generation subjects who were interviewed as young adults (Time 4) were reinterviewed during the fourth decade of life. Of the 6,074 subjects interviewed at Time 4, 5,468 were located and reinterviewed when they were 35–39 years of age (Time 5). For different analyses, various combinations of interview waves were used.

For the first three waves, data were collected by self-administered questionnaires at school in group settings. During Waves 4 and 5, data were collected by lengthy in-person home interviews using structured instruments including self-administered questionnaires that reproduce many of the items used in the first three waves. The percentage distributions of the subjects returning questionnaires at the first and fourth testing according to selected demographic characteristics are presented in Table 1.

Table 1. Selected Demographic Characteristics (Percentages) of the Time 1 and Time 4 Waves

	Time 1	Time 4
Gender		
Male	49	47
Female	51	53
Race/Ethnicity		
White-Anglo	61	62
African American	28	28
Mexican-American	11	10
Mother's Education		
Did not complete elementary school	4	4
Completed elementary school	13	21
Graduated high school	54	55
Graduated college	30	20
Age in 7th Grade		
11 or younger	4	3
12	33	36
13	48	48
14 or older	16	13
Religion		
Protestant	59	60
Catholic	25	20
Jewish	3	4
Other non-Christian	4	6
Unaffiliated	9	10

Sample attrition, particularly over the first three waves, was associated with ethnicity (Mexican-American), mother's education (did not graduate from elementary school), subject's age (older), religious affiliation (unaffiliated), mobility patterns (mobile), deviant behavior of friendship groups, attitudinal predisposition to leave school, and self-reports of early deviant behavior (Kaplan, 1980). In general, we evaluated the effects of sample attrition on hypothesized relationships by comparing the structure of relationships among variables observed for subjects present at the earlier time only with the structure of relationships observed for subjects present at all points in the time that are relevant for the particular analysis (e.g., Kaplan, Johnson, & Bailey, 1986). The relationships observed tend to be quite similar for both groups. Any differences suggest that the conclusions based on subjects present for all waves were conservative and underestimated (that is, the hypothesized relationships tended to be stronger for subjects who were not present for all waves). Further, comparisons of within-wave Time 4 relationships observed for subjects present only at Time 4 with relationships observed for subjects present at both Time 1 and Time 4 suggest minimal selection bias (Kaplan & Johnson, 1992). Attrition between Time 1 and Time 4 was not noteworthy as reference to Table 1 will indicate.

With regard to the second-generation sample, those children of the first generation subjects tested at Time 5 who had reached the age of 12 at the time of the testing were tested in a home interview. Further, all children who will reach the age of twelve by the middle of 2002 will be interviewed as they reach that age. Thus far, 6,414 second-generation subjects have been interviewed. Of these, a subset of 2,222 have been reinterviewed three years after the initial interview.

Analyses and Results

The results of the analyses using these data sources have been reported in over 85 publications (including one book). Only those most directly relevant to testing the guiding theoretical framework will be discussed. Discussions or elaborations of the integrative theory appear in over 20 publications (including three books).

The analyses estimate both linear models and models that specify conditional influences operating on the linear models. Approaches to the linear models include establishing direct linkages (whether through use of partitioning and mean residual gain scores, or through use of multivariate logistic regression) and specification of mediating variables (whether through use of ordinary least squares path analysis or through maximum likelihood estimation structural modeling with latent variables). The models that specify conditional influences are estimated, either using multiple regression with interaction terms or subgroups or multigroup structural equation modeling with the group-defining characteristic interpreted as the conditional variable values. In all instances the analyses produce findings that are compatible with the guiding integrative theoretical framework.

Direct Linear Relationships

Partitioning and Mean Residual Gain Scores

In a series of separate analyses using three-wave panel data and employing partitioning and mean residual gain scores to control on earlier observations of the dependent variables, Kaplan observed the theoretically expected linkages between (1) experiences of rejection by, and failure according to the standards of, conventional groups on the one hand and self-derogation on the other hand (Kaplan, 1976a); (2) self-derogation and disposition to deviance (Kaplan, 1975c); and (3) disposition to deviance and adoption of each of a wide range of deviant responses including substance abuse, interpersonal aggression, and property offenses, as well as other contranormative patterns (Kaplan, 1977a). Kaplan (1975a, 1976b, 1977b) also reported observation of the direct effects of self-derogation on each of a wide range of deviant patterns among subjects who had reported no recent occurrence of the deviant responses. In addition, Kaplan (1978) observed the anticipated relationship between adoption of deviant responses and subsequent self-enhancing effects.

Multivariate Logistic Regression

The generality of the model was tested using multiple logistic function analysis (Kaplan & Robbins, 1983) on the first three waves of data. The elements of the model were the central concept of self-derogation, specified antecedents of self-derogation, and specified sequelae of self-derogation. Four of the variables were self-reports at Time 1, and seven of the variables were expressed as residualized gains between Time 1 and Time 2. The outcome variables were self-reports at Time 3 with regard to performance of deviant acts between Time 2 and Time 3 (after having denied performance of the act between Time 1 and Time 2).

Consistent with aspects of the theory, initiation of four modes of substance abuse was anticipated by earlier self-perceptions of not possessing valued attributes and by not evoking positive responses from representatives of the school environment. Thus, it appears that the failure to achieve according to conventional standards does dispose a person to adopt deviant responses. Also, residualized gains in perceived rejection according to family and school standards are related to subsequent initiation of substance abuse. These measures, in the context of the multivariate model, are understood to reflect both increased experience of failure and the recognition by the subject of the role played by the conventional structure in the genesis of self-devaluing experiences.

In a multivariate context, perceived rejection by peers was inversely related to initiation of substance use (Kaplan & Robbins, 1983). Here, theoretical implications relate to the rejection of substance abuse patterns when the patterns are endorsed by groups (peers) that are the sources of distressful self-devaluing experiences and to the absence of both the opportunities and occasions for substance use that are associated with peer group acceptance. In this connection, the independent effect of residualized gains in awareness of deviant activities among peers (the kids at school) upon initiation of substance abuse supports the theoretically indicated proposition that self-devaluing experiences in conventional groups lead to the search for potentially self-enhancing alternative deviant response patterns.

Mediating Variables

Path Analysis

The general theory was applied again to adolescent drug use using the first three waves of data. Here, though, using ordinary least squares procedures, we examined relationships among the explanatory variables in a five-stage model consisting of eleven constructs measured at two points in time and one construct (drug use) measured at three points in time (Kaplan, Martin, & Robbins, 1982). The results of the analyses are consistent with the representation of drug use as the outcome of (1) the student's recognition of the self-devaluing implications of membership group experiences; (2) exacerbation of the self-esteem motive; and (3) the effects of these two concurrent processes, including decreased identification with the normative structure, increased perception of the self-enhancing potential of deviant responses, increased perception of the prevalence of drug use, and increased association with friends who use drugs.

Self-derogation is, in part, the consequence of the independent effects (net of the effects of earlier self-derogation) of perceived failure according to membership groups' (kids at school, family, or school authorities) standards, the perceived lack of valued peer-endorsed attributes, and the emotional identification with the conventional world that makes the person vulnerable to adverse attitudinal responses by representatives of that world. The awareness of the self-devaluing implications of membership group experiences leads to loss of motivation to conform and to motivation to deviate from membership group norms, as well as to the attenuation of effective social controls in these groups. All of these consequences encourage behaviors, such as drug use, that are deviant from the point of view of those membership groups. If drug use is deviant in the rejecting groups, the effect will be increased awareness of drug use in other groups, increased affiliation with drug-using friends, and increased use of drugs. In rejecting groups where drug use is normative, the effect will be attraction to alternative groups, decreased affiliation with drug-using peers, and decreased drug use.

The continuing inability of membership groups to assuage self-devaluing feelings leads to exacerbation of the self-esteem motive and, thereby, to increased sensitivity to the potential of deviant responses to yield self-enhancement, increased awareness of the prevalence of drug use among the kids at school, increased affiliation with groups using drugs, and increased drug use. At the same time, however, self-rejection makes the person more sensitive to rejecting attitudes of others, which mitigates somewhat the impulse to perform deviant acts.

Self-derogation is involved in all of the direct effects of Time 2 variables on drug use at Time 3: self-derogation at Time 1 is antecedent to felt rejection by peers, family, and school, to awareness of kids at school using drugs, and to association with drug-using friends at Time 2; and we observed a direct path from self-derogation at Time 2 to drug use at Time 3.

The Time 1 variables that had direct effects on illicit drug use at Time 3 are interpretable as indicating the effects of social evaluations of drug use on the performance of this activity. Drug use at Time 3 is anticipated by low perceived failure according to peer group (kids at school) standards, high perceived failure according to school standards, low endorsement of conventional adult values, and reports that good friends use drugs at Time 1. It is possible that two of the Time 1 predictors of drug use at Time 3 (felt rejection by peers and drug-using friends) are indicative of early involvement in a drug-using peers' subculture, which influences later adoption or continuation of drug use patterns. In like manner, Time 1 felt rejection by school and lack of adult-endorsed attributes may reflect the influence of identification with a contranormative or alternative subculture where drugs are used. Whether the subcultural affiliation is independent of or consequent to any earlier self-derogation-related processes is problematic.

In this model we also observed (consistent with the theory) a negative path between drug use and self-derogation *where the total effect was zero*, suggesting the existence of countervailing effects and the need to model the variables mediating the self-enhancing vs. self-devaluing effects of drug abuse.

Using the same dataset but only including respondents who reported not using drugs at Time 1, we tested the complementarity of four explanatory constructs that are reflected in different aspects of the general theory that guides this research. A six-stage path analysis tested a model that incorporated twenty indicators of four explanatory constructs: self-derogation, peer influence, social control, and early substance use (Kaplan, Martin, & Robbins, 1984). Indicators of all four constructs are entered into the model at the earliest point in time and at a later point in time. Thus, each of the constructs is specified as playing an independent primary role (by initiating a chain of influence at the earliest point in time in the model), as well as intervening roles in the explanation of adolescent drug use. The four constructs clearly complement each other in predicting subsequent adoption of drug use.

Important confirmatory and novel findings derive from these analyses of the influence of the four constructs. Consistent with the general theory of deviant behavior, self-derogation leads to drug use through two different routes: (1) Self-derogation leads to loss of motivation to conform to expectations of one's membership groups, which in turn leads to deviant associations and the adoption of deviant patterns; and (2), the exacerbation of the self-esteem motive disposes one to adopt patterns that might assuage the self-rejecting feelings. Regarding peer influence, involvement in the general peer culture appears to have different and opposing implications for subsequent drug use. On the one hand, acceptance by peers increases the likelihood of initiation into early stages of substance use. On the other hand, low levels of rejection by peers increases the likelihood of acceptance by normative groups, which militates against subsequent drug use. The attenuation of relationships with agents of social control and a lack of commitment to social values influence early drug use directly and indirectly via early use of other substances, the onset of self-derogation, and increased affiliation with drug-using peers. The observed relationships also reflect the mediating role of early substance use upon further attenuation of social controls and emotional commitment to social values. Early substance use also has direct effects upon later drug use, and it has indirect effects on later drug use via self-derogation and increased involvement with drug-using friends. The direct effects confirm the general sequence of stages of substance use observed by others. At the same time, these results reveal gaps in our understanding of this general process. We observe direct paths from Time 1 and Time 2 alcohol and marijuana use and from Time 2 drug use to drug use at Time 3. This pattern suggests that the influence of early substance use may operate as well through mechanisms other than self-derogation, increased affiliation with drug-using peer networks, and the effects on these of attenuated commitment to the normative structure.

Structural Equation Models

Building on an increasingly elaborated series of models (Kaplan, Martin, & Johnson, 1986; Kaplan, Johnson, & Bailey, 1986, 1987), the most inclusive structural model postulates relationships between six latent constructs: "Self-rejection" (modeled in terms of global self-derogation, and experiences of rejection and failure in family and school) at Time 1; "disposition to deviance" (measured in terms of indices of disaffection with, and readiness to adopt, antisocial alternatives to conventional family, school, and community patterns) at Time 2; "deviance" (reflecting the commonality underlying the adoption of any of a range of deviant behaviors in three different groupings based on probability of occurrence) at Time 3; "deviance" measured at Time 1; "deviant peer associations" at Time 2; and "social sanctions" (reflected in coming to the attention of the authorities and being the object of punitive responses by school authorities) modeled as occurring between Time 1 and Time 2. Times 1, 2, and 3 reflect, respectively, the seventh, eighth, and ninth grade testings (Kaplan & Johnson, 1991).

As expected, the association of negative self-feelings with perceptions of rejection and failure in family and school (self-rejection) leads to the loss of motivation to conform and the motivation to deviate from conventional expecta-tions (disposition to deviance). Self-rejection is, in part, the consequence of failure to approximate conventional expectations (deviance at Time 1). The disposition to deviate is the result, not only of earlier self-rejection, but also of the negative social sanctions that were elicited by earlier deviant behavior. Negative social sanctions further alienate the individual from the normative order (disposition to deviance).

Both the disposition to deviance and the stigma associated with earlier social sanctions increase the likelihood of association with deviant peers. Net of these direct positive effects of dispositions to deviance and social sanctions upon asso-ciations with deviant peers, self-rejection at Time 1 has a direct inverse influence upon deviant peer associations. Presumably, self-rejection, net of its indirect (via disposition to deviance) effect upon deviant peer association, increases the per-son's motivation to conform and be accepted by normative groups. One manifes-tation of the exacerbation of the need for acceptance is the attempt to avoid deviant activities, including association with deviant peers. In addition, it is pos-sible that the inverse association between self-rejection and deviant peer associa-tions may reflect avoidant tendencies on the part of individuals who have a history of rejection and failure experiences.

Deviant peer associations, the result of rejection of conventional norms, the stigmatization of negative social sanctions, and the attractiveness of deviant sub-jects to deviant peers has a direct effect upon later deviant behavior. Presumably, the deviant peer associations provide the opportunities, the social definitions of the situation, and social support for engaging in deviant behavior. Deviant peer association provides the strongest direct effect upon deviant behavior. However, independent of this effect, social sanctions and earlier deviant behavior have direct positive effects on deviance. Social sanctions increase the need of the indi-vidual for self-justification of the deviant behavior that is accomplished through repetition of the act. Although the intervening effects of social sanctions and deviant peer associations accounted for most of the stability of the deviant behav-ior, some of the stability coefficient has yet to be decomposed.

The theoretical model accounts for 51% of the variance in Time 3 deviant behavior. In view of the facts that the explanatory factors occurred at an earlier point in time than the dependent variable, and that the undecomposed portion of the stability coefficient for deviant behavior is quite modest, the explanatory value of the theoretically informed model is noteworthy (Kaplan & Johnson, 1991). The same model, accounting for 42% of the variance in a measure of drug use over the same (seventh- to ninth-grade) period, was observed with the excep-tion of the absence of the inverse effect of self-rejection on association with drug-using peers. Perhaps association with drug-using peers was not interpreted as deviant or threatening to public and private self-image as association with other deviants, and so the need for approval by self and others did not inhibit the association with drug-using peers (Kaplan, Johnson, & Bailey, 1988).

Consistent with our guiding theoretical framework, the general model was elaborated by specifying the theoretically indicated mediating role of self-rejecting attitudes and coping dispositions. In the former case, theoretical premises derived from the labeling perspective and a more inclusive theory of deviant behavior suggest that negative social sanctions in response to deviant behavior affects rejection that, in turn, has independent effects on attitudes toward conventional society and attitudes toward deviant behaviors and identities. Self-rejection leads to the loss of motivation to conform to, and the genesis of motivation to deviate from, conventional expectations (disposition to deviance) and, independently, to the positive reevaluation of and identification with deviant identities and behaviors. These premises are tested by estimating an elaborated model that specifies self-rejection as mediating and decomposing previously hypothesized and observed direct effects of negative social sanctions on disposition to deviance and drug use (Kaplan et al., 1988). The hypothesized effects were observed, thus lending greater credibility to positions that focus on the mediating role of self-rejection in relationships between negative social sanctions and continuity or amplification of deviance (Kaplan & Fukurai, 1992).

In another elaboration, consistent with the theoretical position that interprets deviant patterns as attempts to cope with self-devaluing experiences in conventional groups, a model was proposed in which the relationships between self-rejection and specific forms of deviant behavior were mediated by coping styles (attack and avoidance) with which the deviant patterns were functionally compatible. Self-rejection at Time 1 was hypothesized and observed to influence both avoidant and attack coping styles measured at Time 2. Also as expected, avoidant coping at Time 2 was related specifically to drug use at Time 3; and attack coping style at Time 2 was related specifically to violence and theft at Time 3. In addition to supporting the position that deviant behaviors serve, or are expected to serve, self-protective and self-enhancing functions, the findings contribute to understanding why one rather than other patterns of deviance are adopted (Kaplan & Peck, 1992).

Moderating Influences

Arguably the major limitation in a number of long-term studies is the failure to test for the scope conditions that are implicit or explicitly stated in the outlines of the guiding theoretical frameworks. A number of the analyses were carried out to test the validity of the integrative theory's premises regarding the conditions under which hypothesized linear relationships will be observed. The analyses used either (1) ordinary least squares regression with interaction terms or multiple groups, or (2) structural equation models.

Regression Models

A significant feature of the theory relates to the conditions under which deviant behavior has self-enhancing as opposed to self-derogating outcomes. Based on the premise that weak ties to the conventional order is a precondition for experiencing reduced self-derogation through deviant adaptations, a two-part hypothesis was tested: (1) Participation in social protest activities in the seventh grade has self-enhancing outcomes in the ninth grade and in young adulthood for subjects in the seventh grade who express alienation from the conventional social order, but (2) participation in social protest activities in the seventh grade is expected to have self-devaluing consequences in the ninth grade and young adulthood for subjects in the seventh grade who do not express alienation from the conventional social order. The results of OLS multiple regression analyses with interaction terms were consistent with the hypothesis. As predicted, among subjects who rejected the idea that one can get ahead by working hard, seventh grade social protest was inversely related to self-derogation; and, among subjects who affirm the idea that one can get ahead by working hard, social protest activities were related to higher subsequent levels of self-derogation (Kaplan & Liu, 2000).

Consistent with the theoretical orientation, we observed positive main effects of participation in social movements and denial that kids like the subjects can get ahead by working hard on later self-derogation. The assumption that ordinary individuals will think less positively of themselves when they fail to conform to the standards of their membership group is consistent with the observation in the multiple regression models that participation in social movements is positively related to later self-derogation scores (controlling on earlier self-derogation). Similarly, consistent with the premise that perceived inability to satisfy one's needs in the context of the conventional social order anticipates self-derogation is the observation, in the multiple regression models, that denial of the statement that kids like the subjects can get ahead if they work hard is positively related to later self-derogation.

More significantly, however, we observed the predicted effect of the interaction between social movement participation and denial that kids like the subjects can get ahead by working hard on lower levels of self-derogation. Among subjects who indicated that kids like the subjects can get ahead by working hard, participation in social protest activities in the seventh grade was positively related to later self-derogation scores. Presumably, belief that working hard is associated with rewards reflects an internalization of conventional norms and identification with the membership groups that adhere to these norms. Among individuals who have internalized conventional norms, participation in activities that question the validity of the conventional normative structure should be associated with negative attitudes toward one's self. Participation in social protest activities reflects deviation from conventional norms. Insofar as individuals who internalize these norms judge themselves according to the degree that they approximate the normative standards, failure to do so by engaging in social protest activities would lead to self-devaluation.

In contrast, for subjects who deny that individuals can get ahead by working hard, participation in social protest activities has salutary consequences for their self-attitudes. The greater the degree of participation in social protest activities, the lower the level of future self-derogatory attitudes. This was the case whether the later self-derogatory activities were measured in the ninth grade or as young adults, although the effect was more apparent in later adolescent years. The decrease in self-derogation that followed participation in social movements (controlling on earlier self-derogation) for subjects who believed that it was not possible to get ahead even with working hard, may be accounted for by any of a number of mechanisms. Subjects who believe that it is not possible to get ahead by working hard likely have lower levels of perceived self-efficacy. Participation in social protest activities perhaps testifies to the individual's capability of controlling his own destiny, albeit outside of conventional parameters.

At the same time, participation in social protest activities reflects affiliation with a group that conforms to different standards than the ones the person was presumably unable to approximate (as reflected in the belief that even with hard work, kids like him will not be able to get ahead). By adopting and conforming to the normative standards of the new reference group, the person is enabled to evaluate himself positively by virtue of conforming to the now-valued standards (including participation in social protest related activities). Further, by engaging in contranormative activities, subjects who believe that they cannot get ahead even by working hard express their contempt for the normative activities according to which they must judge themselves to be failures. By rejecting the validity of the standards, these subjects reject the bases for self-derogatory judgments (Kaplan & Liu, 2000).

In another series of analyses, we estimated models that specify theoretical conditions under which subjects escalate drug use (Kaplan & Johnson, 1992). Stepwise regression analyses predicted escalation of use from nine circumstances surrounding initial use among a subset of the population who had ever engaged in illicit drug use (other than marijuana). The analyses were conducted separately for males and females and within each grouping of males and females for individuals who were high and low, respectively, on each of twelve variables characterizing the subjects' personal and social circumstances at the time of initial test administration.

For three of the independent variables, the effects on escalation of drug use were gender-specific. For males, increased experiences of potency following initial drug use were associated with escalation of drug use at a later point in time. For males, the initiation of drug use following anger at significant others was associated with escalation of drug use at a later point in time. For female subjects, the weakening of interpersonal ties as a result of initial drug use was positively associated with the escalation of drug use.

The association between the circumstances surrounding initial use and escalation of use for either males or females was contingent upon the characteristics of the individual and his or her environment in the seventh grade. Thus, under conditions of high self-derogation, but not under conditions of low self-derogation, was the experience of increased potency occasioned by initial drug use influential on escalation of drug use. External locus of control serves as a moderating variable for a number of antecedents of escalation of drug use for males, but not for females. This is congruent with the understanding that masculine identity in our society is much more concerned with issues of autonomy and dependence than is feminine identity.

The meaning of the moderating variables is influenced by their interaction with gender. For males, initial drug use in response to anger at significant others had significant effects on escalation of drug use only for individuals who were high on a tendency toward avoidance (measured in the seventh grade). This suggests that for individuals who need to avoid others, feelings of anger would be more distressful than for individuals who are less avoidant. Drugs, insofar as they assuage angry feelings, would be more positively reinforcing for high avoidant than low avoidant individuals. On the other hand, for females, only those who were low on a need to avoid were positively reinforced by drug use in response to anger. For women, the higher motivation to maintain interpersonal relationships (reflected in low tendencies to avoid) is gratified by drug use in response to the experiences of anger at significant others. For men, the motivation among high avoidant subjects is to reduce the feelings of anger; for women the motivation is to maintain the relationships (Kaplan & Johnson, 1992). Again, the general theoretical framework appears valid in a numbers of respects.

Structural Equation Models

Recent analyses illustrate the use of structural equation modeling to test theoretically informed hypotheses regarding moderators of the effects of (1) negative self-feelings on deviant behavior, and (2) deviant behavior on negative self-feelings.

Informed by the general theory of deviant behavior, it was hypothesized that the positive effect of negative self-feelings on later deviant behavior would be observed only for youth that are not characterized by a deviant identity. Data from a second-generation panel of youths tested during early adolescence and retested three years later ($N = 1,041$) were used to estimate the structural equations models. As hypothesized, for youths without a deviant identity, negative self-feelings had both direct and indirect (via contemporary deviant behavior) positive effects on later deviant behavior. For youths characterized by deviant identities, however, no overall effect of negative self-feelings on deviant behavior was observed due to the operation of countervailing effects. Countering the indirect positive effects of negative self-feelings (presumably reflecting alienation from the conventional order) were inverse direct effects of negative self-feelings on later deviant behavior (presumably reflecting alienation from the deviant identity stemming from its association with concomitant negative self-feelings) (Kaplan & Lin, 2000).

The findings provide direct empirical support for the significance of at least one of the theoretical conditions that are believed to moderate the relation between negative self-feelings and deviant behavior, in particular, (non)deviant identity. Informed by a general theory of deviant behavior, it was hypothesized that the experience of negative self-feelings would dispose youth to adopt deviant patterns of behavior. It was expected, further, that this effect would be observed only among participants who were categorized as not having a deviant identity—that is, who were conventional. It was reasoned that if people develop negative self-feelings in the course of conventional group experiences, they would be alienated from the normative system (that is, lose motivation to conform) and would seek alternative (deviant) responses through which they might assuage distressful self-feelings.

However, according to the general theory, it was predicted that the positive effect of negative self-feelings would not be observed for participants who were classified as having a deviant identity. It was reasoned that for those individuals, countervailing processes would be at work. On the one hand, deviant identities connote alienation from the conventional world and, therefore, were expected to have the potential to contribute to continuation of deviant adaptations. On the other hand, the development of negative self-feelings, while having a deviant identity, suggests that an attenuation of ties to the deviant identity also should occur, and, as a result, that conventional patterns of behavior would become more likely as an attempt to assuage self-rejecting feelings. These countervailing tendencies were expected to be reflected in a near-zero relation between self-feelings and deviant behavior.

The results of the analyses supported the theoretical models. For the sample as a whole, negative self-feelings predicted deviant behavior. However, further analysis revealed that the subgroup of participants who were classified as not having a deviant identity accounted for this overall effect. For these youth, negative self-feelings were indicated to have both direct and indirect (via contemporary deviant behavior) positive effects on later deviant behavior. However, for youth classified as deviant, the overall effect of negative self-feelings on deviant behavior was non-significant; specifically, a direct inverse effect was counterbalanced by an indirect (via contemporary deviant behavior) positive effect. Deviant identity thus appears to moderate the influence of self-feelings on deviant behavior, at least during the period of adolescence that was the focus of the present research (Kaplan & Lin, 2000).

The influence of deviant behavior on self-derogation was also hypothesized to be contingent on the presence of other theoretically indicated conditions, in particular, stage in the life course, gender, and race/ethnicity. Specifically, we examined the effectiveness of the disposition to engage in aggressive strategies on coping with (that is, reducing) self-derogation. We expected that for social identities in which a salient source of self-derogation is the perceived barrier against self-assertiveness, empowerment, or taking action on one's own behalf, the adoption of aggressive dispositions would be self-enhancing. If the source of self-derogation for females and Mexican-Americans is perceived to be the social disempowerment of these identities, then the adoption of aggressive stances by persons characterized by these identities will result in the reduction of self-derogation. If the perceived disempowerment is experienced more intensely at earlier stages in the life course, then the reduction in self-derogation consequent upon the adoption of aggressive behaviors will be associated with earlier stages in the life course (Kaplan & Halim, 2000).

Similarly, we expected that for social identities in which the adoption of aggressive dispositions is deplored, the adoption of such strategies will increase rather than decrease self-derogation. If females, particularly during adulthood, view aggression as inappropriate and are negatively sanctioned for their disposition to aggressively respond to self-devaluing circumstances, then they will experience exacerbation of their self-derogation following adoption of aggressive coping dispositions.

These expectations were tested using data from a panel tested at three points during the life course (early adolescence, young adulthood, and the latter half of the fourth decade of life). The basic model specified effects of self-derogation on aggression at each point in time, stability effects of self-derogation and aggression between adjacent stages of the life course, and lagged effects of aggression at earlier points in time on self-derogation at later points in time.

This model was estimated for males and females separately, and for White-Anglo, African American, and Mexican-American subjects separately. We expected that gender and race/ethnicity would moderate the model in accordance with the expectations specified above. In general, the estimation of the structural equations models were congruent with our expectations. As expected, for females only, aggression in early adolescence anticipated decreases in self-derogation in young adulthood; and, aggression increased self-derogation between the third and fourth decades of life. For White-Anglo and African American subjects, aggression in early adulthood was related to increased self-derogation in later adulthood, but for Mexican-American subjects, early adult aggression decreased self-derogation by later adulthood. The results are interpretable in terms of self-enhancing implications of aggression for disempowered groups, and in terms of subcultural differences in acceptability of aggressive adaptations to stress at different stages in the life course.

Conclusion

Our work is guided by an integrative theory of deviant behavior that has evolved over the years into what has proved to be a viable framework for integrating findings regarding the antecedents and consequences of deviant behavior. Our research program has estimated increasingly elaborated models that specify theoretically indicated mediating and moderating variables. The results of our analyses indicate that the integrative theory that guides our analysis shows great promise as a valid explanation of deviant adaptations to life stress as well as an inclusive organizing device for ordering the findings of others that operate within other theoretical frameworks. Our research agenda will continue to call for ever more detailed specifications of mediating and moderating variables and, thus, more inclusive explanations of deviant behavior. Where this is called for by our empirical findings or the results of analyses by other investigators, our integrative theory will evolve further toward the goal of providing a guide for a fruitful research agenda that will eventuate in a fuller understanding of the direct, indirect, and conditional causes and consequences of deviant behavior over the life course.

ACKNOWLEDGMENT. This work was supported by research grants (R01 DA 02497 and R01 DA 10016) and by a Career Scientist Award (K05 DA 00136) to the author from the National Institute on Drug Abuse.

References

Akers, R. L. (2000). *Criminological theories: Introduction, evaluation and application* (3rd ed.). Los Angeles, CA: Roxbury Publishing.

Gibbons, D. C., & Krohn, M. D. (1991). *Delinquent behavior*. Englewood Cliffs, NJ: Prentice Hall.

Kaplan, H. B. (1972). Toward a general theory of psychosocial deviance: The case of aggressive behavior. *Social Science and Medicine, 6*, 593–617.

Kaplan, H. (1975a). Increases in self-rejection as an antecedent of deviant response. *Journal of Youth and Adolescence, 4*, 281–292.

Kaplan, H. (1975b). *Self-attitudes and deviant behavior*. Pacific Palisades, CA: Goodyear.

Kaplan, H. (1975c). Sequelae of self-derogation: Predicting from a general theory of deviant behavior. *Youth and Society, 7*, 171–197.

Kaplan, H. (1976a). Antecedents of negative self-attitudes: Membership group devaluation and defenselessness. *Social Psychiatry, 11*, 15–25.

Kaplan, H. (1976b). Self-attitudes and deviant response. *Social Forces, 54*, 788–801.

Kaplan, H. (1977a). Antecedents of deviant responses: Predicting from a general theory of deviant behavior. *Journal of Youth and Adolescence, 6*, 89–101.

Kaplan, H. (1977b). Increase in self-rejection and continuing/discontinued deviant response. *Journal of Youth and Adolescence, 6*, 77–87.

Kaplan, H. (1978). Deviant behavior and self-enhancement in adolescence. *Journal of Youth and Adolescence, 7*, 253–277.

Kaplan, H. (1980). *Deviant behavior in defense of self*. New York: Academic Press.

Kaplan, H. (1982). Self-attitudes and deviant behavior: New directions for theory and research. *Youth and Society, 14*, 185–211.

Kaplan, H. (1983). Psychological distress in sociological context: Toward a general theory of psychosocial stress. In H. B. Kaplan (Ed.), *Psychosocial stress: Trends in theory and research* (pp. 195–264). New York: Academic Press.

Kaplan, H. (1984). *Patterns of juvenile delinquency.* Beverly Hills, CA: Sage Publications.

Kaplan, H. (1986). *Social psychology of self-referent behavior.* New York, NY: Plenum Press.

Kaplan, H. (1995). Drugs, crime, and other deviant adaptations. In H. B. Kaplan (Ed.), *Drugs, crime, and other deviant adaptations: Longitudinal studies* (pp. 3–46). New York, NY: Plenum Press.

Kaplan, H. (1996). Psychosocial stress from the perspective of self theory. In H. B. Kaplan (Ed.), *Psychosocial stress: Perspectives on structure, theory, life-course, and methods* (pp. 175–244). San Diego, CA: Academic Press.

Kaplan, H. B., & Fukurai, H. (1992). Negative social sanctions, self-rejection, and drug use. *Youth and Society, 22,* 275–298.

Kaplan, H. B., & Halim, S. (2000). Aggression and self-derogation: Moderating influences of gender race/ethnicity, and stage in the life course. *Advances in Life Course Research, 5,* 1–32.

Kaplan, H. B., & Johnson, R. L. (1991). Negative social sanctions and juvenile delinquency: Effects of labeling in a model of deviant behavior. *Social Science Quarterly, 72,* 98–122.

Kaplan, H. B., & Johnson, R. L. (1992). Relationships between circumstances surrounding initial illicit drug use and escalation of drug use: Moderating effects of gender and early adolescent experiences. In M. Glantz & R. Pickens (Eds.), *Vulnerability to drug abuse* (pp. 299–358). Washington, DC: American Psychological Association.

Kaplan, H. B., & Lin, C. H. (2000). Deviant identity as a moderator of the relation between negative self-feelings and deviant behavior. *Journal of Early Adolescence, 20,* 150–177.

Kaplan, H. B., & Liu, X. (2000). Social protest and self-enhancement: A conditional relationship. *Sociological Forum, 15*(4), 595–616.

Kaplan, H. B., & Peck, B. M. (1992). Self-rejection, coping style, and mode of deviant response. *Social Science Quarterly, 73,* 903–919.

Kaplan, H. B., & Robbins, C. A. (1983). Testing a general theory of deviant behavior in longitudinal perspective. In K. T. Van Dusen & S. A. Mednick (Eds.), *Prospective studies in delinquent and criminal behavior* (pp. 117–146). Boston, MA: Kluwer-Nijhoff.

Kaplan, H. B., Martin, S. S., & Robbins, C. A. (1982). Applications of a general theory of deviant behavior: Self-derogation and adolescent drug use. *Journal of Health and Social Behavior, 23,* 274–294.

Kaplan, H. B., Martin, S. S., & Robbins, C. A. (1984). Pathways to adolescent drug use: Self-derogation, peer influence, weakening of social controls, and early substance use. *Journal of Health and Social Behavior, 25,* 270–289.

Kaplan, H. B., Martin, S. S., & Johnson, R. J. (1986). Self-rejection and the explanation of deviance: Specification of the structure among latent constructs. *American Journal of Sociology, 92,* 384–411.

Kaplan, H. B., Johnson, R. J., & Bailey, C. A. (1986). Self-rejection and the explanation of deviance: Refinement and elaboration of a latent structure. *Social Psychology Quarterly, 49,* 110–128.

Kaplan, H. B., Johnson, R. J., & Bailey, C. A. (1987). Deviant peers and deviant behavior: Further elaboration of a model. *Social Psychology Quarterly, 50,* 277–284.

Kaplan, H. B., Johnson, R. J., & Bailey, C. A. (1988). Explaining adolescent drug use: An elaboration strategy for structural equation modeling. *Psychiatry, 51,* 142–163.

Messner, S. F., Krohn, M. D., & Liska, A. E. (1989). *Theoretical integration in the study of deviance and crime: Problems and prospects.* Albany, NY: State University of New York Press.

Shoemaker, D. J. (1990). *Theories of delinquency: An examination of explanations of delinquent behavior* (2nd ed). New York, NY: Oxford University Press.

Wells, L. E. (1978). Theories of deviance and the self-concept. *Social Psychology, 41,* 189–204.

7

The Montreal Longitudinal and Experimental Study

Rediscovering the Power of Descriptions

Richard E. Tremblay, Frank Vitaro, Daniel Nagin,
Linda Pagani, and Jean R. Séguin

Aims and Design of the Study

The Montreal Longitudinal and Experimental Study (MLES) began in 1984. The original aim was to study the development of antisocial behavior from kindergarten to high school with a specific focus on the role of parent-child interactions. By the beginning of the 1980s, it was clear that the source of antisocial behavior could be found in the early years. The retrospective work of Lee Robins making a clear case for early onset of chronic antisocial behavior was already 18 years old (Robins, 1966). However, most, if not all, of the large longitudinal studies aiming specifically to unravel the origins of delinquency had started after age 7, the traditional "age of reason".

Our initial plan was to assess all the kindergarten boys in 53 schools of low socioeconomic areas in Montreal, to identify those who were most disruptive, and to intensively study the parent-child social interactions of a subset of approximately 80 of them until high school. The rationale was that disruptive kindergarten boys from low socioeconomic environments in large urban areas are more at risk of frequent and serious delinquent behavior compared to other males and females from the same environment, and compared to population samples of males

Taking Stock of Delinquency: An Overview of Findings from Contemporary Longitudinal Studies,
edited by Thornberry and Krohn. Kluwer Academic/Plenum Publishers, New York, 2003.

and females. Some would become delinquent, others would not, and comparing the development of these two groups would provide cues to the causes of delinquency development in this high-risk group. We were also hoping that the results would provide indications of parenting targets for preventive interventions.

In the spring of 1984, the kindergarten teachers of each of the 53 schools in the low socioeconomic areas of Montreal were asked to rate the behavior of each of their male students. Teachers typically had a morning and an afternoon group, each consisting of approximately 8 boys and 8 girls. Ratings were returned by 87% of the teachers, and 1,161 boys were rated. The next step involved identifying those who were the most disruptive. First, to control for cultural effects, we included in the longitudinal study only the boys with biological parents who were born in Canada and whose mother tongue was French. After applying these criteria and eliminating families who refused to participate further in the study, or who could not be traced after the initial assessment, 1,037 boys remained. We then used 13 items of the Preschool Behavior Questionnaire to identify the most disruptive boys: Bullies; kicks, bites, hits; fights; disobedient; blames others; irritable; destroys things; restless; inconsiderate; tells lies; squirmy; doesn't share; not liked (Tremblay, Desmarais-Gervais, Gagnon, & Charlebois, 1987; Tremblay, Loeber, Gagnon, Charlebois, Larivée, & LeBlanc, 1991).

A sub-sample of disruptive boys was created by selecting those above the 70th percentile of the disruptive behavior scale from teacher ratings. At this point, we realized that we had enough disruptive subjects to add a preventive experiment to the intensive longitudinal study of parent-child interactions, if funds became available. Three groups of disruptive kindergarten boys were thus randomly created: An intensive longitudinal observation group (Group A, $N = 82$), an experimental intervention group (Group B, $N = 43$), and a third group of subjects (Group C, $N = 41$) which would be assessed yearly and would thus serve as a control group for the intervention, as well as a control group for the possible effects of the intensive longitudinal observations of Group A. From this perspective, Group A was also an attention-control group for the experimental group (Group B).

After we obtained funds to conduct the intensive longitudinal study of parent-child interactions and the experimental preventive intervention, it became clear that a follow-up of all the boys assessed in kindergarten would create an important longitudinal study. The financial resources for this large-scale data collection became available in time to assess all the boys when the majority of them were finishing Grade 4, and turning ten years of age. Table 1 presents the different points in time when data were collected. It also represents the different sources of the data.

When in kindergarten, the majority of the boys lived with both their biological parents (67%), but one out of four (24%) was living alone with his mother, and 5% were living with their mother and a man who was not the boy's father; the rest (4%) were living in other family arrangements (e.g., with grand-parents, with father and stepmother). Parents' mean age at the birth of their son was

Table 1. Overview of the MILES Research Design. Data Collection Times

	1984 (6)	1985 (7)	1986 (8)	1987 (9)	1988 (10)	1989 (11)	1990 (12)	1991 (13)	1992 (14)	1993 (15)	1994 (16)	1995 (17)	1996 (18)	1997 (19)	1998 (20)	1999 (21)	2000 (22)
G.A. $N=82$	P_LB_{LO} B_{HO} B_{SO} TP_Q P_{SS}	P_LB_{LO} B_{HO} B_{SO} TP_Q P_{SS}	P_LB_{LO} B_{HO} B_{SO} TP_Q P_{SS}	P_LB_{LO} B_{HO} B_{SO} TP_Q P_{SS}	P_LB_{LO} B_{HO} B_{SO} P_{SL}	P_LB_{LO} B_{HO} B_{SO} P_{SL}	P_LB_{LO} B_{HO} B_{SO} P_{SL}	P_L B_{LO}	P_L B_{LO}	P_L B_{LO}							
G.B. $N=43$		TP_Q	Ex TP_Q P_{SS}	Ex TP_Q P_{SS}													
G.C. $N=41$		P_Q	P_Q	TP_Q P_{SS}													
G.D.* $N=203/336$								B_{LO} P_{SL}	B_{LO} P_{SL}	B_{LO} P_{SL}	B_{LO}	B_{LO}			B_{LO}	B_{LO}	B_{LO}
Total **TP_T** $N=1,037$				P_T	TP_Q B_Q P_{SS}	TP_Q B_Q P_{SS}	TP_Q B_Q P_{SS}	TP_Q B_Q	TP_Q B_Q	TP_Q B_Q	TP_Q B_Q	TP_Q					

Group A: Observaion group; Group B: Intervention group; Group C: Control group; Group D: Bio-psycho-social study group.

* The N varied depending on the specific problems studied. $N=203$ from 1991 to 1996; $N=336$ from 1998 to 2000.

T = Teacher questionnaire; P_T = Parent telephone; P_Q = Parent questionnaire; P_L = Parent laboratory; B_{LO} = Boys laboratory observation; B_Q = Boys questionnaire; B_{HO} = Boys home observations; B_{SO} = Boys school observations; P_{SS} = Peers sociometric data at school; P_{SL} = Peers sociometric data in laboratory; Ex = Experimental intervention.

25.4 ($SD = 4.8$) for mothers, and 28.4 ($SD = 5.6$) for fathers. This varied from 15 to 45 years for mothers, and from 16 to 56 years for fathers. The mean number of school years completed by the mothers was 10.5 ($SD = 2.8$), and 10.7 ($SD = 3.2$) for fathers. The majority of the parents were unskilled workers. The mean score on the Canadian socioeconomic index for occupations (Blishen, Carroll, & Moore, 1987) was 38.15 for mothers and 39.19 for fathers. This index ranges from 17.81 for the lowest status to 101.74 for the highest status, with a mean of 42.74 ($SD = 13.28$). The mean and median family income when the boys were age 10 years (1988) was between $25,000 and $30,000 (Canadian dollars; $19,000 to $23,000 in U.S. dollars) compared with a median income of $44,000 (Canadian dollars) for couples with children in Canada in 1987 (Mitchell, 1991).

Before the major data collection instruments are described, it is useful to note how quickly research on the development and prevention of juvenile delinquency has moved forward in the past century. With its 1,161 kindergarten boys from low SES environments, the MLES still appears, at the beginning of the 21st century, to be the largest longitudinal and experimental study specifically designed to understand the development and prevention of delinquency with subjects first assessed before Grade 1. Consider this quote from Donald West who pioneered the longest running, post 1950, longitudinal study specifically targeting early delinquency. The study started in 1960 with 8–9-year-old boys. He wrote in 1982: "Our plans were inspired by previous American surveys, the work of Glueck and Glueck (1950) and McCord, McCord, and Zola (1959), which pointed to the strong and continuing influence of early upbringing and family circumstances in determining who became delinquent" (p. 3). One of the American surveys West was referring to (McCord et al., 1959; the Cambridge-Somerville Youth Study) had started in 1937 with the aim of preventing delinquency, as Gordon Allport wrote, "*starting at as early an age as possible*"[1] (Allport, 1951, p. vii). There were, in fact, 62 subjects below age 7, 334 were distributed between 7 and $10\frac{1}{2}$, and 254 between $10\frac{1}{2}$ and 12. The intervention was meant to last 10 years and the subjects had been randomly allocated to treatment and control groups. This study initiated by Richard C. Cabot (1940) may be the best-designed longitudinal-experimental study of the prevention of delinquency in the 20th century. Consider now that, more than 40 years after the start of the study designed by Cabot, and more than 20 years after the study designed by West, the MLES began with boys only two years younger than those in the West study and randomly allocated only 46 disruptive boys to an intervention which lasted only 2 years, an intensive intervention by the standards of the experimental intervention studies of the 1980s. Clearly, between 1935 and 1984, the delinquency-prevention science did not make major leaps forward.

---

[1] Emphasis is ours.

Although the original focus of the MLES was on the development of antisocial behavior, investigators became interested in the development of many other dimensions of human development, some closely related to antisocial behavior, such as hyperactivity (e.g., Pulkkinen & Tremblay, 1992; Soussignan et al.), anxiety (e.g., Dobkin, Treiber, & Tremblay, 2000; Kerr, Tremblay, Pagani-Kurtz, & Vitaro, 1997), substance use and abuse (e.g., Carbonneau et al., 1998; Dobkin, Tremblay, Mâsse, & Vitaro, 1995; Dobkin, Tremblay, & Sacchitelle, 1997; Mâsse & Tremblay, 1997), gambling (e.g., Vitaro, Arseneault, & Tremblay, 1997; Vitaro, Arseneault, & Tremblay, 1999), school performance (e.g., Haapasalo, Tremblay, Boulerice, & Vitaro, 2000; Pagani, Tremblay, Vitaro, Boulerice, & McDuff, 2001), accidents (e.g., Junger & Tremblay, 1999; Tremblay, Boulerice, Junger, & Arseneault, 1995), heart rate variability (e.g., Kindlon et al., 1995; Mezzacappa et al., 1997), pubertal maturation, sexual intercourse and testosterone (e.g., Malo & Tremblay, 1997; Schaal, Tremblay, Soussignan, & Susman, 1996; Tremblay et al., 1997; Tremblay et al., 1998), perinatal complications (Arseneault, Tremblay, Boulerice, & Saucier, 2002; Pagani, Tremblay, Vitaro, & Parent, 1998), physical anomalies (Arseneault, Tremblay, Boulerice, Séguin, & Saucier, 2000), poverty (Pagani, Boulerice, Vitaro, & Tremblay, 1999), and others less closely related, such as nutrition (e.g., Laurent, Tremblay, Charlebois, Gagnon, & Larivée, 1988; Laurent, Tremblay, Larivée, Charlebois, & Gagnon, 1988), olfaction (Schaal, Rouby, Marlier, Soussignan, Kontar, & Tremblay, 1998), pain sensitivity (Ditto, Séguin, Boulerice, Pihl, & Tremblay, 1998), and physical health (Dobkin, Tremblay, & Treiber, 1998; Jutras, Tremblay, & Morin, 1999).

The main instruments used in the MLES to assess behavior problems are mother and teacher ratings and self-reported delinquency. Behavior ratings were also obtained annually from mothers and from classroom peers at ages 10, 11, and 12. A structured psychiatric interview was conducted with the boys and their mothers when the boys were 15 years of age. Annual questionnaires completed by mothers provided information on family background, life events, parenting behavior, domestic relationships, and social support. Annual interviews with the boys provided information on a variety of dimensions including personality, life events, perceptions of parenting, domestic relationships, friendships, attitudes toward school and the law, sleep and leisure activities. Direct observations of social interactions were made at school, at home, and in laboratory situations with sub-samples between ages 7 and 15. Psychophysiological and neuropsychological tests, as well as different biological assessments, were also made on sub-samples between age 7 and 20.

Teachers and mothers rated the boys' behavior in the spring, from age 6, at the end of the kindergarten year, to age 15. The six scales derived from teacher and mother ratings were: Physical aggression (fights with other children; kicks, bites, or hits other children; bullies or intimidates other children); Opposition (doesn't share materials; irritable; disobedient; blames others; inconsiderate); Covert conduct problems (destroys property, lies, steals, truants), Anxiety (tends to be fearful or afraid of new things or new situations; cries easily; appears miserable, unhappy, fearful, or distressed); Inattention (has poor concentration or short attention span; inattentive); Hyperactivity (restless, runs about or jumps up and down, does not keep still; squirmy, fidgety); and Prosocial behavior (comforts upset child; helps sick child; helps hurt child; praises other; helps with task difficulty; helps clear up mess; shows sympathy; invites bystander; stops quarrels; helps pick up objects).

Self-reported delinquency was assessed every year from ages 10 to 17 and around age 20. The boys were seen in small groups at their schools between March and May; they answered 27 self-reported delinquency items which were distributed in a questionnaire pertaining to school, family, friends, and leisure activities. The items were: steal from school; steal from store; steal from home; keep object worth less than $10; steal bicycle; sell stolen goods; keep object worth between $10 and $100; steal object worth more than $100; breaking and entering; enter without paying; trespassing; take drugs; take alcohol; get drunk; destroy school material; destroy other material; vandalism at school; destroy objects at home; vandalize car; set a fire; strong-arm; gang fights; use weapon in a fight; fist fight; beat up someone; carry a weapon; throw objects at persons. The 27 items had a 1 to 4 score (never, once or twice, often, very often).

Key Findings

Kindergarten Disruptive Behavior Predicts Delinquency During the Transition from Childhood to Early Adolescence

From most of the data available in the early 1980s, it appeared obvious that boys from low socioeconomic environments who had disruptive behavior problems (aggression, hyperactivity, impulsivity, opposition) during the elementary school years were most at risk of serious delinquency during adolescence and adulthood (Farrington, 1985). If these high-risk children could be identified during the kindergarten year, they could then be offered a prevention program, which would possibly deflect them from their antisocial trajectory.

The MLES did show that higher levels of disruptive behavior during the kindergarten year predicted higher levels of delinquency before entry into high school. Using a "variable" approach (see Magnusson & Bergman, 1990), we compared the predictive value of five behavioral dimensions rated by kindergarten teachers: physical aggression, hyperactivity, inattention, prosocial behavior, and anxiety (Haapasalo et al., 2000). Results showed that, after controlling for preschool family adversity, teacher ratings of physical aggression were the best predictor of the total self-reported delinquency score between 10 and 12 years of age. Using a "person" approach rather than a variable approach (see Magnusson & Bergman, 1990), the data analysis showed that the kindergarten boys most at risk of early delinquency were physically aggressive, but also non prosocial, hyperactive, not anxious, and not inattentive (see also Pulkkinen & Tremblay, 1992).

Kindergarten Personality Predicts Delinquency During the Transition from Childhood to Adolescence

The results presented above indicate that physical aggression during the kindergarten year is the best behavioral predictor of later delinquency. This predictive power is probably largely based on the stability of physical aggression, from early childhood to adolescence (see Tremblay & LeMarquand, 2001). The issue of stability of antisocial behavior will be discussed later in this chapter. A number of theories suggest that the stability of antisocial behavior from early childhood to adulthood is largely based on behavioral dispositions (either genetically determined or acquired early) labeled *temperament* or *personality* (e.g., Cloninger, Svrakic, & Svrakic, 1997; Eysenck, 1997; Gottfredson & Hirschi, 1990; Gray, Owens, Davis, & Tsaltas, 1983; Lahey, Waldman, & McBurnett, 1999; Quay, 1993).

Tremblay, Pihl, Vitaro and Dobkin (1994) tested the hypothesis that stable personality characteristics present during the preschool years could predict the level of delinquent involvement during pre- and early adolescence. Items from the kindergarten teacher ratings were selected to measure temperament dimensions, which had been hypothesized to form the basis of the "antisocial personality": high impulsivity, low anxiety, and lack of regard for others (e.g., Cloninger, 1987; Eysenck, 1964; Lahey et al., 1999; Quay, 1993). Items referring to antisocial behaviors (e.g., physical aggression, indirect aggression, opposition) were not included in an attempt to ensure that the prediction was not simply due to the continuity of antisocial behavior.

To select the boys, who had frequent delinquent behaviors between ages 10 and 13, the total delinquency score was first computed for each year. Those above the 80th percentile on that score for a given year were considered to be highly delinquent that year. Those who were found to be among the high delinquency group for at least two-thirds of their ratings were retained as the frequent delinquency group ($N = 92$; 10.6% of the total sample). Of these boys, 80% reported having beaten someone who had not done anything to them, compared to 23% for the rest of the sample; 90%, compared to 33%, reported shoplifting; 89%, compared to 32%, reported using a weapon in a fight; 71%, compared to 16%, reported breaking or stealing part of a car; and 71%, compared to 25%, reported having been drunk.

The results of a logistic regression analysis showed that high levels of hyper-activity rated by kindergarten teachers was the personality dimension which best predicted boys who had the highest self-reported delinquency scores from ages 10 to 13 years. Anxiety and prosocial behavior also made small independent con-tributions to the prediction. Thus the three personality dimensions, as rated by teachers in kindergarten, did contribute to explaining delinquent behavior during the transition from pre- to early adolescence, but hyperactivity made the major contribution. As suggested by Newman (1987) and Quay (1988), these results confirmed that Gray's behavioral activating system (BAS) may be the major dimension underlying the propensity towards antisocial behavior (see also Gottfredson & Hirschi, 1990). The significant anxiety effect, albeit weak, indi-cated, that the behavioral inhibition system (BIS) may play a role in both pre-venting or fostering antisocial behavior (see Kerr et al., 1997; Lahey et al., 1999). Prosocial behavior, labeled *reward dependence* by Cloninger (1987) made the smallest contribution. We then used Cloninger's classification of extreme person-ality types to verify to what extent boys with stable delinquent behavior during

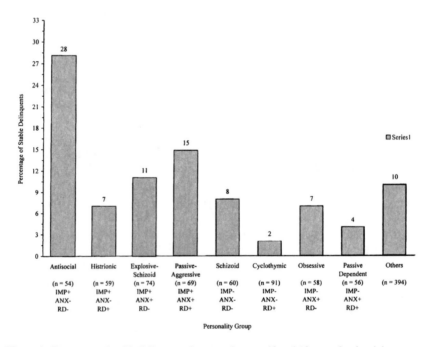

Figure 1. Percentage of stable delinquents between the ages 10 and 13 years for the eight extreme kindergarten personality groups and all other subjects (others). IMP indicates impulsive; ANX, anxious; RD, reward dependent; plus sign, high on the given dimension; and minus sign, low on the given dimension.

the transition from childhood to adolescence were found in specific personality categories. Results confirmed Cloninger's prediction that high impulsive low anxious low reward dependent subjects were the most at risk for antisocial behavior (see Figure 1). The proportion of delinquent boys was significantly higher in the antisocial category when compared to each of the other categories, except for the passive-aggressive one. It should be noted that the antisocial and passive-aggressive categories shared only the high impulsive dimension. These results reflected the interaction between impulsivity and anxiety predicted by Lahey and colleagues. In contrast, the antisocial and histrionic categories shared both the high impulsive and low anxiety dimensions, but had significantly different proportions of highly delinquent boys. Reward dependence of the histrionic boys did appear to protect them from high involvement in delinquency, although they were highly hyperactive and low on anxiety. Thus, the analyses of differences between categories show the importance of the interactions between the three personality dimensions when extreme personality categories are associated with an extreme behavior such as stable high antisocial behavior. Although the logistic regression, which used the whole continuum of each personality dimension, showed only modest predictive values of anxiety and reward dependence, and no significant interaction effects, the categorical analyses revealed statistically significant and theoretically meaningful

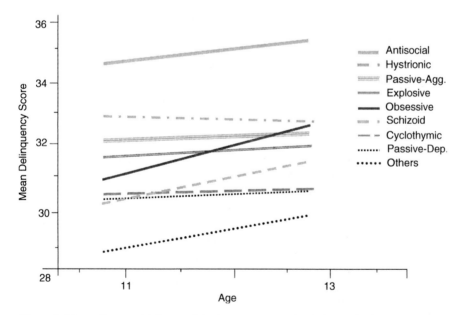

Figure 2. Mean self-reported delinquent behavior score at ages 11 and 13 years for the eight extreme kindergarten personality groups and all other subjects (others).

differences between categories of subjects who shared two of the three dimensions, including hyperactivity. The difference between the antisocial and histrionic groups was remarkable in this respect. This result confirmed the usefulness of the person-approach advocated by Cairns, Cairns, and Neckerman (1988), Hinde and Dennis (1986), and Magnusson and Bergman (1990). The study also demonstrated that the association between personality in kindergarten and later antisocial behavior was the same when delinquency at ages 10 and 13 was taken as the outcome, although the latter age involves one of life's most important transition periods (Figure 2).

Similar results were obtained when the kindergarten personality predictors were used to predict early use of cigarettes and drugs, as well as alcohol abuse (Mâsse & Tremblay, 1997). The results suggested that hyperactivity and anxiety significantly predicted the age of onset of cigarette smoking, getting drunk, and using drugs up to 15 years of age. As expected, boys who had a high score on hyperactivity and a low score on anxiety were more likely to use substances at an early age. However, we did not find that prosocial behavior significantly moderated the risk of early onset of substance use.

We then compared the stability of the personality characteristics at ages 6 and 10 in predicting the early onset of substance use. The results indicated that early (6 years of age) and late (10 years of age) childhood personality dimensions had similar powers of prediction and that they both significantly predicted onset of substance use in pre- and early adolescents.

Although our results indicated that behavioral inhibition (anxiety) assessed by kindergarten teachers protected boys from high levels of delinquency, previous studies had suggested that inhibited elementary school children, especially those who were both inhibited and aggressive, were more at risk of delinquency (Moskowitz & Schwartzman, 1989; Serbin, Schwartzman, Moskowitz, & Ledingham, 1991). In those studies, however, anxiety and shyness were confounded with social withdrawal. Using classmate peer ratings between 10 and 12 years of age we differentiated assessments of shyness and assessments of withdrawal (Kerr et al., 1997). We found that withdrawn-disruptive boys were at increased risk for delinquency at ages 13 to 15, but shy-disruptive boys were less at risk of delinquency at those ages (Figure 3). Social withdrawal appears comparable to lack of social reward dependence in Cloninger's et al.'s (1997) model, and psychotism in Eysenck's model (Eysenck, 1997), whereas behavioral inhibition is comparable to Cloninger's harm avoidance or Gray's (1982) behavioral inhibition. Cloninger postulates that specific brain systems, with their associated neuromodulators, underlie these dimensions. Furthermore, these systems interact differently with the system that underlies the third dimension, novelty seeking, which is most highly correlated with delinquency. High harm avoidance (behavioral inhibition) reduces novelty-seeking tendencies, whereas low reward dependence (withdrawal) potentiates novelty-seeking tendencies.

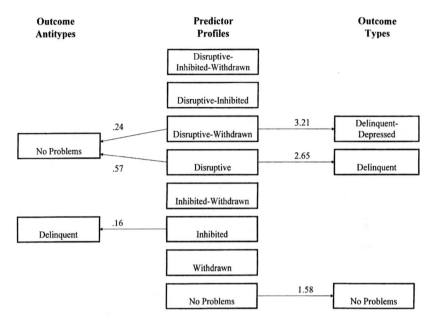

Figure 3. Predictor-outcome combinations that are likely (types) and unlikely (antitypes) along with odd ratios.

In Summary

Kindergarten children who have high levels of hyperactivity are more at risk of frequent delinquent behavior during the transition from childhood to adolescence. The risk will be increased if they have low levels of anxiety and prosocial behavior, and decreased if they have high levels of anxiety and prosocial behavior.

Biological Correlates of Delinquency

Most personality theories of antisocial behavior suggest that inherited and acquired biological structures and processes lead to the development of antisocial personalities (see e.g., Cloninger et al., 1997; Eysenck, 1997; Lahey, McBurnett, & Loeber, 1999). Many studies have shown that physiological and neuropsychological characteristics do correlate with the frequency of delinquent behavior. The MLES provided the opportunity to study the association of chronic physical aggression with the autonomous nervous system activity, with neuro-cognitive deficits, and with testosterone levels.

Concerning the activity of the nervous system, we found that boys with high levels of fighting between 5 and 12 years of age had low heart rate at 11 and 12 years of age, controlling for body size, pubertal status, and level of family adversity (Kindlon et al., 1995). Raine, Venables, and Mednick (1997) showed that this difference in heart rate was present by 3 years of age in a sample of Mauritius children. Controlling for similar confounds, we also found that high levels of self-reported delinquent behavior from 10 to 15 years of age were related to disruption of vagal nerve control over respiratory effects on heart rate (Mezzacappa et al., 1997). This relationship is consistent with the hypothesis that antisocial adolescents have a deficit in control of volitional behaviors involving higher cortical functions (see Moffitt, 1993). We tested this hypothesis by comparing, at age 13, the executive function of boys with different levels of physical aggression between 6 and 12 years of age: those who were chronically physically aggressive, those who were occasionally physically aggressive, and those who were never physically aggressive (Séguin, Pihl, Harden, Tremblay, & Boulerice, 1995). Chronically aggressive boys performed poorly on executive function measures and did not benefit from increases in IQ, while non-aggressive boys performed best and were not disadvantaged by lower general memory abilities. This link between aggression and executive function has sometimes been attributed to the association between aggression and hyperactivity (Pennington & Ozonoff, 1996). This suggestion rests on the hypothesis that hyperactivity is the expression of neuro-cognitive deficits and that it is a precursor of aggression (Lahey et al., 2000; Moffitt, 1993). However, results from our analyses suggest that a relationship exists between certain aspects of executive function (i.e., working memory, deductive, and inductive reasoning abilities) and a history of physical aggression regardless of ADHD and IQ (Séguin, Tremblay, Boulerice, Pihl, & Harden, 1999). This means that physically aggressive adolescent boys have trouble in processing information on-line, in figuring out the underlying rules that govern some situations, in applying known rules in situations that require more flexibility, and in shifting away from maladaptive action even when more appropriate alternatives are objectively accessible. Finally, these difficulties would be severely compounded when the situation is new or unexpected, and for some aggressive boys, when they become aroused (see also Séguin, Arseneault, Boulerice, Harden, & Tremblay, 2001).

The rapid biological changes at the end of the second decade after birth have often been hypothesized to be a cause of the "turbulent" adolescent years. Studies of male antisocial behavior have focused on the increasing levels of testosterone. Testosterone has been associated with aggression in humans, and may be causally contributory. However, the reverse relationship has more often been noted: testosterone levels are directly affected by social experience (Archer, 1991). Analyses of the MLES data showed that levels of testosterone at the beginning of puberty (age 12 years) predicted peer perceived dominance status one year later (age 13), but did not predict the level of physically aggressive delinquency. Body mass at age 12 rather than testosterone level predicted physically aggressive delinquency

at age 13 (Tremblay et al., 1998). At age 13, physically aggressive bo
nificantly lower salivary testosterone levels relative to physically no~ ~~
boys (Schaal et al., 1996). However, the difference became progressively smaller
at age 14 and disappeared by age 15. At age 16, physically aggressive boys had
higher salivary testosterone levels than physically nonaggressive boys (Tremblay
et al., 1997). Because genetic effects on testosterone have been shown for
adolescents and adults (Harris, Vernon, & Boomsma, 1998; Meikle, Stringham,
Bishop, & West, 1988), one explanation for these results is that the full influence
of genetic factors on testosterone is not yet expressed at the onset of puberty.

Clearly, the link between aggression and testosterone is complex, and further
research on this link from early childhood onwards is needed. This conclusion
can be generalized to most biological correlates of antisocial behavior. We need
longitudinal studies of the development of antisocial behavior that will provide
bio-psycho-social data from the prenatal period to adulthood.

Family Poverty, Family Structure, Parenting Process, and School Failure as Predictors of Delinquency

Delinquency is often attributed to poverty, divorce, poor parenting and
school failure. Pagani et al. (1999) reported on an analysis of the predictive power
of family poverty, family structure, and parenting process on school failure and
delinquency during adolescence. The temporal characteristics of economic hardship were studied by dividing the poverty intensity variable by timing and duration. By categorizing poverty and family configuration status temporally, we were
attempting to disentangle the effects of these variables. However, in order to maximize the reliability of the observed results, we began by controlling for maternal
education. Because all boys started school in low-income districts, our methodology allowed us to further distinguish SES from poverty. That is, the research
design offered the opportunity to separate being poor from living in a poor neighborhood but not being poor. The overall advantage was that we could compare the
effects of varying intensity of deprivation in boys living in the same underprivi-
leged environment.

As expected from previous work that had used the same design with the
companion study of the MLES, the Longitudinal Study of Québec Kindergarten
Children, a population sample of children from the province of Québec, family
poverty predicted academic failure at age 16 (Pagani, Boulerice, & Tremblay,
1997). This was in comparison to families that were never poor. Persistent financial hardship from ages 10 through 15 predicted not being in an age-appropriate
grade. These results are consistent with change model studies by Duncan, Brooks-
Gunn, and Klebanov (1994) and Pagani et al. (1997). They support the notion that
financial disadvantage reduces youngsters' ability to compete in the school environment. Whether that effect is due to a school context that is value-laden with

middle-class criteria remains unknown. Although they both predicted academic failure, a lack of parental supervision and enforced home rules did not explain the relation between poverty and school failure. Brooks-Gunn, Klebanov, and Liaw (1995) found that poor families experience multiple risk factors and tend to score lower on learning, physical, emotional, and family environmental measures. It is likely that adolescents who experienced persistent financial hardship throughout their childhood might be more at risk of poor academic performance by virtue of their limited exposure to environmental stimulation (i.e., books, cultural, scientific, and verbal activities). Alternatively, the effects of economic conditions on academic performance could have been accounted for by chronic financial pressures and parental responses (conflicts and strained relationships) to such pressures (Conger, Conger, & Elder, 1997). The limits of our data set precluded the verification of these explanations.

Family poverty predicted delinquency as well, but only more serious manifestations of adolescent antisocial behavior (Table 2). Surprisingly, unlike academic failure, *persistent poverty* was not the risk factor. Unstable financial hardship, wherein family poverty varied in opposing directions at two or more assessments over the 6-year period, predicted twice the risk of reporting extreme delinquency (breaking and entering; purposely set a fire in a public place; coercion; steal objects worth more than $100; vandalize a car; beating someone up) than being in a situation where the family had never been poor. Family poverty did not have an effect on other types of self-reported delinquency such as theft, substance abuse, and physical violence.

Table 2. Self-reported Extreme Delinquency at Age 16

	Model 1	*Model 2*	*Model 3*	*Model 4*	*Model 5*
Maternal education	0.94	0.94	0.95	0.94	0.97
Disruptiveness at age 6	1.04*	1.05**	1.04*	1.04*	1.03
Parental supervision at age 12				0.67***	0.70***
Classroom placement at age 16					2.14**
Family status (Reference group: Intact family)	$p = .045$		$p = .047$	$p = .050$	$p = .048$
Long-term single ≥4	1.67		1.65	1.57	1.49
Short-term single <4	4.18**		4.52**	4.23**	4.51**
Long-term remarried ≥4	1.23		1.04	0.97	1.00
Short-term remarried <4	1.06		1.00	0.73	0.66
Multiple marital transitions	1.57		1.55	1.42	1.41
Duration/timing of poverty (Reference group: Never poor)		$p = .044$	$p = .044$	$p = .044$	$p = .028$
Always poor		1.16	0.93	0.93	0.80
Poor early		1.78	1.64	1.80	1.68
Poor late		0.57	0.39	0.38	0.37
Transitory poverty		2.14*	1.89*	2.14*	2.00*

* $p < .10$; ** $p < .05$; *** $p < .001$.

Not being in an age-appropriate classroom at age 16 was associated with delinquency at age 16. This result was obtained after having controlled for maternal education, early childhood disruptiveness, and inattentiveness. This significant relationship between academic failure and delinquency allowed us to examine its role as a mediator of the impact of poverty. Although not doing well at school predicted extreme delinquency, academic failure did not mediate the effects of poverty on extreme delinquency. Poor boys were not found at risk for serious forms of delinquency by virtue of their academic failure (see Table 2).

Similarly, less parental monitoring was associated with an increased risk of self-reported extreme delinquency. However, parental monitoring did not seem crucial in explaining the effects of poverty on this type of delinquency (see Table 2). If a mediational model explained the effects of financial hardship, then the addition of home rules and parental supervision would have helped account for the effects of poverty on both academic failure and extreme delinquency. It did not.

One limitation of this finding is that we do not know if parent-child attachment processes during early childhood would have mediated the effects of poverty. It is very plausible, but beyond the limits of our data bank. The advantage of this study was that we assessed two family process variables that are important in the rearing of adolescents: structure and monitoring through home rules and supervision.[2] Our classification of family configuration status (both temporally and by type of marital transition) may have shared much of the variance explaining family processes suggested by others (e.g., Sampson & Laub, 1993, 1994).

Our results also bear upon the effects of family break-up, a correlate of poverty, on deviant activities during adolescence. Divorce during early-adolescence (i.e., between ages 12 and 14), placed boys at greater risk for both theft and fighting. However, the results only suggest a mediational model of the effects of divorce on self-reported fighting by the adolescent boys. Independent of financial hardship, a divorce in the last four years (between ages 12 and 14) increased the risk for self-reported acts of physical violence at age 16 by 346%, in comparison to the risk associated with being in an intact family. Child-rearing practices of supervision at age 12 significantly predicted self-reported fighting behavior at age 16. High versus low monitoring by parents was associated with 46% less physical violence. Once

---

[2] When subjects were 12 years old, they reported on parental supervision (2 items, alpha = .71) and home rules (5 items, alpha = .62). These factors were used as covariates when found to be by four-year intervals related to the outcome variables measured at age 16. Each item is scored on a Likert-type scale (never, once or twice, often, and very often.) The supervision questions included: "Do your parents know where you are when you go out?" and "Do your parents know who you hang around with?" The home rules items included: "Do you have rules in your family for the amount of time spent watching TV?", "Do you have a curfew?", "Do you have rules in your family for being home for dinner?", "Does your family have rules for the number of times you can go out during weekdays or weekends?", and "Do your parents supervise your selection of friends?"

this variable was included in the model, divorce was no longer significant as a predictor. This suggests that family break-up has an impact on boys' fighting behavior through its negative influence on parental supervision practices during adolescence, a time when monitoring represents a crucial child-rearing practice.

In Summary

Results from this study revealed that when maternal education and early childhood behavior were controlled for, family poverty had an effect on both academic failure and serious delinquency. This effect was independent of family configuration. Although academic failure and parental supervision predicted extreme delinquency on their own, they did not mediate the relationship between poverty and delinquency. Divorce increased the risk of theft and fighting at age 16, regardless of financial hardship. Parental supervision helped explain the effects of divorce on boys' fighting.

Deviant Friends During Pre-Adolescence and Early Delinquency

Using peer ratings collected in the boys' classrooms when they were 10, 11, and 12 years of age, Vitaro, Tremblay, Kerr, Pagani-Kurtz, and Bukowski (1997) tested the validity of alternative models for the association between delinquency and behavior of friends. Results presented in Table 3 indicate that friends with differing behavioral characteristics (including absence of friends) had no differential impact on the delinquency of boys with a history of high levels of disruptive behavior or conforming behavior, thus supporting the Individual Characteristics model proposed by Tremblay, Mâsse, Vitaro, and Dobkin (1995). Boys who were highly disruptive since kindergarten were the most delinquent at age 13 years, irrespective of their friends' characteristics. One clear exception to the Individual Characteristics model, however, was that moderately disruptive boys with aggressive-disturbing friends reported more delinquency at age 13 than their counterparts with average or nonaggressive-nondisturbing friends or no friends, even after controlling for delinquency at ages 11–12. They even reported delinquency levels similar to highly disruptive boys' levels at age 13. These results are consistent with the Peer Influence model. With nuances suggested by Dishion, French, and Patterson (1995), this alternate model predicted that deviant friends would influence disruptive boys but not nondisruptive boys even though the basic Peer Influence model predicted that deviant friends should lead to more delinquency, irrespective of boys' disruptiveness. This prediction was supported, except that moderately, not highly, disruptive boys were influenced by their aggressive-disturbing friends. The present results are consistent with findings

Table 3. Boys' Delinquency and Disruptiveness at Age 13 (and Standard Deviations) by Group and Friends' Subgroup Membership

Boy's Group	No Friend	Aggressive-disturbing	Average	Nonaggressive-nondisturbing
		Friends' Subgroup		
Self-reported delinquency				
Highly disruptive	32.46[a] (8.21)[b]	36.04 (8.27)	33.32 (7.89)	32.77 (6.00)
	32.89[c]	35.29	33.22	33.54
Moderately disruptive	32.26 (6.54)	35.67 (9.39)	31.28 (4.53)	30.36 (2.94)
	32.05	34.91	31.45	31.16
Moderately conforming	31.10 (4.38)	32.73 (5.62)	31.04 (5.12)	30.29 (3.82)
	31.14	32.10	31.18	30.74
Highly conforming	29.56 (3.54)	30.89 (4.61)	30.00 (4.09)	29.23 (3.23)
	29.09	30.41	30.32	29.84
Teacher-rated disruptiveness				
Highly disruptive	9.51[d] (5.61)	9.20 (6.47)	8.95 (5.84)	9.24 (5.68)
Moderately disruptive	6.77 (5.83)	5.96 (5.06)	5.26 (4.96)	3.21 (2.83)
Moderately conforming	3.89 (4.21)	3.78 (3.15)	2.80 (3.22)	1.66 (1.94)
Highly conforming	1.27 (2.39)	2.15 (3.73)	1.11 (1.84)	0.98 (1.86)

[a] Mean raw score; [b] Standard deviation.
[c] Mean score adjusted for covariates (i.e., SRDQ and parental occupational prestige averaged scores across ages 11 and 12).
[d] Mean score adjusted for age 11–12 years disruptiveness and parental occupation.

from O'Donnell, Hawkins, and Abbott (1995) indicating that aggressive boys who became involved in serious delinquency reported higher levels of involvement with deviant peers than those who did not become delinquent. These authors, however, did not distinguish the highly aggressive and the moderately aggressive boys in their sample. According to their selection criteria, it could be that many moderately aggressive boys might have been included in their sample.

The Peer Influence model also predicted that disruptive boys with no friends would report less delinquency than disruptive boys with friends. At first sight, this prediction was not supported by our data. First, highly disruptive boys with no friends did not report less delinquency than other highly disruptive boys; second, moderately disruptive boys with no friends reported less delinquency only when compared with moderately disruptive boys with aggressive-disturbing friends. However, a closer look at the data revealed that moderately disruptive boys with no friends were more disruptive at age 13 than their counterparts with average or nonaggressive-nondisturbing friends. Moreover, moderately disruptive boys with no friends were already more disruptive at age 6 and more anxious-withdrawn and inattentive at age 11–12 than the three other subgroups of moderately disruptive boys. Even so, they did not report more delinquency than their counterparts with average or nonaggressive-nondisruptive friends. These boys even reported less delinquent behaviors at age 13 than moderately disruptive boys with aggressive-disturbing friends despite their more negative behavioral profile at ages 13, 12, 11, and 6.

These results indicate that moderately disruptive boys with no friends are somewhat protected from delinquency (but not from disruptiveness), possibly because they are protected from deviant peers' influences. They may also be protected from delinquency either because they have no friends outside the classroom or because they have nondeviant friends outside the school. As suggested by the data presented above on personality dimensions (Kerr et al., 1997; Tremblay et al., 1994), they might also be protected because they are behaviorally inhibited. For highly disruptive boys, however, having no friends was not protective, possibly (1) because these boys would not need peer influences (at least from classmates during early adolescence) to become involved in delinquency; or (2) because these boys may have friends in their neighborhood that are deviant even though they have no friends in the classroom.

Finally, the Peer Influence model predicted that nonaggressive-nondisturbing friends would benefit highly and moderately disruptive boys. This protective effect was not supported in this data. Nonaggressive-nondisturbing friends did not influence disruptive boys' trajectories toward delinquency, despite the fact that they were as nonaggressive-nondisturbing, according to peers, as conforming boys' nonaggressive-nondisturbing friends. However, nonaggressive-nondisturbing friends seemed to protect moderately disruptive boys against delinquency.

The fact that moderately but not highly disruptive boys were influenced toward delinquency by disruptive friends leads us to draw at least two tentative conclusions. First, during pre-adolescence, highly disruptive boys do not need to be influenced by deviant peers to become delinquent. This does not rule out the possibility that the influence might have occurred during childhood. The phenomenon of increasing similarity between friends (Epstein, 1983) would be limited here by the fact that highly disruptive boys and their disruptive friends are already similar. Most of them have disruptive friends, which may be viewed as correlates of their disruptiveness, unrelated to their delinquent trajectory. Second, although they are not influenced, negatively or positively, by their friends, highly disruptive boys can influence their friends, some of whom are moderately disruptive. Moderately disruptive boys, then, may engage in delinquent acts under the influence of their deviant friends. This influence is important, since moderately disruptive boys with deviant friends are as delinquent as highly disruptive boys at age 13. These results may help explain findings by Fergusson and Horwood (1996) indicating that peer influences partially mediated the link between early conduct problems and delinquency. They also found a moderate direct link between early conduct problems and delinquency. Each effect may have been accounted for by different groups of subjects with greater or lesser conduct problems; for some subjects peer influences may have been important (i.e., moderately-conduct disordered at risk of becoming the adolescence-limited delinquents); for others, it may not have been the case (i.e., highly-conduct disordered subjects at risk for life-course persistent delinquency).

Replications of our findings are needed. If they are replicated, then we could conclude that mere association with deviant peers causes delinquency, but this statement would only apply to boys with moderate disruptiveness profiles. According to the present findings, this scenario would be operative by early adolescence and possibly beyond.

Several authors have argued that problem boys who are influenced toward delinquency by deviant friends are those who have difficulties with their parents (Oswald & Süss, 1994; Simons, Wu, Conger, & Lorenz, 1994). Our results did not support this hypothesis. Moderately disruptive boys with disruptive friends who became more delinquent did not differ on self-reported family variables compared with other moderately disruptive boys. The present results are consistent with data reported by Hoge, Andrews, and Leschied (1994), which did not detect interaction between family relationship variables and association with deviant peers in predicting severe delinquency. They also concur with findings from O'Donnell et al. (1995) indicating that family bonding and parent management practices contribute little in discriminating early adolescent-aggressive boys who become delinquent from those who do not. Similarly, the measure of best friend's support did not help explain why moderately disruptive boys with disruptive friends became more delinquent than other subgroups of moderately disruptive boys. However, no measure of conflict between friends or reinforcement for deviant behaviors was used in our study. In consequence, the present results do not contradict results from Dishion, Andrews, and Crosby (1994) showing that deviant friends are more coercive and reinforce deviant behaviors more than nondeviant friends.

It is noteworthy that 21% of highly disruptive boys had disruptive friends. In this study as in others, however (Boivin & Vitaro, 1995; Cairns, Cairns, Neckerman, Gest, & Gariépy, 1988) a majority of highly (and moderately) disruptive boys associated with disruptive or average friends. Similarly, a majority of conforming boys associated with average or nonaggressive-nondisturbing friends. Nonetheless, a small proportion (13.7%) of highly conforming boys and a larger proportion of moderately conforming boys (20.5%) associated with disruptive friends, and these friends were as aggressive-disturbing, according to peers, as highly disruptive boys' disruptive friends.

One important question that remains open is why some boys from each group associate with deviant friends whereas others associate with nondeviant friends? The present data do not help us address this issue since the boys who associated with deviant friends did not differ from their counterparts who had nondeviant friends on parental communication, supervision, punishment, or household rules. Nor did they differ on teacher-rated anxiety-withdrawal, inattention, or prosociality. On the other hand, because no differences were found on family and personal characteristics, these variables cannot account for the fact that moderately disruptive boys with deviant friends became more delinquent than the other subgroups of moderately disruptive boys.

In Summary

Findings from these analyses clearly suggest that friends' characteristics may influence some boys' developmental trajectories, but this influence is not independent of the boys' own behavioral characteristics. Some (i.e., highly disruptives) do not require the influences of deviant peers to become involved in delinquent behavior, and others (i.e., nondisruptives) are partially invulnerable to friends' influences (with respect to delinquency up to age 13, at least). Yet others (i.e., moderately disruptives) are adversely influenced by deviant peers and are involved (possibly temporarily) in delinquency despite their non-at-risk behavioral profiles. Vitaro, Brendgen, and Tremblay (2001) showed, furthermore, that attachment to parents also moderated the influence of deviant friends.

Developmental Trajectories to Physically Violent and Nonviolent Juvenile Delinquency

Most longitudinal studies in the field of juvenile delinquency have been concerned with the problem of predicting later antisocial behavior. As can be seen from the data presented above, the MLES followed that tradition. The problem of prediction is important for practical and theoretical reasons. From a practical perspective, it is important to identify as soon as possible those who are at highest risk for delinquency or recidivism so that preventive interventions can be delivered at the appropriate time. The thinking concerning these preventive interventions is generally that the earlier would be the better (Karoly et al., 1998; Mrazek & Haggerty, 1994; Tremblay, LeMarquand, & Vitaro, 1999a). From a theoretical perspective, the identification of predictors of later antisocial behavior is often considered a demonstration of causal effects, and thus a test of a theoretical model concerning the development of antisocial behavior.

Longitudinal studies are certainly a better test of causal theories than cross-sectional studies, which have constituted the majority of studies of delinquent behavior. However, longitudinal studies are still only correlational studies, and the strong association between a predictor variable at Time 1 and an outcome variable at Time 2 does not necessarily imply a causal relationship. In fact most Time 1–Time 2 correlations are probably not causal.

It is important to note that most of our recent theoretical thinking concerning the development of juvenile antisocial behavior had to rely either on analyses of cross-sectional data or analyses of longitudinal data which generally used two data points and focused on differential stability rather than absolute or ipsative stability (Caspi & Bem, 1990). Analyses of developmental trajectories of behavior problems from childhood to adolescence have been extremely rare (for examples see: Cairns, Cairns, Neckerman, Fergusson, & Gariépy, 1989; Moffitt, 1990). If antisocial behavior is stable over time and its appearance at any point during development is caused by the same factors, cross-sectional data could be sufficient to reveal the concurrent relation among the causal factor and the outcome (Gottfredson & Hirschi, 1990), while Time 1–Time 2 longitudinal studies would be sufficient to show that the putative causal factor appears before the outcome and is strongly related to this outcome. However, to understand how antisocial behavior appears and disappears over long periods of time requires relatively frequent repeated measures over long periods of time. One of the major advances in longitudinal studies over the past two decades is the use of multiple measurement points at relatively short intervals and the creation of statistical models to analyze data from numerous assessments over time (Bryk & Raudenbush, 1987; Goldstein, 1995; Muthen, 1989; Nagin, 1999).

Over the past decade, a number of developmental models have suggested that the paths to both physically violent and nonphysically violent delinquency are preceded by oppositional behavior and lack of self-control revealed by impulsive and hyperactive behavior during childhood (e.g., Gottfredson & Hirschi, 1990; Loeber & Stouthamer-Loeber, 1998; Moffitt, 1993; Satterfield, 1987). An alternative model proposes that physically violent delinquency, especially its chronic form, has a specific developmental trajectory, which starts with failure to learn to regulate physical aggression in early childhood (e.g., Cairns, 1979; Tremblay, 2000). The U.S. National Research Council's Panel on Understanding and Preventing Violence (Reiss & Roth, 1993) gave the following formulation of the problem:

> What constructs underlie aggressive and violent behavior, and how general or specific should they be? Should we assume that all persons can be ordered on a dimension of violence potential at any given age, or can they be ordered on a more general dimension such as antisocial personality or *potential for antisocial behavior*? (p. 361)

Nagin and Tremblay (1999) studied this issue by tracing the developmental trajectories of physical aggression, opposition, and hyperactivity from kindergarten to mid-adolescence. The trajectories were estimated with a semi-parametric group-based statistical procedure rather than by subjective classification rules. These trajectories were used to predict different forms of delinquent behavior at the end of adolescence. The results revealed that as boys grow older they generally show less and less hyperactivity, opposition, and physical aggression. Figure 4, which presents the trajectories of physical aggression, illustrates the patterns of behavior with respect to hyperactivity, opposition, and physical aggression. The results for physical aggression replicate previous studies (Cairns & Cairns, 1994;

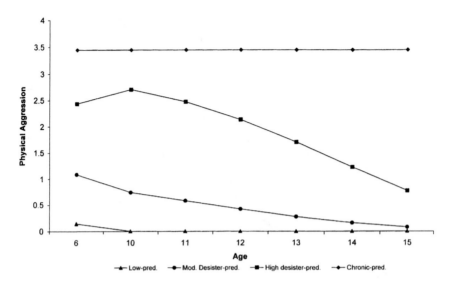

Figure 4. Trajectories of physical aggression.

Tremblay et al., 1996) and contradict the popular belief that as boys become older they increase the frequency of their oppositional and physically aggressive behavior. Instead, we found that the oppositional and physically aggressive adolescents were oppositional and physically aggressive children. Further, contrary to the idea that there is a group of males who have a late onset trajectory of problem behaviors (Haapasalo & Tremblay, 1994; Moffitt, 1993; Moffitt, Caspi, Dickson, Silva, & Stanton, 1996; Patterson, DeBaryshe, & Ramsey, 1989), such a group was not identified. However, there were clearly many boys with high levels of externalizing behavior problems at school entry who became better adjusted as they grew older. This is consistent with an observation made more than two decades ago by Robins (1978) who concluded that "adult antisocial behavior virtually requires childhood antisocial behavior [yet] most antisocial children do not become antisocial adults." (p. 611). For each type of externalizing problem behavior, the relative size of the high level-near desistor group compared to the chronic group provided still further evidence of "Robins' Maxim." For example, for physical aggression, about 28% of the sample was estimated to be in the high level near desistor group, but only 4% was estimated to be in the chronic group. Thus, of the boys who displayed elevated levels of physical aggression in kindergarten, only 1 in 8 continued to exhibit elevated levels of physical aggression in later adolescence.

Using the same semi-parametric, group-based method, Brame, Nagin, and Tremblay (2001) estimated the developmental trajectories for repeated measures of two different response variables: physical aggression in childhood as measured by teacher reports and physical aggression in adolescence as measured by

Table 4. Joint Distribution of Childhood and Adolescent Physical Aggression

Trajectories Based on Classify-Analyze Method on Marginal Outcomes

Adolescent Physical Aggression Trajectories	Childhood Aggression Trajectory # 1 (Low aggression)		Childhood Aggression Trajectory # 2 (Medium aggression)		Childhood Aggression Trajectory # 3 (High aggression)		Total	
	N	%	N	%	N	%	N	%
T_1: No aggression	358	75.9	167	57.6	66	40.2	591	63.8
T_2: Increasing aggression	60	12.7	50	17.2	36	22.0	146	15.8
T_3: Decreasing aggression	46	9.8	54	18.6	40	24.4	140	15.1
T_4: High aggression	8	1.7	19	6.6	22	13.4	49	5.3
Total	472	51.0	290	31.3	164	17.7	926	100.0

$\gamma = +0.462; p < .05.$
Note: Since γ is an ordinal measure of association, we calculate it after combining the adolescent aggression T_2 and T_3 trajectory groups into a single group.

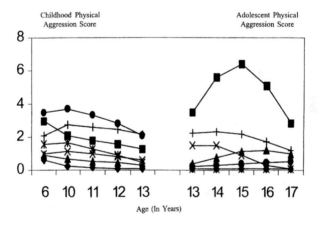

Figure 5. Joint trajectories of childhood physical aggression and adolescent physical aggression ($N = 926$).

self-reported violent delinquency. They found considerable change in the levels of childhood and adolescent physical aggression (see Table 4 and Figure 5). Thus, there was little evidence of stability of behavior in an absolute sense. A second key finding was the connection of childhood aggression to adolescent aggression. Boys with higher childhood physical aggression trajectories were far more likely to transition to a higher-level adolescent aggression trajectory than boys from lower childhood physical aggression trajectories. However, for all childhood physical aggression trajectory levels, the modal transition was to a relatively low-level adolescent aggression trajectory. Third, there was little evidence of "late onset" of high-level physical aggression. Specifically, the joint trajectory analysis found no evidence of transition from a low physical aggression trajectory in childhood to a high trajectory in adolescence.

In the second stage of their analysis, Nagin and Tremblay (1999) used the model coefficient estimates to compute the "posterior probability of group membership" for each individual in the estimation sample. For each individual these probabilities estimate the likelihood of belonging to each trajectory group identified in the analysis. For example, for an individual who displayed persistently high physical aggression from childhood through adolescence, the posterior probability estimate of his belonging to the low aggression trajectory group would be near zero, whereas the estimate for the chronic group would be near one. These probabilities created the basis for examining the differences in annual self-reports of delinquent behavior between ages 15 and 17 for groups of boys who showed different developmental trajectories between 6 and 15 years of age. The purpose was to test different models of the paths from childhood externalizing problem behaviors to juvenile delinquency. Results clearly indicated that boys who show high levels of hyperactive behavior from kindergarten to high school are much less at risk of juvenile delinquency than those who show high levels of physical aggression or opposition. This finding suggests that studies that have found hyperactivity to be a good predictor of juvenile delinquency had failed to control for physical aggression and opposition (Farrington, Loeber, & Van Kammen, 1990; Satterfield, Hoppe, & Schell, 1982; Weiss & Hechtman, 1993). Lahey et al. (1999) came to the same conclusion as we did concerning the developmental links between childhood ADHD and adolescent conduct disorder. Our findings also suggest that Gottfredson and Hirschi's (1990) hypothesis of low self-control as the underlying cause of most criminal and delinquent behavior must be reconsidered. Only 13% of the chronically physically aggressive and 23% of the chronically oppositional were chronically hyperactive. Many chronically antisocial boys are not among the most impulsive, and many chronically impulsive are not chronically antisocial.

Since there were few additive effects in the regression, Yoshikawa's (1994) hypothesis that childhood problem behaviors accumulate to increase the risk of all forms of delinquent behavior did not get strong support from our results either. It was the hypothesis of specific pathways to overt and covert delinquency (Loeber, 1991; Loeber et al., 1993) that was most strongly supported by our results. A chronic oppositional trajectory, with the physical aggression and hyperactivity trajectories being held constant, led to covert delinquency (theft) only, while a chronic physical aggression trajectory, with the oppositional and hyperactivity trajectories being held constant, led to overt delinquency (physical violence) and to the most serious delinquent acts.

Loeber's (Loeber, 1991; Loeber & Hay, 1994; Loeber, Keenan, & Zhang, 1997) model suggested that the overt pathway starts in early childhood with oppositional behavior, leads to physically aggressive behavior during middle childhood, and is transformed into violent delinquency during adolescence. Our results do not support the idea that chronic physical aggression appears after oppositional behavior, because we did not have a late onset group for physical aggression. It could be argued that our study, which began during the kindergarten year, started too late to observe the path from opposition to physical aggression. However, the available data on physical aggression before entry in kindergarten indicates that the frequency of physical aggression reaches its peak around age two and then slowly declines up to adolescence (Restoin et al., 1985; Tremblay et al., 1996; Tremblay, Japel, Pérusse, Boivin, Zoccolillo, Montplaisir, & McDuff, 1999b). Based on longitudinal studies of physical aggression during the preschool years (Cummings, Iannotti, & Zahn-Waxler, 1989; Hay, Castle, & Davies, 2000; Keenan & Shaw, 1994; Keenan & Wakschlag, 2000), it is most likely that the boys in the high level and chronic physically aggressive trajectories were already highly physically aggressive by age 2. For opposition to be antecedent to physical aggression, we would probably need to be referring to opposition in the first year of life.

We have the impression that the boys on the overt delinquency or physical aggression path are those who did not learn to regulate the physically aggressive reactions that most children manifest from the beginning of their second year after birth (Tremblay et al., 1998). This behavioral trajectory appears to begin with physical aggression as soon as the child is sufficiently coordinated to do so. The changes in behavior are probably changes in the frequency, means, context, victims, and consequences of his physical aggression, which are probably related to his physical, cognitive, emotional, and social development.

In Nagin and Tremblay (2001), we find that only two characteristics distinguish the boys who follow such a trajectory of chronic physical aggression from their counterparts who display high levels of physical aggression in kindergarten but who subsequently show greater restraint, namely the high level near desistors: mothers' teen onset of parenthood and low educational attainment. For example, more aggressive young women are more likely to become teen mothers and to drop out of school, and are also more likely to be unresponsive parents. There is also evidence that women who begin childbearing early are more likely to use harsh and erratic discipline. These mothers may also be more prone to birth complications which have been shown to be related to subsequent conduct problems in the child (Arseneault et al., 2000; Raine, Brennan, & Mednick, 1997). These findings suggest that the mothers themselves may be the agents of the intergenerational transfer of chronic physical aggression. The results are not nearly definitive about the specifics of the transfer mechanism in terms of the separate and interactive roles of biology, parenting practices (including those of the father), and the larger social environment. Notwithstanding, they do suggest that the intergenerational transfer mechanism may have profound consequences for the child and society at large.

Our results for the oppositional trajectory appear to confirm that subjects who follow Loeber et al. (1993) covert pathway from pre- to late adolescence begin with early childhood oppositional behavior (Loeber's authority conflict pathway). Thus the chronic covert behavior problem trajectory would start with preschool oppositional behavior problems. Future longitudinal studies of preschool children should focus on the factors that put some children on the chronic oppositional trajectory and others on the chronic physical aggression trajectory. Early temperamental characteristics certainly need to be taken into account (e.g., Kagan & Snidman, 1991; Lahey et al., 1999; Tremblay et al., 1994), but complex early interactions among bio-psycho-social factors are probably major determinants of these chronic trajectories (see Raine, Farrington, Brennan, & Mednick, 1997).

A Preventive Experiment to Test Causal Hypotheses and Identify Effective Interventions

Experimental interventions, or randomized clinical trials, as they are called in the medical literature, are useful to assess the impact of programs designed to prevent the development of antisocial behavior. However, the experimental design can also provide a more adequate test of causal hypotheses than longitudinal studies, since there is an experimental manipulation of hypothesized causal factors and control of the other putative causal factors by the randomization process (Schwartz, Flamant, & Lellouch, 1980).

The aim of the MLES randomized trial was to test to what extent an intensive multimodal preventive intervention for disruptive kindergarten boys could prevent the development of antisocial behavior. When the intervention was planned in the early 1980s, parent training and social skills training were perceived as the alternative to the traditional psycho-dynamic approach to prevent delinquent behavior (e.g., Meichenbaum, 1977; Michelson, Sugai, Wood, & Kazdin, 1983; Patterson, 1982; Patterson, Reid, Jones, & Conger, 1975). Most experiments targeted either children's social-cognitive skills or parenting skills (e.g., Lochman, Nelson, & Sims, 1981; Patterson et al., 1975). The interventions were also generally aimed at children older than 10 years of age and had a relatively short duration, usually less than one year, and often less than 6 months. To increase the chance of obtaining positive effects we decided to target younger children, as well as parents, to include well-adjusted peers, and to maintain the intervention for two years.

The parent-training component was based on a model developed at the Oregon Social Learning Center (Patterson, 1982; Patterson et al., 1975). The procedure involved (1) giving parents a reading program, (2) training parents to monitor their children's behavior, (3) training parents to give positive reinforcement for prosocial behavior, (4) training parents to punish effectively without being abusive, (5) training parents to manage family crises, and (6) helping parents to generalize what they had learned. Having the professional who worked with a family meet the boy's teacher to discuss his adjustment and means of helping him complemented this component. Teachers, however, were generally not able to spend much time discussing teaching strategies for one child, and resources to implement a structured teacher-training program were not available.

Work with parents and teachers was carried out by two university-trained childcare workers, one psychologist, and one social worker all working full-time. The professionals were trained for 10 months before the start of the program and received regular supervision for the duration of the experiment. Each of these professionals had a caseload of 12 families. The team was coordinated by a fifth professional who worked on the project part-time. Work with the parents was planned to last for two school years with one session every 2 or 3 weeks. The professionals, however, were free to decide that a given family needed more or fewer sessions at any given time. The maximum number of sessions given to any family was 46 and the mean number of sessions over the two years was 17.4, including families that refused to continue. The social skills training component was implemented in the schools. One or two disruptive boys were included in groups of three to five peers who were identified by teachers as highly prosocial. The same group of professionals who conducted the parent training offered the training during lunchtime. To create a team approach, different professionals were responsible for the parent and child training with each family. The two professionals responsible for a given family met regularly to discuss treatment strategy. The multidisciplinary team of professionals also met weekly to study a few cases. This helped maintain a consistent treatment approach. For the social skills training component of our intervention, two types of training were given to the disruptive boys within a small group of prosocial peers in school. During the first year, a prosocial skills program was devised based on other programs (Cartledge & Milburn, 1980; Michelson et al., 1983; Schneider & Byrne, 1987). Nine sessions were given on themes such as "How to make contact," "How to help," "How to ask *why*," and "How to invite someone in a group." Coaching, peer modeling, role-playing, and reinforcement contingencies were used during these sessions. The program was aimed at self-control during the second year. Using material from previous studies (Camp, Blom, Hebert, & Van Doorninck, 1977; Goldstein, Sprafkin, Gershaw, & Klein, 1980; Kettlewell & Kausch, 1983; Meichenbaum, 1977), ten sessions were developed on themes such as "Look and listen," "Following rules," "What to do when I am angry," "What to do when they do not want me to play with them," and "How to react to teasing." Coaching, peer modeling, self-instructions, behavioral rehearsal, and reinforcement contingencies were also used during these sessions.

As described in the introduction to this chapter, from the total sample of boys assessed in kindergarten, those above the 70th percentile on the kindergarten teacher-rated disruptive behavior scale were randomly allocated to a treatment or control group. From the end of the two-year intervention to the second year after the intervention, no significant differences were observed between the treated and the control groups. Because of these disappointing results, it is likely that the follow-up of the preventive experiment would not have continued had it not been part of a longitudinal study. Most preventive delinquency interventions have follow-up periods of less than one year (Tremblay & Craig, 1995; Tremblay et al., 1999a).

Three years after the end of the intervention, when most of the boys were in their last year of elementary school, the annual assessments revealed statistically significant positive effects. The boys from the treatment group reported less delinquent behavior, they were rated by their teachers and their peers as being less disruptive, more of them were still in an age-appropriate classroom, and they tended to have less disruptive friends than the control group boys (McCord, Tremblay, Vitaro, & Desmarais-Gervais, 1994; Tremblay et al., 1991; Tremblay et al., 1992; Vitaro & Tremblay, 1994).

Assessments of the boys up to 17 years of age revealed that the intervention had long-term beneficial influences on the boys' development, but these depended on age, domain, and data source. With respect to global school adjustment, measured by being in an age-appropriate regular classroom, the intervention appeared to have a positive impact during the elementary school years; however, that impact disappeared by age 15 years when the boys should have been in their third year of high school (Figure 6). This result was somewhat disappointing. It was intuitively expected that success in elementary school would have a positive effect upon success in secondary school. However, when consideration is given to the level of success for the whole sample of boys who were in the low SES kindergarten classes, a majority (59.3%) were not in an age-appropriate regular classroom by age 15. Given that poor school adjustment at age 15 is the norm for this sample of boys from low SES environments, it was unlikely that an intervention directed at disruptive behavior would have enabled disruptive kindergarten boys to have more success in high school than the majority of their peers. It is important to note that this phenomenon could not have been observed if the experiment had not been nested within a longitudinal study of a population-based age cohort.

Nonetheless, the importance of the beneficial impact upon elementary school adjustment should not be overlooked. The boys who remained in an age-appropriate regular classroom during elementary school were in a very different social and intellectual environment compared to those who were held back or placed in special classes or schools. The quality of that environment may have had beneficial effects upon other aspects of their development during high school (e.g., self-esteem, attitudes toward school, delinquency). Because being placed out of an age-appropriate regular classroom *in high school* appears to be normative for this

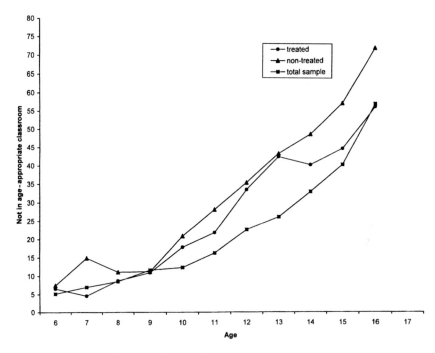

Figure 6. Boys not in age-appropriate classroom.

cohort of boys, it is reasonable to speculate that being out of an age-appropriate classroom may not have the negative impact that it could have if it happened during the elementary school years. This was confirmed by the school dropout data observed when the boys were 17 years of age: the control group had twice the school drop-out rate (21.6%) of the treated group (10.5%) (Vitaro, Brendgen, & Tremblay, 1999).

Delinquency was assessed both with self-reports and court records. The latter did not reveal any significant differences between the groups. One would have hoped that an intensive early intervention with disruptive boys would have reduced the number of boys who were officially treated by the courts as juvenile offenders. Clearly, such a procedure is costly both in terms of social resources and human suffering for the boys and their families, and it was not a negligible phenomenon; 3.1% of the kindergarten boys from the low SES schools and 5.8% of the disruptive kindergarten boys from that cohort were placed under the Young Offenders' Act (6.5% of the treated and 4.8% of the untreated).

Thus, from the perspective of official delinquency (and physical aggression), this type of intervention with these at-risk boys does not appear to have achieved its aim. However, from the perspective of self-reported delinquency, the intervention has reduced the number of delinquent behaviors from age 13 to 16.

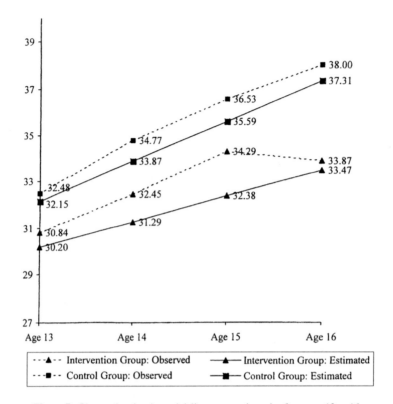

Figure 7. Observed and estimated delinquency trajectories from age 13 to 16.

Figure 7 (Vitaro et al., 2001) summarizes the results from a growth-curve analysis. It shows that the level of delinquency for the prevention group was lower at 13 years (i.e., the intercept) than in the control group. There was, however, no direct effect of the program on the growth (i.e., the slope) of delinquency from 13 through 16 years of age. Path analysis showed that reduction in disruptiveness and increase in parental supervision by age 11, as well as association with non-deviant peers by age 12, were part of a chain of events that was found to mediate the effect of the program on the initial level of delinquency at 13 years (Figure 8). The analysis also showed that the program had an indirect effect through these variables on the growth of delinquency from 13 to 16 years of age.

Taken together, these results indicate that the intervention did not have an impact on the worst cases (i.e., those with official juvenile delinquency records), but it did have an impact by significantly reducing the frequency of delinquent behaviors for a group of high-risk boys. This could be an important effect since each delinquent behavior is a socially meaningful event for a number of persons (e.g., the victim, the delinquent, the families involved, the social control agents).

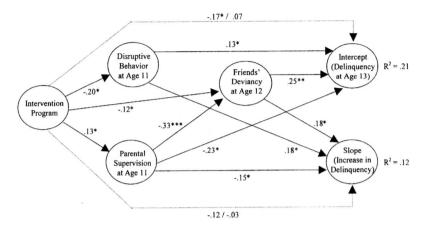

Figure 8. Model of direct and indirect intervention effects. $*p < .05$; $**p < .01$; $***p < .001$.

It may be a meaningful effect for the development of the disruptive kindergarten boys as well, if reducing the frequency of their delinquent behavior has an impact on key developmental sensitive periods.

The findings suggest that the comparative changes in delinquent behavior and the significantly higher levels of academic adjustment observed in youngsters from the experimental group may be attributable to the treatment. Improving parental practices and children's social competence during the early elementary school years does appear to influence the outcomes over the long term, supporting the hypotheses that parent effectiveness and social skills are related to delinquent behavior. Once modified, these elements appear to trigger a chain of events that will result in lowered delinquency. Results concerning peer association indicate that association with less deviant peers might be part of the process.

Not all interventions are successful, however, and there are critical components that can lead to maintenance or worsening of target problem behaviors. Dishion, McCord, and Poulin (1999) reported on two prevention experiments that seemed to have unintentionally produced iatrogenic effects by increasing at risk boys' behavior problems. The negative impact of this often-used treatment strategy could be through contagion. We chose to create treatment groups with a majority of non-problematic boys for the social and social-cognitive skills training sessions. The initial reasons for this were to avoid labeling of the problem children and to capitalize on the positive influence of highly prosocial peers. It seems that this strategy paid off although it meant many more training groups, and consequently more investment of money and time. Now that we are aware of the possible iatrogenic effects of aggregating at risk youth, the extra cost in money and time required by individual or mixed group (i.e., disruptive and prosocial peers) interventions seems to be a necessity rather than a luxury.

A meta-analysis by Ang, Woldbeck, Arnold, and Hughes (1998), showing that social skills training in groups of mixed peers produced stronger effects than in groups of deviant only children, supports this important point.

Our intervention experiment nested within a longitudinal study has shown that intensive interventions with disruptive kindergarten boys can have statistically significant positive results in the long term, and that it can help us understand causal mechanisms leading to delinquent behavior. However, results did not indicate a significant impact on official delinquency and on physical violence. Because we now know that physical aggression begins early and that risk factors are present before conception, we believe that intensive interventions starting as early as pregnancy are more likely to significantly reduce the risk of chronic violence (Tremblay et al., 1999a; Tremblay et al., 1999b). To test this hypothesis would mean the undertaking of a large longitudinal-experimental study starting during pregnancy with a firm commitment to follow these children into adolescence and adulthood.

Beyond the MLES

Our work on the MLES and its companion study, the Longitudinal Study of Québec Kindergarten Children, convinced us that we needed to start earlier than school entry to understand and prevent the development of antisocial behavior. At the beginning of the 1990s, we were invited by the Canadian Ministry of Health and Social Welfare to participate in the planning of an accelerated longitudinal study of a random sample of more than 22,000 Canadian children aged 0 to 11 years at the start of the study. Cross-sectional data from the first data collection point indicated that physical aggression decreased from the third year after birth to 11 years of age (Tremblay et al., 1996). It also indicated that indirect aggression (e.g., getting others not to play with someone you do not like) increased from 4 to 11 years of age (Figure 9). These results suggest that during the preschool years children learn to replace physical aggression by indirect aggression in response to frustration as well as to get what they want. Because the study included up to four children per family, we were also able to examine the concentration of aggression in families. Multilevel statistical analyses indicated that family concentration was higher for physical and indirect aggression than for hyperactivity and anxiety. The analyses also indicated that physical aggression concentration was higher in families of low socioeconomic status than in families of high socioeconomic status, suggesting that the difference in frequency of physical aggression between high and low socioeconomic status children is mainly due to a greater number of low SES status families with many aggressive children, rather than to a wider distribution of aggressive individuals in low SES families (Tremblay et al., 1996). The Ministry intends to assess this sample of children every two years until early adulthood.

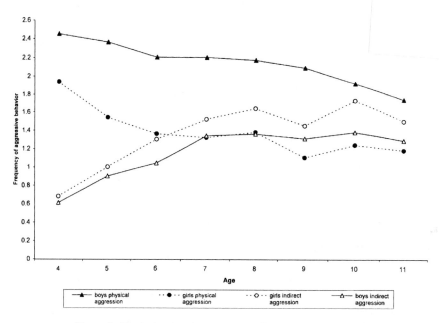

Figure 9. Physical and indirect aggression from 4 to 11 years of age.

We also initiated a longitudinal study of a birth cohort with annual assessments to obtain a more detailed understanding of the development of antisocial behavior during the preschool years. Two different samples were recruited: a random sample of all newborn in the province of Québec in 1997–98 ($N = 2,300$) and a sample of newborn twins in the Montréal area ($N = 600$). Data analyses of the pilot sample for that study ($N = 572$) have already provided important information about the onset of physical aggression. Tremblay et al. (1999b) have shown that almost all children are reported by their mothers to have initiated some form of physical aggression by 17 months of age. Mothers' report of the age of initiation of physically aggressive behaviors indicated that most children initiate these behaviors during the first 6 months of the second year after birth (Figure 10). One of the important analyses from that study concerns mothers' recall of the initiation of physical aggression. When their child was 17 and 30 months old, mothers were asked if the child physically aggressed and, if so, at what age the behavior had started. This procedure is the same as the one used by Loeber and Stouthamer-Loeber (1998) when the Pittsburgh oldest cohort was 13 years of age. Figure 11 shows that the cumulative age of onset curve for physical attacks is very similar to the one presented by Loeber and Stouthamer-Loeber (1998), although in their case the ages range from 3 to 16 years while in our case they range from birth to 30 months of age. Clearly, the age of onset of physical aggression occurs much earlier than 3 years of age as suggested by the Pittsburgh data.

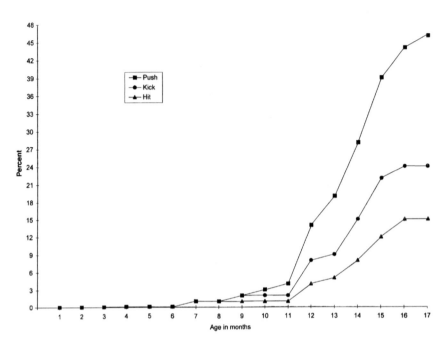

Figure 10. Physical aggression from birth to 17 months of age.

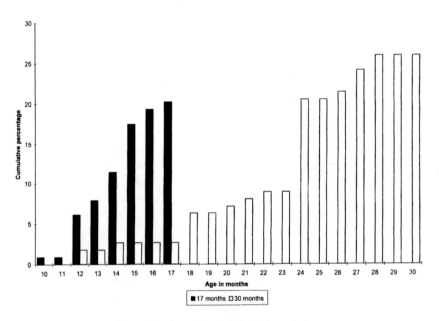

Figure 11. Age of onset of physical aggression.

We believe that the difference here is due to the problem of recall. Figure 11 clearly illustrates this problem. Mothers who reported that their 17-month-old child had started to physically aggress had forgotten this. Twelve months later they were reporting that he had started to physically aggress during the past year. Thus, mothers forget from one year to another when their child initiated physical aggression and they will clearly not be able to recall the age of initiation of physical aggression when their child is in elementary or secondary school.

Results from bivariate correlations between the level of physical aggression at 17 months of age and possible explanatory variables showed that boys' level of physical aggression at that age was significantly correlated with mothers' failure to complete high school, mothers' alcohol consumption, mothers' depression, quality of family functioning, difficult temperament of the boy, and mothers' coercive behavior towards the boy. The association between physical aggression and presence of a sibling also indicated that the presence of a target increases the risk of physical aggression (Table 5).

To identify a plausible developmental sequence of risk factors, the predictors were introduced chronologically in a hierarchical multiple regression (Tremblay et al., in press). Results (Table 6) indicated that mothers' failure to finish high school and their alcohol consumption were the best prenatal predictors of their sons' level of physical aggression at 17 months. Poor family functioning and presence of a sibling were the two best birth predictors, after having controlled for the pre-birth predictors. Finally, difficult temperament was the best of the 5-month predictors, after having controlled for the pre-birth and birth predictors.

Table 5. Correlations Between Variables ($N = 228$)

	2	3	4	5	6	7	8	9	10	11	12	13
Prenatal variables												
1-Income	−.32	.35	−.33	−.10	−.21	.07	−.20	−.28	−.04	−.13	.03	−.12
2-Family type		−.27	.26	.13	.15	.06	.24	.21	.09	.14	−.06	.12
3-Mother's age			−.32	−.15	−.12	−.28	−.06	−.16	.05	−.04	−.12	−.11
4-Mother's education				.01	.26	.10	.10	.21	.05	−.03	.05	.15
5-Mother drinks					.27	−.01	.11	.14	.07	.16	.03	.16
6-Mother smokes						.03	.09	.18	.07	.17	−.05	.05
Birth variables												
7-Siblings							.11	.07	.02	−.06	−.05	.24
8-Family functioning								.44	.10	.23	−.25	.19
9-Mother's depression									.21	.14	−.30	.15
Five month's variables												
10-Temperament										.28	−.36	.21
11-Mother coercive											−.26	.17
12-Mother effective												.01
13-Physical aggression at 17 months												

Table 6. Multiple Regression Analysis to Predict Physical Aggression at 17 Months

	Model 1 Pre-birth Predictors			Model 2 Pre-birth + Birth Predictors			Model 3 Pre-birth + Birth + 5 Months Predictors		
	β	SE (β)	Sign. T	β	SE (β)	Sign. T	β	SE (β)	Sign. T
Pre-birth variables									
Mother's education	1.47	.65	.024	1.13	.63	.08	.93	.62	.137
Mother's alcohol consumption	1.19	.49	.016	1.08	.48	.024	.93	.47	.049
Birth variables									
Siblings				1.16	.34	.001	1.17	.34	.001
Family functioning				.17	.08	.032	.19	.08	.019
Five month's variables									
Child temperament							.34	.10	.001
Mother feeling effective							.29	.15	.047
Total R^2 (in %)		3.9%			10.2%			14.2%	

Mothers' parenting behaviors at 5 months just failed to enter the equation once child temperament was entered.

These results indicate that, although most children use physical aggression by the end of the second year after birth, the frequency of these behaviors reported by their mothers is associated with characteristics that have been shown to predict antisocial behavior: mothers' low education (Farrington, 1998; Nagin & Tremblay, 2001), mothers' substance use (Farrington, 1998; Pihl et al., 1998), poor family functioning (Deater-Deckard, 1998; Farrington, in press; McCord, 1991), and difficult temperament (Caspi, Henry, McGee, Moffitt, & Silva, 1995; Deater-Deckard, 1998; Kingston & Prior, 1995).

The important point for parents, educators and clinicians is that high levels of physical aggression during early childhood must be taken seriously. If most children learn to inhibit physical aggression during the first few years after birth, it may be the best time to help those who appear to have problems in learning to inhibit these behaviors, and in learning to use alternative ways of achieving their goals.

Most of the research on the onset of violent behavior has focused on preadolescents and adolescents. To understand the process by which 17-month-old children have become more physically aggressive than their same-age peers, we will need to focus on the first two years of life. The results described above confirm those from many other studies indicating that mothers' history of social adjustment before the children's birth may play a significant role. Mothers who have a history of behavior problems are less likely to provide the prenatal and postnatal environment necessary for preventing deviant biological and psychosocial development (Castaignede & Tremblay, 1984; Nagin, Pogarsky, & Farrington,

1997; Robins, West, & Herjanic, 1975; Serbin et al., 1998). However, after having controlled for mothers' history of psychosocial adjustment, family income and family functioning, we observed that difficult temperament at 5 months was still a significant predictor. These temperamental dispositions can be the product of pre-natal and postnatal environmental effects, but they can also be the result of genetic effects (Cloninger, Svrakik, & Przybeck, 1993; Kagan, Reznick, & Snidman, 1988; Rutter, 1998). Cognitive development should also be considered. One would expect that the 17-month-old boys with higher levels of physical aggression would have lower levels of cognitive functioning and lower verbal ability (Moffitt, 1993; Stattin & Klackenberg-Larsson, 1993). To disentangle these different processes we need twin studies with good information on parents' cognitive functioning, their social development, on the pregnancy, on parent-child interactions, and on the bio-psycho-social development of the child during the first months after birth. Our latest round of longitudinal studies should help achieve these aims.

Conclusion

The original aim of the MLES was to understand the role parents play in the development of male antisocial behavior from kindergarten to adolescence. The analyses of the developmental trajectories of antisocial behavior led to two extremely important findings: first, the boys were generally at their peak for frequency of physical aggression, opposition, and hyperactivity during their kinder-garten year, when the study began; second, no significant group of boys started to show chronic problems of physical aggression, opposition, or hyperactivity after their kindergarten year.

From these descriptive data a number of causal hypotheses can be ruled out: parenting behaviors, peer association, school failure, or any other factor appear-ing after kindergarten cannot be the cause of the initiation of chronic physical aggression, opposition, or hyperactivity after kindergarten. These factors can play a role in sustaining the antisocial behavior or in reducing it, but they cannot be the cause of the initiation of a chronic trajectory if there is no initiation of such a trajectory after kindergarten.

These results from the trajectory analyses give a very good example of the power of extensive descriptive data. We often waste a lot of time trying to explain the cause of a phenomenon that does not exist. Sometimes we even create the phenomenon in order to show that our favorite independent variable is its cause. Some of the predictive studies did show that family events such as parents' separation or peer association were significantly associated with future antisocial behavior. However, in most of these cases, the covariates used to control for antecedent behavior problems were based on an assessment at only one point in time, and the outcome was also generally limited to one point in time, thus we were not predicting a trajectory of chronic antisocial behavior. The behavioral trajectory analyses show the importance of taking into account the individual's antecedent life course when the aim is to test a causal factor. Attribution of causal consequences in correlational studies with limited data sets is a high-risk scientific enterprise. Unfortunately, most of our knowledge on the development of antisocial behavior relies on such studies.

Future correlational analyses of the causes leading to chronic antisocial behavior should trace the developmental trajectories of antisocial behavior and test whether a putative cause has an impact on the trajectory. We can continue to correlate putative causal variables, assessed at a given point in time, with antisocial behavior assessed at another point in time, but these studies will simply continue to show significant and nonsignificant correlations of variables, which largely depend on the sample which is used and measurement error. They will not provide a comprehensive picture of the life-span development of chronic antisocial behavior.

Some will argue that their aim is to predict short-term changes in the level of antisocial behavior involvement. They will argue that most delinquent behaviors during mid-adolescence are exhibited by those who do not have a chronic history. This is true (Reiss & Roth, 1993), but cross-sectional studies may be the best approach to this problem since the occasional delinquent behavior is probably determined by the current conditions or context. However, if longitudinal data is useful to understand the occasional delinquent act, then the longitudinal studies with frequent repeated measurements over the life span should provide the best data in order to investigate which factors lead to occasional delinquency for individuals with different developmental trajectories.

The experimental intervention was meant to test the impact of a multi-component intervention, but it also provided an important test of causal factors. The intensive two-year intervention which included parent training and social-cognitive skills training was shown to have a significant positive impact on important aspects of the disruptive boys' social adjustment: school adjustment, peer association, substance use, self-reported delinquency, and school drop-out. Linear structural equation analyses indicated that the impact of the intervention on self-reported delinquency was probably mediated through impact on parents' supervision and peer association.

It is important to note that the intervention targeted boys who had high levels of behavior problems in kindergarten. Thus, the impact of the intervention was to reduce the level of the problems of these boys compared to the control group, rather than prevent the onset of antisocial behaviors. A prevention experiment to test the adolescence onset hypothesis (Moffitt, 1993) would have to select children who have no severe problem behaviors by late childhood or early adolescence, provide a preventive intervention, and assess whether the intervention prevented them from initiating antisocial behaviors. To our knowledge, there have been no such tests of the late onset hypothesis.

The fact that the frequency of antisocial behavior was at its peak during the kindergarten year leads to the question, "When does it begin?" We decided to investigate this question with new longitudinal studies beginning at birth and even during pregnancy. The initial results clearly indicate that children initiate oppositional behavior, taking things away from others, and physical aggression as soon as they have the motor coordination and the opportunity to do so. It is extremely unlikely that children need to imitate others to initiate sitting up, standing up, walking and running. Similarly, it is unlikely that they need to imitate others to have a temper tantrum, to kick, slap, punch, throw, and bite. These behaviors must be part of the basic repertoire of human behaviors. Most children appear to reach a peak for frequency of physical aggression during their third year after birth. The minority who will follow a chronic trajectory appear to level off at that point, but most of the others reduce their frequency of involvement with age. The causes of the socialization of physical aggression have not been systematically studied. They are probably numerous, e.g., language development, development of behavioral inhibition, experience of negative consequences from siblings, peers and parents, and learning of alternatives such as indirect aggression.

In contrast to Jean-Jacques Rousseau's main conviction, i.e., children are born good and society makes them bad (1762), which has been shared by most social scientists since then, we are more and more convinced by the developmental data that we have collected that, from infancy onwards, children learn to inhibit behaviors which are socially disruptive; they also learn alternative behaviors that enable them to achieve their aims in a socially acceptable way. This process has been labeled "the socialization process." Children who for any reason do not become socialized at the same time as their same-age peers during the early years will quickly be rejected and labeled deviant by their peers and other members of their environment. These negative interactions between the child and his environment will rapidly set in motion a spiral of negative interactions, which will further handicap the socialization process. Finding the factors which initiated a chronic antisocial behavior trajectory with a study of school age children is probably more difficult than finding the initial causes of a fire after the whole house is in flames.

Studies of the early development of antisocial behavior will need to take a bio-psycho-social approach. The causes leading to a socialization failure will probably be traced to genetic factors, intra-uterine and perinatal factors, parenting and family communication factors, and socioeconomic factors. In most cases, complex interactions will be found among these factors. For example, environmental factors can have an impact on the organization of biological structures which control behavior (e.g., Francis, Diorio, Liu, & Meany, 1999; Keating & Hertzman, 1999), and biological factors can have an impact on the way the environment responds to the individual needs (e.g., Pérusse et al., 2001). Twin and molecular genetic studies, which include assessments of environmental factors, will provide the opportunity to study gene-environment interactions and correlations. However, before investing most resources on these causal studies, we need adequate descriptions of the different developmental trajectories of antisocial behavior that young children follow. If we are to find the causes of a phenomenon, we need adequate description of that phenomenon. This basic rule has too often been forgotten, or we have too often mistakenly believed that we had an adequate description of the phenomenon.

Our last conclusion concerns the sex of the subjects, which have been the focus of most longitudinal studies and preventive interventions related to antisocial behavior. Males have clearly been the main focus of attention, most probably because they are the most physically violent, and commit the largest number of crimes. However, a life span, intergenerational approach to the problem shows that one of the best set of predictors of chronic antisocial behavior is maternal characteristics (Nagin et al., 1997; Nagin & Tremblay, 2001; Robins et al., 1975; Serbin et al., 1998). This may be due to the fact that much of the human brain's organization, which controls behavior throughout a lifetime, occurs during fetal life and the first few years after birth. In all likelihood, mothers' behavior during pregnancy and infancy has an important impact on the organization of their children's brain. Girls who have behavior problems, who use drugs, who fail in school, and mate with a difficult partner will clearly not be in a position to offer the necessary environment for their child's adequate brain development. Poor brain development and disorganized family environments are more likely to lead to poor socialization and hence to antisocial behavior.

It logically follows that interventions involving at-risk young girls and their mate before, during, and after pregnancy should be the most cost-effective form of preventive intervention. Unfortunately, most preventive and corrective efforts targeting aggressive and other forms of antisocial behavior, including the MLES, have been aimed at males because they are more overtly disruptive for society. A true preventive approach, based on our present knowledge of human development, should result in more attention to girls with adjustment problems. Perhaps because they are less of an open threat to society than the antisocial male, they get less attention, including services (Offord, Boyle, & Racine, 1991). Nevertheless, if they mate with antisocial males, smoke, drink and use drugs during pregnancy, and fail to give adequate postnatal care, they are at high risk of becoming the parents of the next generation of antisocial boys.

We need to convince ourselves, policy makers, and the public at large that the basic control of physically violent impulses is learned in the first two to three years of life. If this level of self-control is not learned during the first few years after birth, the child is at high risk of being propelled into a feedback loop where peer, teacher, and parent rejection justifies increasingly aggressive reactions. Mothers are the main care providers during this critical period. In most cases, they provide the care needed to learn self-control and prosocial interactions.

In many cases, they act as a buffer between the child and an inadequate father. However, when a mother has a history of behavior problems, she is unlikely to have a mate who will act as a buffer for the child. This child (male or female) is then unlikely to learn self-control and prosocial skills. Because females are more often the educators of very young children and because they appear to be more receptive to support, putting our limited resources into helping young girls who have adjustment problems would probably be more cost effective in the long run than putting most of our resources into trying to treat aggressive males. Interestingly, this conclusion is similar to the one Lucien Bovet (1951) reached following a review of research on juvenile delinquency for the newly created World Health Organization, more than a half a century ago.

ACKNOWLEDGMENT. The authors wish to thank Michel Boivin, Bernard Boulerice, Bobby Brame, Mara Brendgen, William Bukowski, Patricia L. Dobkin, Christa Japel, Margaret Kerr, Pierre McDuff, Jacques Montplaisir, Daniel Pérusse, Robert O. Pihl, and Mark Zoccolillo for their work on the Montreal Longitudinal and Experimental study; Lyse Desmarais-Gervais for coordinating the GRIP infrastructure; Hélène Beauchesne and Lucille David for coordinating the data collection; Diane Héroux, Pierre McDuff, Muriel Rorive, and Maria Rosa for data management and statistical analyses; Danielle Lebeau and Mihn T. Trinh for the documentation; Chantal Bruneau for secretarial work; and Katia Maliantovitch for revising the text.

This work was supported by grants from the Quebec's Conseil Québécois de la Recherche Sociale (CQRS), and Fonds pour la Formation et l'Aide à la Recherche (FCAR); Canada's Social Sciences and Humanities Research Council of Canada (SSHRC) and National Health Research and Development Program (NHRDP); the Molson Foundation; the Canadian Institute of Advanced Research; the National Consortium on Violence Research; and the National Science Foundation.

And, a very special thank you to the schools, the teachers, the children, and the parents for their ongoing cooperation. Without them this work would not have been possible.

References

Allport, G. W. (1951). Foreword. In E. Powers & H. Witmer (Eds.), *An experiment in the prevention of delinquency: The Cambridge-Somerville Youth Study.* New York: Columbia University Press.

Ang, R. P., Woldbeck, T. F., Arnold, M. E., & Hughes, J. N. (1998). *Effects of group-based skills training for aggressive children and adolescents: A meta-analytic review.* Paper presented at the Annual Meeting of the Association for the Advancement of Behavior Therapy. Washington, DC.

Archer, J. (1991). The influence of testosterone on human aggression. *British Journal of Psychology, 82,* 1–28.

Arseneault, L., Tremblay, R. E., Boulerice, B., Séguin, J. R., & Saucier, J.-F. (2000). Minor physical anomalies and family adversity as risk factors for adolescent violent delinquency. *American Journal of Psychiatry, 157*(6), 917–923.

Arseneault, L., Tremblay, R. E., Boulerice, B., & Saucier, J. F. (2002). Obstetrical complications and violent delinquency: Testing two developmental pathways. *Child Development, 73*, 496–508.

Blishen, B. R., Carroll, W. K., & Moore, C. (1987). The 1981 socioeconomic index for occupations in Canada. *Canadian Review of Sociology and Anthropology, 24*(4), 465–488.

Boivin, M., & Vitaro, F. (1995). The impact of peer relationships on aggression in childhood: Inhibition through coercion or promotion through peer support. In J. McCord (Ed.), *Coercion and punishment in long-term perspectives* (pp. 183–197). New York: Cambridge Press.

Bovet, L. (1951). *Psychiatric aspects of juvenile delinquency.* Geneva: World Health Organization.

Brame, B., Nagin, D. S., & Tremblay, R. E. (2001). Developmental trajectories of physical aggression from school entry to late adolescence. *The Journal of Child Psychology and Psychiatry, 42*, 503–512.

Brooks-Gunn, J., Klebanov, P. K., & Liaw, F. (1995). The learning, physical, and emotional environment in the home in the context of poverty: The Infant Health and Development Program. *Children and Youth Services Review, 17*, 251–276.

Bryk, A. S., & Raudenbush, S. W. (1987). Application of hierarchical linear models to assessing change. *Psychology Bulletin, 101*, 147–158.

Cabot, R. C. (1940). A long-term study of children: The Cambridge-Somerville Youth Study. *Child Development, 11*, 143–151.

Cairns, R. B. (1979). *Social development: The origins and plasticity of interchanges.* San Francisco: W. H. Freeman & Co.

Cairns, R. B., & Cairns, B. D. (1994). *Life lines and risks: Pathways of youth in our time.* New York: Cambridge University Press.

Cairns, R. B., Cairns, B. D., & Neckerman, H. J. (1988). Early school dropout: Configurations and determinants. *Child Development, 60*, 1437–1452.

Cairns, R. B., Cairns, B. D., Neckerman, H. J., Gest, S. D., & Gariépy, J.-L. (1988). Peer networks and aggressive behavior: Social support or social rejection? *Developmental Psychology, 24*, 815–823.

Cairns, R. B., Cairns, B. D., Neckerman, H. J., Ferguson, L. L., & Gariépy, J. L. (1989). Growth and aggression: 1. Childhood to early adolescence. *Developmental Psychology, 25*(2), 320–330.

Camp, B. W., Blom, G. E., Hebert, F., & Van Doorminck, W. J. (1977). Think Aloud. A program for developing self-control in young aggressive boys. *Journal of Abnormal Child Psychology, 5*, 157–169.

Carbonneau, R., Tremblay, R. E., Vitaro, F., Dobkin, P. L., Saucier, J.-F., & Pihl, R. O. (1998). Paternal alcoholism, paternal absence and the development of problem behaviors in boys from age 6 to 12 years. *Journal of Studies on Alcohol, 59*(4), 387–398.

Cartledge, G., & Milburn, J. F. (1980). *Teaching social skills to children. Innovative approaches.* New York: Pergamon Press.

Caspi, A., & Bem, D. J. (1990). Personality continuity and change across the life course. In L. A. Pervin et al. (Eds.), *Handbook of personality: Theory and research* (pp. 549–575). New York: Guilford Press.

Caspi, A., Henry, B., McGee, R. O., Moffitt, T. E., & Silva, P. A. (1995). Temperamental origins of child and adolescent behavior problems: From age three to fifteen. *Child Development, 66*(1), 55–68.

Castaignede, J., & Tremblay, R. E. (1984). Investissement parental et transmission de l'inadaptation sociale chez l'humain. In A. D. Haro & X. Espalader (Eds.), *Processus d'acquisition précoce. Les communications* (pp. 65–99). Rennes: Société Française pour l'Étude du Comportement Animal.

Cloninger, C. R. (1987). A systematic method for clinical description and classification of personality variants. *Archives of General Psychiatry, 44*, 573–588.

Cloninger, C. R., Svrakik, D. M., & Przybeck, T. R. (1993). A psychobiological model of temperament and character. *Archives of General Psychiatry, 50*, 975–990.

Cloninger, C. R., Svrakic, D. M., & Svrakic, N. M. (1997). A multidimensional psychobiological model of violence. In A. Raine, D. Farrington, P. Brennan, & S. A. Mednick (Eds.), *Biosocial bases of violence* (pp. 39–54). New York: Plenum.

Conger, R. D., Conger, J., & Elder Jr., G. H. (1997). Family economic hardship and adolescent adjustment: Mediating and moderating processes. In G. J. Duncan & J. Brooks-Gunn (Eds.), *Consequences of growing up poor* (pp. 288–310). New York: Russell Sage Foundation.

Cummings, E. M., Iannotti, R. J., & Zahn-Waxler, C. (1989). Aggression between peers in early childhood: Individual continuity and developmental change. *Child Development, 60*(4), 887–895.

Deater-Deckard, K. (1998). Parenting stress and child adjustment: Some old hypotheses and new questions. *Clinical Psychology Science & Practice, 5*(3), 314–332.

Dishion, T. J., Andrews, D. W., & Crosby, L. (1994). Antisocial boys and their friends in early adolescence: Relationship characteristics, quality, and interactional processes. *Child Development, 66*, 139–151.

Dishion, T. J., French, D. C., & Patterson, G. R. (1995). The development and ecology of antisocial behavior. In D. Cicchetti & D. J. Cohen (Eds.), *Developmental psychopathology* (Vol. 2, pp. 421–471). New York: Wiley.

Dishion, T. J., McCord, J., & Poulin, F. (1999). Iatrogenic effects in early adolescent interventions that aggregate peers. *American Psychologist, 54*(9), 755–764.

Ditto, B., Séguin, J. R., Boulerice, B., Pihl, R. O., & Tremblay, R. E. (1998). Risk for hypertension and pain sensitivity in adolescent boys. *Health Psychology, 17*(3), 249–254.

Dobkin, P. L., Tremblay, R. E., Mâsse, L. C., & Vitaro, F. (1995). Individual and peer characteristics in predicting boys' early onset of substance abuse: A seven-year longitudinal study. *Child Development, 66*, 1198–1214.

Dobkin, P. L., Tremblay, R. E., & Sacchitelle, C. (1997). Predicting boy's early-onset of substance abuse from father's alcoholism, son's disruptiveness, and mother's parenting behavior. *Journal of Consulting and Clinical Psychology, 65*(1), 86–92.

Dobkin, P. L., Tremblay, R. E., & Treiber, F. A. (1998). Cardiovascular reactivity and adolescent boys' physical health. *Pediatrics, 101*(3), E111–E115.

Dobkin, P. L., Treiber, F., & Tremblay, R. E. (2000). Cardiovascular reactivity in adolescent boys of low socioeconomic status previously characterized as anxious, disruptive, anxious-disruptive, or normal during childhood. *Psychotherapy and Psychosomatics, 69*, 50–56.

Duncan, G. J., Brooks-Gunn, J., & Klebanov, P. K. (1994). Economic deprivation and early childhood development. *Child Development, 65*, 296–318.

Epstein, J. L. (1983). The influence of friends in achievement and affective outcomes. In J. L. Epstein & N. Karweit (Eds.), *Friends in school: Patterns of selection and influence in secondary schools* (pp. 177–200). New York: Academic Press.

Eysenck, H. J. (1964). *Crime and personality*. London: Routledge and Kegan Paul.

Eysenck, H. J. (1997). Personality and the biosocial model of anti-social and criminal behaviour. In A. Raine, D. P. Farrington, P. Brennan, & S. A. Mednick (Eds.), *Biosocial bases of violence* (pp. 21–37). New York: Plenum Press.

Farrington, D. P. (1985). Predicting self-reported and official delinquency. In D. P. Farrington & R. Tarling (Eds.), *Prediction in Criminology* (Vol. 8, pp. 150–173). New York: State University of New York Press.

Farrington, D. (1998). Predictors, causes and correlates of male youth violence. *Crime and Justice*, 421–475.

Farrington, D. P., Loeber, R., & Van Kammen, W. B. (1990). The long term criminal outcomes of conduct problem boys with or without impulsive-inattentive behavior. In L. N. Robins & M. Rutter (Eds.), *Straight and devious pathways from childhood to adulthood* (pp. 62–81). New York: Cambridge University Press.

Fergusson, D. M., & Horwood, L. J. (1996). The role of adolescent peer affiliations in the continuity between childhood behavioral adjustment and juvenile offendings. *Journal of Abnormal Child Psychology, 24,* 205–221.

Francis, D., Diorio, J., Liu, D., & Meaney, M. J. (1999). Nongenomic transmission across generations of maternal behavior and stress responses in the rat. *Science, 286*(5442), 1155–1158.

Glueck, S., & Glueck, E. (1950). *Unraveling juvenile delinquency.* Cambridge: University Press.

Goldstein, H. (1995). *Multilevel statistical models* (2nd ed.). London: Edward Arnold.

Goldstein, A. P., Sprafkin, R. P., Gershaw, N. J., & Klein, P. (1980). The adolescent: Social skills training through structured learning. In G. Cartledge & J. F. Milburn (Eds.), *Teaching social skills to children: Innovative approaches* (pp. 249–277). New York: Pergamon Press.

Gottfredson, M. R., & Hirschi, T. (1990). *A general theory of crime.* Stanford, CA: Stanford University Press.

Gray, J. A. (1982). *The neuropsychology of anxiety.* New York: Oxford University Press.

Gray, J. A., Owens, S., Davis, N., & Tsaltas, E. (1983). Psychological and physiological relations between anxiety and impulsivity. In M. Zuckerman (Ed.), *Biological bases of sensation seeking, impulsivity and anxiety* (pp. 189–218). Hillsdale, NJ: Lawrence Erlbaum Associates.

Haapasalo, J., & Tremblay, R. E. (1994). Physically aggressive boys from ages 6 to 12: Family background, parenting behavior, and prediction of delinquency. *Journal of Consulting and Clinical Psychology, 62*(5), 1044–1052.

Haapasalo, J., Tremblay, R. E., Boulerice, B., & Vitaro, F. (2000). Relative advantages of person- and variable-based approaches for predicting problem behaviors from kindergarten assessments. *Journal of Quantitative Criminology, 16,* 145–168.

Harris, J. A., Vernon, P. A., & Boomsma, D. I. (1998). The irritability of testosterone: A study of Dutch adolescent twins and their parents. *Behavior Genetics, 28,* 165–171.

Hay, D. F., Castle, J., & Davies, L. (2000). Toddlers' use of force against familiar peers: A precursor of serious aggression? *Child Development, 71*(2), 457–467.

Hinde, R. A., & Dennis, A. (1986). Categorizing individuals: An alternative to linear analysis. *International Journal of Behavioral Development, 9,* 105–119.

Hoge, R. D., Andrews, D. A., & Leschied, A. W. (1994). Tests of three hypotheses regarding the predictors of delinquency. *Journal of Abnormal Child Psychology, 22*(5), 547–559.

Junger, M., & Tremblay, R. E. (1999). Self-control, accidents, and crime. *Criminal Justice and Behavior, 26*(4), 485–501.

Jutras, S., Tremblay, R. E., & Morin, P. (1999). La conception de la santé chez des garçons de 14 à 16 ans de milieu défavorisé. *Revue Canadienne des Sciences du Comportement, 31*(3), 188–197.

Kagan, J., & Snidman, N. (1991). Infant predictors of inhibited and uninhibited profiles. *Psychological Science, 2,* 40–44.

Kagan, J., Reznick, J. S., & Snidman, N. (1988). Biological bases of childhood shyness. *Science, 240,* 167–171.

Karoly, L. A., Greenwood, P. W., Everingham, S. S., Houbé, J., Kilburn, M. R., Rydell, C. P., Sanders, M., & Chiesa, J. (1998). *Investing in our children: What we know and don't know about the costs and benefits of early childhood interventions.* Santa Monica, CA: Rand.

Keating, D. P., & Hertzman, C. (Eds.). (1999). *Developmental health and the wealth of nations.* New York: Guilford Press.

Keenan, K., & Shaw, D. S. (1994). The development of aggression in toddlers: A study of low-income families. *Journal of Abnormal Child Psychology, 22*(1), 53–77.

Keenan, K., & Wakschlag, L. S. (2000). More than the terrible twos: The nature and severity of behavior problems in clinic-referred preschool children. *Journal of Abnormal Child Psychology, 28*(1), 33–46.

Kerr, M., Tremblay, R. E., Pagani-Kurtz, L., & Vitaro, F. (1997). Boys' behavioral inhibition and the risk of later delinquency. *Archives of General Psychiatry, 54*(9), 809–816.

Kettlewell, P. W., & Kausch, D. F. (1983). The generalization of the effects of a cognitive behavioral treatment program for aggressive children. *Journal of Abnormal Child Psychology, 11*, 101–114.

Kindlon, D. J., Tremblay, R. E., Mezzacappa, E., Earls, F., Laurent, D., & Schaal, B. (1995). Longitudinal patterns of heart rate and fighting behavior in 9- through 12-year-old boys. *Journal of the American Academy of Child and Adolescent Psychiatry, 34*(3), 371–377.

Kingston, L., & Prior, M. (1995). The development of patterns of stable, transient, and school-age onset aggressive behavior in young children. *Journal of the American Academy of Child and Adolescent Psychiatry, 34*, 348–358.

Lahey, B. B., Waldman, I. D., & McBurnett, K. (1999). Annotation: The development of antisocial behavior, an integrative causal model. *Journal of Child Psychology and Psychiatry, 40*(5), 669–682.

Lahey, B. B., McBurnett, K., & Loeber, R. (2000). Are attention-deficit hyperactivity disorder and oppositional defiant disorder developmental precursors to conduct disorder? In A. Sameroff, M. Lewis, & S. Miller (Eds.), *Handbook of developmental psychopathology* (pp. 431–446). New York: Plenum.

Laurent, D., Tremblay, R. E., Charlebois, P., Gagnon, C., & Larivée, S. (1988). Relation mère-enfant et refus alimentaires chez 4 groupes de garçons agressifs. *Bulletin de psychologie, (387)*, 77–84.

Laurent, D., Tremblay, R. E., Larivée, S., Charlebois, P., & Gagnon, C. (1988). Habitudes alimentaires et comportements agressifs de garçons canadiens-français d'âge scolaire. *Cahiers de Nutrition et de Diététique, XXIII*(6), 418–424.

Lochman, J. E., Nelson, W. M., & Sims, J. E. (1981). A cognitive behavioral program for use with aggressive children. *Journal of Clinical Psychology, 10*(3), 146–148.

Loeber, R. (1991). Questions and advances in the study of developmental pathways. In D. Cicchetti & S. Toth (Eds.), *Models and integrations. Rochester symposium on developmental psychopathology* (Vol. 3, pp. 97–115). Rochester: University of Rochester Press.

Loeber, R., & Hay, D. F. (1994). Developmental approaches to aggression and conduct problems. In M. Rutter & D. F. Hay (Eds.), *Development through life: A handbook for clinicians* (pp. 488–516). Oxford: Blackwell Scientific Publications.

Loeber, R., & Stouthamer-Loeber, M. (1998). Development of juvenile aggression and violence. Some common misconceptions and controversies. *American Psychologist, 53*(2), 242–259.

Loeber, R., Wung, P., Keenan, K., Giroux, B., Stouthamer-Loeber, M., Van Kammen, W. B., & Maughan, B. (1993). Developmental pathways in disruptive child behavior. *Development and Psychopathology, 5*, 103–133.

Loeber, R., Keenan, K., & Zhang, Q. (1997). Boys' experimentation and persistence in developmental pathways toward serious delinquency. *Journal of Child and Family Studies, 6*, 321–357.

Magnusson, D., & Bergman, L. R. (1990). A pattern approach to the study of pathways from childhood to adulthood. In L. N. Robins & M. Rutter (Eds.), *Straight and devious pathways from childhood to adulthood* (pp. 101–116). New York: Cambridge University Press.

Malo, J., & Tremblay, R. E. (1997). The impact of paternal alcoholism and maternal social position on boy's school adjustment, pubertal maturation and sexual behaviour: A test of two competing hypotheses. *Journal of Child Psychology and Psychiatry, 38*(2), 187–197.

Mâsse, L. C., & Tremblay, R. E. (1997). Behavior of boys in kindergarten and the onset of substance use during adolescence. *Archives of General Psychiatry, 54*, 62–68.

McCord, J. (1991). Family relationships, juvenile delinquency, and adult criminality. *Criminology, 29*(3), 397–417.

McCord, J., Tremblay, R. E., Vitaro, F., & Desmarais-Gervais, L. (1994). Boys' disruptive behavior, school adjustment, and delinquency: The Montreal prevention experiment. *International Journal of Behavioral Development, 17*, 739–752.

McCord, W., McCord, J., & Zola, I. K. (1959). *Origins of crime.* New York: Columbia University Press.

Meichenbaum, D. (1977). *Cognitive-behavior modification: An integrative approach.* New York: Plenum Press.

Meikle, A. K., Stringham, J. D., Bishop, D. T., & West, D. W. (1988). Quantitating genetic and non-genetic factors influencing androgen production and clearance rates in men. *Journal of Clinical Endocrinology and Metabolism, 67,* 104–109.

Mezzacappa, E., Tremblay, R. E., Kindlon, D., Saul, J. P., Arseneault, L., Séguin, J., Pihl, R. O., & Earls, F. (1997). Anxiety, antisocial behavior, and heart rate regulation in adolescent males. *Journal of Child Psychology and Psychiatry, 38*(4), 457–469.

Michelson, L., Sugai, D., Wood, R., & Kazdin, A. E. (1983). *Social skills assessment and training with children.* New York: Plenum Press.

Mitchell, A. (1991). Ontario's children and families: A demographic overview. In R. Barnhorst & L. C. Johnson (Eds.), *The state of the child in Ontario* (pp. 1–21). Toronto: Oxford University Press.

Moffitt, T. E. (1990). Juvenile delinquency and attention deficit disorder: Developmental trajectories from age 3 to age 15. *Child Development, 61,* 893–910.

Moffitt, T. E. (1993). The neuropsychology of conduct disorder. *Development and Psychopathology, 5,* 135–151.

Moffitt, T. E., Caspi, A., Dickson, N., Silva, P. S., & Stanton, W. (1996). Childhood-onset versus adolescent-onset antisocial conduct problems in males: Natural history from ages 3 to 18 years. *Development & Psychopathology, 8*(2), 399–424.

Moskowitz, D. S., & Schwartzman, A. E. (1989). Life paths of aggressive and withdrawn children. In N. Cantor & D. Buss (Eds.), *Emerging trends in personality* (pp. 99–114). New York: Springer-Verlag.

Mrazek, P. J., & Haggerty, R. J. (Ed.). (1994). *Reducing risks for mental disorders: Frontiers for preventive intervention research.* Washington, DC: National Academy Press.

Muthen, B. O. (1989). Latent variable modeling in heterogeneous populations. *Psychometrika, 54*(4), 557–585.

Nagin, D. (1999). Analyzing developmental trajectories: A semi-parametric, group-based approach. *Psychological Methods, 4,* 139–177.

Nagin, D., & Tremblay, R. E. (1999). Trajectories of boys' physical aggression, opposition, and hyperactivity on the path to physically violent and nonviolent juvenile delinquency. *Child Development, 70*(5), 1181–1196.

Nagin, D., & Tremblay, R. E. (2001). Parental and early childhood predictors of persistent physical aggression in boys from kindergarten to high school. *Archives of General Psychiatry, 58,* 389–394.

Nagin, D., Pogarsky, G., & Farrington, D. P. (1997). Adolescent mothers and the criminal behavior of their children. *Law and Society Review, 31,* 137–162.

Newman, J. P. (1987). Reaction to punishment in extraverts and psychopaths: Implications for the impulsive behavior of disinhibited individuals. *Journal of Research in Personality, 21,* 464–480.

O'Donnell, J., Hawkins, J. D., & Abbott, R. D. (1995). Predicting serious delinquency and substance use among aggressive boys. *Journal of Consulting and Clinical Psychology, 63*(4), 529–537.

Offord, D., Boyle, M. C., & Racine, Y. A. (1991). The epidemiology of antisocial behavior in childhood and adolescence. In D. Pepler & K. Rubin (Eds.), *The development and treatment of aggression* (pp. 31–54). Hillsdale, NJ: Lawrence Erlbaum.

Oswald, H., & Süss, K. U. (1994). The influence of parents and peers on misconduct at school: Simultaneous and synergistic effects. In K. K. Silbereisen & E. Todt (Eds.), *Adolescence in context: The interplay of family, school, peers, and work in adjustment* (pp. 347–365). New York: Springer-Verlag.

Pagani, L., Boulerice, B., & Tremblay, R. E. (1997). The influence of poverty upon children's classroom placement and behavior problems during elementary school: A change model approach. In G. Duncan & J. Brooks-Gunn (Eds.), *Consequences of growing up poor* (pp. 311–339). New York: Sage.

Pagani, L., Tremblay, R. E., Vitaro, F., & Parent, S. (1998). Does preschool help prevent delinquency in boys with a history of perinatal complications? *Criminology, 36*(2), 245–267.

Pagani, L., Boulerice, B., Vitaro, F., & Tremblay, R. E. (1999). Effects of poverty on academic failure and delinquency in boys: A change and process model approach. *Journal of Child Psychology and Psychiatry, 40*(8), 1209–1219.

Pagani, L., Tremblay, R. E., Vitaro, F., Boulerice, B., & McDuff, P. (2001). Effects of grade retention on academic performance and behavioral development. *Development and Psychopathology, 13*(2), 297–315.

Patterson, G. R. (1982). *Coercive family process.* Eugene, OR: Castalia.

Patterson, G. R., Reid, J. B., Jones, R. R., & Conger, R. R. (1975). *A social learning approach to family intervention: Families with aggressive children (Vol. 1).* Eugene, OR: Castalia.

Patterson, G. R., DeBaryshe, B. D., & Ramsey, E. (1989). A developmental perspective on antisocial behavior. *American Psychologist, 44*, 329–335.

Pennington, B. F., & Ozonoff, S. (1996). Executive functions and develomental psychopathology. *Journal of Child Psychology and Psychiatry, 37*, 51–87.

Pérusse, D., Barr, R. G., Boulerice, B., Camara, K., Turecki, G., Rouleau, G. A., Tremblay, R. E., & Boivin, M. (2001) *Genetic-environmental etiology of infant states.* Manuscript submitted for publication.

Pihl, R. O., McDuff, P., Assaad, J.-M., Dubreuil, E., Strickler, W., & Tremblay, R. E. (1998). *Alcohol and parenting: The effects of maternal heavy drinking.* Working Paper Series. Applied Research Branch, Strategic Policy. Ottawa: Human Resources Development Canada.

Pulkkinen, L., & Tremblay, R. E. (1992). Patterns of boys' social adjustment in two cultures and at different ages: A longitudinal perspective. *International Journal of Behavioural Development, 15*(4), 527–553.

Quay, H. C. (1988). The behavioral reward and inhibition system in childhood behavior disorder. In L. M. Bloomingdal (Ed.), *Attention deficit disorder: Vol. 3. New research in attention, treatment and psychopharmacology* (pp. 176–186). Oxford, UK: Pergamon.

Quay, H. C. (1993). The psychobiology of undersocialized aggressive conduct disorder: A theoretical perspective. *Development and Psychopathology, 5*, 165–180.

Raine, A., Brennan, P., & Mednick, S. A. (1997). Interaction between birth complications and early maternal rejection in predisposing individuals to adult violence: Specificity to serious, early-onset violence. *American Journal of Psychiatry, 154*, 1265–1271.

Raine, A., Farrington, D. P., Brennan, P., & Mednick, S. A. (Eds.) (1997). *Biosocial bases of violence.* New York: Plenum.

Raine, A., Venables, P. H., & Mednick, S. A. (1997). Low resting heart rate at age 3 predisposes to aggression at age 11 years: Evidence from the Mauritius Child Health Project. *Journal of the American Academy of Child and Adolescent Psychiatry, 36*, 1457–1464.

Reiss, A. J., & Roth, J. A. (Ed.). (1993). *Understanding and preventing violence.* Washington, DC: National Academy Press.

Restoin, A., Montagner, H., Rodriguez, D., Girardot, J. J., Laurent, D., Kontar, F., Ullmann, V., Casagrande, C., & Talpain, B. (1985). Chronologie des comportements de communication et profils de comportement chez le jeune enfant. In R. E. Tremblay, M. A. Provost, & F. F. Strayer (Eds.), *Ethologie et développement de l'enfant* (pp. 93–130). Paris: Editions Stock/Laurence Pernoud.

Robins, L. N. (1966). *Deviant children grown up.* Baltimore: Williams & Wilkins.

Robins, L., N. (1978). Sturdy childhood predictors of adult antisocial behavior: Replication from longitudinal studies. *Psychological Medicine, 8*, 611–622.

Robins, L. N., West, P. A., & Herjanic, B. L. (1975). Arrest and delinquency in two generations: A study of black urban families and their children. *Journal of Child Psychology and Psychiatry and Allied Disciplines, 16*, 125–140.

Rousseau, J.-J. (1762/1979). *Emile or on education*. New York: Basic Books.

Rutter, M. (1998). Some research considerations on intergenerational continuities and discontinuities: Comment on the special section. *Developmental Psychology, 34*(6), 1269–1273.

Sampson, R. J., & Laub, J. H. (1993). *Crime in the making: Pathways and turning points through life.* Cambridge, MA: Harvard University Press.

Sampson, R. J., & Laub, J. H. (1994). Urban poverty and the family context of delinquency: A new look at structure and process in a classic study. *Child Development, 65*(2), 523–540.

Satterfield, J. H. (1987). Childhood diagnostic and neurophysiological predictors of teenage arrest rates: An eight-year prospective study. In S. A. Mednick, T. E. Moffitt, & S. A. Stack (Eds.), *The causes of crime: New biological approaches* (Vol. 9, pp. 146–167). New York: Cambridge University Press.

Satterfield, J. H., Hoppe, C. M., & Schell, A. M. (1982). A prospective study of delinquency in 110 adolescent boys with attention deficit disorder and 88 normal adolescent boys. *American Journal of Psychiatry, 139*, 795–798.

Schaal, B., Tremblay, R. E., Soussignan, R., & Susman, E. J. (1996). Male testosterone linked to high social dominance but low physical aggression in early adolescence. *Journal of the American Academy of Child and Adolescent Psychiatry, 35*(10), 1322–1330.

Schaal, B., Rouby, C., Marlier, L., Soussignan, R., Kontar, F., & Tremblay, R. E. (1998). Variabilité et universaux au sein de l'espace perçu des odeurs: Approches inter-culturelles de l'hédonisme olfactif. In R. Dulau & J.-R. Pitte (Eds.), *Géographie des odeurs* (pp. 25–47). Paris: Éditions L'Harmattan.

Schneider, B. H., & Byrne, B. M. (1987). Individualizing social skills training for behavior-disordered children. *Journal of Consulting and Clinical Psychology, 55*, 444–445.

Schwartz, D., Flamant, R., & Lellouch, J. (1980). *Clinical trials*. New York: Academic Press.

Séguin, J. R., Pihl, R. O., Harden, P. W., Tremblay, R. E., & Boulerice, B. (1995). Cognitive and neuropsychological characteristics of physically aggressive boys. *Journal of Abnormal Psychology, 104*(4), 614–624.

Séguin, J., Tremblay, R. E., Boulerice, B., Pihl, R. O., & Harden, P. (1999). Executive functions and physical aggression after controlling for attention deficit hyperactivity disorder, general memory, and IQ. *Journal of Child Psychology and Psychiatry, 40*(8), 1197–1208.

Séguin, J. R., Arseneault, L., Boulerice, B., Harden, P. W., & Tremblay, R. E. (2001). *Response perseveration in adolescent boys with stable and unstable histories of physical aggression: The role of underlying processes.* Manuscript submitted for publication.

Serbin, L. A., Schwartzman, A. E., Moskowitz, D. S., & Ledingham, J. E. (1991). Aggressive, withdrawn and aggressive-withdrawn children in adolescence: Into the next generation. In D. Pepler & K. Rubin (Eds.), *The development and treatment of childhood aggression* (pp. 55–70). Hillsdale, NJ: Lawrence Erlbaum.

Serbin, L. A., Cooperman, J. M., Peters, P. L., Lehoux, P. M., Stack, D. M., & Schwartzman, A. E. (1998). Intergenerational transfer of psychosocial risk in women with childhood histories of aggression, withdrawal, or aggression and withdrawal. *Developmental Psychology, 34*(6), 1246–1262.

Simons, R. L., Wu, C.-I., Conger, R. D., & Lorenz, F. O. (1994). Two routes to delinquency: Differences between early and late starters in the impact of parenting and deviant peers. *Criminology, 32*(2), 247–276.

Soussignan, R., Tremblay, R. E., Schaal, B., Laurent, D., Larivée, S., Gagnon, C., LeBlanc, M., & Charlebois, P. (1992). Behavioural and cognitive characteristics of conduct disordered-hyperactive boys from age 6 to 11: A multiple informant perspective. *Journal of Child Psychology and Psychiatry, 33*(8), 1333–1346.

Stattin, H., & Klackenberg-Larsson, I. (1993). Early language and intelligence development and their relationship to future criminal behavior. *Journal of Abnormal Psychology, 102*(3), 369–378.

Tremblay, R. E. (2000). The development of aggressive behaviour during childhood: What have we learned in the past century? *International Journal of Behavioral development, 24*(2), 129–141.

Tremblay, R. E., & Craig, W. (1995). Developmental crime prevention. In M. Tonry & D. P. Farrington (Eds.), *Building a safer society: Strategic approaches to crime prevention* (Vol. 19, pp. 151–236). Chicago: The University of Chicago Press.

Tremblay, R. E., & LeMarquand, D. (2001). Individual risk and protective factors. In R. Loeber & D. Farrington (Eds.), *Child delinquents: Development, interventions and service needs* (pp. 137–164). Thousand Oaks, CA: Sage Publications.

Tremblay, R. E., & Schaal, B. (1996). Physically aggressive boys from age 6 to 12 years: Their biopsychosocial status at puberty. In G. Ferris & T. Grisso (Eds.), *Understanding aggressive behavior in children* (Vol. 794, pp. 192–208). New York: Annals of the New York Academy of Sciences.

Tremblay, R. E., Desmarais-Gervais, L., Gagnon, C., & Charlebois, P. (1987). The Preschool Behavior Questionnaire: Stability of its factor structure between cultures, sexes, ages and socioeconomic classes. *International Journal of Behavioral Development, 10*(4), 467–484.

Tremblay, R. E., Loeber, R., Gagnon, C., Charlebois, P., Larivée, S., & LeBlanc, M. (1991). Disruptive boys with stable and unstable high fighting behavior patterns during junior elementary school. *Journal of Abnormal Child Psychology, 19*, 285–300.

Tremblay, R. E., McCord, J., Boileau, H., Charlebois, P., Gagnon, C., LeBlanc, M., & Larivée, S. (1991). Can disruptive boys be helped to become competent? *Psychiatry, 54*, 148–161.

Tremblay, R. E., Vitaro, F., Bertrand, L., LeBlanc, M., Beauchesne, H., Boileau, H., & David, H. (1992). Parent and child training to prevent early onset of delinquency: The Montreal longitudinal-experimental study. In J. McCord & R. E. Tremblay (Eds.), *Preventing antisocial behavior: Interventions from birth through adolescence* (pp. 117–138). New York: Guilford Press.

Tremblay, R. E., Pihl, R. O., Vitaro, F., & Dobkin, P. L. (1994). Predicting early onset of male antisocial behavior from preschool behavior. *Archives of General Psychiatry, 51*, 732–738.

Tremblay, R. E., Mâsse, L. C., Vitaro, F., & Dobkin, P. L. (1995). The impact of friends' deviant behavior on early onset of delinquency: Longitudinal data from 6 to 13 years of age. *Development and Psychopathology, 7*(4), 649–668.

Tremblay, R. E., Boulerice, B., Junger, M., & Arseneault, L. (1995). Does low self-control during childhood explain the association between delinquency and accidents in early adolescence? *Journal of Criminal Behavior and Mental Health, 5*, 330–345.

Tremblay, R. E., Boulerice, B., Harden, P. W., McDuff, P., Pérusse, D., Pihl, R. O., & Zoccolillo, M. (1996). Do children in Canada become more aggressive as they approach adolescence? In Human Resources Development Canada & Statistics Canada (Eds.), *Growing up in Canada: National longitudinal survey of children and youth* (pp. 127–137). Ottawa: Statistics Canada.

Tremblay, R. E., Schaal, B., Boulerice, B., Arseneault, L., Soussignan, R. G., & Pérusse, D. (1997). Male physical aggression, social dominance and testosterone levels at puberty: A developmental perspective. In A. Raine, D. P. Farrington, P. Brennan, & S. A. Mednick (Eds.), *Biosocial bases of violence* (pp. 271–291). New York: Plenum Press.

Tremblay, R. E., Schaal, B., Boulerice, B., Arseneault, L., Soussignan, R. G., Paquette, D., & Laurent, D. (1998). Testosterone, physical aggression, dominance, and physical development in early adolescence. *International Journal of Behavioral Development, 22*(4), 753–777.

Tremblay, R. E., LeMarquand, D., & Vitaro, F. (1999a). The prevention of ODD and CD. In H. C. Quay & A. E. Hogan (Eds.), *Handbook of disruptive behavior disorders* (pp. 525–555). New York: Kluwer Academic/Plenum Publishers.

Tremblay, R. E., Japel, C., Pérusse, D., Boivin, M., Zoccolillo, M., Montplaisir, J., & McDuff, P. (1999b). The search for the age of onset of physical aggression: Rousseau and Bandura revisited. *Criminal Behavior and Mental Health, 9*, 8–23.

Tremblay, R. E., Larocque, D., Boivin, M., Pérusse, D., Zoccolillo, M., & Pihl, R. O. (in press). Physical agression during infancy and onset of male conduct disorder. In W. Koops, N. W. Slot, & R. Loeber (Eds.), *A developmental approach of antisocial behavior*. Abingdon, UK: Psychology Press.

Vitaro, F., & Tremblay, R. E. (1994). Impact of a prevention program on aggressive-disruptive children's friendships and social adjustment. *Journal of Abnormal Child Psychology, 22*(4), 457–475.

Vitaro, F., Arseneault, L., & Tremblay, R. E. (1997). Dispositional predictors of problem gambling in adolescent males. *The American Journal of Psychiatry, 154*(12), 1769–1770.

Vitaro, F., Tremblay, R. E., Kerr, M., Pagani-Kurtz, L., & Bukowski, W. M. (1997). Disruptiveness, friends' characteristics, and delinquency in early adolescence: A test of two competing models of development. *Child Development, 68*(4), 676–689.

Vitaro, F., Arseneault, L., & Tremblay, R. E. (1999). Impulsivity predicts problem gambling in low SES adolescent males. *Addiction, 94*(4), 565–575.

Vitaro, F., Brendgen, M., & Tremblay, R. E. (1999). Prevention of school dropout through the reduction of disruptive behaviors and school failure in elementary school. *Journal of School Psychology, 37*(2), 205–226.

Vitaro, F., Brendgen, M., & Tremblay, R. E. (2001). Preventive intervention: Assessing its effects on the trajectories of delinquency and testing for mediational processes. *Applied Developmental Science, 5(4)*, 201–213.

Weiss, G., & Hechtman, L. T. (1993). *Hyperactive children grown up: ADHD in children, adolescents, and adults*. New York: Guilford.

West, D. W. (1982). *Delinquency – its roots, careers and prospects*. Cambridge, MA: Harvard University Press.

Yoshikawa, H. (1994). Prevention as cumulative protection: Effects of early family support and education on chronic delinquency and its risks. *Psychological Bulletin, 115*, 28–54.

8

Understanding and Preventing Crime and Violence

Findings from the Seattle Social Development Project

J. David Hawkins, Brian H. Smith, Karl G. Hill, Rick Kosterman, Richard F. Catalano, and Robert D. Abbott

Introduction

This chapter reviews the results of the Seattle Social Development Project related to crime and violence. The Seattle Social Development Project is a longitudinal study of 808 multiethnic urban children sampled and surveyed in 1985 at age 10 as they entered the fifth grade and most recently surveyed in 1999–2000 at the age of 24. The sample included all consenting fifth-grade students in 18 Seattle public elementary schools selected because they served high crime neighborhoods. The SSDP is grounded in the Social Development Model (SDM), an integrated developmental theory of behavior. A preventive intervention trial, guided by the social development model, was nested within the study. The chapter reviews three types of findings:

- The prevalence, distribution, and patterns of development of offending,
- Using the social development model to predict offending,
- Effects of the SSDP intervention test in the nested trial.

In each section, we locate the research findings in the context of criminological theory and research to indicate the contribution of the findings to the field.

Taking Stock of Delinquency: An Overview of Findings from Contemporary Longitudinal Studies, edited by Thornberry and Krohn. Kluwer Academic/Plenum Publishers, New York, 2003.

Sample Description, Interventions, and Participation

The Seattle Social Development Project (SSDP) studies both positive and antisocial development. The panel study was created in 1985 by nesting an intervention study, initiated in 1981 at first-grade entry, within a larger longitudinal panel study. Eighteen elementary schools serving high crime neighborhoods of Seattle were assigned nonrandomly to conditions in the fall of 1985, and from that point all consenting fifth-grade students in these 18 schools participated in the study.

From the population of 1,053 students entering Grade 5 in participating schools in the fall of 1985, 808 students (76.7%) consented to participate in the longitudinal study and constitute the SSDP sample. That acceptance rate (76.7%) is comparable to other studies attempting to recruit children or adolescents (Ellickson & Bell, 1990; Elliott, Huizinga, & Ageton, 1985; Thornberry, Lizotte, Krohn, & Farnworth, 1990). Of the 808 youths, 396 are females, and 372 European Americans, 195 African Americans, 170 Asian Americans, and 71 Native American or other ethnic group identity. Over 52% of the sample were from low-income families as evidenced by participation in the National School Lunch/School Breakfast Program between the ages of 10 and 12. It should be noted that during this study the Seattle School District used mandatory busing to achieve racial equality in schools. As a result, all schools in this study served a heterogeneous population of students drawn from at least two different neighborhoods of the city.

Youth participants have been interviewed nine times and their parents have been interviewed six times over the ensuing $11\frac{1}{2}$ years as shown in Table 1. Participants' teachers completed the Child Behavior Checklist (CBCL) at the end of five school years from 1985 to 1989. For ease of presentation, the ages presented in Table 1 and throughout this chapter indicate the mean age at each assessment. In the 1996 assessment, we interviewed 765 participants (95% of the

Table 1. Participation at Each Year of Survey

Year of Survey*	F-1985	S-1986	1987	1988	1989	1990	1991	1993	1996	1999
Mean Age	10	11	12	13	14	15	16	18	21	24
Subjects N	808	703	558	654	778	783	770	757	765	752
(%)		(87%)	(69%)	(81%)	(96%)	(97%)	(95%)	(94%)	(95%)	(93%)
Parent Survey N	na	605	623	626	742	719	728	na	na	na
(%)		(75%)	(77%)	(77%)	(92%)	(89%)	(90%)			

* Interviews were conducted in the fall of 1985 and in the spring of each subsequent year. na = Interviews were not conducted with parents during these waves.

initial 808, or 96% of 797 still-living participants). In the 1999–2000 assessment, we interviewed 752 participants (93% of the initial 808, or 95% of 793 still-living participants). Retention rates for the sample still living have remained above 94% since 1989, when participants were 14 years old. These retention rates exceed Hansen, Tobler, and Graham's (1990) estimated target retention rate of 87% for studies of three or more years' duration required to minimize threats to internal and external validity. Approximately 91% of the sample were interviewed in at least 7 of the 9 data assessment waves. Nonparticipation at each assessment wave was not related to gender; lifetime use of tobacco, alcohol, or participation in delinquency by age 10; nor consistently related to ethnicity.

Data Set Description

As shown in Table 2, the data set contains indicators of major psychosocial risk factors for crime, violence, and substance use, indicators of all social development model constructs, and indicators of child and adolescent internalizing and externalizing problem behaviors including measures of delinquent, criminal, and violent behavior. Indicators of positive development are included across all ages. These indicators were developed through reviews of research on predictors of behavior (e.g., Catalano & Hawkins, 1996; Hawkins, Arthur, & Catalano, 1995; Hawkins, Catalano, & Miller, 1992a) and the instruments used in those studies. Items measuring these factors and SDM constructs have been reviewed repeatedly to assure that they are developmentally appropriate congeneric measures of key constructs.

Multiple informants and multimethod measurement have been emphasized. Measures have been obtained from youths, their parents or adult caretakers, teachers, school records, Seattle Police records, and King County and Washington State court records. Police records were searched annually through 1993 (age 18), and individual arrest and related information were collected. We have also collected court record data for the sample through age 21 from all Washington juvenile and superior courts, the Washington Department of Corrections sentencing records, and the Federal Bureau of Investigation. School records were collected annually through 1991 and include achievement test scores, grades, special education needs, student demographics, and disciplinary actions.

New items and scales have been added to surveys to measure behaviors and activities such as sexual activity, work, marriage, pregnancy, and parenting that emerge as participants mature. New items have also been added to measure constructs of interest emerging in the literature and to provide more developmentally appropriate measures of key constructs. Retrospective assessments of childhood abuse and neglect, age of disorder onset and symptom duration, family health history, and history of depression have been added to the age 24 interview.

Table 2. Measures of Risk and Protective Factors, Social Development Constructs and Outcome Variables, Seattle Social Development Project, 1985–1999

Position in the Social Structure
   Income
   Economic Deprivation
   Living Arrangements
   Ethnicity
   Gender
   Age

External Constraints
   Parenting
   Neighborhood Characteristics
   Prevalence and Frequency of Victimization

Individual Constitutional Factors
   Diagnostic Interview Schedule (DIS): Diagnostic Categories
   Global Assessment of Functioning
   Child Temperament
   Prosocial Opportunities
   School
   Family
   Neighborhood
   Peer
   Work
   Intimate/Marital Relationships

Skills
   Social skills, academic and work skills, refusal skills

Prosocial Involvement
   School
   Family
   Neighborhood
   Peer
   Work
   Intimate/Marital Relationships
   Religious Services Attendance

Prosocial Rewards
   School
   Family
   Neighborhood
   Peer
   Work
   Intimate/Marital Relationships

Prosocial Bonding
   School Commitment and Attachment
   Parent-Child Attachment
   Peer
   Intimate/Marital Relationships

Table 2. Continued

Belief in the Moral Order/Antisocial Opportunities
  Drug Availability
  Antisocial Behavior of Others
  Substance Use of Parents, Peers, Partners and Coworkers
  Neighborhood
  Parental Norms and Attitudes Favorable to Drug Use

Antisocial Involvement
  Neighborhood
  Peer

Antisocial Rewards and Costs
  Neighborhood
  Peer
  Family (Consistent and Moderate Discipline)

Antisocial Bonding
  Peer

Belief in Antisocial Values
  Respondent Norms and Attitudes Favorable to Drug Use and Delinquency

Outcomes
  Educational Achievement
  Educational Attainment
  Work Force Attainment
  Relationship Involvement
  Birth Control
  Safe Sex
  Number of Sexual Partners
  Pregnancies
  Sexually Transmitted Diseases
  Substance Use During Pregnancy
  High Risk Sexual Behavior
  Sexual Violence and Rape
  Prevalence, Setting, Severity of Injuries
  Substance Involvement in Injuries: Accidental, Self-inflicted, or Other-inflicted
  Frequency of Utilization: Health, Mental Health, and Substance Abuse Services
  Substance Use: Frequency of Use: Cigarettes, Smokeless Tobacco, Alcohol, Marijuana,
    Cocaine (any form), Amphetamines, Tranquilizers, Psychedelics, Narcotics, Injection Drug
    Use, Overall Drug Use
  Alcohol and Drug Problem Use
  Frequency of Delinquency: Vandalism, Theft/Robbery, Assault/Violence, Using Weapons,
    Drug Selling, Trouble with Police, Moving Violations, White Collar Crime, Gambling,
    Gang Involvement, Domestic Violence

Other Risk Factors
  Stressful Life Events and Conditions
  Transitions and Mobility

Cronbach's reliability coefficients have been calculated for all scales for which this is appropriate. All scales have demonstrated adequate to excellent internal reliability, with Cronbach's alpha internal consistency coefficients of .60 to .92 for scales created from youth and parent surveys.

Methodological Issues: Intervention Effects

Special care must be taken when conducting studies of causal mechanisms on samples that contain interventions, because analyses which do not take the intervention into account may be subject to threats to validity. While our analyses of intervention effects have found differences in the levels and prevalence of certain risk and protective factors, social development model constructs and outcomes between groups (Hawkins, Catalano, Kosterman, Abbott, & Hill, 1999), we have found little evidence of differences among the different groups in the relationships among variables (i.e., covariance matrices) related to the etiology of problem behaviors (Abbott et al., 1991). However, to be cautious, in our etiological studies we have used analysis methods that model and control for the presence of a nested intervention (e.g., Catalano, Kosterman, Hawkins, Newcomb, & Abbott, 1996; Huang, Kosterman, Catalano, Hawkins, & Abbott, 2001). These studies have indicated a high goodness of fit with the data when the parameters of the intervention and control groups were constrained to be equal (comparative fit index, or CFI = .93 to .94).

Prevalence, Frequency, and Onset of Offending in the SSDP Sample

Dimensions of Criminal Careers in the SSDP Sample

The criminal career approach to understanding offending is influential in criminology (Blumstein, Cohen, Roth, & Visher, 1986). It emphasizes the need to investigate specific dimensions of offending including what fraction of the population commits offenses (prevalence), the frequency of offending per year by active offenders, when criminal careers begin and end and the duration of careers between onset and desistance, and the extent to which a small fraction of the population (chronic offenders) account for the majority of all offenses. Because some criminal career dimensions require information regarding exact dates of offenses, which are available in official records but not self-reports, most knowledge about criminal careers has been derived from official records of arrests, court referrals, or convictions (Farrington, 1997). However, official records only capture a small fraction of the true number of offenses committed. Therefore, conclusions about criminal career features based only on official records may be inaccurate or even misleading. Self-reports of offending capture a larger fraction of the true number of offenses committed and may, therefore, yield more accurate information about criminal career features.

Farrington et al., (in press) systematically examined the criminal careers of the SSDP sample using official records and self-reports to understand similarities and differences in the two types of measures of offending across eight specific offenses for which data were available from both self-reports and court records at the same ages: burglary, vehicle theft, larceny, robbery, assault, vandalism, marijuana use, and drug selling.

Prevalence of Offending

Table 3 shows the annual prevalence of offending for all eight offenses at each age from 11 to 17, according to both court referrals and self-reports. As expected, the prevalence of offending was much higher in self-reports at all ages.

Table 3. Prevalence and Frequency of Offending in the SSDP Sample

	Prevalence		Frequency	
	Court	*Self-Report*	*Court*	*Self-Report*
Age				
11	1.7	30.3	1.1	2.9
12	2.1	27.9	2.1	4.6
13	8.0	41.6	2.8	11.6
14	10.8	45.6	2.7	13.5
15	13.1	47.7	3.1	16.8
16	13.6	51.3	2.2	18.3
17	12.7	61.1	2.4	21.8
Total	33.8	86.3	4.6	49.2
Offense Type				
Burglary	4.7	22.3	1.6	3.2
Vehicle theft	23.6	32.7	1.8	5.9
Larceny	25.8	66.2	2.0	11.6
Robbery	3.3	8.5	1.2	5.6
Assault	12.5	61.1	2.4	11.3
Vandalism	8.1	48.1	1.9	8.2
Marijuana use	1.8	50.2	1.2	29.9
Drug selling	3.9	21.5	1.6	28.8
Property	27.7	71.7	3.6	14.3
Violence	16.9	70.3	2.9	16.1
Drug	4.5	51.7	1.8	41.1
Arrest		26.3		4.8

In total, 86.3% of youths admitted committing at least 1 of these 8 offenses, and 33.8% were referred to court for at least one offense.

Table 3 also shows the prevalence of offenses of different types according to court referrals and self-reports. Again, the prevalence of offending was higher in self-reports for each of the eight types of offenses. The two prevalence estimates were most similar for vehicle theft (court 23.6%, self-report 32.7%) and most dissimilar for marijuana use (court 1.8%, self-report 50.2%). In general, the most prevalent offenses according to court referrals were also the most prevalent according to self-reports. The major exceptions were vehicle theft (relatively more prevalent in court referrals) and marijuana use (relatively more prevalent in self-reports).

Individual Offending Frequency

While the variation in the prevalence of offending with age is well established, this is not true of the variation in the frequency of offending with age. The total number of offenses committed at any age can be disaggregated into the number of different offenders (prevalence) and the average number of offenses committed per offender (the individual offending frequency, termed "lambda" by Blumstein et al., 1986). The individual offending frequency is a crucial criminal career parameter with important theoretical and policy implications (such as for estimating the incapacitative effects of incarceration).

The studies reviewed by Farrington (1986) suggested that individual offending frequency does not vary systematically with age, in official records or self-reports. However, based on a large sample of juvenile court careers in Arizona, Loeber and Snyder (1990) found that offending frequency increased steadily from age 9 to age 16. It also increased between ages 10 and 14 according to self-reports in Denver, Pittsburgh, and Rochester longitudinal surveys (Kelley, Huizinga, Thornberry, & Loeber, 1997). In a systematic comparison of official records in London and Stockholm, Farrington and Wikstrom (1994) concluded that the individual offending frequency stayed constant with age in London but increased to a peak at age 15 (and then decreased) in Stockholm. Changes in the individual offending frequency with age have theoretical significance in criminology. Hirschi and Gottfredson (1983) argued that prevalence and individual offending frequency both reflected the same underlying construct of criminal propensity, and hence that both should vary similarly with age.

Table 3 shows the individual offending frequency (the average number of offenses per offender) for the SSDP sample. This was much higher in self-reports (49.2 per offender on average) than in court records (4.6 per offender on average). For all eight offenses, there was no significant tendency in court records for the individual offending frequency to vary with age; for each offense at each age, the individual offending frequency varied only between 1.0 and 1.8. Therefore, it was rare to be referred to court more than once for any given type of offense at any given age. However, as indicated in Table 3, the self-report data show a steady increase in individual offending from age 11 to age 17 in the SSDP sample. Court referrals and self-reports in the SSDP sample clearly differed in their conclusions about whether the individual offending frequency stayed constant or increased with age. It appears that offending frequency truly increased with age, but that this increase was not seen in court referrals perhaps because of system limitations on the number of court referrals per offender per year. These findings indicate the importance of self-report data for accurately estimating offending frequency (lambda).

Continuity

Generally, there is a significant continuity between offending in one age range and offending in another. Establishing the degree of continuity is important in predicting future criminal careers. In Farrington's (1992) study of London boys, 73% of those convicted as juveniles at age 10–16 were reconvicted as young adults at age 17–24, in comparison with only 16% of those not convicted as juveniles, yielding an odds ratio of 14.6 for adult conviction for convicted juveniles compared with those not convicted as juveniles. Also, for 10 specified offenses, the significant continuity between offending in one age range and offending in a later age range held for self-reports as well as official convictions (Farrington, 1989). The similarity between continuity in official records and continuity in self-reports has not previously been studied in an American sample.

Farrington and colleagues (in press) investigated the continuity in the prevalence of offending between ages 12–13 and 14–15 and between ages 14–15 and 16–17 separately for court referrals and self-reported offenses in the SSDP sample. The results were consistent, showing significant continuity for all types and categories of offenses between all age ranges and across court referrals and self-reports. These data replicate Farrington's London results on continuity of offending.

Chronic Offenders

A frequently cited finding from the Philadelphia cohort study of Wolfgang, Figlio, and Sellin (1972) is that 6% of the males (the "chronic offenders") accounted for about half (52%) of the juvenile arrests. Similar results were obtained in London. In Stockholm, the concentration of offending was greater; only 2% of the males accounted for about half of all the offenses (Farrington & Wikstrom, 1994). Whether the concentration of offending is greater or less in self-reports than in official records has not previously been investigated, and neither has the question of whether self-reports and official records identify the same people as chronic offenders.

Following Wolfgang et al. (1972), Farrington et al. (in press) operationally defined "chronic offenders" in the SSDP sample as those who commit half of all offenses. In court referrals, 40 youths (5.5% of the sample and 16.2% of offenders) accounted for half of all offenses. For self-reported offenses, 56 youths (7.0% of the sample and 8.1% of offenders) accounted for half of all offenses. There was significant overlap between official and self-reported chronic offenders. Nearly half (48.8%) of the official chronics were also self-reported chronics, compared with only 4.7% of official nonchronics (odds ratio = 19.5, $p < .05$).

Age of Onset

In the SSDP data, an early age of onset predicted a larger number of offenses. Nagin and Farrington (1992) concluded that this was because of the persistence of a previously existing criminal potential rather than because of any causal impact of early onset. An early age of onset (11–12) also predicted a high rate of offending after onset in court referrals, but not in self-reports in the SSDP data. This may be a consequence of the apparent reluctance, found in these data, to refer youths aged 11–12 (in Grades 5 and 6) to court after offending. Those youths who were referred at ages 11–12 may have been relatively extreme in their criminal potential.

The first self-reported offense was, on average, 1.8 years before the first court referral. Given the average self-reported rate of offending after early onset of about 11 offenses per year, it can be estimated that the average offender in the SSDP sample committed about 20 offenses before the first referral to juvenile court. The criminal justice system is not very efficient at bringing offenders (especially drug offenders) to court. Overall, less than half of all offenders were referred to court, and the probability of an offender being referred to court was greater than 50% for only one type of offense—vehicle theft. The probability of an offender being referred to court increased sharply between ages 11–12 and 13–15. It is noteworthy that the probability of an offense leading to a court referral decreased with increasing numbers of offenses committed, suggesting that more prolific offenders were more skilled at evading capture, or that the juvenile justice system could not cope with prolific offenders.

To summarize the results on criminal career dimensions in the SSDP sample, in self-reports prevalence and individual offending frequency were higher, the age of onset was earlier, and the concentration of offending was greater than in court records. Self-reports and court referrals yielded similar results demonstrating continuity in offending. The main differences in delinquency career results concerned the sharp increases in the prevalence of court referrals and in the probability of an offender being referred to court at age 13, the fact that early onset (age 11–12) predicted a high frequency of offending in court referrals but not in self-reports, and the fact that individual offending frequency increased with age from 11 to 17 in self-reports but not in court referrals. The findings from these analyses underscore the importance of collecting longitudinal self-report data on offending in order to accurately understand criminal careers.

Trajectories of Offending

Traditionally, most studies on offending have focused on differences between offenders and nonoffenders (Farrington, 1997). However, developmental and life-course perspectives (Catalano & Hawkins, 1996; Le Blanc, 1997; Loeber, 1996; Moffitt, 1993; Patterson & Yoerger, 1993; Sampson & Laub, 1993; Thornberry & Krohn, 2001) suggest the importance of understanding the developmental course of offending. Specifically, theory and research suggest that, within the offender population, there are distinctive groups that follow distinctive trajectories of offending with distinctive etiologies. Identifying distinct groups of individuals who follow different criminal trajectories is important both for theory and practice. With regard to theory, different causal mechanisms and pathways may be needed to understand distinct patterns of criminal behavior over time. From a practice perspective, it is possible that different preventive interventions are needed to forestall or interrupt different criminal trajectories.

To illustrate, the developmental theories of both Moffitt and Patterson have divided offenders into two categories, referred to by Moffitt (1993) as "life-course persistent" and "adolescence-limited" and Patterson and Yoerger (1993) as "early and late starters." The life-course-persistent group is characterized by early conduct and behavioral problems followed by a gradual development of offending that can occur over many years. The adolescence-limited group members start their offending careers in adolescence and desist from offending during adolescence.

There has been considerable debate on the number of distinct developmental offense trajectories (D'Unger, Land, McCall, & Nagin, 1998; Tolan & Gorman-Smith, 1998). To examine this question, Chung, Hill, Hawkins, Gilchrist, and Nagin (2002) employed a semiparametric, group-based modeling (SGM) approach developed by Nagin and colleagues (Fergusson, Horwood, & Nagin, 2000; Jones, Nagin, & Roeder, 2001; Nagin, 1999; Nagin & Land, 1993; Nagin & Tremblay, 1999) to identify and characterize naturally occurring, self-reported offense trajectories from age 13 to 21 in the SSDP panel. Using a dependent variable of self-reported offense seriousness, a five-group solution proved to be the most efficient balance between parsimony and goodness of fit. Figure 1 shows the observed trajectories for the five groups.

These trajectory groups are labeled: nonoffenders, late onsetters, desistors, escalators, and chronics. The nonoffender group is comprised of individuals who never reported any offending. This group is about 24% of the sample. The late onsetter group (14.4% of sample) reported no offenses at age 13 but gradually increased to low seriousness of offending by age 21. The desistor group (35.3% of sample) reported low seriousness of offending at age 13 and by age 21 largely desisted, though we recognize that some may reoffend later. The escalator group (19.3% of sample) started off reporting low seriousness of offending at age 13 but by age 21 reported serious offenses. Finally, the chronic group (7% of sample)

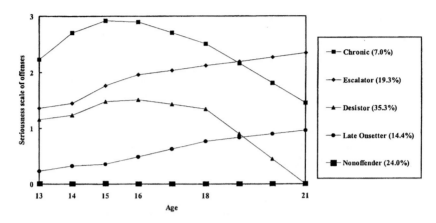

Figure 1. Developmental trajectories of offending from ages 13 to 21.

Chung, I.-J., Hill, K. G., Hawkins, J. D., Gilchrist, L. D., & Nagin, D. S. (2002). Childhood predictors of offense trajectories. *Journal of Research in Crime and Delinquency, 39*(1), 60–90.
Copyright © 2002 by Sage Publications
Reprinted by permission of Sage Publications, Inc.

reported serious levels of offending throughout the adolescent period. By age 21, they had reduced their serious offenses but stayed at a moderately serious level of offending. Note the similarity in size of the chronic offender group using this method and the 7% of chronic offenders found in the SSDP sample by Farrington et al. (in press) using the Wolfgang et al. (1972) criteria of responsibility for half of the offenses committed by the panel.

Chi-square tests were conducted to determine if the trajectory groups identified in Figure 1 differed in terms of demographics. Offense trajectories did not differ significantly by poverty status but were significantly different at the .10 level when an extreme-groups comparison strategy was used (comparing only nonoffender and chronic offender groups by poverty status). The size of the nonoffender group was greater in the nonpoor subsample (24.8%) when compared with the poor subsample (21.6%), whereas the size of the chronic offender group was greater in the poor subsample (8.6%) when compared with the nonpoor subsample (5.9%). Offense trajectories were significantly different by gender and ethnicity ($p < .001$). A greater proportion of males (9.9%) than females (4.1%) were chronic offenders, while only 16.0% of the males were nonoffenders compared with 32.2% of females. About 12% of African American youths, 7% of European Americans, 2% of Asian Americans, and 7% of Others were identified as in the chronic offender group. Asian Americans were most likely to be nonoffenders.

The offense pattern of the chronic group in the SSDP sample is consistent with the early starters and life-course persistent offenders described by Patterson, Reid, and Dishion (1992) and Moffitt (1993), respectively. This group is defined in terms of the dual criteria of childhood onset and a tendency to persist into late adolescence and early adult life. Moffitt (Moffit, 1993; Moffitt, Caspi, Dickson, Silva, & Stanton, 1996) suggested that this group comprises about 6% of the general population. This is similar to the size of the chronic offender group in this study (7%).

The late onsetter group members are somewhat consistent with Moffitt's (1993) adolescence-limited offenders and Patterson et al.'s (1992) late starters. This group met the criterion of adolescent onset, but they did not desist from offending by age 21 as predicted by Moffitt and Patterson. This late onsetter group may be heterogeneous, with some members desisting later in adulthood. Future waves of analyses of SSDP data are needed to determine this. Nevertheless, the late onsetters in this study did not limit their offending to the adolescent period as suggested by Moffitt and Patterson. These results are similar to the finding reported by Nagin, Farrington, and Moffitt (1995) that the reformation of "adolescence-limited" offenders was less than complete. They found that although such "adolescence-limited" offenders had desisted from officially recorded offending near age 20, it was not uncommon for them to continue to self-report drinking heavily, using drugs, getting into fights, and committing minor offenses up to age 32.

Perhaps most interestingly, these analyses identified two groups of offenders not identified by Moffitt's or Patterson's theories. Neither the escalator nor the desistor groups is described in their theories. The escalator group in particular, involving almost 20% of the SSDP sample and escalating to a serious level of offending by age 21, appears to be an important target for prevention and intervention efforts. In this study we also identified factors at age 10–12 that predict membership in the different offending trajectories. These predictors and the implications of these analyses for prevention and intervention programming are discussed later.

The Structure of Deviance

General Deviance Theory and Dimensions of Problem Behavior

The question of whether different problem behaviors reflect a single underlying factor such as criminal propensity (Gottfredson & Hirschi, 1990), or whether they are better conceived as multidimensional phenomena has importance for both theory and intervention design. Research on this question has yielded contradictory evidence. Donovan, Jessor, and Costa (1988) and Farrell, Danish, and Howard (1992) found empirical support for a general syndrome of deviance among high school adolescents. Donovan and Jessor (1985) reported support for the one-factor hypothesis in their studies of young adults. On the other hand, McGee and Newcomb (1992) found that multiple factors were needed to explain problem behavior in young adults.

In Gillmore et al. (1991), we used confirmatory factor analysis to examine this question in the SSDP data set when panel members were aged 11–12. Four hypothetical factor structures for the observed correlations among different forms of problem behaviors were examined. Results for both boys and girls suggested that a three-factor solution was the best fitting model. That model differentiated school problem behaviors from delinquent behaviors, and from substance use, although for boys the improvement in fit over a two-factor model combining delinquent behaviors and substance use was minimal.

These results do not support the general deviance thesis in which different types of problem behaviors are hypothesized to reflect a single underlying proneness to deviance. However, it is important to remember that these analyses focused on youths aged 11–12. It is possible that these behaviors become more linked later in adolescence. Nevertheless, the results suggest that researchers studying younger populations should be cautious in combining measures of problem behaviors.

Dimensions of Problem Behavior in African American and European American Adolescents

Williams, Ayers, Abbott, Hawkins, and Catalano (1996) investigated possible differences in the structure of deviance across racial groups in the SSDP sample later in adolescence. Although a number of studies have found significant differences in the prevalence of deviant behavior across racial groups (Barnes & Farrell, 1992; Beck & Zannis, 1992; Johnston, O'Malley, & Bachman, 1993), few have directly addressed the question of whether there are differences in the structure of problem behavior in different racial groups.

Williams et al. (1996) examined this question by comparing the SSDP data on self-reported drug use, self-reported delinquency, and self-reported juvenile justice system involvement from African American and European American SSDP adolescents at ages 15–16. Multiple group confirmatory factor analysis showed that the fit of the models for both African American and European American adolescents was stronger when two or more factors were used to describe problem behavior, indicating that these behaviors cannot be explained by a single underlying construct of deviance, regardless of the strong positive correlations found among various adolescent problem behaviors.

This study also found evidence that African American adolescents are disproportionately involved in the juvenile justice system in comparison to their self-reported delinquent behavior. For European American adolescents, juvenile justice system involvement was more highly correlated with self-reported delinquency than it was for African American adolescents. European Americans who reported engaging in more delinquent activity reported higher rates of juvenile justice system involvement, as indicated by correlations and standardized coefficients.

However, this was not true for African American adolescents, who reported high rates of juvenile justice system involvement but not equally high rates of self-reported delinquency (Williams, 1994). The differences across racial groups indicate an effect of race on juvenile justice system involvement. In the SSDP sample, the overrepresentation of African American adolescents in the juvenile justice system did not reflect greater self-reported rates of delinquent behavior.

Tracking Progressions of Problem Behavior

Another perspective on the observed high correlations among problem behaviors views certain behaviors as gateways or stepping stones to involvement in increasingly deviant behaviors. Research has shown developmental pathways in the sequencing of initiation of the use of alcohol, tobacco, marijuana, and other illicit drugs (Brook, Whiteman, & Cohen, 1995; Donovan & Jessor, 1983; Huizinga & Elliott, 1981). Recently, Hawkins, Hill, Guo, and Battin-Pearson (2002) confirmed this progression in the SSDP sample, finding the most common transition sequence in the SSDP sample to be from alcohol to tobacco to marijuana to other illicit drug use.

Given the close link between crime and drug use, we asked if the initiation sequence identified for the use of drugs could be expanded to include delinquent behaviors. There is disagreement about the extent to which individuals' development of delinquency is orderly rather than random, and whether a single pathway or multiple pathways best capture individuals' development (Loeber & Stouthamer-Loeber, 1998). Some have linked drug use to stages of antisocial behavior generally (Brook et al., 1995; Jessor, Donovan, & Kosta, 1991; Kaplan & Damphousse, 1995). Loeber and Stouthamer-Loeber (1998) and Loeber and Wikstrom (1993) have proposed a model with separate progressions along different pathways of delinquent and drug-using behavior.

Elliott (1994) proposed a mixed developmental progression wherein youths move sequentially from minor delinquency to alcohol use, marijuana use, index crime (aggravated assault, robbery, or rape), and finally illicit "hard" drug use. This model had three key points of uncertainty: whether delinquency or alcohol use begins the sequence, whether marijuana use or index offending follows next, and whether there is a consistent ordering in the initiation of hard drug use and index offenses.

In contrast, Loeber and Wikstrom (1993) identified separate delinquency-crime and substance-use-only pathways. Analyses reported by Hill, Collins, and Hawkins (2001) sought to determine the degree of support for these different pathways in the SSDP data using Latent Transition Analysis, a method designed to test stage-sequential models (Collins, Hyatt, & Graham, 2000; Collins & Wugalter, 1992).

The Latent Transition Analyses of the SSDP data strongly supported Elliott's mixed model pathway including both substance use and delinquency. A model preventing transitions from delinquency-only and substance-use-only pathways to mixed statuses provided a significantly worse fit indicating the better fit of the mixed model pathway. The specialized pathways of delinquency-only and substance-use-only suggested by Loeber and Wikstrom (1993) were rare in the SSDP data. Only 4% of the sample followed the Delinquency + Index Crime-only pathway, and only 1% had followed the Alcohol + Marijuana + Hard Drugs-only pathway by age 18.

Uncertainties in Elliott's model regarding the sequencing of initiation of index crime versus marijuana use after initiation of alcohol use were clarified in the SSDP data. Hill et al. (2001) found that the elementary to middle school transition was more likely to include the alcohol-to-index crime path, while the middle to high school transition was more likely to include the alcohol-to-marijuana path. A possible explanation for this finding is that early initiation of alcohol use in the elementary grades is more deviant than later initiation of alcohol use and is, therefore, more likely to be followed by more serious forms of deviance such as index crimes. Later initiation of alcohol use in middle school is more likely to be followed by more normative outcomes like marijuana initiation rather than index crimes.

These results suggest that, while structurally, drug use and delinquency may be distinct forms of deviance, analyses of the development of crime in childhood and adolescence should take concomitant development of substance use into account and vice versa. It is possible that their progressive, joint escalation is due to common factors such as deviant peers, or that the behaviors themselves compound one another (e.g., increasing substance use may escalate violence or increase the likelihood of theft). Further, given this joint development, studies of the consequences of adolescent substance use which do not control for adolescent crime may confound the effects of the two.

These findings are important for prevention practice and policy. They suggest that prevention efforts should seek to interrupt a mixed pathway of drug use and delinquency rather than focusing only on drugs or only on crime. If we are to prevent youths from becoming involved and staying involved in substance use and crime, we will have to address both behaviors at developmentally appropriate points in comprehensive prevention efforts.

Predictors of Violence and Delinquency

The prevention of crime and violence requires knowledge of the predictors of these behaviors. To be effective in stopping crime before it happens, crime prevention efforts must address factors that predict crime. The Seattle Social

Development Project has contributed to knowledge regarding the predictors of crime. Those contributions are reviewed in this section.

A broad range of risk factors that predict increased probabilities of adolescent delinquency and substance use have been identified (Farrington & West, 1993; Hawkins et al., 1992a; Hawkins et al., 1992b; Lipsey & Derzon, 1998; Resnicow, Ross Gaddy, & Vaughan, 1995; Stouthamer-Loeber et al., 1993; Williams, 1994). Increasing exposure to risk factors is hypothesized to lead youths on a pathway to involvement in problem behaviors (Barnes & Welte, 1986; Maddahian, Newcomb, & Bentler, 1986; Pollard, Hawkins, & Arthur, 1999).

Researchers have also investigated the effects of positive influences, or protective factors, that inhibit the development of problem behaviors (Farrington & West, 1993; Rutter, 1985, 1990; Stouthamer-Loeber et al., 1993; Werner, 1989). Protective factors are hypothesized to reduce the influence of risk factors on behavior, thus helping reduce involvement in delinquency and substance use (Hawkins et al., 1992a). The Social Development Model (see Figure 2), the theoretical foundation for the research of the Seattle Social Development Project, specifies how risk and protective factors interact in the development of prosocial behavior and antisocial behavior. The SDM is an integrated developmental theory that seeks to explain behavior by combining hypotheses of social learning, differential association, and social control theories.

Differential association theory (Cressey, 1953; Matsueda, 1982, 1988; Matza, 1969; Sutherland, 1973; Sutherland & Cressey, 1970) posits that delinquency, like many other behaviors, is learned in interaction with other persons in a process of communication within intimate personal groups. A person is more likely to become delinquent if exposed to a preponderance of persons favorable to violations of the law relative to those unfavorable to violations of the law. There is substantial evidence for the effects of delinquent peers on delinquent behavior during adolescence (Agnew, 1991; Benda & Whiteside, 1995; Reinarman & Fagan, 1988; Thornberry, Lizotte, Krohn, Farnworth, & Jang, 1994).

Social learning theory also suggests that criminal behavior including violence, is learned (Akers, 1977; Akers, Krohn, Lanza-Kaduce, & Radosevich, 1979; Bandura, 1973, 1977; Burgess & Akers, 1966; Conger, 1976, 1980; Krohn & Massey, 1980). This theory emphasizes that learning occurs through the reinforcement and punishment of behavior. It hypothesizes that criminal behavior is primarily learned in those groups or contexts which comprise the individual's major source of reinforcements.

Social control theory suggests that crime is made possible by weak bonding with prosocial groups like school and family (Hirschi, 1969). Many studies have examined social bonds and delinquent behavior. Social bonds to family and school have been found to inhibit deviant and violent behavior, as predicted by control theory (Cernkovich & Giordano, 1987; Hindelang, 1973; Kempf, 1993; Krohn & Massey, 1980; Massey & Krohn, 1986).

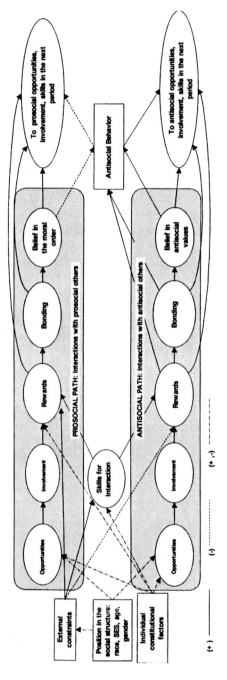

Figure 2. The social development model: general model.

Each of these theories only partially accounts for observed processes in the etiology of delinquency. For example, control theory does not account for antisocial influences in shaping behavior. Social learning theory does not specify the role of bonding in the etiology of behavior. None of these theories explicitly describes etiology developmentally (Le Blanc & Loeber, 1993; Thornberry, 1997).

The social development model integrates key features of differential association, social learning, and social control theories in a developmental theory of behavior. This integrated theory seeks to more adequately describe causal and mediating processes hypothesized to predict behavior over the course of development (Catalano & Hawkins, 1996; Hawkins & Weis, 1985; Weis & Hawkins, 1981).

We present an overview of the social development model here and then examine the degree to which social development model constructs have been found in analyses of the SSDP data to predict violence and delinquency. The section concludes with the results of tests of the social development model itself.

The SDM hypothesizes parallel developmental processes leading to prosocial and antisocial outcomes. The model seeks to explain a broad range of behaviors through specification of predictive developmental relationships.

The prosocial path of the SDM specifies how protective processes of opportunities, involvement, skill development, and recognition/reinforcement for prosocial behavior build prosocial bonds and beliefs or norms that are protective against antisocial behavior. The antisocial path of the SDM specifies how risk factors interact in processes similar to those operating on the prosocial path to produce antisocial behavior. According to this model, intervention and prevention strategies can be effective through reducing risks and by enhancing positive protective influences.

The SDM hypothesizes a sequence of processes in each of a series of submodels specific to stages of development from early childhood through adolescence that lead to behavioral outcomes through the cumulative effects of prosocial and antisocial influences. The model specifies three types of exogenous factors: position in the social structure (including age, race, gender, and SES); individual characteristics (including temperament and intelligence); and external constraints (the behavioral norms or standards of the social contexts in which the individual participates). The SDM hypothesizes that these exogenous factors are mediated by the processes of socialization or social development that occur along the two major pathways of the model.

The model has both a prosocial and an antisocial pathway. The constructs that form these paths are the same except for their prosocial or antisocial valencing. Opportunities, involvement, skills, and reinforcement are the basic building blocks of the model. These constructs operate on the prosocial path as protective factors. The SDM hypothesizes that the interplay of specific factors during development influences the degree to which children develop strong social bonds to school and family. The factors that affect children's prosocial bonding are the degree of opportunity for active involvement available in the family and classroom, the skills possessed and applied by children during participation in these social groups, and the reinforcements provided to children in response to their behavior in these groups. That is, opportunities to interact with prosocial others or participate in prosocial activities are expected to increase actual interaction with prosocial others and involvement in prosocial activities. Successful involvement depends, in part, on the individual's skills to interact and participate in these activities. Thus, skills are hypothesized to moderate the degree to which involvement in prosocial activities leads to recognition and reinforcement for that involvement. The SDM hypothesizes that when individuals perceive their involvement with prosocial others and in prosocial activities as rewarding or reinforcing, they develop bonds of attachment to those prosocial others and commitment to those prosocial activities. Individuals are likely to adopt the normative beliefs or standards for behavior of those to whom they are bonded. Thus, bonding to prosocial others and prosocial activities is hypothesized to increase the individual's belief in the moral order, which is, in turn, expected to prevent antisocial behavior.

On the antisocial path, these same constructs of opportunities for involvement, involvement skills, and rewards operate as risk factors. That is, opportunities for interactions with others involved in antisocial behavior are expected to increase interactions with antisocial others. Again, the individual's skills are expected to influence the degree to which those interactions are experienced as rewarding or reinforcing. If interactions with antisocial others are rewarding to the individual, the SDM hypothesizes that the individual will be more likely to become bonded to these antisocial others, to develop norms favorable to antisocial behavior, and to engage in antisocial behavior. However, on the antisocial path, the model also hypothesizes direct paths from antisocial rewards to antisocial behavior and from bonding to antisocial others to antisocial behavior.

In the SDM, an individual's beliefs or norms (belief in the moral order or norms favorable to antisocial behavior) are hypothesized to guide behavior across social contexts and developmental periods. The beliefs and behavioral outcomes at the end of one developmental stage determine the starting point for the next developmental period by affecting both skills and the perception and availability of future opportunities for prosocial and antisocial involvement.

Analyses of the SSDP data have investigated the degree to which the constructs specified in the SDM predict violence and crime. With regard to external constraints, we have found that parental attitudes favorable to violence predict later self-reported violent behavior of the children in the SSDP sample. Kosterman, Graham, Hawkins, Catalano, and Herrenkohl (2001) found that parental attitudes favorable to violence measured when children were aged 10 predicted their children's violence in adolescence and the persistence of violent behavior into adulthood. Herrenkohl et al. (2000) found that parental attitudes favorable to violence at age 10 directly predicted children's violence at 18. This relationship held after controlling for the age of onset of violence and for the later effects of factors in the family, school, and peer domains measured at age 14 (Herrenkohl et al., 2001a).

In contrast, positive external constraints in the family domain, such as consistent rules and clear behavioral limits, have been found to have clear and positive effects in preventing antisocial behavior in the SSDP sample during adolescence (Kosterman, Hawkins, Guo, Catalano, & Abbott, 2000), even among boys rated aggressive by their teachers at age 10 (O'Donnell, Hawkins, & Abbott, 1995a).

With regard to the exogenous, individual constitutional factors of the SDM, teacher-rated hyperactivity measured at age 10 has been found to predict later violence (Herrenkohl et al., 2000; Kosterman et al., 2000), even after controlling for age 14 family, school, and peer factors. (Herrenkohl et al., 2001b.)

The SDM hypothesizes a recursive process in which behavioral outcomes at each age affect later developmental trajectories by affecting the subsequent opportunities encountered by an individual. We have found across a number of studies of the SSDP sample that elementary school age problem behaviors predict later antisocial behavior. Early aggressive behavior predicted both later gang involvement and sustained gang membership in the SSDP sample (Battin-Pearson, Guo, Hill, Abbott, & Hawkins, 1998; Hill, Howell, Hawkins, & Battin-Pearson, 1999). Early aggressive behavior predicted violence at age 18 (Herrenkohl et al., 2000), and persistence of violence into adulthood in the sample (Kosterman et al., 2000). Huang et al. (2001) found consistency in aggressive behavior in the sample from age 14 through age 18, though as discussed later, this test of the SDM found that this relationship was partially mediated by hypothesized SDM processes.

The first construct on the SDM path of prosocial development is opportunity for prosocial involvement. Across several studies of the SSDP sample, prosocial opportunity has failed to predict delinquency, crime or violent behavior outcomes in bivariate analyses (Ayers et al., 1999; Battin-Pearson et al., 2000; Kosterman et al., 2000). The SDM hypothesizes that prosocial opportunities play a positive role in preventing crime only when they lead to greater levels of involvement, when that involvement is skillful, and when that involvement is followed by recognition for skillful involvement. Both the theory and current findings suggest that, by itself, providing opportunities for children and youth to be involved in positive activities is not likely to prevent criminal or violent behavior.

We have investigated the predictive power of skills for interaction and involvement. Ayers et al. (1999) found that both social skills and substance use refusal skills distinguished delinquent offenders at age 12–13 who desisted from delinquent behaviors at age 13–14 from those who were still engaged in delinquent behavior at age 13–14. In another study, Williams, Ayers, Abbott, Hawkins, and Catalano (1999) found that poor social skills measured at age 12–13 predicted delinquency at age 15–16 for both African American and White youths.

Academic achievement, another indicator of skills, has been shown to predict problem behaviors when measured at different developmental points. Hill et al. (1999) found that low academic achievement and being identified as learning disabled at ages 10–12 predicted joining a gang between ages 13 and 18. Williams et al. (1999) showed that poor academic skills at ages 12–13 predicted delinquency at ages 15–16 equally well for African American and White youths. Teacher rated schoolwork skills, school grades, and California Achievement Test performance were all predictive of changes in delinquency status from ages 12–13 to 14–15 (Ayers et al., 1999). Low academic performance measured in elementary, middle, and high school was significantly predictive of violence at age 18 (Herrenkohl et al., 2000). The predictive effect of low academic performance on later violence was still significant after controlling for the effects of factors in the family and peer domains (Herrenkohl et al., 2001a).

The SDM hypothesizes that young people with prosocial opportunities and skills required for successful prosocial involvement will become bonded to prosocial individuals and institutions to the extent that their involvement is rewarded or recognized (Rewards for Prosocial Involvement). Our studies have shown that the rewards students experience for success at school are predictive of less violence later (Kosterman et al., 2000) and predictive of deescalation of delinquent behavior (Ayers et al., 1999).

Attachment and commitment to prosocial others constitute the prosocial bond in the Social Development Model. This bond is hypothesized to result from opportunities, skills, and rewards for prosocial interaction and involvement. One of the main settings for prosocial bonding is school. Low bonding to school repeatedly has emerged in SSDP studies as a predictor of later crime (Ayers et al., 1999; Chung et al., 2002). Low school commitment at both ages 14 and 16 predicted violence at age 18 (Herrenkohl et al., 2000), and low school bonding combined with low school achievement at age 10–11 predicted involvement in serious delinquency at age 13–14 for boys, regardless of aggressiveness at ages 10–11 (O'Donnell et al., 1995a). Both low school commitment and low attachment to prosocial peers were found to distinguish between those youths who never joined a gang and those who remained in a gang for multiple years (Battin-Pearson et al., 1997).

Bonding to family may also be a form of attachment to prosocial others. However, several analyses of the SSDP data set have failed to find bonding to family to be protective against crime or violence (Ayers et al., 1999; Hill et al., 2001; Kosterman et al., 2000; O'Donnell et al., 1995a). These findings may result from the failure of these analyses to take into account the degree to which family members are, themselves, engaged in, or hold norms favorable toward, criminal, violent, or other problem behaviors. We have seen in analyses of SSDP data that parental violence and criminality and parents who condone violence predict later violent behavior of their children (Herrenkohl et al., 2000; Kosterman et al., 2000).

The SDM hypothesizes that children will embrace the beliefs and behaviors supported and modeled by those individuals to whom they form a bond. Our failure to account for possible antisocial behaviors and norms of family members in assessing the effect of family bonding on behavior is likely to have attenuated the observed relationship. Our analyses have not insured that the family bonding we have measured is, in fact, bonding to prosocial others. This interpretation is consistent with results of a test of the SDM on another data set that included prosocial and antisocial valencing of family members (Catalano, Oxford, Harachi, Abbott, & Haggerty, 1999). In that analysis, bonding to prosocial family members inhibited problem behavior while bonding to antisocial family members led to an increase in children's problem behaviors as hypothesized by the SDM.

The SDM hypothesizes that prosocial bonding leads to belief in the moral order, which directly influences behavior. Support for this was found by Ayers et al. (1999); both belief in the moral order and norms against drug use directly predicted a decrease in delinquency status from age 12 to 15. O'Donnell et al. (1995a) found that norms against drug use at age 12–13 predicted less involvement in serious delinquency at age 13–14 among aggressive boys.

The first construct on the SDM's antisocial path of development is opportunities for antisocial interaction. One way we have measured this factor at the neighborhood level is through youths' self-reports of opportunities to obtain and try marijuana. Opportunities to get and try marijuana predicted violence at age 18 after controlling for school and family factors (Herrenkohl et al., 2001a), whether measured in elementary, middle, or high school (Herrenkohl et al., 2000). Opportunities to get marijuana predicted membership in diverse violence trajectories from ages 13 to 21 (Chung et al., 2002), and violence in adolescence and early adulthood (Kosterman et al., 2000). Self-reported opportunities to get and try marijuana also predicted joining a gang (Battin-Pearson et al., 1998; Hill et al., 1999). Both opportunities to get marijuana and other neighborhood opportunities for involvement in antisocial activities predicted change in delinquent behavior from ages 12 to 15 (Ayers et al., 1999).

Peers are another source of opportunities for antisocial interaction. Kosterman et al. (2000) found that having friends at age 10 who did things that got them in trouble with teachers, who had tried liquor without parental permission, and who did not try to do well in school predicted violence in adolescence and early adulthood. Herrenkohl et al. (2000) found that age 18 violence was predicted by peer delinquency measured at ages 10, 14, and 16 and by sibling delinquency at age 16. Both sibling antisocial behavior and neighborhood youth in trouble, measured at age 10–12, increased the risk of joining a gang between ages 13 and 18 (Hill et al., 1999).

As noted earlier, opportunities for antisocial involvement may also come from parents and other adults. Herrenkohl et al. (2000) found that parental violence and criminality and neighborhood adults involved in crime predicted violent behavior in the sample at age 18. O'Donnell et al. (1995a) found that knowing adults involved in antisocial behavior at age 12–13 predicted serious delinquency at age 13–14 among aggressive boys.

The construct following opportunities on the antisocial path of the SDM is interaction with antisocial others. Involvement with antisocial peers has been a significant predictor of poor outcomes in a number of studies. Hill et al. (1999) measured association with friends who engage in problem behaviors at age 10–12 and found that it predicted joining a gang between ages 13 and 18. Chung et al. (2002) found that a composite antisocial peer factor representing peer deviance and interaction and extent of bonding with those peers predicted membership in diverse violence trajectories from ages 13 to 21. In another study, violent behavior at age 18 was also predicted by involvement with antisocial peers even after controlling for the influence of predictors in the family and school domains (Herrenkohl et al., 2001a). O'Donnell et al. (1995a) found that interactions with both antisocial peers and antisocial adults predicted later involvement in serious delinquency among 12 to 13-year-old aggressive boys. In Ayers et al. (1999), involvement with antisocial peers, both as reported by students and by their teachers, distinguished those on paths to greater delinquency from ages 12 to 15.

Both involvement with delinquent peers and gang membership have been shown to predict crime and violent behavior across multiple studies (Howell, 1997). Herrenkohl et al. (2000) replicated previous gang studies in finding that gang membership at ages 14 and 16 predicted violence at age 18. However, it has not been clear whether gang membership predicts crime and violent behavior over and above the influence of antisocial peers. Battin, Hill, Abbott, Catalano, and Hawkins (1998) sought to gain a clearer understanding of the effects of gang membership over and above the effects of associating with delinquent friends. We distinguished between three groups of youths: (1) self-reported gang members, (2) individuals who were not gang members but were involved with delinquent peers, and (3) individuals who were not in a gang and had few or no delinquent friends. As expected, those who were neither in a gang nor had delinquent friends were less delinquent than either of the other groups. However, in comparison to youths who were not in a gang but had delinquent friends, gang members committed significantly more delinquent acts. At age 14–15 gang members reported more violent crimes, general delinquency, drug selling, and alcohol use, when compared with nongang youths with delinquent friends. Gang membership appeared to intensify violent delinquent acts, but did not appear to increase nonviolent crimes such as theft or other property crimes.

Battin et al. (1998) also modeled the relationship between gang membership and delinquency measured through both court records and self-reports, controlling for the proportion of delinquent friends reported by subjects and prior delinquency, using structural equation modeling. This analysis confirmed that gang membership uniquely and significantly contributed to delinquency after controlling for associations with delinquent friends and even beyond prior delinquency. Gang membership contributed to both court-reported and self-reported delinquency, above and beyond having delinquent peers and beyond prior delinquency, indicating that gang membership is a strong and important criminogenic influence.

Having established the importance of gang membership in predicting crime, we also examined whether the length of time involved with a gang had predictive power (Battin-Pearson et al., 1998). For most youths in the SSDP sample that joined a gang, membership was a transitory phenomenon. Approximately two-thirds of the sample who joined a gang belonged for one year or less, while only one-third of gang members belonged for multiple years. Comparisons between sustained gang members and transient members indicated that sustained gang members had significantly higher rates of violent, property, and substance use offenses during their time of membership than transient gang members, indicating that remaining in a gang for multiple years is associated with increased offending.

The consequences or rewards an individual experiences as a result of interaction and involvement with antisocial others are hypothesized in the SDM to directly affect the likelihood and degree of involvement in antisocial behavior itself and also to predict the development of bonding to antisocial others. Ayers et al. (1999) used a four-item scale to measure rewards for antisocial involvement and found it predicted changes in delinquency status from ages 12–13 to 14–15.

In the SDM, bonding to antisocial others is expected to directly predict antisocial behavior and to predict the development of beliefs favorable to antisocial behavior. Adherence to antisocial beliefs is, in turn, hypothesized to directly predict antisocial behavior. Herrenkohl et al. (2000) showed that attitudes favorable to violent behavior at age 14 significantly predicted violence at age 18. Antisocial beliefs at age 10 predicted violence in adolescence and young adulthood (Kosterman et al., 2000), and antisocial beliefs at ages 10–12 also predicted joining a gang between ages 13 and 18 in the SSDP sample (Hill et al., 2001).

Having reported the direct relationships between SDM constructs and crime and violence outcomes, we turn to analyses that tested the SDM itself to determine which pathways hypothesized in the model are supported in the SSDP panel.

Tests of the Social Development Model

The social development model organizes a broad range of risk and protective factors into a model specifying causal hypotheses to capture key elements of socialization. Huang et al. (2001) sought to test the causal and mediating processes of social development model constructs measured at ages 10, 13, 14, and 16 and their ability to predict violent behavior at age 18 as measured by self-reported fighting, hitting, beating, and threatening someone with a weapon.

A confirmatory factor analysis (CFA) was run on the social development model constructs. All factor loadings were significant and in the expected direction corresponding to the structural model, and the CFA model fit the data well. All factor intercorrelations were in the expected direction, with positive correlations among prosocial constructs and among antisocial constructs, and negative correlations between prosocial and antisocial constructs. These results provide evidence that the scales indicating each factor shared substantial common variance across indicators, and that relationships among factors were consistent with distinctions hypothesized by the SDM between prosocial and antisocial constructs. Figure 3 presents the estimated path coefficients for the structural relationships hypothesized by the social development model.

All but one path specified by the SDM were significant and in the expected direction. With the exception of the path from antisocial bonding to violence at age 18, all social development model hypotheses were confirmed. The overall model fit the data reasonably well, $\chi^2(740, n = 807) = 2412.79$, CFI = .90 and RMSEA = .05. As noted above, the SDM has hypothesized multiple possible pathways to antisocial behavior, directly from rewards for antisocial involvement and interaction, from bonding to antisocial others, and from the adoption of antisocial beliefs. Social learning theory (Bandura, 1977) and social control theory (Hirschi, 1969) suggest the existence of a direct path from rewards to antisocial behavior without bonding to antisocial others. Differential association theories suggest the inclusion of the antisocial bonding construct with a path from

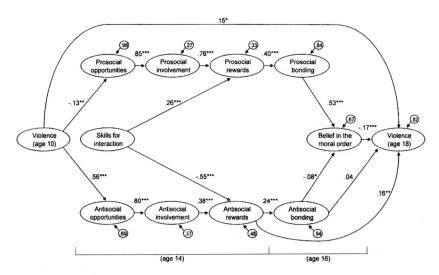

Figure 3. Structural path estimates for the social development model.

Huang, B., Kosterman, R., Catalano, R. F., Hawkins, J. D., & Abbott, R. D. (2001). Modeling mediation in the etiology of violent behavior in adolescence: A test of the social development model. *Criminology, 39*(1), 75–107.

antisocial bonding to antisocial behavior, while cultural deviance theory suggests the addition of the construct of antisocial beliefs or norms and a path from these norms to antisocial behavior. While all these pathways are plausible, only two were supported in this test of the SDM. The nonsignificance of the path from antisocial bonding to violence at age 18 indicates little support for the differential association hypothesis that antisocial behavior results because youths develop strong bonds to others engaged in antisocial behavior. These results support the SDM hypotheses derived from control theory and social learning theory that perceptions of rewards for antisocial involvement lead directly to violent behavior.

There was notable stability in behavior in this model. Violent behavior from age 10 had a significant direct effect on violence at age 18. However, social developmental constructs played an important predictive and mediational role as hypothesized. Adding the direct path from prior violence did not change other hypothesized structural paths in the model. While we found an important direct effect of earlier violence, social development processes in adolescence affected later violence even after considering earlier violence, and they mediated a significant portion of the effects of earlier violence, as hypothesized.

Interventions to prevent or reduce antisocial behavior, most basically conceived, seek to interrupt the causal processes that lead to antisocial outcomes and strengthen the processes that lead to prosocial outcomes. The results of this test indicate the utility of the SDM for understanding both prosocial and antisocial causal processes.

Five specific implications can be drawn from this model test:

(1) With the exception of antisocial bonding, each of the constructs in the social development model is a viable focus for violence prevention and intervention.

(2) Multiple interventions may be required because there are multiple direct and indirect paths to violent behavior.

(3) Interventions to interrupt the causal processes in the development of violent behavior should include components seeking to promote processes that enhance constructs on the prosocial path as well as to interrupt processes on the antisocial path.

(4) The direct and indirect influence of prior behavior on future behavior suggests the importance of intervening early in development to reduce early violent behavior.

(5) Among youths who manifest violent behavior in childhood or early adolescence, disrupting antisocial socialization influences or teaching skills to resist these influences should be emphasized.

Longitudinal studies have shown that those who initiate violent behavior in childhood are at particularly high risk for serious violent offending in adolescence and adulthood (see reviews by Farrington, 1998; Hawkins et al., 1998).

Risk for later violent offending typically diminishes with later ages of initiation (Elliott, 1994; Thornberry, Huizinga, and Loeber, 1995), although initiation of violence at any age through adolescence is associated with an increased proba- bility for violence at subsequent ages (Farrington, 1998). Consistent with this, Moffitt (1993) and Patterson and Yoerger (1993) suggested that youths who initi- ate violence early and then persist in offending through adolescence follow a dif- ferent etiological process than youths who engage in violence only during adolescence.

In Herrenkohl et al. (2001b), we asked whether socialization processes in the social development model similarly predict violence in late adolescence (age 18) for childhood initiators of violence (ages 10–11) and adolescent initiators of vio- lence (ages 12–16). The analyses did not seek to explain the etiology of initiation of violence, but focused on predicting persistent violence through age 18 among those who had already initiated violent behavior in an earlier period.

The portion of the SDM tested in this study is shown in Figure 4. Measures of prosocial and antisocial opportunities, prosocial and antisocial involvement, skills for interaction, and prosocial and antisocial rewards were measured at age 14 with reports from youths, parents, and teachers. The prosocial and antisocial bonding constructs were measured at age 16 with data from those same sources.

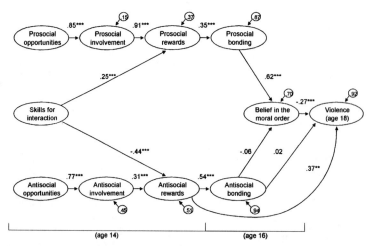

Chi-Square=2560, df=1296; Nonnormed Fit Index=.88; Comparative Fit Index=.89; residual mean square error of approximation=.04.

Figure 4. Constrained multiple group structural equation model.

Herrenkohl, T. I., Huang, B., Kosterman, R., Hawkins, J. D., Catalano, R. F., & Smith, B. H. (2001b). A compari- son of the social development processes leading to violent behavior in late adolescence for childhood initiators and adolescent initiators of violence. *Journal of Research in Crime and Delinquency, 38*(1), 45–63.

A measure of belief in the moral order at age 16 also was included. Three indicators formed each latent construct in the model. Whenever possible, items in each construct represented four different domains of influence (community, school, family, and peer) (Bollen & Lennox, 1991; Newcomb, 1990).

Controlling for gender and race in the analyses, we found that a model in which we constrained factor loadings and path coefficients to be the same for childhood and adolescent initiators of violence fit the data as well as an unconstrained model. The change in chi-square from the unconstrained to the constrained model was not significant ($\Delta\chi^2$ (40) = 52.366, $p > .05$), indicating that the overall fit of the model was not impaired by the constraints imposed. In short, during the middle and high school periods, the social development model predicted later violent behavior equally well for both childhood and adolescent initiators of violence.

As shown in Figure 4, with the exception of paths from the antisocial bonding factor to belief in the moral order factor, and from the antisocial bonding factor to the violence outcome measure—which were nonsignificant—all paths in the portion of the SDM tested here were strong and in the direction specified by the model's hypotheses. On both the prosocial and antisocial paths, opportunities for involvement in activities and interactions with others predicted youths' degree of involvement and interaction in those activities and interactions at age 14. Degree of involvement, in turn, predicted perceived rewards (reinforcement), which predicted bonding to prosocial or antisocial others at age 16. Skills for interaction were positively associated with prosocial rewards at age 14 and negatively associated with antisocial rewards at that age. Having prosocial bonds at age 16 was associated with having more belief in the moral order at age 16 and belief in the moral order at age 16 was predictive of lower involvement in violence at age 18.

On the antisocial path, rewards coming from involvement in activities with antisocial others at age 16 predicted greater involvement in violence at age 18, whereas rewards did not predict bonding to antisocial others. As previously noted, bonding to antisocial others at age 16 was not predictive of violence at age 18. The direct path from antisocial rewards to later violence again indicates that the likelihood of violence among youths in adolescence may depend less on the strength of relationship ties to other antisocial youths and adults than it does on the degree to which young people view antisocial involvement as rewarding or not.

As reported above, the final constrained multiple group structural equation model in Herrenkohl et al. (2001b) showed that factor loadings and structural paths in the SDM were similar in magnitude and direction for the childhood and adolescent initiators of violence. No meaningful etiological differences between the two groups during the adolescent period were found. While the SSDP data identify youths on different developmental trajectories of antisocial behavior as shown earlier in Figure 1, the Herrenkohl et al. (2000) analyses do not support the suggestion that different etiological models are needed to explain the adolescent violent behavior of early starters versus those who begin violent behavior in adolescence. These findings are important for the design of violence prevention and control strategies during the adolescent developmental period. If, from age 14 to 16, different processes promoted later violence among childhood versus adolescent initiators, then different prevention and control strategies would be needed for these groups during adolescence. The evidence reported by Herrenkohl et al. (2001b) suggests that, since the processes leading to violence at age 18 are similar for childhood and adolescent initiators of violence, the same prevention and control strategies should be useful for both groups during adolescence. This also suggests that opportunities for intervention to reduce violence are available well into adolescence even for youths that have engaged in violent behavior from an early age.

Intervention Effects on Delinquent Behaviors and Social Development Constructs

The Seattle Social Development Project included an intervention study nested within the panel study. Students were nonrandomly assigned to "full intervention," "late intervention," "parent-training only intervention," and control conditions in the fall of 1985. The full intervention group received a social development intervention package from Grade 1 through Grade 6. The late intervention group received the intervention package in Grades 5 and 6 only. A third group received a parent training intervention only in fifth and sixth grades, and the control group received no special intervention (Hawkins et al., 1999).

In the social development intervention conditions (the full and late intervention groups), classroom teachers were trained to use proactive classroom management, interactive teaching, and cooperative learning techniques in their classrooms. In addition, all students in those conditions received social skills training in the classroom. In the social development intervention conditions and the parent-training only condition, parenting evenings provided developmentally adjusted training in skills for effective parenting and supporting their children's educational success.

Program Goals and Rationale

The social development intervention sought to reduce specific risk factors and to increase protective factors for adolescent health and behavior problems specified in the social development model. The intervention sought to help teachers increase the *clarity of norms and rules about behavior* (Rutter, Maughan, Mortimore, Ouston, & Smith, 1979) and *consistently enforce expectations regarding behavior* (Gottfredson & Gottfredson, 1985). The intervention targeted family factors of *poor family management practices* including unclear rules, poor monitoring of behavior, and inconsistent or harsh discipline (Widom, 1989;

Yoshikawa, 1994); *favorable parental attitudes toward problem behavior, family conflict*, and sought to strengthen *family bonding* (Hawkins et al., 1992a). Peer focused interventions sought to strengthen attachment to prosocial peers (Mrazek & Haggerty, 1994) and provide skills to resist *influences of delinquent peers*. By initiating the full intervention in Grade 1, we sought to reduce *early and persistent antisocial behavior* (Elliott, 1994; Farrington, 1989, 1991), *antisocial peer influence* (Kellam, Rebok, Ialongo, & Mayer, 1994; Mrazek & Haggerty, 1994), *early involvement in substance use* (McCord, 1983), and *academic failure* (Maguin & Loeber, 1995), and to strengthen *attachment and commitment to school* (Gottfredson, 1988; Johnston, O'Malley, & Bachman, 1985). Because being raised in poverty increases risk for crime, school failure, and school dropout (Blumstein et al., 1986; Elliott, Huizinga, & Menard, 1989; Goodlad, 1984), effects of the intervention on children from poverty have been of particular interest in our analyses.

Research has shown that teachers can improve children's attitudes towards school, behavior at school, and academic achievement through the use of effective methods of instruction and management (Bloom, 1976; Brophy & Good, 1986; Mortimore, 1995; Slavin, Karweit, & Wasik, 1994). Studies have also identified child-rearing methods that reduce conduct problems and improve school performance of elementary-aged children (Bank, Patterson, & Reid, 1987; Dumas, 1989; Tremblay et al., 1991; Tremblay et al., 1992).

To change the risk and protective factors affecting the SSDP sample, we designed interventions with teachers, parents, and children themselves. To ensure that the component interventions would complement each other, the components were explicitly grounded in the social development model (Catalano & Hawkins, 1996; Hawkins & Weis, 1985).

We hypothesized that training teachers to teach and manage their classrooms in ways that promote bonding to school, training parents to manage their families in ways that promote bonding to family and to school, and providing children with training in skills to enhance their involvement and rewards for interaction with prosocial others would positively affect children's attitudes toward school, behavior at school, and academic achievement. These methods further seek to reduce children's opportunities and rewards for antisocial involvement. We thought that these changes would, in turn, set children on a different developmental trajectory observable in more positive academic outcomes and fewer delinquent and health-risk behaviors later in adolescence.

Study Design

To assess the effects of "full intervention," "late intervention," and a "parent-training-only intervention," a nonrandomized, controlled trial with four conditions was created in 1985 by nesting an experimental intervention initiated in 1981 at first-grade entry, within the longitudinal panel study. Schools were assigned nonrandomly to conditions in the fall of 1985, and from that point, all fifth-grade students in each school participated in the same interventions. New schools added for the panel study were matched to the intervention schools with respect to grades served and inclusion of students drawn from high crime neighborhoods of Seattle. Schools added for the panel study were assigned to conditions to achieve balanced numbers across conditions.

The full intervention group consists of all students who were randomly assigned to intervention classrooms in Grades 1 through 4 in eight elementary schools participating in the earlier experimental study, and who remained in schools assigned to the intervention condition in Grades 5 or 6 in the present study. The late intervention group consists of students in intervention schools who were in intervention classrooms in Grades 5 and 6 only, some of whom were controls in the earlier intervention study. The parent-training-only group consists of students whose parents were offered parent training only when their children were in Grades 5 and 6 and no other intervention. The control condition consists of students in schools assigned to receive no intervention in Grades 5 and 6 and who were not in intervention classrooms in Grades 1 through 4.

Intervention Program Description

Classroom Instruction and Management

Each year, as the panel moved through the elementary grades, teachers in intervention classrooms received five days of in-service training in a package of instructional methods with three major components: *proactive classroom management* (Cummings, 1996); *effective instruction strategies* (Barber, 1981; Hawkins, Doueck, & Lishner, 1988b); and *cooperative learning* (Slavin, 1980, 1991). **Proactive classroom management** is aimed at establishing an environment that is conducive to learning and that promotes appropriate student behavior while minimizing disruption of classroom activities. In this intervention, teachers established and taught classroom routines at the beginning of the year to create a consistent pattern of expectations. Prior to the beginning of each year, intervention teachers were taught to give clear expectations and explicit instructions about attendance, classroom procedures, and student behavior, and to recognize and reward attempts to comply. Teachers were also taught methods to maintain classroom order that minimize interruptions to instruction and learning. Teachers were taught to provide frequent, specific, and contingent encouragement and praise for student effort and progress that identified the specific student behavior being rewarded. These methods are described in *Managing to Teach* (Cummings, 1996). **Direct instruction** is based on the premise that virtually all students can develop the skills necessary to succeed in the classroom under appropriate instructional conditions. The components of direct instruction used in this project were assessment, mental set, objectives, input, modeling, checking for understanding, and remediation (Barber, 1981). **Cooperative learning** involves teachers' use of small groups of students as learning partners. Students of differing abilities and backgrounds are provided the opportunity to work together in teams to master curriculum materials and receive recognition as a team for their group's academic performance. The cooperative learning techniques used in this intervention were Student Teams Achievement Divisions and Teams-Games-Tournaments developed by Slavin (1980, 1991).

Child Skill Development

First-grade teachers of the full treatment group also received instruction in the use of a cognitive and social-skills-training curriculum, Interpersonal Cognitive Problem Solving (Shure, 1992; Shure & Spivak, 1980, 1988), which teaches skills to children to think through and use alternative solutions to problems with peers. This curriculum developed children's skills for involvement in cooperative learning groups and other social activities without resorting to aggressive or other problem behaviors.

In addition, when students in both intervention conditions were in Grade 6, they received four hours of training from project staff in skills to recognize and resist social influences to engage in problem behaviors, and to generate and suggest positive alternatives in order to stay out of trouble while keeping friends (Comprehensive Health Education Foundation, 1999).

Parent Intervention

Parent training classes appropriate to the developmental level of the children were offered on a voluntary basis to parents or adult caretakers of children. Parents in the full intervention condition were offered training in child behavior management skills when their children were in the first and second grades through a seven-session curriculum, "Catch 'Em Being Good" (McCarthy & Brown, 1983), grounded in the work of Gerald Patterson (Patterson, 1982). In the spring of second grade and again in the third grade, parents of children in the full intervention also were offered a four-session curriculum, "How to Help Your Child Succeed in School," (Developmental Research and Programs, 1991) to strengthen their skills for supporting their children's academic development.

When their children were in Grades 5 and 6, parents of children in both the full and the late intervention conditions were offered a five-session curriculum, "Preparing for the Drug (Free) Years"® (Hawkins et al., 1988), to strengthen their skills to reduce their children's risks for drug use. Preparing for the Drug (Free)

Years (PDFY) is a research-based program that has been found to be effective in helping parents of children ages 9–14 protect their children from substance abuse (Kosterman, Hawkins, Spoth, Haggerty, & Zhu, 1997; Spoth et al., 1998). PDFY seeks to reduce drug abuse and related behavior problems by helping parents:

- create opportunities for children to be involved in meaningful ways with their families,
- strengthen family bonds,
- set clear expectations for their children's behaviors,
- teach their children skills to resist peer pressure,
- reduce family conflict and control emotions, and
- practice consistent family management.

Table 4 provides an overview of the intervention components.

Effects on Problem Behaviors and Social Development Constructs

Hawkins, Von Cleve, and Catalano (1991) examined the early effects of the full intervention at the end of the second grade, following two years of intervention. At this point in the study, eight Seattle public elementary schools were participating. In six of these schools, first-grade teachers and students were randomly assigned to experimental or control classrooms. One of the eight schools was assigned to a full experimental condition, where all first-grade students and teachers in the school were assigned to the experimental condition, and one school was assigned to a full control condition. In total, 520 participating students were in project schools at the end of the second grade (spring of 1983), of which 458 (88%) provided posttest data (285 in the experimental group, 173 in the control group). Participants were 52% female, 46% European American, 32% African American, 16% Asian American, and 5% Native American. No significant demographic differences between experimental and control groups were found.

The Teacher Report Form of the Child Behavior Checklist (CBCL) was used to assess the effects of the intervention at the end of the second grade (Achenbach & Edelbrock, 1983, 1986). All comparisons controlled for socioeconomic status.

Two significant intervention effects were found for males at the end of second grade. Teachers reported that boys in the experimental group were significantly less aggressive and demonstrated significantly less externalizing antisocial behavior than boys in the control group. When analyzed separately for European Americans and African Americans, significant effects on aggressive behavior and externalizing antisocial behavior were found only for European American boys.

Table 4. Seattle Social Development Project Interventions

Teacher Training in Classroom Instruction and Management
  Proactive classroom management
    Establish consistent classroom expectations and routines at the beginning of the year
    Give clear, explicit instructions for behavior
    Recognize and reward desirable student behavior and efforts to comply
    Use methods that keep minor classroom disruptions from interrupting instruction
  Interactive teaching
    Assess and activate foundation knowledge before teaching
    Teach to explicit learning objectives
    Model skills to be learned
    Frequently monitor student comprehension as material is presented
    Re-teach material when necessary
  Cooperative learning
    Involve small teams of students of different ability levels and backgrounds as learning partners
    Provide recognition to teams for academic improvement of individual members over past
    performance

Child Social and Emotional Skill Development
  Interpersonal problem solving skills
  Communication
  Decision-making
  Negotiation
  Conflict resolution
  Refusal skills
  Recognize social influences to engage in problem behaviors
  Identify consequences of problem behaviors
  Generate and suggest alternatives
  Invite peer(s) to join in alternatives

Parent Training
  Behavior management skills
    Observe and pinpoint desirable and undesirable child behaviors
    Teach expectations for behaviors
    Provide consistent positive reinforcement for desired behavior
    Provide consistent and moderate consequences for undesired behaviors
  Academic support skills
    Initiate conversation with teachers about children's learning
    Help children develop reading and math skills
    Create a home environment supporting of learning
  Skills to reduce risks for drug use
    Establish a family policy on drug use
    Practice refusal skills with children
    Use self-control skills to reduce family conflict
    Create new opportunities in the family for children to contribute and learn

Hawkins, J. D., Catalano, R. F., Kosterman, R., Abbott, R., & Hill, K. G. (1999). Preventing adolescent health-risk behaviors by strengthening protection during childhood. *Archives of Pediatrics and Adolescent Medicine, 153*(3), 226–234.

One significant intervention effect was found for females at the end of second grade. Teachers reported experimental girls to be less self-destructive than control girls. When ethnic groups were examined separately, this pattern of results held for European American girls, but not African American girls.

Hawkins et al. (1992b) reported intervention effects for the full intervention group at fifth-grade entry. The full intervention group consisted of students exposed to at least one semester of intervention in Grades 1 to 4 ($n = 199$). In this analysis, the control group consisted of students enrolled in control classrooms during Grades 1 to 4 plus unexposed students who were added to the project in the fall of fifth grade when the panel was expanded ($n = 709$). An accretion analysis compared the initial control group with the additional available control students on each of the intervening and outcome variables assessed and found no significant overall differences. However, when analyzed separately by gender, the added control girls had significantly higher mean California Achievement Test scores than did girls from the initial control group, suggesting a possible accretion effect on this variable for control girls.

Analyses of covariance controlling for ethnicity, socioeconomic status, and mobility showed intervention effects across a number of risk and protective factors. Intervention students reported significantly better family management, family communication, family involvement, attachment to family, school reward, school attachment, and school commitment compared to controls. Intervention students also reported nonsignificant improvements in their parents' use of restrained punishment, belief in the moral order, perceived drug use risk, and expected drug use punishment. Contrary to hypotheses, control students scored significantly higher than intervention students on the California Achievement Test. However, analyses showed that this finding reflected the anomalous effects of accretion for female students only and was no longer in evidence at Grade 6. Effects of the intervention were found on alcohol initiation and on delinquency initiation by fifth grade, with intervention students reporting significantly less initiation for both behaviors than control students.

O'Donnell, Hawkins, Catalano, Abbott, and Day (1995b) investigated the effects of the full intervention on students from low-income families at the end of Grade 6. The full intervention group consisted of students exposed to at least one semester of intervention in Grades 1 through 4 and to at least one semester of intervention in fifth or sixth grades. The control group included students who did not receive the intervention in Grades 1 through 6. Students included in the analysis were those eligible for the National School Lunch Program in the fall of fifth grade ($n = 177$). At the end of the sixth grade, 106 (60%) low-income students completed surveys (intervention group $n = 44$, control $n = 62$). The low-income sample for these analyses was 54% female, 42% African American, 25% Asian American, 24% European American, 6% Native American, and 3% other ethnicities. No significant ethnic differences were found between conditions in either the male or female sample. There was no evidence of differential attrition by condition, with one exception. At fifth-grade entry, girls attriting from the intervention condition reported more antisocial opportunities while attriting control girls reported fewer antisocial opportunities than those who remained.

Low-income girls in the full intervention condition reported significantly more classroom and team learning opportunities, more classroom participation, more bonding and commitment to school, and fewer opportunities to get marijuana than controls at the end of Grade 6. Significantly fewer had initiated cigarette use than had their control counterparts. Fewer low-income intervention girls had initiated alcohol and marijuana use by the end of Grade 6, though this was a nonsignificant trend ($p < .10$).

Boys from low-income families in the full intervention condition evidenced significantly better social skills and schoolwork skills and fewer antisocial friends as rated by their teachers than did their control counterparts. They reported significantly more commitment to school and had significantly better achievement test scores and grades than their control counterparts at the end of Grade 6. Low-income boys in the full intervention group were somewhat less likely to report having initiated delinquency by the end of the sixth grade than were low-income control boys ($p < .10$).

Hawkins et al. (1999) investigated the long-term effects of the full and late interventions on study participants at age 18, six years after all intervention had ended. The analyses included all fifth-grade children assigned to full intervention, late intervention, and control conditions in 1985 whose parents provided written consent to their involvement in the longitudinal follow-up study ($n = 643$). The sample for this analysis was 51% male, 44% Caucasian American, 26% African American, 22% Asian American, 5% Native American, and 3% classified as other ethnicities. Over 56% were from low-income families. In 1993, at age 18, 93% of the original consenting sample assigned to these three conditions were successfully interviewed. These 598 participants were distributed across full intervention ($n = 149$), late intervention ($n = 243$), and control ($n = 206$) conditions. No significant differences were found between intervention and control groups with respect to residential stability, socioeconomic status, single-parent families, proportion of boys, proportion of Whites or non-Whites, living in disorganized neighborhoods, or high schools attended. Attrition analyses showed that attrition was not significantly related to gender, ethnicity, poverty, or intervention condition, nor were there any significant attrition-by-condition interactions on fifth-grade measures related to the outcome variables.

Chi-square tests and analysis of variance procedures were used to examine intervention effects across delinquency, substance use, sexual behavior, and school outcomes. At age 18, six years after intervention ended, those in the full intervention condition were significantly more attached to school and more committed to school than were controls. They reported significantly better school grades and achievement and significantly less misbehavior at school than did the control group. These significant findings were paralleled by Seattle school data showing trends ($p < .10$) of better school grades and fewer disciplinary action reports during high school for full intervention students compared with controls. Significantly fewer participants in the full intervention condition reported violent behavior in their lifetimes to age 18, heavy alcohol use in the past year, lifetime sexual activity, and having had multiple sex partners in their lifetimes by age 18, compared to controls. Results are shown in Table 5; fewer full intervention participants than controls also reported lifetime nonviolent crime and having been arrested, and fewer had been charged with delinquent offenses according to court records, but these differences did not reach statistical significance.

The pattern of effects shown in Table 5 suggests a "dose effect" of the intervention. For both crime and sexual activity outcomes, the full intervention group had the best outcomes, followed by the late intervention group, followed by the control group. Significant effects of intervention were observed primarily for the full intervention group. These findings indicate that interventions grounded in the social development model, seeking to promote the development of bonding to school and family as protective against later criminal behavior, are most likely to be effective when initiated early in development and maintained across the elementary grades.

Measuring SDM Mediators in the Intervention Study

A number of scholars have called for research on the mechanisms through which preventive interventions have their effects (Chen & Rossi, 1989; Durlak & Wells, 1997; Maggs & Schulenberg, 2001; Spoth, Redmond, Haggerty, & Ward, 1995). In theory-guided intervention studies, this involves specifying the chain of causation in the theory that guides the preventive intervention and assessing the degree to which that chain of causation is supported by data.

Tests of preventive intervention hold promise for improving the effectiveness of preventive services in communities by identifying interventions that have the desired preventive effects. Tests of preventive intervention can also be useful for testing theory. For both purposes, it is important to measure the degree to which the intervention tested is actually implemented. Implementation measurement allows a determination of the degree to which the intervention was, in fact, delivered to the group designed to receive it in the study. For those concerned with improving the effectiveness of preventive services, this is important. If positive effects are found, they can be plausibly linked to the intervention only if the intervention was, in fact, implemented. If no effects are found, this indicates that the intervention was not effective only if it was well implemented.

Measuring implementation in intervention studies is also important for achieving the promise of such studies for testing theory. Measures of implementation

Table 5. Comparisons of Control, Late, and Full Intervention Groups across Targeted Delinquency, Substance Use, and Sexual Behavior Outcomes

Outcome	N	Prevalence			Control v. Full		Control v. Late	
		Control	Late	Full	Difference (95% CI)	p	Difference (95% CI)	p
Crime								
Lifetime violence	598	59.7	56.4	48.3	−11.4 (−21.3 to −0.4)	.04	−3.3 (−12.0 to 6.3)	.54
Lifetime nonviolent crime	598	63.1	58.4	57.7	−5.4 (−15.1 to 5.5)	.36	−4.7 (−13.3 to 4.8)	.36
Lifetime arrested	598	24.8	24.7	18.8	−6.0 (−14.0 to 3.2)	.23	−0.1 (−7.6 to 8.4)	>.99
Lifetime court charges from County records	542	37.8	36.9	29.9	−7.9 (−17.5 to 3.1)	.18	−0.9 (−9.8 to 9.0)	.93
Substance Use								
Lifetime cigarette use	598	54.4	52.7	53.7	−0.7 (−10.6 to 10.4)	.98	−1.7 (−10.5 to 8.0)	.79
Lifetime alcohol use	598	72.8	72.0	71.8	−1.0 (−9.9 to 9.0)	.93	−0.8 (−8.6 to 7.9)	.93
Lifetime marijuana use	598	44.7	45.7	42.3	−2.4 (−12.2 to 8.6)	.74	1.0 (−8.7 to 9.8)	.90
Lifetime other drugs use	598	20.9	21.8	20.8	−0.1 (−8.1 to 9.1)	>.99	0.9 (−7.1 to 8.1)	.90
Sexual Activity								
Lifetime sexually active	591	83.0	76.1	72.1	−10.9 (−19.2 to −1.4)	.02	−6.9 (−14.0 to 1.0)	>.09
Lifetime multiple sex partners	589	61.5	59.1	49.7	−11.8 (−21.7 to −0.7)	.04	−2.4 (−11.1 to 7.2)	.68
Lifetime been or gotten a woman pregnant	581	26.4	27.4	17.1	−9.3 (−17.3 to 0.0)	.06	1.0 (−7.8 to 8.9)	.90
Lifetime had or fathered a baby	589	14.7	14.3	9.5	−5.2 (−11.4 to 2.2)	.20	−0.4 (−6.6 to 6.6)	>.99

Note: Prevalences compared with χ^2 statistic based on 2 × 2 tables with Yates' correction for continuity. CI indicates confidence interval.

Hawkins, J. D., Catalano, R. F., Kosterman, R., Abbott, R., & Hill, K. G. (1999). Preventing adolescent health-risk behaviors by strengthening protection during childhood. *Archives of Pediatrics and Adolescent Medicine, 153*(3), 226–234.

quality allow assessment of the theory underlying intervention. Theories are chains of hypotheses that specify causal relationships. To illustrate, the social development model hypothesizes that teaching practices affect opportunities, skills, and rewards in school classrooms as experienced by students. These skills, opportunities, and rewards are hypothesized to build bonding to school and prosocial peers. In turn, bonds to school and prosocial peers are expected to increase prosocial beliefs which, in turn, will reduce the likelihood that youths will engage in problem behaviors such as violence. Good teachers who promote the development of bonding to school through the development of skills and the provision of opportunities and rewards should help to prevent problem behaviors, regardless of the condition to which they have been assigned in an intervention study. Therefore, to test theory in intervention studies, it is important to measure the degree to which the hypothesized mediating variables in the theory's causal chain are present in both intervention and control conditions. The use of implementation scores allows assessment of the degree to which the behaviors of the teachers are related to the mediating variables specified by theory, regardless of intervention condition. In this example, they allow assessment of the links between the behavior of teachers and the social development model's mediating variables of students' skills and perceptions of classroom opportunities, rewards, and bonding.

Abbott et al. (1998) used measures of implementation of the SSDP teaching practices both to assess the efficacy of the project's teacher training and coaching system on implementation of the desired teaching practices and to test the hypothesis that the desired teaching practices would affect classroom opportunities and rewards, student bonding to school, and achievement outcomes. This investigation used the entire SSDP panel. Analyses examined data collected in the fifth and sixth grades, from fall 1985 to spring 1987. The study employed hierarchical linear modeling and empirical Bayesian estimation to appropriately take missing data and the nesting of children in classrooms into account (Bryk & Raudenbush, 1992; Little & Rubin, 1987). Students were distributed across 20 intervention and 22 control classrooms in 18 schools.

The implementation measure was derived from classroom observation ratings by trained project classroom observers during Grade 6. Observers, blind to experimental condition, used the Interactive Teaching Map (Kerr, Kent, & Lam, 1985) to evaluate the extent to which intervention and control teachers used the targeted teaching practices. Each teacher was observed for four observation periods during the year. Each observation period was broken into minute-by-minute sampling time frames and lasted 50 minutes. Targeted teaching practices applied with fidelity were scored $+1$, nontarget classroom practices or ineffectively used targeted practices were scored 0, and teaching strategies in conflict with the targeted teaching strategies were scored -1 for each minute they occurred. A scoring algorithm developed by Kerr et al. (1985) then transformed the observations into a single implementation score for each teacher that reflected the teacher's appropriate use of the targeted teaching strategies during the four separate observations. The implementation scores ranged from -23 to 46 (Mean $= 7.2$, $sd = 14.4$).

Three analyses were conducted. First, to assess whether intervention teachers used the project teaching strategies more than control teachers, the implementation scores during sixth grade were compared. Second, to assess the effects of the teacher training and coaching intervention on students, measures of outcomes at the end of Grade 6 were compared for intervention versus control children controlling for baseline measures of these outcomes at fifth-grade entry using hierarchical linear models (Bryk, Raudenbush, & Congdon, 1996). Third, we assessed the hypothesized effects of the degree of use of targeted teaching practices by sixth-grade teachers, regardless of condition, on the mediators specified by the SDM using hierarchical linear models. Again, outcome analyses controlled for fall fifth-grade baseline data.

Results from the observations showed that sixth-grade teachers in the intervention condition (Mean $= 10.033$, $sd = 14.24$) implemented the project's teaching strategies more than teachers in the control condition (Mean $= 5.811$, $sd = 15.82$). Because of the large variability within condition, however, this difference was not statistically significant ($t(40) = .91$, $p < .37$). Of the teachers in the intervention condition, 65% were above the overall mean in implementation, compared to 40% of those in the control condition.

The second analysis, comparing outcomes for students in intervention versus control classrooms, found significant effects on California Achievement Test (CAT) scores favoring those in intervention classrooms ($t = 2.69$; $p < .02$), but no significant differences in SDM mediating variables between the intervention and control students. However, this analysis by condition did not directly assess the hypothesized effects of the targeted teaching practices on the theoretically relevant mediating variables of the SDM. For a more accurate assessment of this relationship, we analyzed the relationship between teacher implementation scores and the SDM mediating variables, regardless of teachers' condition assignment. High implementation of project teaching practices was marginally predictive of higher standardized achievement tests scores on the CAT at the end of Grade 6 after controlling for fourth-grade CAT scores. Importantly, after controlling for baseline measures on each measure, teachers' degree of implementation of the targeted teaching practices was significantly predictive of increases in the theoretically specified constructs of opportunities for classroom involvement ($p < .004$), actual involvement in the classroom ($p < .009$), reinforcement for classroom involvement ($p < .023$), and bonding to school ($p < .032$) among students.

Absent measures of implementation of project teaching practices by both control and intervention teachers that allowed modeling of the effects of teacher practices on mediating variables regardless of condition assignment, we might have inaccurately concluded from the intervention condition comparisons that the targeted teaching practices were not related to the constructs of opportunities for involvement, reinforcement, and bonding to school. But the intervention/control comparison is really a test of the effectiveness of teacher training, not of the theoretically specified links between teaching and social development model constructs. The model's operating constructs of opportunity, involvement, reward, and bonding to school are experienced in classrooms as teaching practices, regardless of the condition to which a teacher has been assigned by researchers. Good teaching should increase opportunities, skills, and rewards for student involvement in the classroom regardless of whether the teacher is an "intervention" or "control" teacher. While the intervention teachers used the targeted practices more than did control teachers, there were teachers with more and less skill in both conditions. When the teacher's implementation score was used to measure use of the targeted teaching strategies, the analyses show that these teaching strategies influenced students' levels of classroom opportunity, involvement, reinforcement, and bonding to school as hypothesized by the social development model.

Findings from the present study, like others (Gottfredson, Gottfredson, & Hybl, 1993; Slavin, 1991), suggest that it is possible to improve academic achievement as well as to promote bonding to school by changing teaching practices in mainstream classrooms. It also appears, as hypothesized, that the teaching practices used in this intervention test can increase opportunities, skills, involvement, and reinforcement in classrooms as well as students' bonding to school.

These analyses illustrate the importance of including measurement of implementation in prevention studies. Clearly, measures of implementation quality allow assessment of the degree to which the preventive intervention was actually implemented (in this case through the use of the targeted teaching strategies by intervention teachers) and, therefore, the degree to which changes in hypothesized outcomes should be expected in association with the intervention. But, as illustrated here, measures of implementation quality also allow assessment of the theory underlying intervention. In this case, they allowed assessment of the links between the behavior of teachers and the mediating variables of students' skills and perceptions of classroom opportunities and rewards and school bonding.

As noted earlier, analyses of SSDP data have shown that bonding to school is an important protective factor against delinquent and violent behavior. Research suggests that academic motivation declines during adolescence (Eccles & Midgley, 1990; Epstein & McPartland, 1976; Hirsch & Rapkin, 1987; Oldfather & Wigfield, 1996; Schulenberg, Asp, & Petersen, 1984; Simmons & Blyth, 1987). Hawkins, Guo, Hill, Battin-Pearson, and Abbott (2001) examined whether the SSDP intervention in the elementary grades retarded the decline in school bonding during the middle and high school periods following the elementary SSDP intervention. The level of school bonding was assessed at five time points following the intervention (ages 13, 14, 15, 16, and 18). The question of interest here was whether developmental trajectories in bonding to school in the three intervention groups would be similar or different over a six-year follow-up period absent additional intervention or boosters. Several possible correlates of school bonding beyond intervention condition were included in the analysis. These included academic achievement in the elementary grades measured by student fifth-grade California Achievement Test scores, gender, ethnicity, and low-income background—measured by a student's eligibility for the National School Lunch/School Breakfast program. Measures of school success and failure, school misbehavior, crime, substance use, and sexual activity at age 18 reported in Hawkins et al. (1999) were included to assess the relationship of these outcomes to school bonding.

The first analysis examined the relationships of school bonding with behavioral outcomes at age 18. Specifically, we examined whether changes in school bonding in adolescence (controlling for the student's level of school bonding at age 13) were related to behavioral outcomes at age 18 and whether the student's final level of school bonding at age 18 was related to these outcomes.

Table 6 shows that increasing school bonding in adolescence was correlated with higher levels of school achievement and official GPA and was correlated with less school misbehavior, substance use, and sexual activity. Table 6 also shows that higher levels of school bonding at age 18 were positively correlated with school achievement and official GPA and negatively correlated with other problem behaviors such as school misbehavior, crime, substance use, and sexual activity at age 18. This pattern of results was maintained after controlling for gender, ethnicity, and poverty in elementary school (not tabled). These results indicate that both the change in school bonding from ages 13 to 18 and the level of school bonding at age 18 were significantly associated with behavioral outcomes at age 18.

A second analysis examined whether the SSDP intervention affected changes in school bonding from ages 13 to 18. Figure 5 provides the observed mean level of school bonding from ages 13 to 18 (Grade 7 to Grade 12) for the three intervention groups.

As can be seen in Figure 5, at age 13, one year after the intervention ended, the full treatment group had the highest mean level of school bonding of the three groups. The mean level of school bonding declined after age 13 for all three groups. However, the mean level of school bonding in the full treatment group stabilized while the mean level of school bonding continued to decline to age 18 for the other two groups. As a result, the full treatment group again reported the highest mean level of school bonding among all three groups at ages 16 and 18. The next analyses examined whether there was a significant intervention effect on the change in school bonding during the period from ages 13 to 18. We found that the full intervention group had a significantly higher level of school bonding at age 18 than the control group, while there was no significant difference in school bonding at age 18 between the late treatment group and the control group. At age 18, the average level of school bonding was decreasing among controls. The average level of bonding appeared to be slightly increasing in the late treatment group at

Table 6. Correlation between Change in School Bonding and Behavioral Outcomes in School, Delinquency, and Substance Use at Age 18

Outcome	Rate of Change (from Age 13 to 18)		Est. Level of Bonding at Age 18	
	Partial Correlation[†]	n	Pearson Correlation	n
School Success/Failure				
School achievement (age 17)	0.22***	480	0.22***	597
Official GPA (age 17)	0.17**	280	0.27***	352
Repeated a grade (lifetime prevalence)	−0.02	480	−0.09*	597
Dropped out of school (lifetime prevalence)	0.00	479	−0.12**	595
Official California Achievement Test score (age 17)	0.01	223	−0.04	277
School Misbehavior				
Cheated on tests, skipped school/classes, sent from class for misbehavior (past year frequency)	−0.27***	425	−0.34***	528
Official disciplinary action report (high school prevalence)	−0.05	339	−0.21***	425
Suspended or expelled (lifetime prevalence)	−0.04	479	−0.13***	596
Crime				
Lifetime violence	−0.03	480	−0.19***	597
Lifetime nonviolent crime	−0.02	480	−0.20***	597
Lifetime arrested	−0.05	480	−0.18***	597
Lifetime court charges from county records	−0.08[+]	435	−0.12**	541
Substance Use				
Lifetime cigarette use	−0.12**	480	−0.26***	597
Lifetime alcohol use	−0.10**	480	−0.27***	597
Lifetime marijuana use	−0.08[+]	480	−0.25***	597
Lifetime other drug use	−0.08[+]	480	−0.25***	597
Sexual Activity				
Lifetime sexually active	−0.12**	474	−0.22***	590
Lifetime multiple sex partners	−0.09*	472	−0.21***	588
Lifetime been pregnant or gotten a woman pregnant	−0.05	465	−0.07[+]	580
Lifetime had or fathered a baby	−0.02	472	−0.04	588

[+]$p < 0.1$; *$p < 0.05$; **$p < 0.01$; ***$p < 0.001$.
[†]Partial correlation coefficients were calculated by controlling the observed level of school bonding at the 7th grade (age 13).

Hawkins, J. D., Guo, J., Hill, K. G., Battin-Pearson, S., & Abbott, R. D. (2001). Long term effects of the Seattle Social Development intervention on school bonding trajectories. *Applied Developmental Science: Special Issue: Prevention as Altering the Course of Development*, 5(4), 225–236.

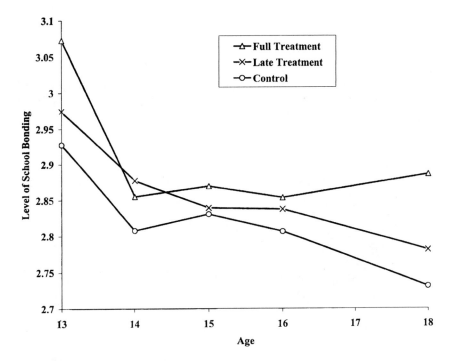

Figure 5. Observed mean level of school bonding by intervention groups.

Hawkins, J. D., Guo, J., Hill, K. G., Battin-Pearson, S., & Abbott, R. D. (2001). Long term effects of the Seattle Social Development intervention on school bonding trajectories. *Applied Developmental Science: Special Issue: Prevention as Altering the Course of Development*, 5(4), 225–236.

age 18, however, it was not significantly different from that in the control group. For the full treatment group, the average level of school bonding was clearly increasing at age 18, and this increased slope was significantly different from that in the control group. In addition, the average rate of acceleration was significantly higher for the full treatment group than for the control group. There was no significant difference in the rate of acceleration between the late treatment and the control group.

Thus, the full treatment group had a significantly curved pattern of school bonding (first declining, leveling off, then increasing to age 18), while the late treatment and control groups had linearly decreasing levels of school bonding through age 18.

It is noteworthy that late intervention (in Grades 5 and 6) was not enough to significantly affect bonding to school in the secondary grades. These findings suggest that interventions seeking to promote bonding to school as a mechanism for preventing later delinquent and violent behavior should be initiated early in the elementary years and maintained through the elementary grades.

Finally, we examined whether the effect of the intervention on school bonding remained when other factors such as gender, ethnicity, poverty, and academic achievement at the fifth grade were included. The effects of SSDP intervention condition on the mean level of school bonding at age 18, the mean rate of change at age 18, and the rate of acceleration remained significant even after the effects of gender, ethnicity, poverty, and earlier academic achievement were considered.

These findings suggest that preventive interventions in elementary school, focusing on teachers, students, and parents, can have a long-term positive effect on changes in and levels of school bonding. It is interesting that the effects of this elementary school intervention on school bonding were not significant at age 14 (two years after intervention ended) but reappeared later in adolescence.

The present data call into question the common assumption that it is only worth looking for long-term effects of preventive interventions if short-term effects are found and maintained. The results suggest that intervention during childhood can change developmental trajectories leading to greater differences at long-term follow-up than at one-year posttest. These findings parallel those reported by Tremblay, Masse, Pagani, and Vitaro (1996); Pentz et al. (1994); and Botvin, Baker, Dusenbury, Botvin, and Diaz (1995). They suggest the importance of long-term follow-up, even when short-term effects are small or seem to disappear. Further, the assumption that effects of preventive intervention deteriorate over time without boosters is not supported by these results. The present data suggest that interventions that change the course of development during childhood can have long-term effects, even without boosters, though it may take time for these effects to appear.

The analyses reported here found that both changes in school bonding from ages 13 to 18 and levels of bonding to school at age 18 predicted health and behavior problems at age 18. These findings are consistent with the social development model that guided the intervention that posits a mediating role of bonding to school in influencing health and behavior outcomes during adolescence. The results suggest that school bonding during the secondary school years was a mediating mechanism associated with observed behavioral effects of the intervention at age 18 reported in Hawkins et al. (1999).

Summary

This chapter reviewed the findings from the Seattle Social Development Project related to crime and violence. Our analyses comparing the features of criminal careers in self-report and official records identified important differences in estimates of offending that appear to reflect limitations in court records. These findings underscore the importance of self-reports of delinquent and criminal behavior for understanding the features of criminal careers.

We have identified five offending trajectories in the SSDP panel: nonoffenders (24%), late onsetters (14.4%), desistors (35.3%), escalators (19.3%), and chronic offenders (7%). Neither the escalator (low offending at age 13, increasing to relatively high offending by age 21) nor the desistor (low offending at age 13, desisting by age 21) group has been identified by major theories of delinquency. The escalator group in particular, involving roughly one fifth of the sample and escalating to serious offending by age 21, appears to be an important target for prevention and intervention efforts and deserves further investigation and theoretical attention.

Our analyses of the structure of deviance have not supported general deviance theories of delinquency. We have found that a model differentiating school problem behaviors from delinquent behaviors and from substance use provides the best fit for the SSDP data across genders. However, for boys in the sample, it is clear that delinquent behaviors and substance use often co-occur and should both be considered when seeking to understand adolescent behavior. We also have found that delinquent behavior resulted in disproportionate involvement in the juvenile justice system for African American adolescents in comparison to European American youths in this sample.

We have examined the progression of problem behaviors to determine whether the initiation of delinquency and substance use follow a predictable sequence as suggested by Elliott's mixed model pathway or whether the data better fit a model of separate pathways for the two classes of behavior. Analyses of the SSDP data strongly supported a mixed model pathway of behavioral initiation that includes both substance use and delinquency. We have found little evidence of delinquency-only or substance-use-only behavioral pathways in our data.

The prevention of crime and violence requires knowledge of the predictors of these behaviors. To be effective in stopping crime before it happens, crime prevention efforts must address factors that predict crime. Analyses of the SSDP data have provided empirical support for the social development model. We have found all the pathways specified in the model to be significant except the path from antisocial bonding to violence. We have also found that the socialization processes specified in the model predict violence at age 18 equally well for youths who initiated violent behavior in childhood (ages 10–11) and for youths who initiated violence in adolescence (ages 12–16). The implications of our findings for preventive intervention are clear:

(1) With the exception of antisocial bonding, each of the constructs in the social development model is a viable focus for violence prevention action.
(2) Multiple interventions may be required because there are multiple direct and indirect paths to violent behavior.
(3) Interventions to interrupt the causal processes in the development of violent behavior should include components seeking to promote processes

that enhance constructs on the prosocial path as well as to interrupt processes on the antisocial path.

(4) The direct and indirect influence of prior behavior on future behavior suggests the importance of intervening early in development to reduce early violent behavior.

(5) The same prevention and control strategies should be useful during adolescence for both early and late initiators of violence.

(6) Opportunities for intervention to reduce violence are available well into adolescence even for youths who have engaged in violent behavior from an early age.

(7) Among youths who manifest violent behavior in childhood or early adolescence, disrupting antisocial socialization influences or teaching skills to resist these influences should be emphasized.

The Seattle Social Development Project included an intervention study nested within the panel study. The tested intervention package sought to strengthen prosocial developmental processes and to interrupt antisocial developmental processes specified by the social development model through training of parents, teachers, and children themselves during the elementary grades. Positive effects of the theoretically grounded package of interventions have been found at the end of Grade 2, at the beginning of Grade 5, at the end of Grade 6, and at age 18, six years after the interventions ended.

At age 18, a broad range of effects of the full intervention were found. Participants in the full intervention condition were significantly more attached and committed to school than were controls. They reported significantly better school grades and achievement and significantly less misbehavior at school than did the control group. These significant findings were paralleled by Seattle school data showing trends ($p < .10$) of better school grades and fewer disciplinary action reports during high school for full intervention students compared with controls. Significantly fewer participants in the full intervention condition reported violent behavior in their lifetimes to age 18, heavy alcohol use in the past year, lifetime sexual activity, and having had multiple sex partners in their lifetimes by age 18, compared with controls. These findings indicate that this package of preventive interventions grounded in the social development model has wide-ranging benefits in promoting positive social development and preventing antisocial and health-compromising behaviors through adolescence.

Moreover, analyses of the effects of the full social development intervention on bonding to school over time indicate that intervention during childhood can change developmental trajectories through adolescence leading to greater differences at long-term follow-up than at one-year posttest. The assumption that effects of preventive intervention deteriorate over time without boosters is not supported by these results. These data suggest that interventions that change the course of development during childhood can have long-term positive effects in promoting prosocial bonding and reducing violence.

ACKNOWLEDGMENT.   The work reported in this chapter was made possible by grant number T32 MH20010 from the National Institute on Mental Health, number 5 R01 DA12138-02 from the National Institute on Drug Abuse, and by grants from the Office of Juvenile Justice and Delinquency Prevention and the Robert Wood Johnson Foundation. We would like to thank David Farrington, Michael Newcomb, and Lee Robins for their encouragement and guidance in the development of the Seattle Social Development Project and this chapter.

References

Abbott, R. D., Hawkins, J. D., Catalano, R. F., Peterson, P. L., O'Donnell, J., Day, L. E., & Cheney, D. (1991, November). *Structure of problem behavior during transition from childhood to adolescence: A multigroup longitudinal analysis.* Paper presented at the American Society of Criminology, San Francisco.

Abbott, R. D., O'Donnell, J., Hawkins, J. D., Hill, K. G., Kosterman, R., & Catalano, R. F. (1998). Changing teaching practices to promote achievement and bonding to school. *American Journal of Orthopsychiatry, 68,* 542–552.

Achenbach, T. M., & Edelbrock, C. (1983). *Manual for the Child Behavior Checklist and Revised Child Behavior Profile.* Burlington: University of Vermont Press.

Achenbach, T. M., & Edelbrock, C. (1986). *Manual for the Teacher's Report Form and Teacher Version of the Child Behavior Profile.* Burlington: University of Vermont Press.

Agnew, R. (1991). The interactive effects of peer variables on delinquency. *Criminology, 29,* 47–72.

Akers, R. L. (1977). *Deviant behavior: A social learning approach* (2nd ed.). Belmont, CA: Wadsworth Publishing Company.

Akers, R. L., Krohn, M., Lanza-Kaduce, L., & Radosevich, M. (1979). Social learning and deviant behavior: A specific test of a general theory. *American Sociological Review, 44,* 636–655.

Ayers, C. D., Williams, J. H., Hawkins, J. D., Peterson, P. L., Catalano, R. F., & Abbott, R. D. (1999). Assessing correlates of onset, escalation, deescalation, and desistance of delinquent behavior. *Journal of Quantitative Criminology, 15,* 277–306.

Bandura, A. (1973). *Aggression: A social learning analysis.* Englewood Cliffs, NJ: Prentice Hall.

Bandura, A. (1977). *Social learning theory.* Englewood Cliffs, NJ: Prentice Hall.

Bank, L., Patterson, G. R., & Reid, J. B. (1987). Delinquency prevention through training parents in family management. *Behavior Analyst, 10,* 75–82.

Barber, C. (1981). *Methods of instruction: Interactive teaching component III: Trainer's manual.* Columbia, MD: Westinghouse National Issue Center.

Barnes, G. M., & Farrell, M. P. (1992). Parental support and control as predictors of adolescent drinking, delinquency, and related problem behaviors. *Journal of Marriage and the Family, 54,* 763–776.

Barnes, G. M., & Welte, J. W. (1986). Patterns and predictors of alcohol use among 7–12th grade students in New York State. *Journal of Studies on Alcohol, 47,* 53–62.

Battin, S. R., Hill, K. G., Abbott, R. D., Catalano, R. F., & Hawkins, J. D. (1998). The contribution of gang membership to delinquency beyond delinquent friends. *Criminology, 36,* 93–115.

Battin-Pearson, S., Guo, J., Hill, K. G., Abbott, R. D., Catalano, R. F., & Hawkins, J. D. (1997, November). *Early predictors of sustained adolescent gang membership.* Paper presented at the American Society of Criminology Annual Meeting, San Diego, CA.

Battin-Pearson, S., Guo, J., Hill, K. G., Abbott, R. D., & Hawkins, J. D. (1998). *Early predictors of sustained adolescent gang membership*. Unpublished manuscript.

Battin-Pearson, S., Newcomb, M. D., Abbott, R. D., Hill, K. G., Catalano, R. F., & Hawkins, J. D. (2000). Predictors of early high school dropout: A test of five theories. *Journal of Educational Psychology, 92*, 568–582.

Beck, K. H., & Zannis, M. (1992). Patterns of alcohol consumption among suburban adolescent black high school students. *Journal of Alcohol and Drug Education, 37*, 1–13.

Benda, B. B., & Whiteside, L. (1995). Testing an integrated model of delinquency using LISREL. *Journal of Social Service Research, 21*, 1–32.

Bloom, B. S. (1976). *Human characteristics and school learning*. New York: McGraw-Hill.

Blumstein, A., Cohen, J., Roth, J. A., & Visher, C. A. (1986). *Criminal careers and career criminals* (Vol. 1). Washington, DC: National Academy Press.

Bollen, K., & Lennox, R. (1991). Conventional wisdom on measurement: A structural equation perspective. *Psychological Bulletin, 110*, 305–314.

Botvin, G. J., Baker, E., Dusenbury, L., Botvin, E. M., & Diaz, T. (1995). Long-term follow-up results of a randomized drug abuse prevention trial in a white middle-class population. *Journal of the American Medical Association, 273*, 1106–1112.

Brook, J. S., Whiteman, M., & Cohen, P. (1995). Stage of drug use, aggression, and theft/vandalism: Shared and unshared risks. In H. B. Kaplan (Ed.), *Drugs, crime, and other deviant adaptations: Longitudinal studies. Longitudinal research in the social and behavioral sciences: An interdisciplinary series* (pp. 83–96). New York: Plenum.

Brophy, J., & Good, T. L. (1986). Teacher behavior and student achievement. In M. C. Wittrock (Ed.), *Handbook of research on training* (3rd ed., pp. 328–375). New York: MacMillan.

Bryk, A. S., & Raudenbush, S. W. (1992). *Hierarchical linear models: Applications and data analysis methods*. Newbury Park, CA: Sage.

Bryk, A. S., Raudenbush, S. W., & Congdon, R. T. (1996). *Hierarchical linear and nonlinear modeling with the HLM/2L and HLM/3L programs*. Chicago, IL: Scientific Software International.

Burgess, R. L., & Akers, R. L. (1966). A differential association-reinforcement theory of criminal behavior. *Social Problems, 4*, 128–147.

Catalano, R. F., & Hawkins, J. D. (1996). The social development model: A theory of antisocial behavior. In J. D. Hawkins (Ed.), *Delinquency and crime: Current theories* (pp. 149–197). New York: Cambridge University Press.

Catalano, R. F., Kosterman, R., Hawkins, J. D., Newcomb, M. D., & Abbott, R. D. (1996). Modeling the etiology of adolescent substance use: A test of the social development model. *Journal of Drug Issues, 26*, 429–455.

Catalano, R. F., Oxford, M. L., Harachi, T. W., Abbott, R. D., & Haggerty, K. P. (1999). A test of the social development model to predict problem behaviour during the elementary school period. *Criminal Behaviour and Mental Health, 9*, 39–56.

Cernkovich, S. A., & Giordano, P. C. (1987). Family relationships and delinquency. *Criminology, 25*, 295–319.

Chen, H., & Rossi, P. H. (1989). Issues in the theory-driven perspective. *Evaluation and Program Planning, 12*, 299–306.

Chung, I.-J., Hill, K. G., Hawkins, J. D., Gilchrist, L. D., & Nagin, D. (2002). Childhood predictors of offense trajectories. *Journal of Research in Crime and Delinquency, 39*, 60–90.

Collins, L. M., & Wugalter, S. E. (1992). Latent class models for stage-sequential dynamic latent variables. *Multivariate Behavioral Research, 27*, 131–157.

Collins, L. M., Hyatt, S. L., & Graham, J. W. (2000). Latent transition analysis as a way of testing models of stage-sequential change in longitudinal data. In T. D. Little, K. U. Schnabel, & J. Baumert (Eds.), *Modeling longitudinal and multilevel data: Practical issues, applied approaches, and specific examples* (pp. 147–161, 269–281). Mahwah, NJ: Erlbaum.

Comprehensive Health Educational Foundation (1999). *Here's looking at you 2000*. Seattle, WA: Author.

Conger, R. D. (1976). Social control and social learning models of delinquent behavior. *Criminology: An Interdisciplinary Journal, 14*, 17–40.

Conger, R. D. (1980). Juvenile delinquency: Behavior restraint for behavior facilitation. In T. Hirschi & M. Gottfredson (Eds.), *Understanding crime* (pp. 131–142). Beverly Hills: Sage.

Cressey, D. R. (1953). *Other people's money: A study of the social psychology of embezzlement.* New York: The Free Press.

Cummings, C. (1996). *Managing to teach*. Edmonds, WA: Teaching, Inc.

Developmental Research and Programs. (1991). *How to help your child succeed in school.* Seattle, WA: Author.

Donovan, J. E., & Jessor, R. (1983). Problem drinking and the dimension of involvement with drugs: A Guttman scalogram analysis of adolescent drug use. *American Journal of Public Health, 73*, 543–552.

Donovan, J. E., & Jessor, R. (1985). Structure of problem behavior in adolescence and young adulthood. *Journal of Consulting and Clinical Psychology, 53*, 890–904.

Donovan, J. E., Jessor, R., & Costa, F. M. (1988). Syndrome of problem behavior in adolescence: A replication. *Journal of Consulting and Clinical Psychology, 56*, 762–765.

Dumas, J. E. (1989). Treating antisocial behavior in children: Child and family approaches. *Clinical Psychology Review, 9*, 197–222.

D'Unger, A. V., Land, K. C., McCall, P. L., & Nagin, D. S. (1998). How many latent classes of delinquent criminal careers? Results from mixed Poisson regression analyses of the London, Philadelphia and Racine cohorts studies. *American Journal of Sociology, 103*, 1593–1630.

Durlak, J. A., & Wells, A. M. (1997). Primary prevention mental health programs for children and adolescents: A meta-analytic review. *American Journal of Community Psychology, 25*, 115–152.

Eccles, J. S., & Midgley, C. (1990). Changes in academic motivation and self-perception during early adolescence. In R. Montemayor, G. R. Adams, & T. P. Gullotta (Eds.), *Advances in adolescent development: Vol. 2. From childhood to adolescence: A transitional period?* (pp. 134–155). Newbury Park, CA: Sage.

Ellickson, P. L., & Bell, R. M. (1990). Drug prevention in junior high: A multisite longitudinal test. *Science, 247*, 1299–1305.

Elliot, D. S. (1994). Serious violent offenders: Onset, developmental course, and termination. The American Society of Criminology 1993 Presidential Addresss. *Criminology, 32*, 1–22.

Elliott, D. S., Huizinga, D., & Ageton, S. S. (1985). *Explaining delinquency and drug use*. Beverly Hills, CA: Sage.

Elliott, D. S., Huizinga, D., & Menard, S. (1989). *Multiple problem youth: Delinquency, substance use, and mental health problems*. New York: Springer-Verlag.

Epstein, J., & McPartland, J. (1976). The concept and measurement of the quality of school life. *American Educational Research Journal, 50*, 13–30.

Farrell, A. D., Danish, S. J., & Howard, C. W. (1992). Risk factors for drug use in urban adolescents: Identification and cross-validation. *American Journal of Community Psychology, 20*, 263–286.

Farrington, D. P. (1986). Stepping stones to adult criminal careers. In D. Olweus, J. Block, & M. Radke-Yarrow (Eds.), *Development of antisocial and prosocial behavior: Research, theories, and issues* (pp. 359–384). Orlando, FL: Academic Press.

Farrington, D. P. (1989). Early predictors of adolescent aggression and adult violence. *Violence and Victims, 4*, 79–100.

Farrington, D. P. (1991). Childhood aggression and adult violence: Early precursors and later-life outcomes. In D. J. Pepler & K. H. Rubin (Eds.), *The development and treatment of childhood aggression* (pp. 5–29). Hillsdale, NJ: Erlbaum.

Farrington, D. P. (1992). Criminal career research in the United Kingdom. *British Journal of Criminology, 32*, 521–536.

Farrington, D. P. (1997). Human development and criminal careers. In M. Maguire, R. Morgon, & R. Reiner (Eds.), *The Oxford handbook of criminology* (pp. 361–408). Oxford: Clarendon Press.

Farrington, D. P. (1998). Predictors, causes, and correlates of male youth violence. In M. Tonry & M. H. Moore (Eds.), *Crime and justice: A review of research* (Vol. 24, pp. 421–475). Chicago: University of Chicago Press.

Farrington, D. P., & West, D. J. (1993). Criminal, penal and life histories of chronic offenders: Risk and protective factors and early identification. *Criminal Behaviour and Mental Health, 3*, 492–523.

Farrington, D. P., & Wikstrom, P.-O. H. (1994). Criminal careers in London and Stockholm: A cross-national comparative study. In E. G. M. Weitekamp & H.-J. Kerner (Eds.), *Cross-national longitudinal research on human development and criminal behavior*. Dordrecht, Netherlands: Kluwer.

Farrington, D. P., Joliffe, D., Hawkins, J. D., Catalano, R. F., Hill, K. G., & Kosterman, R. (in press). Comparing delinquency careers in court records and self-reports. *Criminology*.

Fergusson, D. M., Horwood, L. J., & Nagin, D. S. (2000). Offending trajectories in a New Zealand birth cohort. *Criminology, 38*, 525–551.

Gillmore, M. R., Hawkins, J. D., Catalano, R. F., Jr., Day, L. E., Moore, M., & Abbott, R. (1991). Structure of problem behaviors in preadolescence. *Journal of Consulting and Clinical Psychology, 59*, 499–506.

Goodlad, J. (1984). *A place called school: Prospects for the future*. New York: McGraw-Hill.

Gottfredson, D. C., Gottfredson, G. D., & Hybl, L. G. (1993). Managing adolescent behavior: A multiyear, multischool study. *American Educational Research Journal, 30*, 179–215.

Gottfredson, G. D. (1988). *A workbook for your school improvement program*. Baltimore, MD: Johns Hopkins University.

Gottfredson, G. D., & Gottfredson, D. C. (1985). *Victimization in schools*. New York: Plenum.

Gottfredson, M. R., & Hirschi, T. (1990). *A general theory of crime*. Stanford, CA: Stanford University Press.

Hansen, W. B., Tobler, N. S., & Graham, J. W. (1990). Attrition in substance abuse prevention research: A meta-analysis of 85 longitudinally followed cohorts. *Evaluation Review, 14*, 677–685.

Hawkins, J. D., & Weis, J. G. (1985). The social development model: An integrated approach to delinquency prevention. *Journal of Primary Prevention, 6*, 73–97.

Hawkins, J. D., Catalano, R. F., Brown, E. O., Vadasy, P. F., Roberts, C., Fitzmahan, D., Starkman, N., & Ransdell, M. (1988a). *Preparing for the drug (free) years: A family activity book*. Seattle, WA: Comprehensive Health Education Foundation.

Hawkins, J. D., Doueck, H. J., & Lishner, D. M. (1988b). Changing teaching practices in mainstream classrooms to improve bonding and behavior of low achievers. *American Educational Research Journal, 25*, 31–50.

Hawkins, J. D., Von Cleve, E., & Catalano, R. F., Jr. (1991). Reducing early childhood aggression: Results of a primary prevention program. *Journal of the American Academy of Child and Adolescent Psychiatry, 30*, 208–217.

Hawkins, J. D., Catalano, R. F., & Miller, J. Y. (1992a). Risk and protective factors for alcohol and other drug problems in adolescence and early adulthood: Implications for substance abuse prevention. *Psychological Bulletin, 112*, 64–105.

Hawkins, J. D., Catalano, R. F., Morrison, D. M., O'Donnell, J., Abbott, R. D., & Day, L. E. (1992b). The Seattle Social Development Project: Effects of the first four years on protective factors and problem behaviors. In J. McCord & R. E. Tremblay (Eds.), *Preventing antisocial behavior: Interventions from birth through adolescence* (pp. 139–161). New York: Guilford Press.

Hawkins, J. D., Arthur, M. W., & Catalano, R. F. (1995). Preventing substance abuse. In M. Tonry & D. Farrington (Eds.), *Crime and justice: Vol. 19. Building a safer society: Strategic approaches to crime prevention* (pp. 343–427). Chicago: University of Chicago Press.

Hawkins, J. D., Herrenkohl, T., Farrington, D. P., Brewer, D., Catalano, R. F., & Harachi, T. W. (1998). A review of predictors of youth violence. In R. Loeber & D. P. Farrington (Eds.), *Serious and violent juvenile offenders: Risk factors and successful interventions* (pp. 106–146). Thousand Oaks, CA: Sage.

Hawkins, J. D., Catalano, R. F., Kosterman, R., Abbott, R., & Hill, K. G. (1999). Preventing adolescent health-risk behaviors by strengthening protection during childhood. *Archives of Pediatrics and Adolescent Medicine, 153*, 226–234.

Hawkins, J. D., Guo, J., Hill, K. G., Battin-Pearson, S., & Abbott, R. D. (2001). Long term effects of the Seattle Social Development intervention on school bonding trajectories. *Applied Developmental Science: Special Issue: Prevention as Altering the Course of Development, 5*, 225–236.

Hawkins, J. D., Hill, K. G., Guo, J., & Battin-Pearson, S. R. (2002). Substance use norms and transitions in substance use: Implications for the gateway hypothesis. In D. Kandel (Ed.), *Stages and pathways of drug involvement: Examining the gateway hypothesis* (pp. 42–64). New York: Cambridge University Press.

Herrenkohl, T. I., Maguin, E., Hill, K. G., Hawkins, J. D., Abbott, R. D., & Catalano, R. F. (2000). Developmental risk factors for youth violence. *Journal of Adolescent Health, 26*, 176–186.

Herrenkohl, T. I., Guo, J., Kosterman, R., Hawkins, J. D., Catalano, R. F., Jr., & Smith, B. H. (2001a). Early adolescent predictors of youth violence as mediators of childhood risks. *Journal of Early Adolescence, 21*, 447–469.

Herrenkohl, T. I., Huang, B., Kosterman, R., Hawkins, J. D., Catalano, R. F., & Smith, B. H. (2001b). A comparison of the social development processes leading to violent behavior in late adolescence for childhood initiators and adolescent initiators of violence. *Journal of Research in Crime and Delinquency, 38*, 45–63.

Hill, K. G., Howell, J. C., Hawkins, J. D., & Battin-Pearson, S. R. (1999). Childhood risk factors for adolescent gang membership: Results from the Seattle Social Development Project. *Journal of Research in Crime and Delinquency, 36*, 300–322.

Hill, K. G., Collins, L. M., & Hawkins, J. D. (2001). Examining the progression of offenses in the behavioral repertoire: A latent transition analysis of Elliott's model. Manuscript submitted for publication.

Hindelang, M. J. (1973). Causes of delinquency: A partial replication and extension. *Social Problems, 20*, 471–487.

Hirschi, T. (1969). *Causes of delinquency.* Berkeley, CA: University of California Press.

Hirschi, T., & Gottfredson, M. (1983). Age and the explanation of crime. *American Journal of Sociology, 89*, 552–584.

Hirsh, B. J., & Rapkin, B. D. (1987). The transition to junior high school: A longitudinal study of self-esteem, psychological symptomatology, school life and social support. *Child Development, 58*, 1235–1243.

Howell, J. C. (1997). *Juvenile justice and youth violence.* Thousand Oaks, CA: Sage.

Huang, B., Kosterman, R., Catalano, R. F., Hawkins, J. D., & Abbott, R. D. (2001). Modeling mediation in the etiology of violent behavior in adolescence: A test of the social development model. *Criminology, 39*, 75–107.

Huizinga, D. H., & Elliott, D. S. (1981). *A longitudinal study of drug use and delinquency in a national sample of youth: Assessment of causal order: A report of the National Youths Survey (Project Report No. 16).* Boulder, CO: Behavioral Research Institute.

Jessor, R., Donovan, J. E., & Costa, F. M. (1991). *Beyond adolescence: Problem behavior and young adult development.* New York: Cambridge University Press.

Johnston, L. D., O'Malley, P. M., & Bachman, J. G. (1985). *Drug use, drinking, and smoking: National survey results from high school, college, and young adult populations.* (DHHS Publication No. ADM 89-1638). Washington, DC: U.S. Government Printing Office.

Johnston, L. D., O'Malley, P. M., & Bachman, J. G. (1993). *National survey results on drug use from the Monitoring the Future Study, 1975–1992* (Vol. I). Rockville, MD: National Institute on Drug Abuse.

Jones, B., Nagin, D., & Roeder, K. (2001). A SAS procedure based on mixture models for estimating developmental trajectories. *Sociological Methods and Research, 29*, 374–393.

Kaplan, H. B., & Damphousse, K. R. (1995). Self-attitudes and antisocial personality as moderators of the drug use-violence relationship. In H. B. Kaplan (Ed.), *Drugs, crime, and other deviant adaptations: Longitudinal studies. Longitudinal research in the social and behavioral sciences: An interdisciplinary series* (pp. 187–210). New York: Plenum.

Kellam, S. G., Rebok, G. W., Ialongo, N. S., & Mayer, L. S. (1994). The course and malleability of aggressive behavior from early first grade into middle school: Results of a developmental epidemiology-based preventive trial. *Journal of Child Psychology and Psychiatry and Allied Disciplines, 35*, 259–281.

Kelley, B. T., Huizinga, D., Thornberry, T. P., & Loeber, R. (1997). Epidemiology of serious violence. *Office of Juvenile Justice and Delinquency Prevention Juvenile Justice Bulletin, June.*

Kempf, K. (1993). The empirical status of Hirschi's control theory. In F. Adler & W. S. Laufer (Eds.), *New directions in criminological theory: Advances in criminological theory* (Vol. 4, pp. 143–185). New Brunswick, NJ: Transaction Books.

Kerr, D. M., Kent, L., & Lam, T. C. M. (1985). Measuring program implementation with a classroom observation instrument: The interactive teaching map. *Evaluation Review, 9*, 461–482.

Kosterman, R., Hawkins, J. D., Spoth, R., Haggerty, K. P., & Zhu, K. (1997). Effects of a preventive parent-training intervention on observed family interactions: Proximal outcomes from preparing for the Drug Free Years. *Journal of Community Psychology, 25*, 337–352.

Kosterman, R., Hawkins, J. D., Guo, J., Catalano, R. F., & Abbott, R. D. (2000). The dynamics of alcohol and marijuana initiation: Patterns and predictors of first use in adolescence. *American Journal of Public Health, 90*, 360–366.

Kosterman, R., Graham, J. W., Hawkins, J. D., Catalano, R. F., & Herrenkohl, T. I. (2001). Childhood risk factors for persistence of violence in the transition to adulthood: A social development perspective. *Violence and Victims, 16*, 355–370.

Krohn, M. D., & Massey, J. L. (1980). Social control and delinquent behavior: An examination of the elements of the social bond. *Sociological Quarterly, 21*, 529–543.

Le Blanc, M. (1997). A generic control theory of the criminal phenomenon: The structural and dynamic statements of an integrative multilayered control theory. In T. P. Thornberry (Ed.), *Developmental theories of crime and delinquency* (pp. 215–285). New Brunswick, NJ: Transaction Publishers.

Le Blanc, M., & Loeber, R. (1993). Precursors, causes and the development of criminal offending. In D. F. Hay & A. Angold (Eds.), *Precursors and causes in development and psychopathology. Wiley series on studies in child psychiatry* (pp. 233–263). Chichester, England, UK: John Wiley & Sons.

Lipsey, M. W., & Derzon, J. H. (1998). Predictors of violent or serious delinquency in adolescence and early adulthood: A synthesis of longitudinal research. In R. Loeber & D. P. Farrington (Eds.), *Serious and violent juvenile offenders: Risk factors and successful interventions* (pp. 86–105). Thousand Oaks, CA: Sage.

Little, R. J. A., & Rubin, D. B. (1987). *Statistical analysis with missing data.* New York: John Wiley & Sons.

Loeber, R. (1996). Developmental continuity, change, and pathways in male juvenile problem behaviors and delinquency. In J. D. Hawkins (Ed.), *Delinquency and crime: Current theories* (pp. 1–27). New York: Cambridge University Press.

Loeber, R., & Snyder, H. N. (1990). Rate of offending in juvenile careers: Findings of constancy and change in lambda. *Criminology, 28*, 97–109.

Loeber, R., & Stouthamer-Loeber, M. (1998). Development of juvenile aggression and violence. Some common misconceptions and controversies. *American Psychologist, 53*, 242–259.

Loeber, R., & Wikstrom, P.-O. H. (1993). Individual pathways to crime in different types of neighborhood. In D. P. Farrington, R. J. Sampson, & P.-O. H. Wikstrom (Eds.), *Integrating individual and ecological aspects of crime.* (BRA-report No. 1, pp. 169–204). Stockholm, Sweden: Swedish National Council for Crime Prevention.

Maddahian, E., Newcomb, M. D., & Bentler, P. M. (1986). Adolescents' substance use: Impact of ethnicity, income, and availability. *Advances in Alcohol and Substance Abuse, 5*, 63–78.

Maggs, J. L., and Schulenberg, J. (2001). Editors' introduction: Prevention as altering the course of development and the complementary purposes of developmental and prevention sciences. *Applied Developmental Science. Special Issue: Prevention as Altering the Course of Development, 5*, 196–200.

Maguin, E., & Loeber, R. (1995). Academic performance and delinquency, *Crime and justice: A review of research* (Vol. 20, pp. 145–264). Chicago: University of Chicago Press.

Massey, J. L., & Krohn, M. D. (1986). A longitudinal examination of an integrated social process model of deviant behavior. *Social Forces, 65*, 106–134.

Matsueda, R. L. (1982). Testing control theory and differential association: A causal modeling approach. *American Sociological Review, 47*, 489–504.

Matsueda, R. L. (1988). The current state of differential association theory. *Crime and Delinquency, 34*, 277–306.

Matza, D. (1969). *Becoming deviant*. Englewood Cliffs, NJ: Prentice Hall.

McCarthy, S., & Brown, E. O. (1983). *Catch 'em being good*. Seattle: Center for Law and Justice.

McCord, J. (1983). Alcohol in the service of aggression. In E. Gottheil, K. A. Druley, T. E. Skoloda, & H. M. Waxman (Eds.), *Alcohol, drug abuse, and aggression* (pp. 270–279). Springfield, IL: Thomas.

McGee, L., & Newcomb, M. D. (1992). General deviance syndrome: Expanded hierarchical evaluations at four ages from early adolescence to adulthood. *Journal of Consulting and Clinical Psychology, 60*, 766–776.

Moffitt, T. E. (1993). Adolescence-limited and life-course-persistent antisocial behavior: A developmental taxonomy. *Psychological Review, 100*, 674–701.

Moffitt, T. E., Caspi, A., Dickson, N., Silva, P., & Stanton, W. (1996). Childhood-onset versus adolescent-onset antisocial conduct problems in males: Natural history from ages 3 to 18 years. *Development and Psychopathology, 8*, 399–424.

Mortimore, P. (1995). The positive effects of schooling. In M. Rutter (Ed.), *Psychosocial disturbances in young people: Challenges for prevention* (pp. 333–363). New York: Cambridge University Press.

Mrazek, P. J., & Haggerty, R. J. (1994). *Reducing risks for mental disorders: Frontiers for prevention intervention research*. Washington, DC: National Academy Press.

Nagin, D. S. (1999). Analyzing developmental trajectories: A semiparametric, group-based approach. *Psychological Methods, 4*, 139–157.

Nagin, D. S., & Farrington, D. P. (1992). The stability of criminal potential from childhood to adulthood. *Criminology, 30*, 235–260.

Nagin, D. S., & Land, K. C. (1993). Age, criminal careers, and population heterogeneity: Specification and estimation of a nonparametric, mixed Poisson model. *Criminology, 31*, 327–362.

Nagin, D. S., & Tremblay, R. E. (1999). Trajectories of boys' physical aggression, opposition, and hyperactivity on the path to physically violent and nonviolent juvenile delinquency. *Child Development, 70*, 1181–1196.

Nagin, D. S., Farrington, D. P., & Moffitt, T. E. (1995). Life-course trajectories of different types of offenders. *Criminology, 33*, 111–139.

Newcomb, M. D. (1990). What structural equation modeling can tell us about social support. In B. R. Sarason, I. G. Sarason, & G. R. Pierce (Eds.), *Social support: An interactional view* (pp. 23–63). New York: John Wiley & Sons.

O'Donnell, J., Hawkins, J. D., & Abbott, R. D. (1995a). Predicting serious delinquency and substance use among aggressive boys. *Journal of Consulting and Clinical Psychology, 63*, 529–537.

O'Donnell, J., Hawkins, J. D., Catalano, R. F., Abbott, R. D., & Day, L. E. (1995b). Preventing school failure, drug use, and delinquency among low-income children: Long-term intervention in elementary schools. *American Journal of Orthopsychiatry, 65*, 87–100.

Oldfather, P., & Wigfield, A. (1996). Children's motivations for literacy learning. In L. Baker, P. Afflerbach, & D. Reinking (Eds.), *Developing engaged readers in school and home communities* (pp. 89–113). Mahwah, NJ: Erlbaum.

Patterson, G. R. (1982). *A social learning approach: Vol. 3. Coercive family process.* Eugene, OR: Castalia.

Patterson, G. R., & Yoerger, K. (1993). Developmental models for delinquent behavior. In S. Hodgins (Ed.), *Mental disorder and crime* (pp. 140–172). Newbury Park, CA: Sage.

Patterson, G. R., Reid, J. B., & Dishion, T. J. (1992). *A social interactional approach: Vol. 4. Antisocial boys.* Eugene, OR: Castalia.

Pentz, M. A., Dwyer, J. H., Johnson, C. A., Flay, B. R., Hansen, W. B., MacKinnon, D. P., Chou, C. P., Rohrbach, L. A., & Montgomery, S. B. (1994). *Long-term follow-up of a multicommunity trial for prevention of tobacco, alcohol, and drug use.* Unpublished manuscript.

Pollard, J. A., Hawkins, J. D., & Arthur, M. W. (1999). Risk and protection: Are both necessary to understand diverse behavioral outcomes in adolescence? *Social Work Research, 23,* 145–158.

Reinarman, C., & Fagan, J. (1988). Social organization and differential association: A research note from a longitudinal study of violent juvenile offenders. *Crime and Delinquency, 34,* 307–327.

Resnicow, K., Ross Gaddy, D., & Vaughan, R. D. (1995). Structure of problem and positive behaviors in African American youths. *Journal of Consulting and Clinical Psychology, 63,* 594–603.

Rutter, M. (1985). Resilience in the face of adversity: Protective factors and resistance to psychiatric disorder. *British Journal of Psychiatry, 147,* 598–611.

Rutter, M. (1990). Psychosocial resilience and protective mechanisms. In J. E. Rolf, A. S. Masten, D. Cicchetti, K. Neuchterlein, & S. Weintraub (Eds.), *Risk and protective factors in the development of psychopathology* (pp. 181–214). New York: Cambridge University Press.

Rutter, M., Maughan, B., Mortimore, P., Ouston, J., & Smith, A. (1979). *Fifteen thousand hours: Secondary schools and their effects on children.* Cambridge: Harvard University Press.

Sampson, R. J., & Laub, J. H. (1993). *Crime in the making: Pathways and turning points through life.* Cambridge, MA: Harvard University Press.

Schulenberg, J., Asp, C. E., & Peterson, A. (1984). School from the young adolescent's perspective: A descriptive report. *Journal of Early Adolescence, 4,* 107–130.

Shure, M. B. (1992). *I can problem solve: An interpersonal cognitive problem-solving program.* Champagne, IL: Research Press.

Shure, M. B., & Spivack, G. (1980). Interpersonal problem solving as a mediator of behavioral adjustment in preschool and kindergarten children. *Journal of Applied Developmental Psychology, 1,* 29–44.

Shure, M. B., & Spivack, G. (1988). Interpersonal cognitive problem solving. In R. H. Price, E. L. Cowan, R. P. Lorion, & J. Ramos-McKay (Eds.), *Fourteen ounces of prevention: A casebook for practitioners* (pp. 69–82). Hawthorne, NY: Aldine De Gruyter.

Simmons, R. G., & Blyth, D. A. (1987). *Moving into adolescence: The impact of pubertal change and school context.* Hawthorne, NY: Aldine de Gruyter.

Slavin, R. E. (1980). *Using student team learning.* Baltimore: Johns Hopkins University.

Slavin, R. E. (1991). Synthesis of research on cooperative learning. *Educational Leadership, 48,* 71–82.

Slavin, R. E., Karweit, N. L., & Wasik, B. A. (1994). *Preventing early school failure.* Needham Heights, MA: Allyn & Bacon.

Spoth, R., Redmond, C., Haggerty, K., & Ward, T. (1995). A controlled parenting skills outcome study examining individual difference and attendance effects. *Journal of Marriage and the Family, 57,* 449–464.

Spoth, R., Redmond, C., Shin, C., Lepper, H., Haggerty, K., & Wall, M. (1998). Risk moderation of parent and child outcomes in a preventive intervention: A test and replication. *American Journal of Orthopsychiatry, 68,* 565–579.

Stouthamer-Loeber, M., Loeber, R., Farrington, D. P., Zhang, Q., Van Kammen, W., & Maguin, E. (1993). The double edge of protective and risk factors for delinquency: Interrelations and developmental patterns. *Development and Psychopathology, 5*, 683–701.

Sutherland, E. H. (1973). Development of the theory [Private paper published posthumously]. In K. Schuessler (Ed.), *Edwin Sutherland on analyzing crime* (pp. 13–29). Chicago: University of Chicago Press.

Sutherland, E. H., & Cressey, D. R. (1970). *Criminology.* New York: Lippincott.

Thornberry, T. P. (1987). Toward an interactional theory of delinquency. *Criminology, 25*, 863–891.

Thornberry, T. P. (1997). Introduction: Some advantages of developmental and life-course perspectives for the study of crime and delinquency. In T. P. Thornberry (Ed.), *Developmental theories of crime and delinquency* (pp. 1–10). New Brunswick: Transaction Publishers.

Thornberry, T. P., & Krohn, M. D. (2001). The development of delinquency: An interactional perspective. In S. O. White (Ed.), *Handbook of youth and justice* (pp. 289–305). New York: Plenum.

Thornberry, T. P., Lizotte, A. J., Krohn, M. D., & Farnworth, M. (1990). *The role of delinquent peers in the initiation of delinquent behavior. (Working Paper Series, No. 6).* Albany, NY: University at Albany Press.

Thornberry, T. P., Lizotte, A. J., Krohn, M. D., Farnworth, M., & Jang, S. J. (1994). Delinquent peers, beliefs, and delinquent behavior: A longitudinal test of interactional theory. *Criminology, 32*, 47–83.

Thornberry, T. P., Huizinga, D., & Loeber, R. (1995). The prevention of serious delinquency and violence: Implications from the program of research on the causes and correlates of delinquency. In J. C. Howell, B. Krisberg, J. D. Hawkins, & J. J. Wilson (Eds.), *A sourcebook: Serious, violent, and chronic juvenile offenders* (pp. 213–237). Thousand Oaks, CA: Sage.

Tolan, P. H., & Gorman-Smith, D. (1998). Development of serious and violent offending careers. In R. Loeber & D. P. Farrington (Eds.), *Serious and violent juvenile offenders: Risk factors and successful interventions* (pp. 68–85). Thousand Oaks, CA: Sage.

Tremblay, R. E., McCord, J., Boileau, H., Charlebois, P., Gagnon, C., Le Blanc, M., & Larivée, S. (1991). Can disruptive boys be helped to become competent? *Psychiatry, 54*, 148–161.

Tremblay, R. E., Vitaro, F., Bertrand, L., Le Blanc, M., Beauchesne, H., Boileau, H., & David, L. (1992). Parent and child training to prevent early onset of delinquency: The Montreal Longitudinal-Experimental Study. In J. McCord & R. Tremblay (Eds.), *Preventing antisocial behavior: Interventions from birth through adolescence* (pp. 117–138). New York: Guilford.

Tremblay, R. E., Masse, L. C., Pagani, L., & Vitaro, F. (1996). From childhood physical aggression to adolescent maladjustment: The Montreal Prevention Experiment. In R. D. Peters & R. J. McMahon (Eds.), *Preventing childhood disorders, substance abuse and delinquency* (pp. 268–298). Thousand Oaks, CA: Sage.

Weis, J. G., & Hawkins, J. D. (1981). *Preventing delinquency.* Reports of the national juvenile justice assessment centers. Washington, DC: U.S. Dept. of Justice Office of Juvenile Justice and Delinquency Prevention National Institute for Juvenile Justice and Delinquency Prevention.

Werner, E. E. (1989). High-risk children in young adulthood: A longitudinal study from birth to 32 years. *American Journal of Orthopsychiatry, 59*, 72–81.

Widom, C. S. (1989). The cycle of violence. *Science, 244*, 160–166.

Williams, J. H. (1994). *Understanding substance use, delinquency involvement, and juvenile justice system involvement among African-American and European-American adolescents.* Unpublished dissertation, University of Washington, Seattle.

Williams, J. H., Ayers, C. D., Abbott, R. D., Hawkins, J. D., & Catalano, R. F. (1996). Structural equivalence of involvement in problem behavior by adolescents across racial groups using multiple group confirmatory factor analysis. *Social Work Research, 20*, 168–177.

Williams, J. H., Ayers, C. D., Abbott, R. D., Hawkins, J. D., & Catalano, R. F. (1999). Race differences in risk factors for delinquency and substance use among adolescents. *Social Work Research, 23*, 241–256.

Wolfgang, M. E., Figlio, R. F., & Sellin, T. (1972). *Delinquency in a birth cohort.* Chicago: University of Chicago Press.

Yoshikawa, H. (1994). Prevention as cumulative protection: Effects of early family support and education on chronic delinquency and its risks. *Psychological Bulletin, 115*, 28–54.

9

Common Themes, Future Directions

Marvin D. Krohn and Terence P. Thornberry

This compendium contains summaries from seven contemporary panel studies investigating the causes and consequences of delinquency. Together these studies provide a dynamic portrait of subjects who range in age from infancy to the fourth decade of their lives, who hail from three different nations and diverse geographical locations within the United States, and who are ethnically diverse. The disciplinary backgrounds, theoretical perspectives, and methodological approaches of these studies vary, allowing each one to contribute a different piece to this complex portrait or provide a different hue to a part that is addressed by multiple studies. Although the seven studies differ somewhat in approach, they share a common rationale: the study of crime from a developmental or life-course perspective, using a panel study design that follows the same individuals across the life course.

There are a number of precocious panel studies that early on recognized the need for longitudinal panel studies in the study of criminal behavior (e.g., Elliott & Voss, 1974; Elliott, Huizinga, & Ageton, 1985; Glueck & Glueck, 1950; McCord, 1979). Indeed, two of them are featured in this volume in the chapters by Farrington and by Kaplan, but many large-scale panel studies began in the 1980s. Five of the seven studies included in this book began their data collection efforts in that decade. As we stated in the introductory chapter, the impetus for these studies was both the insights and the limitations of cross-sectional studies on the causes of delinquency and of cohort studies describing the development of criminal careers. With the recognition that the foundations for criminal behavior may begin earlier than adolescence and that the effects of such behavior may linger through the adult stages of the life course, the study of criminal behavior expanded from a somewhat myopic focus on the adolescent years to a much

Taking Stock of Delinquency: An Overview of Findings from Contemporary Longitudinal Studies, edited by Thornberry and Krohn. Kluwer Academic/Plenum Publishers, New York, 2003.

wider focus incorporating broader segments of the life course. Although these seven studies share a common, underlying research approach, they are by no means exact replicates of one another. There is considerable variation across these studies and we begin this chapter with a discussion of these differences.

Different Designs

The seven studies in this volume differ in the time at which they entered the subject's life course. Several studies began to assess their subjects when they were in grade school (Farrington; Hawkins et al.; Huizinga et al.; Loeber et al.; Tremblay et al.) and two first interviewed their subjects in middle school (Kaplan; Thornberry et al.).[1]

The interplay between theory and data in each chapter provides interesting contrasts in their approaches to longitudinal research. Kaplan articulates his integrated theory and reviews only those findings from the Houston study that address that theory. Thornberry et al. and Hawkins et al. rely heavily on their theoretical approaches to organize the presentation of their results, but also review studies that do not directly bear on their respective theories. Huizinga et al. acknowledge that the organizing force behind the development of the survey for the Denver project was the integrated theory developed with Elliott and others (Elliott et al., 1985), but they do not use the theory in their discussion of the results, choosing instead to take a risk factor approach. The other three projects also adopt a risk factor approach, although Farrington develops a theoretical perspective based on the results from the Cambridge study and Loeber et al. discuss the theoretical implications of their research.

An intriguing aspect of the chapters that do take a more theoretical approach is how, in essence, the theories change with the subjects. That is, as the subjects age within a longitudinal design, the theories are expanded and modified to accommodate the different stages of the life course that are being examined. For example, Thornberry (1987) began with a theory that focused almost exclusively on adolescence. Interactional theory then expanded to account for the transition from adolescence to young adulthood (Thornberry & Krohn, 2001) and was later modified again to address early childhood and the intergenerational transmission of antisocial behavior (Thornberry, Freeman-Gallant, Lizotte, Krohn, & Smith, 2002). As the Kaplan et al. article illustrates, a theory also changes as empirical results suggest modifications. The results from the Houston project both confirm the general tenets of Kaplan's theory and help to elaborate it as mediating and modifying variables are identified. Kaplan's work is a prime example of the value of using a unifying theoretical perspective in conducting longitudinal research.

---

[1] In this chapter, references without years refer to the earlier chapters in this book.

In addition to design differences and varying theoretical approaches, these seven projects are also distinct in terms of the interplay between social policy and the theoretical and research effort. Two of the projects embedded an intervention program in the longitudinal panel design. The Montreal study (Tremblay et al.) included a preventive experiment focusing on training parents in effective parenting strategies and improving social skills among the children. The program was effective in reducing disruptive behavior, self-reported delinquency, and dropping out of school. However, it did not affect rates of official delinquency or physical violence.

The Seattle study incorporated a school-based prevention program derived from the Social Development Model (Catalano & Hawkins, 1996; Hawkins & Weiss, 1985). It also targeted schools, parents, and children's social skills, but with more emphasis on the school setting than was evident in the Montreal program. The program proved to be effective in improving behavior in the school setting, as well as in reducing the risk of violent behavior, heavy alcohol use, and sexual promiscuity at age 18. What is especially significant about the Seattle study is the way in which the results from the intervention program informed the theory and the results from the longitudinal analysis informed the intervention program. It represents a model for how theory, research, and policy can be integrated effectively in a single enterprise.

There are many other differences in the studies reviewed in this volume. Among them are the differences in research sites, the demographic characteristics of the samples, measurement strategies, and the length of intervals between survey administration. In spite of these differences, the studies serve to both replicate and complement each other's findings.

Similar Results

Each chapter presents many findings from the respective studies, so it would be both difficult and redundant to try to summarize all that has been reported. Rather, we will briefly focus on several general issues that the studies address, such as the developmental pattern of delinquency, the role of parents, school, peers, and social structure, and the transition from adolescence to adulthood. As will become evident, there is a great deal of similarity in findings across these somewhat different studies. We do not want to overstate the level of similarity, however, for, indeed, there are differences in results. Differences are more evident with respect to specific variables and less so with respect to general concepts; and there are differences in the emphasis given to different findings across the studies. Nevertheless, the results reported in the previous chapters point to some important generalized findings about the causes, course, and consequences of delinquency.

The Developmental Pattern of Delinquency

A number of the studies have provided descriptive information on the developmental pattern of delinquent behavior. One of the most consistent findings across them is that the earlier the age at which children begin offending, the more likely are the delinquent careers to be chronic and serious, with an increased probability of official delinquency (Farrington; Hawkins et al.; Huizinga et al.; Loeber et al.; Thornberry et al.). This finding underscores the need to study very early patterns of development, even before children enter school. Tremblay et al. have begun this analysis, finding that mothers report that physical aggression begins as early as 13 months of age. This finding, coupled with results that suggest that physical aggression in kindergarten predicts aggression during adolescence, leads Tremblay et al. to suggest that we should begin studying causal processes during pregnancy. Consistent with these findings, a number of projects have begun, or are planning to begin, data collection efforts targeted at preschool children (Hill, Hawkins, Catalano, McMahon, & Gilchrist, 1999; Thornberry et al.; Tremblay et al.). These efforts are designed to identify very early markers of aggressive behaviors and to enable researchers to more adequately address intergenerational issues.

In addition to the impact of the age of onset on subsequent delinquency, there has been much focus on the pathways and trajectories of delinquent behavior. Loeber et al. have taken the lead in identifying and verifying the multiple pathways that lead to delinquent behavior. Observing that the development toward serious delinquency was orderly, they identified three pathways that characterize different ways in which individuals come to commit serious delinquent behavior. These findings have been replicated with several other data sets, some of which are represented in this volume.

Using the approach developed by Nagin and Land (1993), the development of delinquency has also been depicted in a more dynamic way in these projects (Farrington; Hawkins et al.; Loeber et al.; Thornberry et al.; Tremblay et al.). This semiparametric group-based modeling approach characterizes the course of offending by grouping together respondents who follow distinctive offense trajectories. Although identical offense trajectories are not found across the data sets, similar patterns are observed. These studies all identify groups of nonoffenders and low-rate offenders, on the one hand, and chronic high-rate offenders on the other. There is also consistent evidence of desistors and of very late onset offenders. As Hawkins et al. observe, the discovery of groups characterized by escalating their offending at later ages is a particularly important contribution.

Parents, School, Peers, and Social Structure

Whether a risk factor approach or a theoretically directed approach is taken, all seven chapters include a discussion of results that focus on the factors in children's lives that are most likely to influence and be influenced by delinquent behavior: parents, school, peers, and social structure. Although the results are not entirely consistent across research sites, there are a number of common findings.

A major focus across the projects concerns the importance of effective parenting on the behavior of both young children and adolescents. Tremblay et al. found that family functioning predicts physical aggression in children as young as two years of age. The influence of effective parenting is also observed in the other studies at least through early adolescence. Monitoring and supervision appear to be the most important parenting variables in predicting delinquent behavior. Although there is some discrepancy in the results regarding whether the effects of parenting fade as youth move into later adolescence, the weight of the evidence appears to suggest that this does occur.

The projects have also begun to explore the intergenerational transmission of delinquent behaviors. Findings suggest a correlation between the criminal behavior of the parents and the delinquent behavior of children. Several of the projects have initiated studies that will try to explore mediating processes by including the children of the original target subjects in these longitudinal investigations. Given the wealth of information gathered on the target subjects, these intergenerational studies hold great promise for improving our understanding of the effect of parents and parenting on delinquent behavior.

Children spend a substantial portion of their lives in school. What they learn and the completion of a high school education can have an important effect on their life chances. All of the projects included measures of school commitment, performance, and achievement. Low school performance and commitment to school are consistent predictors of delinquency and other problematic behaviors. The main measure of school achievement, failure to graduate from high school, is predicted by delinquency and drug use; in turn, failure to graduate from high school also increases the probability of subsequent problematic behavior.

The relationship between associating with delinquent peers and delinquent behavior is one of the more consistent findings in the criminological literature (Thornberry & Krohn, 1997). A few of the studies in this volume make use of longitudinal panel data to examine the causal role that peers play. Kaplan found that associating with delinquent peers is directly related to delinquent behavior within a complex chain of causal factors. Hawkins et al. found that involvement with delinquent peers is indirectly related to delinquent behavior through peer reactions or reinforcement. This finding is consistent with Thornberry et al.'s results that suggest that peer associations, peer reinforcement, and delinquent behavior are involved in a reciprocal causal process in which delinquent behavior increases the probability both of association with delinquent peers and of being reinforced by peers for delinquent behavior which, in turn, increases the probability of subsequent delinquent behavior.

The effect of one type of peer network, the delinquent street gang, is especially significant. Several of the studies (Hawkins et al.; Huizinga et al.; Thornberry et al.)

explored the impact of gang membership on several forms of deviant behavior. They all found that, while in a gang, members have higher rates of delinquency and drug use. More interestingly, they also found that the rates of delinquent behavior are typically lower before and after gang membership, suggesting that gangs facilitate deviant behavior rather than simply selecting those individuals most prone to delinquency. The gang appears to be more facilitative of delinquency than are delinquent peer groups, even those groups with many friends who commit delinquent acts. Overall, there appears to be something about the gang that is particularly conducive to delinquency.

Social structural and neighborhood measures of disadvantage are prominently featured in the research reviewed in this volume. Measures of economic disadvantage (poverty, welfare, social class) have been found to be either directly or indirectly related to delinquent behavior. Ethnicity and race are related to some forms of delinquent behavior and, in some instances, have been found to interact with other risk factors to generate delinquent behavior.

Several studies examined the effect of neighborhood context on both aggregate-level delinquency and individual-level delinquent behavior. Huizinga et al. found that differences in the neighborhoods of Denver predict the overall rate of delinquency but are only indirectly related to individual-level delinquency. Thornberry et al. reached similar conclusions. Loeber et al. found that neighborhood context interacts with other variables to predict individual-level delinquency as well as having an indirect effect on this behavior.

Overall, many theories of delinquency focus attention on the impact of parenting behaviors, school performance, peer influence, and structural position in accounting for delinquency. The longitudinal studies represented in this volume converge in providing empirical support for the importance of these conceptual domains as antecedents of delinquency. Each study also provides a great deal of specific information about how these interactional processes unfold over time.

Life-Course Transitions

Longitudinal panel studies are particularly valuable for studying the consequences of delinquent behavior. As noted above, many of these projects have followed and continue to follow the same subjects from childhood or adolescence into young adulthood and beyond. Having extensive measurement packages containing data not only on early misbehavior but also on a myriad of potential correlates, these studies are well-equipped to examine how delinquent behavior affects not only subsequent criminality but also life-course transitions in areas such as education, work force participation, and the family.

Farrington, who has followed his subjects longer than any of the other projects, found that convicted offenders are more likely to be divorced or separated (at age 32), unemployed or have low take-home pay, and are more likely to report subsequent delinquent behavior. Thornberry et al. focused on the effect of delinquent behavior and drug use on transitions that may be problematic for success as an adult. They found that delinquent behavior and drug use are related to failure to graduate from high school, teenage parenthood, and living independently from the family of origin before graduating from high school. Such precocious transitions can place individuals at a disadvantage in competing for success in the adult world. Making use of similar measures, most of these results were replicated when the Denver and Pittsburgh data were added to the analysis.

Unexpected Results

The results summarized thus far focus on traditional concerns of scholars studying the etiology of drug use, delinquency, and crime. Of course, they go well beyond what cross-sectional studies were able to examine, placing these concerns within a developmental perspective. By so doing, these studies can better assess causal order, more fully explore the consequences of delinquent behavior, and determine if the risk and protective factors play a different role at different stages in the life course.

The nature of large-scale panel studies allows for the opportunity to study many other issues that are not of traditional concern. In some cases, these studies have generated unexpected findings that have important implications both for understanding crime and delinquency and for suggesting strategies to prevent and control such behavior. In this section, we review a few of these more unexpected findings.

A key feature of the studies reviewed here is their ability to follow subjects through a substantial portion of their life course. It is, therefore, not surprising that many of the unanticipated findings concern behaviors that occur at different stages of development.

The Montreal study began collecting data on children when they were in kindergarten. Tremblay et al. reported that the amount of physical aggression exhibited by these young children is surprisingly high. Indeed, physical aggression is higher during kindergarten than it is at subsequent ages. These findings suggest that it is necessary to begin observing children at even younger ages if one wants to address the onset of physical aggression. Tremblay and colleagues have begun to do so and have found that there is a substantial amount of physical aggression exhibited by children by their second year of life, as soon as children obtain the motor skills and opportunity for such behavior. They suggest that children reach their peak in the frequency of physical aggression in their third year of life. Moreover, they found that characteristics of parents and family functioning can significantly explain physical aggression at these very young ages.

If these results extend our focus to ever-younger ages, the results from other longitudinal studies regarding criminal careers extend the focus well beyond the adolescent years. In examining the parents of his subjects, Farrington found that the average age of conviction was 30 for fathers and 35 for mothers, while the average age of desistance was 36 and 38. The duration of criminal careers was 16 years for fathers and 15 years for mothers. Clearly, crime is not just for the young who will subsequently grow out of it as they reach adulthood.

Concern for older offenders is also triggered by the findings regarding the group that has been labeled "late starters" (Hawkins et al.; Thornberry et al.). These are individuals who begin their offending trajectories in their late adolescent years. Unlike adolescence-limited offenders, they do not desist as they approach young adulthood, but continue to offend at relatively high rates. The discovery of these late starters challenges a number of assumptions of prior theory and research on criminal careers and poses a number of questions. Most importantly we need to know why, after so many years of no or limited delinquent activity, these late starters begin to spurt. Additionally, we need to determine why they persist at a relatively high rate of offending and how long their careers last.

Following individuals through the life course affords the opportunity to examine the effects of different risk factors at different ages or developmental stages. Such analysis provides results that challenge a fairly well-established assumption concerning the effect of child maltreatment on later delinquency and drug use. Ireland, Smith, and Thornberry (2002), using the Rochester data, found that maltreatment that occurs only in childhood does not significantly increase the risk of delinquent outcomes. Rather, it is maltreatment that occurs either in adolescence or that continues from childhood through adolescence that predicts these deviant outcomes, as well as other problematic outcomes (Thornberry, Ireland, & Smith, 2001). If these findings are replicated in other data sets, they could have important implications for both theory and policy. For example, much more attention needs to be paid to adolescent maltreatment rather than a singular focus on maltreatment during childhood.

Farrington observed an interesting anomaly regarding the effect of poverty on rates of offending. He found that, as expected, male offenders had relatively low incomes at the age of 32. This is not surprising as it probably reflects the problematic impact that delinquency and crime have on acquiring the necessary social and human capital to compete successfully in the adult world. What is surprising is that at the age of 18 offenders actually were relatively better off than non-offenders. A plausible explanation for these findings is that offenders make precocious transitions to adult statuses by leaving school and getting a job early in the life cycle. Thus, they may initially be economically better off than non-offenders who may delay entry into the work force in order to finish their education or to acquire a more career-oriented position. By age 32, the failure to acquire the necessary human and social capital catches up with offenders and affects their economic well-being.

Loeber et al., as well as a number of other studies represented in this volume, found that the more risk factors one has the greater the likelihood of delinquent behavior. They also found that protective factors serve to reduce the impact of risk factors. In comparing the ratio of risk to protective factors and analyzing the effect of this risk score within neighborhoods, Loeber et al. found that the neighborhood has an impact on delinquency only when there is a balance of risk and protective factors. When risks outweigh protective factors, the SES of the neighborhood does not matter.

The findings reviewed in this section just begin to touch on some of the interesting and perhaps unanticipated findings from these large-scale panel studies. Given that both data analysis and data collection is ongoing, we can anticipate even more contributions that challenge some of our basic assumptions and expand our understanding of delinquent and criminal behavior.

General Conclusions

The seven studies represented in this volume have produced a host of findings that have contributed substantially to our knowledge of the development of deviant behavior and its impact on the life course. Because of their volume and range, it is very difficult to summarize and to limit the discussion of general conclusions. We have chosen, therefore, to highlight just two general conclusions that we feel are representative of all the studies included.

The Impact of Deviant Behavior

The traditional concern in the study of delinquent behavior has been to identify the factors that influence the etiology of delinquency. Delinquent behavior is typically seen as an outcome of biological, psychological, and sociological forces in a recursive causal model. Regardless of how serious or prolonged the behavior may be, it has been traditionally seen as having little causal impact on other aspects of the individual's life such as relationships with family and friends, and success in school and at work. Recent developmental theories of delinquency have corrected this image (e.g., Catalano & Hawkins, 1996; Moffitt, 1997; Sampson & Laub, 1993; Thornberry, 1987). The research results summarized in this volume serve to underscore how delinquent, aggressive, and other problematic behaviors influence most other arenas and relationships in people's lives.

The results have illustrated how physical aggression and coercive behavior exhibited at very young ages can impact parental behavior and the relationships between parent and child. Delinquent behavior has an impact on commitment to and success in school. Participating in delinquency increases the chances of associating with delinquent others which can increase embeddedness in delinquent behavior. And delinquency and drug use have an important impact on life chances in establishing a family, a career, and economic security.

The implications for our understanding of delinquency and our attempts to prevent and limit delinquent behavior are profound. Theories that do not incorporate reciprocal effects involving delinquency and other forms of problematic behavior are not providing a complete picture of how delinquent behavior develops over time. Incorporating bidirectional causality into our understanding of delinquency makes the task more complex. However, such complexity is necessary for a more complete understanding of delinquent behavior.

The implications for policy are equally significant. We need to deal with aberrant behavior and its effects at any age, including very young ages, to prevent the spiral of delinquency from continuing. We need also to understand that the source of family problems or school problems may be delinquent behavior itself rather than assuming that the flow of causality is always to delinquency. Again, this adds a significant layer of complexity to the task but it is one which the results presented here suggest must be taken into account to generate effective social policy concerning delinquency.

Continuity and Change

Perhaps the most significant advantage of a longitudinal panel study is the ability to study both continuity and change in delinquent behavior and the factors that cause both. The results from the summarized research confirm that there is a significant amount of continuity in deviant behavior. Early aggression predicts later delinquency and the early onset of delinquency predicts later criminal behavior. These findings may suggest that there is an underlying potential for antisocial behavior that is distributed heterogeneously in the population and manifests itself throughout the life course (Nagin & Farrington, 1992).

However, there is also a great deal of change in behavior as respondents traverse the life course, suggesting a more dynamic or state-dependent explanation. The weight of the evidence found by these studies suggests that changing situations over the life course also contribute to the explanation of both continuity and change in delinquency. To some extent, delinquency is perpetuated by the consequences it generates in the person's life. For, as we saw in the previous section, delinquency has feedback effects that disrupt the normal course of adolescent development and interferes with the accumulation of human and social capital. Thus, the forces that produce continuity in antisocial behavior are not entirely determined by factors occurring early in the life course.

The factors that produce behavioral change such as desistance may also be developmentally specific. For example, during adolescence, protective factors like prosocial friends (Hawkins, Catalano, & Miller, 1992) may play a particularly important role in steering youth away from antisocial behavior. As people make the transition to adulthood, the completion of their education or successfully establishing a commitment to a partner may change the trajectory of their behavior. Longitudinal studies have only begun to identify why some individuals who manifest early behavior problems do not continue to commit deviant acts and why some individuals who delay participating in delinquency do so at high frequency in late adolescence. Clearly, the ability to examine these issues represents one of the critical advantages of long-term panel studies.

Future Directions

Each of the articles in this volume identified future directions for research that were suggested by the results obtained thus far. A full compilation of the list would represent a daunting agenda. Here, we identify a few of what we think are the more important directions.

Although these research studies have extended the age span at which data are collected on respondents, the findings reviewed here serve to strongly suggest that the age span be extended even further to include both very young children and to follow subjects beyond their early adult years. Many of the studies began their data collection while the subjects were in early childhood. They found that even at these young ages children exhibited patterns of antisocial conduct that predicted subsequent problematic behavior. To assess the causes of such early onset, and even to determine how early the onset actually is, we need to begin assessments at much younger ages. Among the projects represented in this volume, Tremblay et al. have taken the lead in doing this by beginning with observations of infants at birth.

In addition to extending the age downward to include infants, we must continue our efforts to follow our subjects through a greater span of their life course. Our understanding of the impact of delinquent behavior on life-course transitions and trajectories has been enhanced by some of the findings reported in this volume. However, with the exception of the Cambridge and Houston studies, the studies have followed their subjects only through their early to mid twenties. At this age, employment and family trajectories have not necessarily been established. Hence, to determine how delinquent behavior affects life-course outcomes, we need to follow subjects well past this early adulthood stage.

In addition to focusing on life-course outcomes, extending the age range upward will also allow us to study the critical issues of desistance and late starters. Much of the desistance research only follows subjects into their early adult years. It is not clear if these respondents have truly desisted or whether there is a temporary break in their behavior. We need to focus on desistance as a process rather than as a static outcome and to do so we need to continue to follow respondents for a much longer period of time (Bushway, Piquero, Broidy, Cauffman, & Mazerolle, 2001).

A few of the studies in this volume report finding a group of truly late starters who do not engage in delinquent behavior or have very low levels of delinquency up until their late adolescent years. At that time, their rate of delinquency or crime increases substantially and, by their early twenties, they are among the high frequency offenders. Because this group of offenders has relatively high crime rates in their early twenties and because they represent a phenomenon that is relatively new to the field, they are very important to study. To do so, we must extend the age range to which we follow our subjects.

An important focus of research on deviant behavior including crime and delinquency is the degree to which it is common across generations of individuals from the same family. The longitudinal panel studies included in this volume provide a unique opportunity to investigate this issue. All of the studies have information on the parents of focal subjects. Some questions of intergenerational transmission can be addressed with these data. However, the data are problematic for several reasons. Some are based only on the focal subject's perception of parental behaviors and attitudes, while others measure parental behavior either at a time when parents are substantially older than the focal subjects or rely on retrospective data on parental behavior from when they were adolescents. It is far better to assess behaviors at the same or similar ages in the different generations. This, of course, requires studying a new generation of subjects in order to assess their behaviors at the same ages as the assessment of the focal subjects. Such research is beginning. For example, Kaplan is surveying the children of his original subjects at the same ages as the original subjects were surveyed. Thornberry et al. are examining the third generation at much younger ages, but are planning to follow them through their adolescent years. Once these data are collected, data on three generations will be able to explore a variety of issues regarding the intergenerational transmission of deviant behavior.

So far we have mentioned extensions of the projects that are either in their beginning stages or are being planned. Two other future directions, however, are suggested by limitations in these projects and would require that new longitudinal projects be designed. First, most of the projects reviewed in this volume either do not include females as focal subjects or underrepresent them. The decision to do so stems from a focus on serious delinquent behavior and chronic delinquents. Because females constitute a minority of serious and chronic delinquents, they are not as well represented in the samples as males. However, evidence from the studies that do include females indicates that this assumption may be both biased and limiting; adolescent females are clearly involved in serious delinquency and other problem behaviors. Thornberry et al., for example, found that about an equal percentage of females as males joined a gang and that the impact of the gang on their behavior and development was every bit as serious as it was for the males. Moreover, when we take into account co-occurring problem behaviors such as drug use and risky sex, females require the full attention of researchers. We need longitudinal studies that include a sufficient number of females so that analyses can be done within categories of variables such as race and gang membership. Fortunately, Loeber et al. have just begun a replication and extension of the Pittsburgh Youth Study using a female sample. These and similar studies will begin to fill this gap in our knowledge base.

Second, although many of the studies reviewed here included a substantial sample of African Americans and Latinos, they do not include a strong minority perspective in the explanation of delinquent and criminal careers. Given the over-representation of people of color in the juvenile and criminal justice systems (Snyder & Sickmund, 1995), this is a particularly serious issue. We need to develop and incorporate theoretical models that are culturally sensitive and culturally specific into our longitudinal investigations. For example, there may be both risk and protective factors that are unique to the history and current circumstances of African American and Latino youth that are not being considered or measured in current studies (Tatum, 2000, in press). Failure to include them may weaken our explanatory power and the effectiveness of intervention programs. Systematically including culturally-specific perspectives, both in ongoing studies and in the design of new studies, is one of our highest priorities.

A Final Word

We hope the chapters in this volume adequately reflect our belief that research on the causes and consequences of delinquency has come a long way in the recent past. In less than half a century, we have moved from relatively small, cross-sectional studies to larger, long-term studies with detailed measures of a wide range of developmental domains and sophisticated analytic strategies. The projects included in this volume reflect some, but by no means all, of those projects. We hope that the summaries of key findings presented here give the reader a sense of the richness and diversity of scientific information currently available. We also hope that they stimulate renewed interest in more accurately understanding the causes and consequences of delinquency and in developing effective programs to reduce it.

References

Bushway, S., Piquero, A., Broidy, L., Cauffman, E., & Mazerolle, P. (2001). An empirical framework for studying desistance as a process. *Criminology, 39*, 491–515.

Catalano, R. F., & Hawkins, J. D. (1996). A social development model: A theory of antisocial behavior. In J. D. Hawkins (Ed.), *Delinquency and crime* (pp.149–197). New York: Cambridge University Press.

Elliott, D. S., & Voss, H. (1974). *Delinquency and dropout*. Lexington, KY: Heath.

Elliott, D. S., Huizinga, D., & Ageton, S. S. (1985). *Explaining delinquency and drug use*. Beverly Hills: Sage Publications.

Glueck, S., & Glueck, E. T. (1950). *Unraveling juvenile delinquency*. New York: Commonwealth Fund.

Hawkins, J. D., & Weis, J. G. (1985). The social development model: An integrated approach to delinquency prevention. *Journal of Primary Prevention, 6*, 73–97.

Hawkins, J. D., Catalano, R. F., & Miller, J. Y. (1992). Risk and protective factors for alcohol and other drug problems in adolescence and early adulthood: Implications for substance abuse prevention. *Psychological Bulletin, 112*, 64–105.

Hill, K. G., Hawkins, J. D., Catalano, R., McMahon, R., & Gilchrist, L. (1999). Intergenerational influence of substance use on children. Grant proposal funded by the National Institute on Drug Abuse.

Ireland, T. O., Smith, C. A., & Thornberry, T. P. (2002). Developmental issues in the impact of child maltreatment on later delinquency and drug use: Reconsidering the strength and boundaries of the relationship. *Criminology, 40*, 359–399.

McCord, J. (1979). Some child-rearing antecedents of criminal behavior in adult men. *Journal of Personality and Social Psychology, 37*, 1477–1486.

Moffitt, T. E. (1997). Adolescence-limited and life-course-persistent offending: A complementary pair of developmental theories. In T. P. Thornberry (Ed.), *Developmental theories of crime and delinquency: Vol. 7. Advances in criminological theory* (pp. 11–54). New Brunswick, NJ: Transaction Publishers.

Nagin, D. S., & Farrington, D. P. (1992). The stability of criminal potential from childhood to adulthood. *Criminology, 30*, 235–260.

Nagin, D. S., & Land, K. C. (1993). Age, criminal careers, and population heterogeneity: Specification and estimation of a nonparametric, mixed Poisson model. *Criminology, 31*, 327–362.

Sampson, R. J., & Laub, J. H. (1993). *Crime in the making: Pathways and turning points through life*. Cambridge, MA: Harvard University Press.

Snyder, H. N., & Sickmund, M. (1995). *Juvenile offenders and victims: A focus on violence*. Washington, DC: U.S. Department of Justice, Office of Juvenile Justice and Delinquency Prevention.

Tatum, B. (2000). *Crime, violence and minority youths*. Brookfield, VT: Ashgate.

Tatum, B. (In press). *Toward a Black criminology: African American perspectives on deviance, crime, and violence*. Durham, NC: Carolina Academic Press.

Thornberry, T. P. (1987). Toward an interactional theory of delinquency. *Criminology, 25*, 863–891.

Thornberry, T. P., & Krohn, M. D. (1997). Peers, drug use, and delinquency. In D. M. Stoff, J. Breiling, & J. D. Maser (Eds.), *Handbook of antisocial behavior* (pp. 218–233). New York: Wiley.

Thornberry, T. P., & Krohn, M. D. (2001). The development of delinquency: An interactional perspective. In S. O. White (Ed.), *Handbook of youth and justice* (pp. 289–305). New York: Plenum.

Thornberry, T. P., Ireland, T. O., & Smith, C. A. (2001). The importance of timing: The varying impact of childhood and adolescent maltreatment on multiple problem outcomes. *Development and Psychopathology, 13*, 957–979.

Thornberry, T. P., Freeman-Gallant, A., Lizotte, A. J., Krohn, M. D., & Smith, C. A. (2002). Linked lives: The intergenerational transmission of antisocial behavior. Manuscript submitted for publication.

Index

327